IRELAND'S
BEST TRIPS

34 AMAZING ROAD TRIPS

Fionn Davenport
Isabel Albiston, Belinda Dixon,
Catherine Le Nevez, Neil Wilson

SYMBOLS IN THIS BOOK

 Top Tips

History & Culture

Essential Photo

Link Your Trips

Family

Walking Tour

Tips from Locals

Food & Drink

Eating

Trip Detour

Outdoors

Sleeping

☏ Telephone Number

@ Internet Access

🗏 English-Language Menu

🕙 Opening Hours

🛜 Wi-Fi Access

Family-Friendly

P Parking

Vegetarian Selection

Pet-Friendly

Nonsmoking

Swimming Pool

Air-Conditioning

MAP LEGEND

Routes
- Trip Route
- Trip Detour
- Linked Trip
- Walk Route
- Tollway
- Freeway
- Primary
- Secondary
- Tertiary
- Lane
- Unsealed Road
- Plaza/Mall
- Steps
- Tunnel
- Pedestrian Overpass
- Walk Track/Path

Trips
- 1 Trip Numbers
- 9 Trip Stop
- Walking tour
- Trip Detour

Population
- ❂ Capital (National)
- ◉ Capital (State/Province)
- ● City/Large Town
- ● Town/Village

Boundaries
- International
- State/Province
- Cliff

Areas
- Beach
- Cemetery (Christian)
- Cemetery (Other)
- Park
- Forest Reservation
- Urban Area
- Sportsground

Hydrography
- River/Creek
- Intermittent River
- Swamp/Mangrove
- Canal
- Water
- Dry/Salt/ Intermittent Lake
- Glacier

Transport
- ✈ Airport
- Cable Car/ Funicular
- P Parking
- Train/Railway
- Tram

Highway Markers
- E44 E-Road Network
- M100 National Network

PLAN YOUR TRIP

ON THE ROAD

CONTENTS

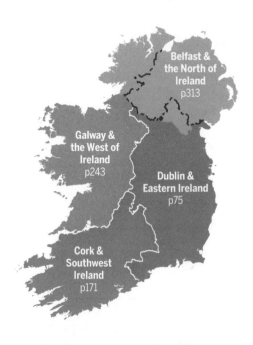

Belfast &
the North of
Ireland
p313

Galway &
the West of
Ireland
p243

Dublin &
Eastern Ireland
p75

Cork &
Southwest
Ireland
p171

3

Contents cont.

Clonmacnoise High Cross at this ancient monstastic site

MICHAEL MANTKE/SHUTTERSTOCK ©

5.

WELCOME TO
IRELAND

Your main reason for visiting? Most likely to experience Ireland of the postcard. The captivating peninsulas of the southwest, the brooding expanse of Connemara and the dramatic wildness of County Donegal. It can also be uncovered in the lakelands of Counties Leitrim and Roscommon and the undulating hills of the sunny southeast.

Scenery, history, culture, bustling cosmopolitanism and the stillness of village life – you'll find all of these along the 34 road trips in this book. You'll visit blockbuster attractions and replicate famous photo ops. But there are plenty of surprises too, and they're all within easy reach of each other.

Whether you want to drive through the wildest terrain or sample great food while hopping between spa treatments, we've got something for you. And if you've only got time for one trip, make it one of our eight Classic Trips, which take you to the very best of Ireland.

Dingle Peninsula Driving the Wild Atlantic Way

IRELAND
HIGHLIGHTS

Classic Trip

2

The Long Way Round
Ireland's crenellated coastlines, vibrant port cities and island treasures. **14 DAYS**

Classic Trip

29

The North in a Nutshell
Big cities, big-name sights, hidden beaches, tiny islands – an epic drive. **10 DAYS**

Classic Trip

22

Best of the West
Enjoy epic landscapes on this tour of Ireland's best westerly sights. **6 DAYS**

North Channel

NORTHERN IRELAND

Ballycastle

Glenariff Forest Park ④

ANTRIM

Larne

Carrickfergus

Coleraine

Kells

Ballymena

Antrim

Bangor

Newtownards

Holywood

BELFAST ★

Strangford Lough

Portstewart

Carndonagh

Limavady

DERRY/ LONDONDERRY

Lisburn

Lurgan

Craigavon

DOWN

Killyleagh

Downpatrick

Castlewellan Forest Park

Portrush

Buncrana

Derry/ Londonderry

Strabane

TYRONE

Gortin Glen ④ Forest Park

Omagh

Portadown

Banbridge

Newcastle

ARMAGH

Newry

Kilbroney Forest Park

Greencastle

Ballyliffin

Dunlewy

Letterkenny

DONEGAL

Castle Caldwell ④ Forest Park

Enniskillen

Monaghan

Armagh

Dundalk

LOUTH

Dunfanaghy

Falcarragh

Gortahork

Glenties

Ardara

Donegal

Bruckless

Clones

MONAGHAN

Carrickmacross

Dún an Rí Forest Park

Slane

Drogheda

Irish Sea

Burtonport

Dungloe

Maghery

FERMANAGH

Lough Navar Lower Forest Park Lough Erne

Cuilcagh Mountain ④ Park

LEITRIM

CAVAN

Killykeen Forest Park

Cavan

Navan

Glencolumbcille

Bundoran

Sligo

Carrick- on-Shannon

Carrick-

LONGFORD

Kells

IRELAND

Sligo Bay

SLIGO

Boyle

ROSCOMMON

Ballycastle

Ballina

Knock

Strokestown

MAYO

Castlebar

Bangor Erris

Ballycroy ④ National Park

Newport

Westport

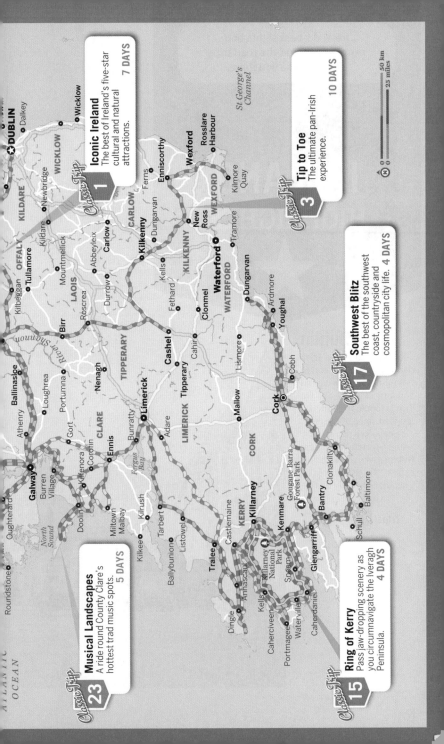

Classic Trip 1

Iconic Ireland
The best of Ireland's five-star cultural and natural attractions.
7 DAYS

Classic Trip 3

Tip to Toe
The ultimate pan-Irish experience.
10 DAYS

Classic Trip 17

Southwest Blitz
The best of the southwest coast, countryside and cosmopolitan city life. **4 DAYS**

Classic Trip 23

Musical Landscapes
A ride round County Clare's hottest trad music spots.
5 DAYS

Classic Trip 15

Ring of Kerry
Pass jaw-dropping scenery as you circumnavigate the Iveragh Peninsula. **4 DAYS**

ATLANTIC OCEAN

St George's Channel

DUBLIN
Dalkey
Wicklow
WICKLOW
Newbridge
KILDARE
Kildare
OFFALY
Tullamore
Kilbeggan
Mountmellick
LAOIS
Abbeyleix
Durrow
Kells
Roscrea
Birr
Portumna
Nenagh
TIPPERARY
Loughrea
Ballinasloe
Athenry
Gort
CLARE
Ennis
Corofin
Kilfenora
Burren Village
North Sound
Doolin
Oughterard
Roundstone
Galway
Miltown Malbay
Fergus Bay
Kilrush
Kilkee
Tarbert
Ballybunion
Listowel
Tralee
Castlemaine
Dingle
Annascaul
Kells
Cahersiveen
Portmagee
Waterville
Caherdaniel
Killarney National Park
Killarney
KERRY
Sneem
Kenmare
Glengarriff
Gougane Barra Forest Park
Bantry
Baltimore
Schull
Clonakilty
CORK
Cork
Cobh
Mallow
LIMERICK
Limerick
Adare
Bunratty
Cashel
Cahir
Tipperary
Clonmel
Lismore
Ardmore
Youghal
WATERFORD
Waterford
Dungarvan
Tramore
New Ross
KILKENNY
Kilkenny
Fethard
Dungarvan
CARLOW
Carlow
Ferns
Enniscorthy
WEXFORD
Wexford
Rosslare Harbour
Kilmore Quay

River Shannon

0   50 km
0   25 miles

Ireland's best sights and experiences, and the road trips that will take you there.

IRELAND
HIGHLIGHTS

Dublin

It's likely that your Irish visit will begin and end in Dublin, Ireland's capital and largest city by far. On **Trip 1: Iconic Ireland**, you can visit some of the city's best-known attractions, while **Stretch Your Legs: Dublin** gives you a chance to explore the city in greater depth, especially its rich Georgian heritage.

Trips

Dublin Christ Church Cathedral

Connemara Lough Derrryclare and Connemara Mountains

Connemara

A kaleidoscope of rusty bogs, lonely valleys and enticing hamlets laid across a patchwork of narrow country roads punctuated by the odd inviting country pub: welcome to Connemara, yours to discover on **Trip 24: Mountains & Moors**. Connemara evokes the very best of Irish scenery and the country itself, unsullied by centuries of history and transformation.

Trips

Galway

Storied, sung-about and snug, Galway is one of Ireland's great pleasures. So much so that it's full of people who came, saw and still haven't managed to leave. Wander the tuneful streets and refuel in any of the city's great pubs on **Trip 23: Musical Landscapes** – it *could* keep you busy for a whole month of nights out.

Trips

Belfast

There's far more to Belfast than its troubled past, as you can discover for yourself on **Trip 29: The North in a Nutshell**. But you can learn about Northern Ireland's recent history on our walking tour, **Stretch Your Legs: Belfast**, on which you'll explore the political murals and peace lines of West Belfast's divided neighbourhoods of the Falls and the Shankill.

Trips

Cork Colourful houses on the River Lee

BEST ROADS FOR DRIVING

R560, County Kerry Drive the spectacular Connor Pass. **Trips** `1` `16` `22`

R115 (Old Military Rd), County Wicklow The loveliest, loneliest road of the east. **Trip** `9`

Ring of Kerry Ireland's most famous circular route. **Trips** `1` `2` `15` `17`

Beara Peninsula Magnificent views and lovely villages. **Trips** `1` `2` `19` `22`

N59, Connemara Mountains, moors and broody boglands. **Trips** `22` `24` `25` `26`

Cork

An appealing waterfront location, some of the best food you'll find, lively craic and a liberal, youthful and cosmopolitan dynamic make Ireland's second city, Cork, hard to resist. Foodies can taste the best of the city's (and county's) eateries and markets on **Trip 18: Southwestern Pantry**, and take in the key sites on our designated walking tour.

Trips `2` `17` `18` `22`

13

Glendalough Monastic ruins

Glendalough

Once one of Ireland's most dynamic universities, the monastic ruins of Glendalough, founded by St Kevin as a spiritual retreat, are now among the country's most beautiful ruined sites. They're easily visited from Dublin on **Trip 4: A Long Weekend Around Dublin**. The remains of the settlement (including an intact round tower), coupled with the stunning scenery, are unforgettable, and are the perfect spot for a leisurely mountain hike.

Trips 4 7 9

BEST TOWNS FOR TRADITIONAL MUSIC

Dingle A handful of bars with nightly music. **Trips** 1 2 16 22

Miltown Malbay Come for the Willie Clancy Festival in July. **Trip** 23

Ennis The capital of music country. **Trips** 1 23 28

Doolin Three pubs host some of the country's best sessions. **Trips** 2 5 23

Dingle Peninsula Dramatic coastline and the Blasket islands

Brú na Bóinne Neolithic necropolis

Dingle Peninsula

It seems that everybody wants to go to Dingle – join them on **Trip 16: Dingle Peninsula**. Luckily, this is one place that transcends the crowds with its allure. Sure you may be stuck behind a bus, but this rocky, striated land has a history as compelling as its beauty, prehistoric monuments, scenic spots and fabulous pubs.

Trips

Brú na Bóinne

The vast neolithic necropolis of Brú na Bóinne in County Meath is 600 years older than the pyramids, 1000 years older than Stonehenge, and designed with a mathematical precision that would have confounded the ancient Greeks. Visit on **Trip 7: Ancient Ireland**, to see the simulated winter sunrise that illuminates the main burial chamber.

Trips 4 6 7 14

Rock of Cashel

The Rock of Cashel, a highlight of **Trip 21: The Holy Glen**, never ceases to startle when you first see it rising from the otherwise mundane plains of Tipperary. And this ancient fortified home of kings is just the tip of the iceberg; moody ruins are hidden in the surrounding green expanse, set neatly atop a rock overlooking pretty Cashel town.

Trips 3 7 21

Ring of Kerry

Yes, it's popular. And yes, it's always choked with bus traffic, especially in summer. But there are about 1000 reasons why the Ring of Kerry is the tourist charm bracelet it is – and gets its own designated itinerary (**Trip 15: Ring of Kerry**). You'll find most of the reasons around the Iveragh Peninsula just west of Killarney; do it counter-clockwise unless you want to get stuck behind a caravan of tour buses!

Trips

Giant's Causeway

The grand geological flourish of the Giant's Causeway is Northern Ireland's most popular attraction and one of the world's iconic natural wonders. Clamber across the 40,000 unique hexagonal basalt columns on **Trip 34: The Antrim Coast**, then decide whether you prefer the scientific explanation or the far more colourful legend that explains them.

Trips

(left) **Giant's Causeway** Basalt columns off the northeast coast;

(below) **Cliffs of Moher** Cliffs and coastline in County Clare

PHOTOS BY W. EBIKO/GETTY IMAGES ©

GREG SINCLAIR/500PX ©

Cliffs of Moher

Bathed in the golden glow of the late afternoon sun, the iconic Cliffs of Moher are one of the west coast's splendours. Witnessed from a boat bobbing below or from dry land as you would on **Trip 1: Iconic Ireland**, the towering stone faces have a jaw-dropping, dramatic beauty that's enlivened by scores of sea birds, including cute little puffins.

Trips

BEST ANCIENT RUINS

Carrowkeel A megalithic tomb atop a scenic hill. **Trip** 27

Dún Aengus A prehistoric fort abutting a sea-lashed cliff. **Trips** 2 4 23 28

Clonmacnoise Ireland's most important monastic university. **Trips** 5 7 8

Loughcrew Cairns A 'forgotten' neolithic passage grave. **Trip** 7

Cruachan Aí Europe's most significant Celtic royal site. **Trip** 7

IF YOU LIKE...

Donegal Dunfanaghy from Horn Head

Ancient Monuments

Ireland is old, as in, older-than-the-pyramids old. Everywhere you go you can find a historic castle, the ruins of a 1500-year-old monastery, or a collection of stones with faded carvings done by prehistoric people so ancient that archaeologists talk of eras rather than centuries.

7 Ancient Ireland The big stars of Ireland's ancient past.

16 Dingle Peninsula Slea Head is littered with prehistoric monuments.

21 The Holy Glen Visit County Tipperary's collection of monastic treasures.

27 Sligo Surrounds A wealth of prehistoric sites within easy reach of each other.

Great Views

What do you fancy? A jagged coastline pounded by the waves? A desolate mountain range with a brooding, low-slung sky? Or perhaps an emerald valley stretched out below you, dotted with clusters of sheep and criss-crossed by stone walls? In Ireland, keep your camera close by.

9 Wicklow Mountains Mountain passes and glacial valleys are the scenic highlights.

15 Ring of Kerry Virtually every corner on this iconic drive reveals a postcard view.

24 Mountains & Moors A trip through broody, beautiful Connemara.

30 Delights of Donegal The stunning scenery of Ireland's northwestern corner.

Hidden Treasures

Exploring the best of Ireland is not just about five-star attractions or the bustling crowds that won't get out of your perfect picture. Beyond the tourist chart-toppers there's a host of sights and towns that have escaped mass attention, but are just as worthy of your time.

10 Carlow Back Roads A marvellous county untouched by mass tourism.

20 Shannon River Route Ireland's mightiest river has a host of little-visited delights.

25 Loughs of the West The west's lesser-known backwaters.

31 Inishowen Peninsula Remote and hard to get to, but worth the effort.

Newgrange Passage graves at Brú na Bóinne neolithic site

Traditional Music

Western Europe's most vibrant folk music is kept alive by musicians who ply their craft (and are plied with drink) in impromptu and organised sessions in pubs and music houses throughout the country; even the 'strictly for tourists' stuff will feature excellent performances.

16 Dingle Peninsula
Forget yourself in one of Dingle's music pubs.

23 Musical Landscapes
The best of the west's pubs, venues and music festivals.

29 The North in a Nutshell Visit the home of Enya, Clannad and a whole musical movement.

Good Food

Throughout Ireland, there is abundant evidence of the foodie revolution as local chefs and producers combine international experience with the kind of meals that have always been taken for granted on well-run Irish farms.

12 Wexford & Waterford
Parts of west Waterford are a gourmet heaven.

18 Southwestern Pantry County Cork is the flag bearer of the foodie revolution.

19 West Cork Villages
Virtually every village in West Cork has a good restaurant.

22 Best of the West From Sligo to Kerry, there's great grub to be had.

An Adrenalin Rush

Ireland has myriad ways for you to work up a sweat – from chasing chickens around a farmyard to paragliding off the edge of a mountain. There are plenty of family-friendly activities throughout the country, from heritage museums to zip lines across a forest canopy.

14 Family Fun From working farms to adventure centres – fun for the whole family.

16 Dingle Peninsula
Scuba diving and surfing in the beautiful southwest.

32 Northwest on Adrenaline Get breathless in the sea and up a mountain.

NEED TO KNOW

CURRENCY
Republic of Ireland: euro (€)

Northern Ireland: pound sterling (£)

LANGUAGE
English, Irish

VISAS
Not required by most citizens of Europe, Australia, New Zealand, USA and Canada.

FUEL
Petrol (gas) stations are everywhere, but are limited on motorways. Expect to pay €1.35 per litre of unleaded (€1.25 for diesel) in the Republic, £1.25 for unleaded and diesel in Northern Ireland.

RENTAL CARS
Avis (www.avis.ie)

Europcar (www.europcar.ie)

Hertz (www.hertz.ie)

Thrifty (www.thrifty.ie)

IMPORTANT NUMBERS
Country code (☏ 353 Republic, ☏ 44 Northern Ireland)

Emergencies (☏ 999)

Roadside Assistance (☏ 1800 667 788, ☏ 0800 887 766 in Northern Ireland)

Climate

■ Warm to hot summers, mild winters

Belfast GO May–Sep

Dublin GO any time; lots of indoor attractions

Galway GO May–Sep

Killarney GO May–Sep

Cork GO May–Sep

When to Go

High Season (Jun–mid-Sep)
» Weather at its best.

» Accommodation rates at their highest (especially in August).

» Tourist peak in Dublin, Kerry and southern and western coasts.

Shoulder (Easter–May, mid-Sep–Oct)
» Weather often good: sun and rain in May, often-warm 'Indian summers' in September.

» Summer crowds and accommodation rates drop off.

Low Season (Nov–Easter)
» Reduced opening hours from October to Easter; some destinations close.

» Cold and wet weather throughout the country; fog can reduce visibility.

» Big city attractions operate as normal.

Your Daily Budget

Budget: Less than €60
» Dorm bed: €12–20
» Cheap meal in cafe or pub: €6–12
» Pint: €4.50–5 (more in cities)

Midrange: €60–150
» Double room in hotel or B&B: €80–180 (more in Dublin)
» Main course in midrange restaurant: €12–25
» Car rental (per day): €25-45

Top End: More than €150
» Four-star hotel stay: from €150
» Three-course meal in good restaurant: around €50
» Top round of golf from €90

Eating

Restaurants From cheap cafes to Michelin-starred feasts, covering every imaginable cuisine.

Cafes Cafes are good for all-day breakfasts, sandwiches and basic dishes.

Pubs Pub grub ranges from toasted sandwiches to carefully crafted dishes.

Hotels All hotel restaurants take nonguests. A popular option in the countryside.

Eating price indicators represent the cost of a main dish:

Republic of Ireland/ Dublin

€ less than €12/15

€€ €12–25/€15-28

€€€ more than €25/28

Northern Ireland

£ less than £12

££ £12–20

£££ more than £20

Sleeping

Hotels From chain hotels with comfortable digs to Norman castles with rainfall shower rooms and wi-fi.

B&Bs From a bedroom in a private home to a luxurious Georgian townhouse.

Hostels Every major town and city has a selection of hostels, with clean dorms and wi-fi. Some have laundry and kitchen.

Sleeping price indicators represent the cost of a double room in high season:

Republic/Northern Ireland

€ less than €80/£50

€€ €80–180/£50–120

€€€ more than €180/£120

Arriving in Ireland

Dublin Airport
Rental cars Rental agencies have offices at the airport.

Taxis Taxis take 30 to 45 minutes and cost €25 to €30.

Buses Private coaches run every 10 to 15 minutes to the city centre (€6).

Cork Airport
Rental cars There are car-hire desks for all the main companies.

Taxis A taxi to/from town costs €22 to €26.

Bus Every half hour between 6am and 10pm to the train station and bus station (€2.80).

Dun Laoghaire Ferry Port
Train DART (suburban rail) takes about 25 minutes to the centre of Dublin.

Bus Public bus takes around 45 minutes to the centre of Dublin.

Mobile Phones

All European and Australasian phones work in Ireland, as do North American phones not locked to a local network. Check with your provider. Prepaid SIM cards cost from €10/£10.

Internet Access

Wi-fi and 3G/4G networks are making internet cafes largely redundant. Most accommodation places have free wi-fi, or a daily charge (up to €10).

Money

ATMs are widely available. Credit and debit cards can be used in most places, but check first.

Tipping

Not obligatory, but 10% to 15% in restaurants; €1/£1 per bag for hotel porters.

Useful Websites

Entertainment Ireland (www.entertainment.ie) Countrywide listings.

Failte Ireland (www.discoverireland.ie) Official tourist-board website for the Republic.

Lonely Planet (www.lonelyplanet.com/ireland, www.lonelyplanet.com/ireland/northern-ireland) Destination information, hotel bookings, traveller forum and more.

Northern Ireland Tourist Board (www.nitb.com) Official tourist-board site.

For more, see Road Trip Essentials (p372).

CITY GUIDE

DUBLIN

Ireland's largest city by far is also its buzzing capital, with superb restaurants, world-class museums and more nightlife than you could ever use, from theatre to its 1000-plus pubs. Still the *sine qua non* of the city's social life, these watering holes are the best place to take Dublin's pulse.

Dead Zoo Dublin's Natural History Museum

Getting Around

The one-way system makes driving in Dublin tricky; the traffic can make it a test of patience. You can walk pretty much anywhere in the compact city centre.

Parking

There is plenty of paid parking, except on Sundays or after 7pm, when you can park for free on single-yellow lines. Sheltered car parks (around €4 per hour) are your best bet if your hotel doesn't have a car park.

Where to Eat

Temple Bar has the biggest concentration of restaurants, mostly midpriced and often bland; the best options are on the streets on either side of Grafton St. Top-end spots are around Merrion Sq and Fitzwilliam Sq.

Where to Stay

Base yourself in a suburb immediately south of the city centre, such as Ballsbridge, Donnybrook or Ranelagh, to experience the best of the city's B&B culture. The little shops and boutiques immediately west of Grafton St are the best for browsing.

Useful Websites

Dublin Tourism (www.visitdublin.com) Sights, accommodation bookings, discounts.

All The Food (www.allthefood.ie) Up-to-date restaurant reviews for Dublin.

Lonely Planet (www.lonelyplanet.com/ireland/dublin) Travel tips, accommodation and a travellers' forum.

Trips Through Dublin 1 2 5 14

For more, check out our city and country guides.
www.lonelyplanet.com

TOP EXPERIENCES

➡ **Stroll the Elizabethan Cobbles of Trinity College**
Ireland's most famous university is also Dublin's most atmospheric bit of city-centre real estate; it's home to the Book of Kells.

➡ **Discover Ireland's Treasures**
The National Museum of Ireland is where you'll find the country's most complete collection of medieval goldwork, Celtic design and iconic treasures dating back 2500 years.

➡ **Indulge Your Thespian Side**
From classic plays to experimental new works, the city's theatres have something for everyone.

➡ **Saunter Through Georgian Squares**
The Georgian gems of St Stephen's Green and Merrion Sq are the best spots to catch a bit of urban R & R.

➡ **Get to Grips with Irish History**
The tour of Kilmainham Gaol is a hard-hitting exploration of the country's troubled past.

➡ **Tap into Your Inner Victorian Botanist**
Opened by Dr David Livingstone, the Natural History Museum, aka the 'dead zoo', has preserved its 19th-century spirit – as well as some two million stuffed animals.

➡ **Grab a Pint in a Traditional Pub**
There's nowhere better to sample a pint of Guinness – the 'black stuff' or 'liquid gold' – than in one of the city's many traditional pubs.

Galway Bay Oysters A local culinary favourite

GALWAY

Ireland's most bohemian burg has long celebrated difference, which accounts for its vibrant arts scene, easygoing pace and outstanding nightlife. Old-fashioned pubs with traditional sessions, theatres hosting experimental works, designated music venues in thrall to the heartfelt outpourings of the singer-songwriter... It's just another night in Galway.

Getting Around

Traffic in and out of the city centre is a major issue during peak hours. The one-way system and network of pedestrianised streets can make getting around a little tricky.

Parking

Parking throughout Galway's streets is metered. There are several multistorey and pay-and-display car parks around town.

Where to Eat

Seafood is Galway's speciality, be it fish and chips, ocean-fresh chowder or salmon cooked to perfection. Galway Bay oysters star on many menus. Pedestrianised Quay St is lined with restaurants aimed at the tourist throngs.

Where to Stay

Base yourself in the city centre so you can take full advantage of the city's tightly packed attractions. The west side, on the far side of the River Corrib, is where you'll find the best concentration of eateries, classic pubs and music venues.

Useful Websites

Discover Ireland (www.discoverireland.ie) Sights, accommodation bookings, discounts.

Galway Pub Guide (www.galwaycitypubguide.com) Comprehensive guide to the heaving scene.

Galway Tourism (www.galwaytourism.ie) Local tourist information.

Trips Through Galway

1 3 5 22 23 24 25

Belfast Jaffe Memorial Fountain, Victoria Square

BELFAST

Vibrant, confident and fascinating – not words that immediately jump to mind when imagining Belfast. But Northern Ireland's largest city has worked hard to get rid of its reputation as a violence-scarred protagonist of the news, and now offers great museums, fine dining and a wealth of shopping to go with its rich history.

Getting Around

Belfast is easy enough to drive in, with a good road network and signposting enabling you to get where you want to go.

Parking

For on-street parking between 8am and 6pm Monday to Saturday, you'll need to buy a ticket from a machine. For longer periods, head for one of the many multistorey car parks that are dotted around the city centre.

Where to Eat

In the evening, the liveliest part of the city centre stretches south of Donegall Sq to Shaftesbury Sq. During the day, many pubs, cafes and restaurants do a roaring trade. South Belfast is also where you'll find some terrific restaurants.

Where to Stay

Most of Belfast's budget and midrange accommodation is south of the centre, in the university district around Botanic Ave, University Rd and Malone Rd. This area is also crammed with good-value restaurants and pubs, and is mostly within a 20-minute walk of City Hall.

Useful Websites

Belfast City Council (www. belfastcity.gov.uk/events) Information on a wide range of organised events.

Belfast Music (www. belfastmusic.org) Online gig listings.

Belfast Welcome Centre (www.gotobelfast.com) Sights, accommodation bookings, discounts.

Great Belfast Food (www. greatbelfastfood.com) Stay up to date with Belfast's foodie scene.

Trips Through Belfast

CORK

The Republic of Ireland's second city is second only to Dublin in size; in every other respect it considers itself equal to Dublin (or even better). Great restaurants, top-class galleries and a vibrant pub scene lend credence to its claim, while the people are as friendly and welcoming as you'll find anywhere.

Getting Around

Cork's compact centre and easy-to-follow one-way system makes driving a relatively hassle-free experience.

Parking

Streetside parking requires scratch-card parking discs (€2 per hour), obtained from the tourist office and some newsagencies. There are several signposted car parks around the central area, with charges of €2 per hour and €12 overnight.

Where to Eat

The narrow pedestrianised streets north of St Patrick's St are packed with cafes

GABRIEL12/SHUTTERSTOCK ©

TOP EXPERIENCES

➡ Look Upon Cork
Wander up through Shandon and explore the galleries, antique shops and cafes of the city's prettiest neighbourhood, perched on a hill on the northern side of town.

➡ Eyeball the Best of Irish Art
The Crawford Municipal Art Gallery is small, but it's packed with great art by such top Irish names as Jack B Yeats, Nathaniel Hone, Sir John Lavery and Mainie Jellett.

➡ Indulge Your Taste Buds
Cork's foodie scene is made famous by its collection of terrific restaurants, but don't forget the splendid Victorian English Market.

➡ Have a Night on the Town
Atmospheric old pubs, buzzing music venues and a well-respected theatre scene make for a memorable night out.

English Market Cork's produce market

and restaurants, and the place hops day and night. The English Market is *the* place for great produce and outstanding daytime eats.

Where to Stay

Base yourself in town, as close to St Patrick's St and the South Mall as possible. Once you've exhausted the warren of streets between these two locations, venture west across the Lee and wander up to Shandon, where Corkonians regularly take refuge from the city below.

Useful Websites

Cork City Tourism (www.cometocork.com) Sights, accommodation bookings, discounts.

People's Republic of Cork (www.peoplesrepublicofcork.com) Indie guide to what's on in Cork.

WhazOn? (www.whazon.com) Comprehensive entertainment listings.

Trips Through Cork 2 17 18 22

29

IRELAND
BY REGION

Framed by rugged coastlines and peppered with breathtaking scenery, Ireland's compact driving circuit could keep you busy for months. Here's your guide to each region and road trips for the best experiences.

Galway & the West of Ireland (p243)

Connemara has a lyrical beauty that drives artists wild, while County Clare is the spiritual home of traditional Irish music. Between them are the Aran Islands, the very definition of windswept and remote. And don't forget Galway City, Ireland's colourful bohemian capital.

Get musical on Trip 23

Go wild in Connemara on Trip 24

Cork & Southwest Ireland (p171)

The Ireland of the postcard and tourist brochures, the southwest's abundance of stunning drives and iconic scenery will leave you spoilt for choice. From the country's most popular drives to untrodden back roads meandering through the region's gourmet heartland, *this* is the scenic Ireland you came to see.

See the best of Cork on Trip 15

Taste gourmet goodness on Trip 18

Belfast & the North of Ireland (p313)

Beyond the best-known driving routes along the Antrim Coast with its cluster of world-class attractions, the north of Ireland is as delightful as it is surprising, whether you're snaking up a meandering mountain pass in Donegal or exploring the fascinating cities of Belfast and Derry/Londonderry.

Take giant footsteps on Trip

Go mountain wild on Trip

Dublin & Eastern Ireland (p75)

A capital city with all the attractions deserving of the title, Dublin can be explored on foot before you set off to experience its surrounding counties. Within an hour's drive of Dublin there are eye-catching Palladian mansions, remote mountain passes cutting through gorgeous glacial valleys, and prehistoric monuments of world renown.

Explore ancient Ireland on Trip 7

Get mountain fever on Trip 9

IRELAND

Classic Trips

What is a Classic Trip?

All the trips in this book show you the best of Ireland, but we've chosen eight as our all-time favourites. These are our Classic Trips – the ones that lead you to the best of the iconic sights, the top activities and the unique Irish experiences. Turn the page to see our cross-regional Classic Trips, and look out for more Classic Trips throughout the book.

Above: Traditional music session at Matt Molloy's, Westport
Left: Trinity College, Dublin

Classic Trip

Iconic Ireland

1

This trip gives you a glimpse of the best Ireland has to offer, including the country's most famous attractions, most spectacular countryside, and most popular towns and villages.

TRIP HIGHLIGHTS

0 km

Dublin
World-class museums, superb restaurants and terrific nightlife

Roundstone

1 **START**

5

Ennis

460 km

Cliffs of Moher
Majestic sea cliffs rising over 200m from a churning sea

7

Killorglin • **Killarney**
FINISH
Kenmare

670 km

Dingle
Traditional pubs, enticing craft studios and music, music everywhere

7 DAYS
959KM / 596 MILES

GREAT FOR...

BEST TIME TO GO
April to September for the long days and best weather.

ESSENTIAL PHOTO
The Lakes of Killarney from Ladies' View on the Ring of Kerry.

BEST TWO DAYS
The Connemara peninsula and the Ring of Kerry.

larney National Park Ladies' View along the Ring of Kerry

Classic Trip

1 Iconic Ireland

Every time-worn truth about Ireland will be found on this trip: the breathtaking scenery of stone-walled fields and wave-dashed cliffs; the picture-postcard villages and bustling towns; the ancient ruins that have stood since before history was written. The trip begins in Ireland's storied, fascinating capital and transports you to the wild west of Galway and Connemara before taking you south to the even wilder folds of County Kerry.

TRIP HIGHLIGHT

1 Dublin

World-class museums, superb restaurants and the best collection of entertainment in the country – there are plenty of good reasons why the capital is the ideal place to start your trip. Get some sightseeing in on a walking tour (p168) before 'exploring' at least one of the city's storied – if not historic – pubs.

Your top stop should be the grounds of **Trinity College** (☎01-896 1000; www.tcd.ie; College Green; ⏰8am-10pm; 🚌all city centre, 🚆Westmoreland or Trinity), home to the gloriously illuminated **Book of Kells**. It's kept in the stunning 65m Long Room of the **Old Library** (Library Sq; adult/student/family €11/11/28, fast-track €14/11/28; ⏰8.30am-5pm Mon-Sat, from 9.30am Sun May-Sep, 9.30am-5pm Mon-Sat, noon-4.30pm Sun Oct-Apr; 🚌all city centre, 🚆Westmoreland or Trinity).

✕ 🛏 p44, p58, p93, p165

The Drive » It's a 208km trip to Galway city across the country along the M6 motorway, which has little in terms of visual highlights beyond green fields, which get greener and a little more wild the further west you go. Twenty-two kilometres south of Athlone (about halfway) is a worthwhile detour to Clonmacnoise.

----

2 Galway City

The best way to appreciate Galway is to amble (p310) – around Eyre Sq and down Shop St towards the Spanish Arch and the River Corrib, stopping off for a little liquid sustenance in one of the city's classic old pubs. Top of our list is

LINK YOUR TRIP

18 Southwestern Pantry

From Kenmare, it's a 42km drive south to Durrus and the start of the mouth-watering Southwestern Pantry trip.

19 West Cork Villages

You can explore the gorgeous villages of West Cork from Kinsale.

Tig Cóilí (☎091-561 294; www.tigcoiligalway.com; Mainguard St; ☺10.30am-11.30pm Mon-Thu, to 12.30am Fri & Sat, 12.30-11pm Sun), a fire-engine-red pub that draws them in with its two live *céilidh* (traditional music and dancing sessions) each day. A close second is **Tigh Neachtain** (www.tighneachtain.com; 17 Upper Cross St; ☺11.30am-midnight Mon-Thu, to 1am Fri, 10.30am-1am Sat, 12.30-11.30pm Sun), known simply as Neachtain's (*nock*-tans) or Naughtons – stop and join the locals for a pint.

✗ 🏠 p44, p72, p93, p256, p268, p277

The Drive » The most direct route to Roundstone is to cut through Connemara along the N59, turning left on the Clifden Rd – a total of 76km. Alternatively, the 103km coastal route, via the R336 and R340, winds its way around small bays, coves and lovely seaside hamlets.

❸ Roundstone

Huddled on a boat-filled harbour, Roundstone (Cloch na Rón) is one of Connemara's gems. Colourful terrace houses and inviting pubs overlook the dark recess of Bertraghboy Bay, which is home to lobster trawlers and traditional *currachs* (rowing boats) with tarred canvas bottoms stretched over wicker frames.

Just south of the village, in the remains of an old Franciscan monastery, is Malachy Kearns' **Roundstone Musical Instruments** (☎095-35808; www.bodhran.com; Monastery Rd; ☺9.15am-7pm Jul-Sep, 10.30am-6pm Mon-Sat Oct-Jun). Kearns is Ireland's only full-time maker of traditional bodhráns (hand-held goatskin drums). Watch him work and buy a tin whistle, harp or booklet filled with Irish ballads; there's also a small free folk museum and a cafe.

DETOUR: THE SKY ROAD

Start: ❹ Clifden

From the N59 heading north out of Clifden, signs point towards the Sky Road, a 12km route tracing a spectacular loop out to the township of Kingston and back to Clifden, taking in some rugged, stunningly beautiful coastal scenery en route. It's a cinch to drive, but you can also easily walk or cycle it.

The Drive » The 22km inland route from Roundstone to Clifden is a little longer, but the road is better (especially the N59) and the brown, barren beauty of Connemara is yours to behold. The 18km coastal route along the R341 brings you through more speckled landscape; to the south you'll have glimpses of the ocean.

❹ Clifden

Connemara's 'capital', Clifden (An Clochán) is an appealing Victorian-era country town with an amoeba-shaped oval of streets offering evocative strolls. It presides over the head of the narrow bay where the River Owenglin tumbles into the sea. The surrounding countryside beckons you to walk through woods and above the shoreline.

✗ 🏠 p44, p93

The Drive » It's 154km to the Cliffs of Moher; you'll have to backtrack through Galway city (take the N59) before turning south along the N67. This will take you through the unique striated landscape of The Burren, a moody, rocky and at times fearsome space accented with ancient burial chambers and medieval ruins.

TRIP HIGHLIGHT

❺ Cliffs of Moher

Star of a million tourist brochures, the Cliffs of Moher (Aillte an Mothair, or Ailltreacha Mothair) are one of the most popular sights in Ireland.

The entirely vertical cliffs rise to a height of

214m, their edge falling away abruptly into the constantly churning sea. A series of heads, the dark limestone seems to march in a rigid formation that amazes, no matter how many times you look.

Such appeal comes at a price: crowds. This is check-off tourism big time and bus loads come and go constantly in summer. A vast **visitor centre** (☎065-708 6141; www.cliffsofmoher.ie; R478; adult/child incl parking €8/free; ☺8am-9pm May-Aug, to 7pm Mar, Apr, Sep & Oct, 9am-5pm Nov-Feb) handles the hordes.

Like so many over-popular natural wonders, there's relief and joy if you're willing to walk for 10 minutes. Past the end of the 'Moher Wall', a 5km trail leads south along the cliffs to Hag's Head – few venture this far.

The Drive ⟫ The 39km drive to Ennis goes inland at Lahinch (famous for its world-class golf links); it's then 24km to your destination, through flat south Clare. Dotted with stone walls and fields, it's the classic Irish landscape.

 Ennis

As the capital of a renowned music county, Ennis (Inis) is filled with pubs featuring trad music. In fact, this is the best reason to stay here. Where's best changes often; stroll the

streets pub-hopping to find what's on any given night.

If you want to buy an authentic (and well-made) Irish instrument, pop into **Custy's Music Shop** (☎065-682 1727; www.custysmusic.com; Cook's Lane; ☺9am-6pm Mon-Sat), which sells fiddles and other musical items as well as giving general info about the local scene.

🍴🛏️ p45, p268, p309

The Drive ⟫ It's 186km to Dingle if you go via Limerick city, but only 142km if you go via the N68 to Killimer for the ferry across the Shannon estuary to Tarbert. The views get fabulous when you're beyond Tralee on

the N86, especially if you take the 456m Connor Pass, Ireland's highest.

TRIP HIGHLIGHT

⑦ Dingle Town

In summer, Dingle's hilly streets can be clogged with visitors, there's no way around it; in other seasons, its authentic charms are yours to savour. Many pubs double as shops, so you can enjoy Guinness and a singalong among screws and nails, wellies and horseshoes.

🍴🛏️ p45, p59, p195, p257

> ## LOCAL KNOWLEDGE: ENNIS' BEST TRAD SESSION PUBS
>
> **Cíaran's Bar** (☎065-684 0180; Francis St; ☺noon-11.30pm Mon-Sat, to 11pm Sun) Slip into this small place by day and you can be just another geezer pondering a pint. At night there's usually trad music. Bet you wish you had a copy of the Guinness mural out front!
>
> **Brogan's** (☎065-684 4365; www.brogansbarandrestaurant.com; 24 O'Connell St; ☺noon-midnight) On the corner of Cooke's Lane, Brogan's sees a fine bunch of musicians rattling even the stone floors from about 9pm Monday to Thursday, plus even more nights in summer.
>
> **Cruise's Pub** (☎065-682 8963; www.queenshotelennis.com; Abbey St; ☺5.30pm-1am; 📶) There are trad-music sessions most nights from 9.30pm.
>
> **Poet's Corner Bar** (☎065-682 8127; www.flynnhotels.com; Old Ground Hotel, O'Connell St; ☺11am-11.30pm Mon-Thu, to 12.30am Fri & Sat, noon-11pm Sun; 📶) This old pub often has massive trad sessions on Fridays.

Classic Trip

PATRYK KOSMIDER/SHUTTERSTOCK ©

WHY THIS IS A CLASSIC TRIP
FIONN DAVENPORT, WRITER

The loop from Dublin west to Galway and then south through Kerry into Cork explores all of Ireland's scenic heavy hitters. It's the kind of trip I'd make if I was introducing visiting friends to Ireland at its very best, a taster trip that would entice them to come back and explore the country in greater depth.

Above: Old Library Long Run, Trinity College, Dublin
Left: Traditional pub, Dingle Town
Right: Cliffs of Moher, County Clare

PHOTOGRAPHY BY ROBERT RIDDELL/GETTY IMAGES ©

IRELAND'S CLASSIC TRIPS 1 ICONIC IRELAND

The Drive » It's only 17km to Slea Head along the R559. The views – of the mountains to the north and the wild ocean to the south and west – are a big chunk of the reason you came to Ireland in the first place.

----

8 Slea Head

Overlooking the mouth of Dingle Bay, Mt Eagle and the Blasket Islands, Slea Head has fine beaches, good walks and superbly preserved structures from Dingle's ancient past, including **beehive huts**, forts, inscribed stones and church sites. Dunmore Head is the westernmost point on the Irish mainland and the site of the wreckage in 1588 of two Spanish Armada ships.

The Iron Age **Dunbeg Fort** is a dramatic example of a promontory fortification, perched atop a sheer sea cliff about 7km southwest of Ventry on the road to Slea Head. The fort has four outer walls of stone. Inside are the remains of a house and a beehive hut, as well as an underground passage.

The Drive » The 88km to Killarney will take you through Annascaul (home to a pub once owned by Antarctic explorer Tom Crean) and Inch (whose beach is seen in *Ryan's Daughter*). At Castlemaine, turn south towards Miltown then take the R563 to Killarney.

⑨ Killarney

Beyond its proximity to lakes, waterfalls, woodland and moors dwarfed by 1000m-plus peaks, Killarney has many charms of its own as well as being the gateway to the Ring of Kerry, perhaps *the* outstanding highlight of many a visit to Ireland.

Besides the breathtaking views of the mountains and glacial lakes, highlights of the 102-sq-km Killarney National Park include Ireland's only wild herd of native red deer, the country's largest area of ancient oak woods and 19th-century Muckross House.

✕ ⌂ p45, p185, p195

The Drive » It's 27km along the narrow and winding N71 to Kenmare, much of it through magnificent scenery, especially at Ladies' View (much loved by Queen Victoria's ladies-in-waiting) and, 5km further on, Moll's Gap, a popular stop for photos and food.

----

⑩ Kenmare

Picturesque Kenmare carries its romantic reputation more stylishly than does Killarney, and there is an elegance about its handsome central square and attractive buildings. It still gets very busy in summer, all the same. The town stands where the delightfully named Finnihy,

DETOUR:
SKELLIG MICHAEL

Start: ⑫ **Portmagee & Valentia Island**

The jagged, 217m-high rock of **Skellig Michael** (www.heritageireland.ie; ☉mid-May–Sep) (Archangel Michael's Rock, like St Michael's Mount in Cornwall and Mont Saint Michel in Normandy) is the larger of the two Skellig Islands and a Unesco World Heritage site. Early Christian monks survived here from the 6th until the 12th or 13th century; their determined quest for ultimate solitude led them to this remote, windblown edge of Europe.

Skellig Michael featured as Luke Skywalker's secret retreat in the Star Wars movies *The Force Awakens* (2015) and *The Last Jedi* (2017), attracting a whole new audience to the island's dramatic beauty.

It's a tough place to get to, and requires care to visit, but is worth every effort. The 12km sea crossing can be rough, and there are no toilets or shelter, so bring something to eat and drink, and wear stout shoes and weatherproof clothing. Due to the steep (and often slippery) terrain and sudden wind gusts, it's unsuitable for young children or people with limited mobility.

Note that the island's fragility requires limits on the number of daily visitors. The 15 boats are licensed to carry no more than 12 passengers each, for a maximum of 180 people at any one time. It's wise to book ahead in July and August, bearing in mind that if the weather's bad the boats may not sail (about two days out of seven). Trips usually run from Easter until September, depending, again, on weather.

Boats (about €100 per person) leave Portmagee, Ballinskelligs and Derrynane at around 10am, returning at 3pm. Boat owners generally restrict you to two hours on the island, which is the bare minimum to see the monastery, look at the birds and have a picnic. The crossing takes about 1½ hours from Portmagee, 35 minutes to one hour from Ballinskelligs and 1¾ hours from Derrynane.

Roughty and Sheen Rivers empty into Kenmare River. Kenmare makes a pleasant alternative to Killarney as a base for visiting the Ring of Kerry and the Beara Peninsula.

🍴 🛏 p45, p59, p207

The Drive » The 47km to Caherdaniel along the southern stretch of the Ring of Kerry duck in and out of view of Kenmare River, with the marvellous Beara Peninsula to the south. Just before you reach Caherdaniel, a 4km detour north takes you to the rarely visited Staigue Fort, which dates from the 3rd or 4th century.

---

⑪ Caherdaniel

The big attraction here is **Derrynane National Historic Park** (📞066-947 5113; www.derrynanehouse. ie; Derrynane; adult/child €5/3; ⏰10.30am-6pm mid-Mar–Sep, 10am-5pm Oct, to 4pm Sat & Sun Nov–early-Dec; 🅿), the family home of Daniel O'Connell, the campaigner for Catholic emancipation. His ancestors bought the house and surrounding parkland, having grown rich on smuggling with France and Spain. It's largely furnished with O'Connell memorabilia, including the restored triumphal chariot in which he lapped Dublin after his release from prison in 1844.

The Drive » Follow the N70 for about 18km and then turn left onto the Skellig Ring

(roads R567 and R566), cutting through some of the wildest and most beautiful scenery on the peninsula, with the ragged outline of Skellig Michael never far from view. The whole drive is 35km long.

---

⑫ Portmagee & Valentia Island

Portmagee's single street is a rainbow of colourful houses, and is much photographed. On summer mornings, the small pier comes to life with boats embarking on the choppy crossing to the Skellig Islands.

A bridge links Portmagee to 11km-long **Valentia Island** (Oileán Dairbhre), an altogether homier isle than the brooding Skelligs to the southwest. Like the Skellig Ring it leads to, Valentia is an essential, coach-free detour from the Ring of Kerry. Some lonely ruins are worth exploring.

Valentia was chosen as the site for the first transatlantic telegraph cable. When the connection was made in 1858, it put Caherciveen in direct contact with New York. The link worked for 27 days before failing, but went back into action years later.

The island makes an ideal driving loop. From April to October, there's a frequent, quick ferry trip at one end, as well as the bridge to Portmagee

on the mainland at the other end.

The Drive » The 55km between Portmagee and Killorglin keep the mountains to your right (south) and the sea – when you're near it – to your left (north). Twenty-four kilometres along is the unusual Glenbeigh Strand, a tendril of sand protruding into Dingle Bay with views of Inch Point and the Dingle Peninsula.

---

⑬ Killorglin

Killorglin (Cill Orglan) is a quiet enough town, but that all changes in mid-August, when it erupts in celebration for Puck Fair, Ireland's best-known extant pagan festival.

First recorded in 1603, with hazy origins, this lively (read: boozy) festival is based around the custom of installing a billy goat (a poc, or puck), the symbol of mountainous Kerry, on a pedestal in the town, its horns festooned with ribbons. Other entertainment ranges from a horse fair and bonny baby competition to street theatre, concerts and fireworks; the pubs stay open until 3am.

Author Blake Morrison documents his mother's childhood here in *Things My Mother Never Told Me*.

Classic Trip

Eating & Sleeping

Dublin ①

✕ Clanbrassil House   Irish €€

(☑01-453 9786; www.clanbrassilhouse.com; 6 Upper Clanbrassil St; mains €19-28; ⊙5-10pm Tue-Fri, 11.30am-2.30pm & 5-10pm Sat; ☐9, 16, 49, 54A from city centre) With an emphasis on family-style sharing plates, this intimate restaurant consistently turns out exquisite dishes, cooked on a charcoal grill such as rib-eye with bone marrow and anchovy, or ray wing with capers and brown shrimp butter. The hash brown chips are a thing of glory, too.

✕ Greenhouse   Scandinavian €€€

(☑01-676 7015; www.thegreenhouserestaurant. ie; Dawson St; 2-/3-course lunch menu €45/55, 4-/6-course dinner menu €110/129; ⊙noon-2pm & 6-9.30pm Tue-Sat; ☐all city centre, ☐St Stephen's Green) Chef Mickael Viljanen might just be one of the most exciting chefs working in Ireland today thanks to his Scandi-influenced tasting menus, which have made this arguably Dublin's best restaurant. The lunchtime set menu is one of the best bargains in town – a Michelin-starred meal for under 50 bucks. Reservations necessary.

⊨ Cliff Townhouse   Boutique Hotel €€

(☑01-638 3939; www.theclifftownhouse.com; 22 St Stephen's Green N; r from €220; @ 🛜; ☐all city centre, ☐St Stephen's Green) As pieds-à-terre go, this is a doozy: there are 10 exquisitely appointed bedrooms spread across a wonderful Georgian property whose best views overlook St Stephen's Green. Downstairs is Sean Smith's superb restaurant **Cliff Townhouse**.

Galway City ②

✕ Oscar's   Seafood €€

(☑091-582 180; www.oscarsseafoodbistro. com; Upper Dominick St; mains €16-30; ⊙5.30-9.30pm Mon-Sat) The menu changes daily at this outstanding seafood restaurant but it might include monkfish poached in saffron and white wine and served with cockles, seaweed-steamed Galway Bay lobster with garlic-lemon butter, or lemon sole with samphire.

⊨ House Hotel   Boutique Hotel €€

(☑091-538 900; www.thehousehotel.ie; Spanish Pde; d €205-285; 🛜) Inside a former warehouse in the liveliest part of the city, Galway's hippest hotel has a stunning lobby with retro-styled furnishings and modern art, accented with bold shades like fuchsia pink. The 40 soundproofed rooms are small but plush, with vivid colour schemes and quality fabrics. Bathrooms come with toiletries by Irish designer Orla Kiely.

Clifden ④

✕ Mitchell's   Seafood €€

(☑095-21867; www.mitchellsrestaurantclifden. com; Market St; mains lunch €8-16, dinner €18-28; ⊙noon-9pm Mar-Oct) Seafood from the surrounding waters takes centre stage at this elegant spot, from velvety chowder and open crab sandwiches at lunchtime to intricate dinner mains. The highlight is a standout seafood platter (€26), piled high with Ros A Mhil Prawns, Killary mussels, Oranmore oysters, Connemara smoked salmon and Cleggan crab.

⊨ Blue Quay Rooms   B&B €€

(☑087 621 7616; www.bluequayrooms.com; Beach Rd; d €70-100; P 🛜) Painted a vivid shade of blue, this boutique property is even more stunning inside. Adorned with a brass ship's wheel, the nautical-themed lounge has black-and-white chequerboard floor tiles, designer fabrics and fresh flowers. Rooms also blend vintage and contemporary furnishings; all but one have harbour views.

Ennis 6

✕ Rowan Tree Cafe Bar   Fusion €€
(☎065-686 8669; www.rowantreecafebar.ie;
Harmony Row; mains €8-14; ⏱10.30am-11pm;
📶🅿♿) A one-time ballroom, the dining room
here has high ceilings, fairy lights and 18th-
century wooden floors, while tables outside
have river views. Global-themed dishes are
packed with local, seasonal ingredients; treats
include St Tola's goat-cheese fritters, west-
coast crab linguini, and lamb and feta burgers. A
cracking Sunday brunch draws the crowds.

🛏 Old Ground Hotel   Hotel €€€
(☎065-682 8127; www.oldgroundhotelennis.
com; O'Connell St; s €130, d €180-200, ste
€230-275; 📶) Entered through a lobby of
polished floorboards, cornice-work, antiques
and open fires, this prestigious landmark dates
back to the 1800s. The 83 rooms vary greatly
in size and decor, which ranges from historic
to cutting-edge. Kids under 16 staying in their
parents' room are charged €25 per night.

Dingle Town 7

✕ Reel Dingle Fish Co   Fish & Chips €
(☎066-915 1713; Bridge St; mains €5-15; ⏱1-
10pm) Locals queue along the street to get hold
of the freshly cooked local haddock (or cod, or
monkfish, or hake, or mackerel...) and chips at
this tiny outlet. Reckoned to be one of the best
chippies in Kerry, if not in Ireland.

✕ Out of the Blue   Seafood €€€
(☎066-915 0811; www.outoftheblue.ie; The
Wood; mains €19-39; ⏱5-9.30pm Mon-Sat,
12.30-3pm & 5-9.30pm Sun) Occupying a bright
blue-and-yellow waterfront fishing shack, this
rustic spot is one of Dingle's top restaurants,
with an intense devotion to fresh local seafood
(and only seafood). If staff don't like the catch,
they don't open, and they resolutely don't serve
chips. Highlights might include Dingle Bay
prawn bisque with lobster.

🛏 Pax House   B&B €€€
(☎066-915 1518; www.pax-house.com; Upper
John St; d €130-230; ⏱Mar-Dec; 🅿📶) From its
highly individual decor (including contemporary
paintings) to the outstanding views over the
estuary from the glass-framed terrace and
balconies opening from some rooms, Pax House

is a treat. Breakfast incorporates produce
grown in its own garden; families can be
accommodated with fold-out beds.

Killarney 9

✕ Celtic Whiskey Bar & Larder   Gastropub €€
(☎064-663 5700; www.celticwhiskeybar.com;
93 New St; mains €9-27; ⏱food served noon-
9.45pm; 📶) This buzzing gastropub serves
some of the tastiest food in town, with menu
highlights ranging from cheese and charcuterie
platters and aged fillet steaks to brioche sliders
and steamed Glenbeigh mussels.

🛏 Crystal Springs   B&B €€
(☎064-663 3272; www.crystalspringsbandb.
com; Ballycasheen Cross, Woodlawn Rd; s/d
from €98/120; 🅿📶) The timber deck of this
wonderfully relaxing B&B overhangs the River
Flesk, where trout anglers can fish for free.
Rooms are richly furnished with patterned
wallpapers and walnut timber; private
bathrooms (most with spa bath) are huge.

Kenmare 10

✕ Boathouse Bistro   Bistro €€
(☎064-664 2889; www.dromquinnamanor.com;
Dromquinna Manor, Sneem Rd; mains €15-28;
⏱12.30-9pm daily mid-Mar–Sep, Fri-Sun only
Oct–mid-Mar; 🅿) At the water's edge, this
blue-and-white 1870s boathouse 4.5km west
of Kenmare has been stunningly converted
to a beach-house-style bistro specialising in
local seafood delivered daily to its own wharf.
Expertly cooked dishes (Kenmare Bay crab
claws in chilli and garlic butter, beer-battered
fish and chips) are accompanied by a great
selection of by-the-glass wines and craft gins.

🛏 Parknasilla Resort & Spa   Hotel €€€
(☎064-667 5600; www.parknasillaresort.
com; Parknasilla; d/f/ste from €169/195/325;
🅿@📶♿) On the tree-fringed shores of
the Kenmare River with views to the Beara
Peninsula, this hotel has been wowing guests
(including George Bernard Shaw) since 1895.
From the modern, luxuriously appointed
bedrooms to the top-grade spa, private 12-hole
golf course, elegant restaurant and supervised
kids' play area, everything here is done just
right. It's 3km southeast of Sneem.

Classic Trip

The Long Way Round

Why go in a straight line when you can perambulate at leisure? This trip explores Ireland's jagged, scenic and spectacular edges; a captivating loop that takes in the whole island.

2

TRIP HIGHLIGHTS

244 km

Giant's Causeway
One of the natural wonders of the world

600 km

Westport
Photogenic Georgian town with a musical reputation

Belfast

Dublin
START

The Burren
Doolin

Ring of Kerry

Inishmore
Wind-lashed, cliff-protected World Heritage island

740 km

FINISH

1300 km

Ardmore
Secluded seaside village with ancient Christian ruins

**14 DAYS
1300KM /
807 MILES**

GREAT FOR...

BEST TIME TO GO

You'll have the best weather in June and August, but September is ideal.

ESSENTIAL PHOTO

Killahoey Beach from the top of Horn Head.

BEST TWO DAYS

Stops 7 to 9 allow you to experience the very best of the wild west, including a day trip to the Aran Islands.

Dunfanaghy Killahoey Beach from Horn Head

47

Classic Trip

2 The Long Way Round

There's a strong case to be made that the very best Ireland has to offer is closest to its jagged, dramatic coastlines: the splendid scenery, the best mountain ranges (geographically, Ireland is akin to a bowl, with raised edges) and most of its major towns and cities – Dublin, Belfast, Galway, Sligo and Cork. The western edge – between Donegal and Cork – corresponds to the Wild Atlantic Way driving route.

1 Dublin

From its music, art and literature to the legendary nightlife that has inspired those same musicians, artists and writers, Dublin has always known how to have fun and does it with deadly seriousness.

Should you tire of the city's more highbrow offerings, the **Guinness Storehouse** (www.guinness-storehouse.com; St James's Gate, S Market St; adult/child from €18.50/16, Connoisseur Experience €55; ⏰9.30am-7pm Sep-Jun, 9am to 8pm Jul & Aug; 🚌13, 21A, 40, 51B, 78, 78A, 123 from Fleet St, 🚃James's) is the most popular place to visit in town; a beer-lover's Disneyland and multimedia bells-and-whistles homage to the country's most famous export and the city's most enduring symbol. The old grain storehouse is a suitable cathedral in which to worship the black gold; shaped like a giant pint of Guinness, it rises seven impressive storeys high around a central atrium.

✕ 🛏 p44, p58, p93, p165

SCOTLAND

Campbeltown

Giant's
Causeway 3
Ballycastle

North
Channel

Dunfanaghy 4

Buncrana

Coleraine

Rosses
Bay

p51 N56 N13 A2 A37 p50

Letterkenny

Derry

A26

Larne

N56

Strabane

Ballymena

A2

Donegal

A5

Antrim

Omagh

Belfast 2

Donegal
Bay

Lisburn

N15

Dromore

Bundoran

A4

Armagh

Banbridge

Sligo 5

Enniskillen

Monaghan

A1

Ballysadare

Newry

N17

Dundalk

harlestown

N4

N3

Dundalk
Bay

Longford

Drogheda

Irish
Sea

Roscommon

N55

Mullingar

M1

Tuam

M6

Swords

Athlone

Dublin 1 START

Ballinasloe

M6

Tullamore

Naas

Bray

N65

M7

p168

Birr

Portlaoise

Greystones

Wicklow

Nenagh

M7

Carlow

Arklow

Thurles

3

Kilkenny

M11

Limerick

Cashel

M9

Tipperary

Enniscorthy

Clonmel

New Ross

Wexford

M8

Waterford

Rosslare
Harbour

Ballyduff

N25

Mallow

Dungarvan

St George's
Channel

Youghal

13 14 Ardmore

Cork 13

N25

FINISH

Cobh

ATLANTIC
OCEAN

N 0 ——————— 100 km
0 ——————— 50 miles

The Drive » It's 165km of
motorway to Belfast – M1 in the
Republic, A1 in Northern Ireland
– but remember that the speed
limit changes from kilometres
to miles as you cross into the
North.

TRIP HIGHLIGHT

2 Belfast

Belfast is in many ways
a brand-new city. Once
lumped with Beirut,
Baghdad and Bosnia as
one of the four 'Bs' for
travellers to avoid, in
recent years it has pulled
off a remarkable transformation from bombs-
and-bullets pariah to a
hip-hotels-and-hedonism
party town.

The old shipyards on
the Lagan continue to
give way to the luxury
apartments of the Titanic
Quarter, whose centre-
piece, the stunning,

LINK YOUR TRIP

3 Tip to Toe

Kilmore Quay is
134km east of Ardmore,
where you can pick up the
toe part of this trip and do it
in reverse.

**13 Blackwater Valley
Drive**

From Ardmore, it's only 5km
to Youghal, where you can
explore the gorgeous valley
of the Blackwater River.

star-shaped edifice housing the **Titanic Belfast centre** (www.titanicbelfast. com; Queen's Rd; adult/child £18.50/8; ⏰9am-7pm Jun & Jul, to 8pm Aug, to 6pm Apr, May & Sep, 10am-5pm Oct-Mar; 🚍G2), covering the ill-fated liner's construction

here, has become the city's number-one draw.

New venues keep popping up – already this decade historic **Crumlin Road Gaol** (📞028-9074 1500; www.crumlinroadgaol. com; 53-55 Crumlin Rd; tour adult/child £12/7.50; ⏰10am-5.30pm, last tour 4.30pm; 🚍12B, 57) and **SS Nomadic** opened to the public, and WWI warship **HMS Caroline** became a floating museum in 2016.

They all add to a list of attractions that includes beautifully restored Victorian architecture, a glittering waterfront lined with modern art, a fantastic foodie scene and music-filled pubs.

If you're keen on learning more about the city's troubled history, take a walking tour of West Belfast (p368).

🍴 🛏 p58, p359

The Drive » The fastest way to the causeway is to take the A26 north, through Ballymena, before turning off at Ballymoney – a total of 100km – but the longer (by 16km), more scenic route is to take the A8 to Larne and follow the coast through handsome Cushendall and popular Ballycastle.

DETOUR: GIANT'S CAUSEWAY TO BALLYCASTLE

Start: ❸ Giant's Causeway

Between the Giant's Causeway and Ballycastle lies the most scenic stretch of the Causeway Coast, with sea cliffs of contrasting black basalt and white chalk, rocky islands, picturesque little harbours and broad sweeps of sandy beach. It's best enjoyed on foot, following the 16.5km of waymarked **Causeway Coast Way** (www.walkni.com) between the Carrick-a-Rede car park and the Giant's Causeway, although the main attractions can also be reached by car or bus.

About 8km east of the Giant's Causeway is the meagre ruin of 16th-century **Dunseverick Castle**, spectacularly sited on a grassy bluff. Another 1.5km on is the tiny seaside hamlet of **Portbradden**, with half a dozen harbourside houses and the tiny, blue-and-white **St Gobban's Church**, said to be the smallest in Ireland. Visible from Portbradden and accessible via the next junction off the A2 is the spectacular **White Park Bay**, with its wide, sweeping sandy beach.

The main attraction on this stretch of coast is the famous (or notorious, depending on your head for heights) **Carrick-a-Rede Rope Bridge** (📞028-2073 3335; www.nationaltrust.org.uk/carrick-a-rede; 119 Whitepark Rd, Ballintoy; adult/child £9/4.50; ⏰9.30am-6pm Apr-Oct, to 3.30pm Nov-Mar). The 20m-long, 1m-wide bridge of wire rope spans the chasm between the sea cliffs and the little island of Carrick-a-Rede, swaying gently 30m above the rock-strewn water.

TRIP HIGHLIGHT

❸ Giant's Causeway

When you first see it you'll understand why the ancients believed the causeway was not a natural feature. The vast expanse of regular, closely packed, hexagonal stone columns dipping gently beneath the waves looks for all the world like the handiwork of giants.

This spectacular rock formation – a national nature reserve and Northern Ireland's only Unesco World Heritage site – is one of Ireland's most impressive and atmospheric landscape features, but it can get very crowded. If you can, try to visit midweek or out of season to experience it at its most evocative. Sunset in spring and autumn is the best time for photographs.

Visiting the Giant's Causeway itself is free of charge but you pay to use the car park on a combined ticket with the **Giant's Causeway Visitor Experience** (028-2073 1855; www.nationaltrust.org. uk; 60 Causeway Rd; adult/child £12.50/6.25; ⊙9am-7pm Jun-Sep, to 6pm Mar-May & Oct, to 5pm Nov-Feb); parking-only tickets aren't available.

✕ p58

The Drive >> Follow the A29 and A37 as far as Derry/Londonderry, then cross the invisible border into the Republic and take the N13 to Letterkenny before turning northwest along the N56 to Dunfanaghy. It's a total of 136km.

④ Dunfanaghy

Huddled around the waterfront beneath the headland of Horn Head, Dunfanaghy's small, attractive town centre has a surprisingly wide range of accommodation and some of the finest dining options in the county's northwest. Glistening beaches, dramatic coastal cliffs, mountain trails and forests are all within a few kilometres.

✕ ⊨ p58, p327, p335

The Drive >> The 145km south to Sligo town will take you back through Letterkenny (this stretch is the most scenic), after which you'll follow the N13 as far as Ballyshannon and then, as you cross into County Sligo, the N15 to Sligo town.

⑤ Sligo Town

Sligo is in no hurry to shed its cultural traditions but it doesn't sell them out either. Pedestrian streets lined with inviting shopfronts, stone bridges spanning the River Garavogue and céilidh sessions spilling from pubs contrast with genre-bending contemporary art and glass towers rising from prominent corners of the compact town.

✕ ⊨ p58, p72, p293, p301, p351

The Drive >> It's 100km to Westport, as you follow the N17 (and the N5 once you leave Charlestown); the landscape is flat, the road flanked by fields, hedgerows and farmhouses.

Castlebar, 15km before Westport, is a busy county town.

TRIP HIGHLIGHT

⑥ **Westport**

There's a lot to be said for town planning, especially if 18th-century architect James Wyatt was the brain behind the job. Westport (Cathair na Mairt), positioned on the River Carrowbeg and the shores of Clew Bay, is easily Mayo's most beautiful town and a major tourist destination for visitors to this part of the country.

It's a Georgian classic, its octagonal square and tidy streets lined with trees and handsome buildings, most of which date from the late 18th century.

The Drive >> Follow the N5 then the N84 as far as the outskirts of Galway city – a trip of about 100km. Take the

DETOUR: HORN HEAD

Start: ④ Dunfanaghy

Horn Head has some of Donegal's most spectacular coastal scenery and plenty of birdlife. Its dramatic quartzite cliffs, covered with bog and heather, rear over 180m, and the view from their tops is heart-pounding.

The road circles the headland; the best approach by car is in a clockwise direction from the Falcarragh end of Dunfanaghy. On a fine day, you'll encounter tremendous views of Tory, Inishbofin, Inishdooey and tiny Inishbeg islands to the west; Sheep Haven Bay and the Rosguill Peninsula to the east; Malin Head to the northeast; and the coast of Scotland beyond. Take care in bad weather as the route can be perilous.

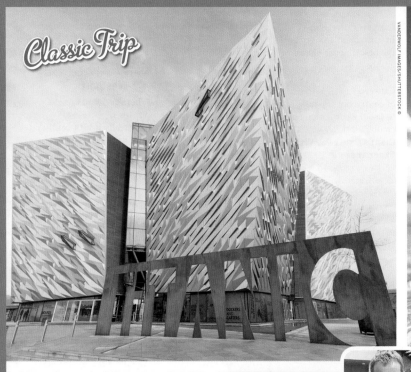

Classic Trip

VANDERWOLF IMAGES/SHUTTERSTOCK ©

GEOSTOCK/GETTY IMAGES ©

WHY THIS IS A CLASSIC TRIP
FIONN DAVENPORT, WRITER

Not only are you covering the spectacular landscapes of mountains and jagged coastlines of the Wild Atlantic Way, but you can explore the modern incarnation of the country's earliest settlements, taking you from prehistoric monuments to bustling cities.

Above: Titanic Belfast Centre, Belfast
Left: Clock Tower, Westport
Right: Giant's Causeway on the Antrim Coast

N18 south into County Clare. At Kilcolgan, turn onto the N67. Ballyvaughan provides a good base to explore the heart of The Burren.

----

⑦ The Burren

The karst landscape of The Burren is not the green Ireland of postcards. But there are wildflowers in spring, giving the 560-sq-km Burren brilliant, if ephemeral, colour amid its austere beauty. Soil may be scarce, but the small amount that gathers in the cracks and faults is well drained and nutrient-rich. This, together with the mild Atlantic climate, supports an extraordinary mix of Mediterranean, Arctic and alpine plants. Of Ireland's native wildflowers, 75% are found here, including 24 species of beautiful orchids, the creamy-white burnet rose, the little starry flowers of mossy saxifrage and the magenta-coloured bloody cranesbill.

The Drive » It's some 40km to Doolin, heading south first via the N67 then onto the R480, which corkscrews over the lunar, limestone landscape of The Burren's exposed hills. Next curve west onto the R476 to meander towards Doolin via more familiar Irish landscapes of green fields, and the villages of Kilfenora and Lisdoonvarna – great for pit stops and trad-music sessions.

⑧ Doolin

Doolin is renowned as a centre of Irish traditional music, but it's also known for its setting – 6km north of the Cliffs of Moher – and down near the ever-unsettled sea, the land is windblown, with huge rocks exposed by the long-vanished topsoil. Many musicians live in the area, and they have a symbiotic relationship with the tourists: each desires the other and each year the music scene grows

a little larger. But given the heavy concentration of visitors, it's inevitable that standards don't always hold up to those in some of the less-trampled villages in Clare.

The Drive ›› Ferries from Doolin to Inishmore take about 90 minutes to make the crossing.

TRIP HIGHLIGHT

⑨ Inishmore

A step (and boat or plane ride) beyond the desolate beauty of The Burren are the Aran Islands. Most visitors are satisfied to explore only Inishmore (Inis Mór) and its main attraction, **Dun Aengus** (Dún Aonghasa; ☑099-61008; www.heritageireland.ie; adult/

child €5/3; ⌚9.30am-6pm Apr-Oct, to 4pm Nov-Mar), the stunning stone fort perched perilously on the island's towering cliffs. Powerful swells pound the 87m-high cliff face. A complete lack of rails or other modern additions that would spoil this amazing ancient site means that you can not only go right up to the cliff's edge but also potentially fall to your doom below quite easily. When it's uncrowded, you can't help but feel the extraordinary energy that must have been harnessed to build this vast site.

The arid landscape west of Kilronan (Cill Rónáin), Inishmore's main settlement, is dominated by stone walls, boulders, scattered buildings and the odd patch of deep-green grass and potato plants.

✕ 🍴 p59, p93, p269, p309

The Drive ›› Once you're back on terra firma at Doolin, it's 223km to Dingle via the N85 to Ennis then the M18 to Limerick city. The N69 will take you into County Kerry as far as Tralee, beyond which it's 50km on the N86 to Dingle.

⑩ Dingle

Unlike the Ring of Kerry, where the cliffs tend to dominate the ocean, it's the ocean that dominates the smaller Dingle Peninsula. The opal-blue

---

DOOLIN'S MUSIC PUBS

Doolin's three main music pubs (others are recent interlopers) are, in order of importance to the music scene:

›› **McGann's** (☑065-707 4133; www.mcgannspubdoolin. com; Roadford; ⌚10am-11.30pm Mon-Wed, to 12.30am Thu-Sat, to 11pm Sun; 🛜) McGann's has all the classic touches of a full-on Irish music pub; the action often spills out onto the street. The food here is the best of the trio.

›› **Gus O'Connor's** (☑065-707 4168; www.gusoconnors doolin.com; Fisherstreet; ⌚9am-midnight Mon-Thu, to 2am Fri-Sun) Right on the water, this sprawling favourite packs them in and has a rollicking atmosphere when the music and drinking are in full swing.

›› **McDermott's** (MacDiarmada's; ☑065-707 4328; www. mcdermottspub.com; Roadford; ⌚10am-11pm Sun-Wed, to 12.30am Thu-Sat) Also known as MacDiarmada's, this simple red-and-white old pub can be the rowdy favourite of locals. When the fiddles get going, it can seem like a scene out of a John Ford movie.

waters surrounding the promontory's multihued landscape of green hills and golden sands give rise to aquatic adventures and to fishing fleets that haul in fresh seafood that appears on the menus of some of the county's finest restaurants.

Centred on charming Dingle town, there's an alternative way of life here, lived by artisans and idiosyncratic characters and found at trad sessions and folkloric festivals across Dingle's tiny settlements.

The classic loop drive around Slea Head from Dingle town is 47km, but allow a day to take it all in – longer if you have time to stay overnight in Dingle town.

✖ 🛏 p45, p59, p195, p257

The Drive » Take the N86 as far as Annascaul and then the coastal R561 as far as Castlemaine. Then head southwest on the N70 to Killorglin and the Ring of Kerry. From Dingle, it's 53km.

- - - - - - - - - - - - - - - - - -

⑪ Ring of Kerry

The Ring of Kerry is the longest and the most diverse of Ireland's big circle drives, combining jaw-dropping coastal scenery with emerald pastures and villages.

The 179km circuit usually begins in Killarney and winds past pristine beaches, the island-dotted Atlantic, medieval ruins, mountains and loughs (lakes). The coastline is at its most rugged between Waterville and Caherdaniel in the southwest of the peninsula. It can get crowded in summer, but even then, the remote Skellig Ring can be uncrowded and serene – and starkly beautiful.

The Ring of Kerry can easily be done as a day trip, but if you want to stretch it out, places to stay are scattered along the route. Killorglin and Kenmare have the best dining options, with some excellent restaurants; elsewhere, basic (sometimes very basic) pub fare is the norm. The Ring's most popular diversion is the Gap of Dunloe, an awe-inspiring mountain pass at the western edge of Killarney National Park. It's signposted off the N72 between Killarney and Killorglin. The incredibly popular 19th-century Kate Kearney's Cottage is a pub where most visitors park their cars before walking up to the gap.

- - - - - - - - - - - - - - - - - -

⑫ Kenmare

If you've done the Ring in an anticlockwise fashion (or cut through the Gap of Dunloe), you'll end up in handsome Kenmare, a largely 18th-century town and the ideal alternative to Killarney as a place to stay overnight.

✖ 🛏 p45, p59, p207

The Drive » Picturesque villages, a fine stone circle and calming coastal scenery mark the less-taken 143km route from Kenmare to Cork city. When you get to Leap, turn right onto the R597 and go as far as Rosscarbery; or, even better, take twice as long (even though it's only 24km more) and make your way along narrow roads near the water the entire way.

AN ANCIENT FORT

For a look at a well-preserved *caher* (walled fort) of the late Iron Age to early Christian period, stop at **Caherconnell Fort** (📞065-708 9999; www.caherconnell. com; R480; adult/child €6/4, sheepdog demonstration €5/3, combination ticket €9.60/5.60; ⏱10am-6pm Jul & Aug, to 5.30pm May, Jun & Sep, 10.30am-5pm mid-Mar–Apr & Oct), a privately run heritage attraction that's more serious than sideshow. Exhibits detail how the evolution of these defensive settlements may have reflected territorialism and competition for land among a growing, settling population. The drystone walling of the fort is in excellent condition. The top-notch visitor centre also has information on many other monuments in the area. It's about 1km south of Poulnabrone Dolmen on the R480.

Classic Trip

⑬ Cork City

The Republic's second city is first in every important respect, at least according to the locals, who cheerfully refer to it as the 'real capital of Ireland'. The compact city centre is surrounded by interesting waterways and is chock full of great restaurants fed by arguably the best foodie scene in the country.

🍴 🛏 p59, p207, p215, p257

The Drive >> It's only 60km to Ardmore, but stop off in Midleton, 24km east of Cork along the N25, and visit the whiskey museum. Just beyond Youghal, turn right onto the R673 for Ardmore.

TRIP HIGHLIGHT

⑭ Ardmore

Due to its location off the main drag, Ardmore is a sleepy seaside village and one of the southeast's loveliest spots – the ideal destination for those looking for a little waterside R&R.

St Declan reputedly set up shop here sometime between AD 350 and 420, which would make Ardmore the first Christian bastion in Ireland – long before St Patrick landed. The village's 12th-century round tower, one of the best examples of these structures in Ireland, is the town's most distinctive architectural feature, but you should also check out the ruins of St Declan's church and holy well, 1km east on a bluff on Ardmore's signposted 5km cliff walk.

LOCAL KNOWLEDGE: THE HEALY PASS

Instead of going directly into County Cork along the N71 from Kenmare, veer west onto the R571 and drive for 16km along the northern edge of the Beara Peninsula. At Lauragh, turn onto the R574 and take the breathtaking **Healy Pass Road**, which cuts through the peninsula and brings you from County Kerry into County Cork. At Adrigole, turn left onto the R572 and rejoin the N71 at Glengarriff, 17km east.

Ruins of St Declan's church and holy well, Ardmore

Eating & Sleeping

Dublin ❶

✖ Pi Pizza

Pizza €€

(www.pipizzas.ie; 73-83 S Great George's
St; pizzas €9-16; ⏰noon-10pm Sun-Wed, to
10.30pm Thu-Sat; 🚊all city centre) Reg White
cut his pie-making teeth at flour + water in
San Francisco before opening this fabulous
restaurant in 2018, and it's already a contender
for best pizzeria in town. The smallish menu has
just eight pizzas, each an inspired interpretation
of a Neapolitan classic. Highly recommended
are the *funghi* or *broccolini*, 'white' pizzas made
without the tomato layer.

🛏 Westbury Hotel

Hotel €€€

(☎01-679 1122; www.doylecollection.com;
Grafton St; r/ste from €430/580; 🅿 @ 🛜;
🚊all city centre, 🚊St Stephen's Green) Tucked
away just off Grafton St is one of the most
elegant hotels in town. The upstairs lobby is a
great spot for afternoon tea or a drink, and the
two restaurants on-site — Balfes and Wilde —
are both exceptional.

Belfast ❷

✖ Saphyre

Modern Irish £££

(☎028-9068 8606; www.saphyrerestaurant.
com; 135 Lisburn Rd; mains lunch £10, dinner
£24-32; ⏰11am-3pm & 5-10pm Wed-Fri, 10am-
3pm & 5-10pm Sat; 🚊9A to 9C) Spectacularly
set inside the 1924 Ulsterville Presbyterian
Church (behind an interior-design showroom),
Saphyre serves some of the most sophisticated
cooking in Belfast today. Menus change
seasonally and include a five-course tasting
menu (£50); each dish is a masterpiece. Brunch
is available from 11am to 3pm and there's live
music on Saturdays from 1pm to 3pm.

🛏 Merchant Hotel

Hotel £££

(☎028-9023 4888; www.themerchanthotel.
com; 16 Skipper St; d/ste from £180/350;

🅿 @ 🛜; 🚊3A, 4D, 5A, 6A) Belfast's most
flamboyant hotel occupies the palatial
former Ulster Bank head office. Rooms are
individually decorated with a fabulous fusion
of contemporary styling and old-fashioned
elegance; those in the original Victorian building
have opulent floor-length silk curtains while
newer rooms have an art deco–inspired theme.
Facilities include a luxurious spa and an eight-
person rooftop hot tub.

Giant's Causeway ❸

✖ Causeway Hotel

Irish ££

(www.thecausewayhotel.com; 40 Causeway Rd;
mains £10-21; ⏰noon-8.30pm) The restaurant
at the Causeway Hotel serves an all-day menu of
hearty dishes like chowder with wheaten bread,
fish and chips, burgers and pasta. The dinner
menu is more refined and features the likes of
oven-baked salmon and cod, crispy duck breast
and sirloin steak.

Dunfanaghy ❹

✖ Cove

Modern Irish €€

(☎074-913 6300; www.facebook.com/
coverestaurantdonegal; off N56, Rockhill, Port-na-
Blagh; dinner mains €20-30; ⏰6.30-9.30pm
Tue-Sun) Owners Siobhan Sweeney and Peter
Byrne are perfectionists who tend to every detail
in Cove's art-filled dining room, and on your
plate. The cuisine is fresh and inventive. Seafood
specials are deceptively simple with subtle Asian
influences, and after dinner you can enjoy the
elegant lounge upstairs. There's an excellent
wine list. Book ahead.

Sligo Town ❺

✖ Lyons Cafe

Irish €

(☎071-914 2969; www.lyonscafe.com; Quay St;
mains €8-16; ⏰9am-6pm Mon-Sat) The cafe in
Sligo's flagship department store, Lyons first

opened in 1926, but the food served in the airy, 1st-floor eatery is bang up to date. Acclaimed chef and cookbook author Gary Stafford offers a fresh and seasonal menu that's inventive yet casual.

🛏 Glass House   Hotel €€

(📞071-919 4300; www.theglasshouse.ie; Swan Point; s €103, d €112-129, ste €138-155; 🛜) You can't miss this cool and contemporary four-star hotel in the centre of town, its sharp glass facade jutting skyward. Inside, the food areas have good river views, there are two bars and the 116 well-equipped rooms come in a choice of zesty colours.

Inishmore ➐

🛏 Kilmurvey House   B&B €€

(📞099-61218; www.aranislands.ie/kilmurvey-house; Kilmurvey; s/d from €60/95; 🕐Apr–mid-Oct; 🛜) There's a dash of grandeur about Kilmurvey House, where 12 spacious rooms sit in an imposing, 18th-century stone mansion. Breakfasts are convivial affairs, with homemade granola, porridge with whiskey and baked scones. It's a 500m stroll east to swim at pretty **Kilmurvey Beach**. Children under 16 aren't permitted.

Dingle Town ➓

🍴 Doyle's   Seafood €€€

(📞066-915 2674; www.doylesrestaurantdingle. ie; 4 John St; mains €25-33; 🕐5-9.30pm Mon-Sat, to 7.30pm Sun) Cherry-red-painted Doyle's serves some of the best seafood in the area (which in these parts is really saying something). Starters such as Dingle Bay crab claws or oysters au naturel team up with mains like fennel-scented Spanish fish stew, seafood linguine and roast monkfish cassoulet.

Kenmare ⑫

🍴 Tom Crean Fish & Wine   Irish €€

(📞064-664 1589; www.tomcrean.ie; Main St; mains €17-31; 🕐5-9.30pm Thu-Mon Sep-Jun, daily Jul & Aug; 🛜) Named for Kerry's

pioneering Antarctic explorer, and run by his granddaughter, this venerable restaurant uses only the best of local organic produce, cheeses and fresh seafood. Sneem lobster is available in season, the oysters au naturel capture the scent of the sea, and the seafood gratin served in a scallop shell is divine. Upstairs, the 19th-century townhouse has boutique rooms with king-size beds (doubles from €75).

🛏 Virginia's Guesthouse   B&B €

(📞086 306 5291; www.virginias-kenmare. com; 36 Henry St; s/d from €40/75; 🛜) You'll be hard-pushed to find better value than this central B&B with eight comfy rooms and a lounge/library with free tea and coffee, but the trade-off is weekend street noise (earplugs are supplied). Other caveats include no breakfast (but there are cafes nearby), no kids under 12 and check-in strictly before 9pm.

Cork City ⑬

🍴 Market Lane   Irish €€

(📞021-427 4710; www.marketlane.ie; 5 Oliver Plunkett St; mains €14-25; 🕐noon-9.30pm Mon-Wed, to 10pm Thu, to 10.30pm Fri & Sat, 1-9.30pm Sun; 🛜🚻) It's always hopping at this bright corner bistro. The menu is broad and hearty, changing to reflect what's fresh at the English Market: perhaps roast hake with wild garlic velouté, or beetroot, walnut and feta cakes? No reservations for fewer than six diners; sip a drink at the bar until a table is free. Lots of wines by the glass.

🛏 Montenotte Hotel   Boutique Hotel €€€

(📞021-453 0050; www.themontenottehotel. com; Middle Glanmire Rd; d/f from €189/229; 🅿🛜🏊) Built as a private residence for a wealthy merchant in the 1820s, the Montenotte has been reimagined as a boutique hotel that skilfully blends its 19th-century legacy with bold designer colour schemes. The hilltop location commands superb views, especially from the roof-terrace bar and restaurant, and guests can enjoy the hotel's sunken Victorian garden, private cinema and luxurious spa.

Classic Trip

Tip to Toe

3

*If this trip were a film it would be a road epic.
Sweep from mountain passes down cliff-side
roads past sandy shores to charismatic cities,
big-name sights and hidden beaches.*

TRIP HIGHLIGHTS

Mt Errigal

1 START

0 km

**Glengesh
Pass**

7

Sligo

Derry
Witness remarkable
attempts to heal the
sectarian past

160 km

Sliabh Liag
Get thrillingly close to
towering, multi-
coloured sea cliffs

Galway

680 km

Kilkenny
Revel in the urban
pleasures of vibrant
Kilkenny

15

620 km

14

**Kilmore
Quay**

FINISH

Rock of Cashel
Explore an ancient
power base of
churchmen and kings

**10 DAYS
950KM /
590 MILES**

GREAT FOR...

BEST TIME TO GO

Spring and autumn
to avoid summer
crowds.

**ESSENTIAL
PHOTO**

Mountainous
Glengesh Pass for a
'did I really drive that?'
snap.

**BEST THREE
DAYS**

Stops 11 to 15 for
party-town Galway,
elegant Birr and iconic
Rock of Cashel.

Classic Trip

3 Tip to Toe

This 10-day trip takes in so much. You'll bob on a boat beneath 600m-high cliffs, clamber over castle ruins and marvel at massive seabird colonies. Scenery-rich routes link sites telling tales of rebellion, the Troubles, famine and faith. Memorable days connect experiences rich in Irish culture, from lyrical poetry to pubs alive with traditional music. On this trip you'll really discover Ireland, tip to toe, head to heart.

TRIP HIGHLIGHT

1 Derry

Derry comes as a pleasant surprise to many visitors: a vibrant, riverside city, encircled by impressive, 17th-century fortifications. Like Belfast it has a past of bitter sectarian divisions, but here too a remarkable healing is underway. Get a true taste of both the enormity of the problems and the progress by walking (p370) around the city, strolling atop the city walls, passing Unionist strongholds and absorbing the powerful murals of the Republican Bogside district. Be sure to visit the **Tower Museum** (www. derrystrabane.com/tower museum; Union Hall Pl; adult/child £3/1.50; ⏱10am-5.30pm, last entry 4pm), where audiovisual exhibits bring the city's rich and complex past to life.

✕🛏 p72, p327, p359

The Drive >> As the A2/N13 heads west out of Derry towards Letterkenny, road signs switch from mph to km/h: you've just entered the Irish Republic. At Bridgend follow signs left up to Grianán of Aileách (12km).

② Grianán of Aileách

This fort encircles Grianán Hill like a halo. Ducking in through its cave-like entrance and clambering up its tiered battlements reveals eye-popping views of Lough Swilly, with Inch Island plumb in the centre; Counties Donegal, Derry and Tyrone stretch out all the way around.

It's thought the site was in use in pre-Celtic times as a temple to the god Dagda, becoming the seat of the O'Neills between the 5th and 12th centuries. It was demolished by Murtogh O'Brien, king of Munster, and most of these remains are a 19th-century reconstruction.

The Drive » The N13 cruises west to traffic-choked Letterkenny (with some handy

LINK YOUR TRIP

12 Wexford & Waterford

Scenic shorelines, birdlife and fishing villages. Start where this trips stops: Kilmore Quay.

24 Mountains & Moors

Drive deep into romantic Connemara. Pick it up from, and return to, Galway city on this trip's route.

Classic Trip

accommodation options). There, climb north gradually on the N56 towards Dunfanaghy, with the distant Glendowan Mountains sliding into view. Once up in the high hills, take the R255 left to Glenveagh National Park (50km) and Glenveagh Castle.

----

❸ Glenveagh National Park

Lakes shimmer like dew in mountainous **Glenveagh National Park** (Páirc Náisiúnta Ghleann Bheatha; www. glenveaghnationalpark.ie), where knuckles of rock alternate with green-gold bogs and oak and birch forest. In delightfully showy **Glenveagh Castle** (www.glenveaghnationalpark.ie;

off R251; adult/child 30min tour €7/5, bus from visitor centre adult/child $3/2; ⏱9.15am-5.30pm Apr-Oct, 9am-5pm Nov-Mar, last tours 45min before closing), rooms combine stuffed stags with flamboyant furnishings, with highlights being the tartan-and-antler-covered music room and the blue single ladies' room (formerly Greta Garbo's).

The exotic gardens are spectacular with their terraces and Italianate style a marked contrast to the wildly beautiful landscape. A shuttle bus runs to the castle from the visitor centre, but the 3.6km walk is a better way to soak up the scenery.

The Drive ›› Head west on the R251, an exhilarating, bouncing drive through cinematic scenery: the Derryveagh Mountains tower to your left,

and the fast-approaching peak of Mt Errigal fills your windscreen ahead. At the hamlet of Dunlewey (Dún Lúiche, 16km), turn left to the lake.

----

❹ Dunlewey

Simply stepping out of your car in this mountain hamlet provides an insight into the isolated way of life this high in the hills. It's underlined at the **Dunlewey Centre** (Ionad Cois Locha; ☎074-953 1699; www.dunleweycentre. com; Dunlewey; cottage or boat trip adult/child €7.25/5.25, cottage & boat €13.50/9.50; ⏱10.30am-5.30pm Easter-Sep, to 4.45pm Oct; ♿), where the 30-minute tour of a thatched weaver's cottage reveals a huge loom, spartan bedroom (complete with chamber pot under the iron bedstead) and snug lounge warmed by a peat fire.

🛏 p72, p335

The Drive ›› The R251, then the N56, begin a slow descent south, bumping past crags and sudden loughs and bogs. Shortly after heritage-town Ardara turn right, following brown signs to Glengesh Pass. It's an ear-popping ascent up hairpin bends and past wayside shrines. Near the top, 60km from Dunlewey, turn right into the walled parking bay.

----

❺ Glengesh Pass

Glengesh Pass provides one of Donegal's most spectacular mountain views, and this parking spot is *the* place to take that holiday snap. A V-shaped valley sweeps

---

↱ DETOUR: LOUGHREA PENINSULA

Start: ❹ **Dunlewey**

This leg's scenery is beautiful enough, but if you fancy some sandy shores with your mountains, try this detour. Around 20km south of Dungloe, at Maas, instead of swinging left on the N56 to Glenties, peel right onto the coastal R261, which winds deep into beautiful Loughrea Peninsula. Next, take a minor road right to **Narin**, following signs to the **beach** (*trá*), a 4km-long, spectacular, dune-backed, sandy stretch, where you can walk out to tiny **Iniskeel Island** at low tide.

Post-stroll, continue on the shoreside road, past Portnoo and Rossbeg, rejoining the R261, then the N56 at Ardara.

away far below, while the Derryveagh Mountains line up far behind. The road you've just driven up is a tiny ribbon, snaking off into the distance. There's a picnic area immediately below the parking spot, ensuring an al-fresco meal with a truly memorable view.

The Drive >> Edging over the pass, a cluster of wind turbines spins into view. Descend gradually, past unfenced grazing land (watch out for free-roaming sheep) and neat piles of drying peat. Suddenly, the sea around Glen Head appears. Head through Glencolumbcille (Gleann Cholm Cille, 16km) on the Malin Beg Rd; the folk village comes soon after.

⑥ Glencolumbcille

Glencolumbcille may feel like the middle of nowhere, but the three-pub village offers scalloped beaches, a strong sense of Irish identity and an insight into a fast-disappearing way of life.
Father McDyer's Folk Village (www.glenfolkvillage. com; Doonalt; adult/child €6/5; ☺10am-6pm Mon-Sat, from noon Sun Easter-Sep, 11am-4.30pm Oct) was set up in 1967 to freeze-frame traditional folk life for posterity. Its six thatched 18th- and 19th-century cottages are packed with everyday items, from beds and cooking pans to tools and open fires.

✗ p72

The Drive >> The R263 snakes south and soon reveals the massive mountain of Sliabh Liag. Edge past it to Carrick (An Charraig) then follow brown Sliabh Liag signs south beside the inlet to tiny Teelin (Tieleann, 9km).

TRIP HIGHLIGHT
⑦ Sliabh Liag

The Cliffs of Moher may be more famous, but the ones at Sliabh Liag (Slieve League) are taller – some of the highest in Europe, in fact. This 600m-high, multicoloured rock face seems stark and otherworldly as it rears up from the Atlantic Ocean. A diminutive 12-seater boat, the **Nuala Star** (☏087 628 4688; www.sliabhleagueboat-trips.com; Teelin Pier; tours per person €20-25; ☺Apr-Oct), sets off from Teelin to the foot of the cliffs. The trips are weather dependent and have to be booked. If the sea is too rough, you can drive or walk to the cliffs.

The Drive >> The drive east from Carrick completes a gradual descent from wild, pitted hills to smoother urban life; remote homesteads give way to garden-fronted houses. The N56 skirts Donegal town, from where the N15 heads south to Sligo, 110km from Sliabh Liag.

----

⑧ Sligo Town

An appealing overnight base, vibrant Sligo combines lively pubs and futuristic buildings with old stone bridges and a historic abbey. It also shines a spotlight on William Butler Yeats (1865–1939), Sligo's greatest literary figure and one of Ireland's premier poets.

DETOUR: DONEGAL CASTLE

Start: ⑦ **Sliabh Liag**
Midway between Sliabh Liag and Sligo, riverside **Donegal Castle** (☏074-972 2405; www.heritageireland. ie; Castle St; adult/child €5/3; ☺10am-6pm daily Easter–mid-Sep, 9.30am-4.30pm Thu-Mon mid-Sep–Easter) makes for a picturesque detour. The original 1474 castle was torched then rebuilt in 1623, along with a neighbouring Jacobean house. It's a deeply attractive spot: grassy lawns lead up to geometric battlements, and rooms are packed with fine furnishings and antiques.

The castle is in the centre of pretty Donegal town. Follow signs from the N56 and afterwards take the N15 to Sligo.

Classic Trip

WHY THIS IS A CLASSIC TRIP
ISABEL ALBISTON,
WRITER

It's not just dizzying clifftops, the wild Atlantic roaring and spraying below, and the only reminder of proximate civilisation drifting over in the scent of tangy peat smoke and the sound of bleating sheep; it's also vibrant cities packed with culture and buzzing with nightlife. From the stark mountains in the north to the gentle lowlands of the south, this trip is one heck of a drive.

Above: Rock of Cashel, County Tipperary
Left: Sliabh Liag, County Donegal
Right: Peace Bridge over the Foyle River, Derry

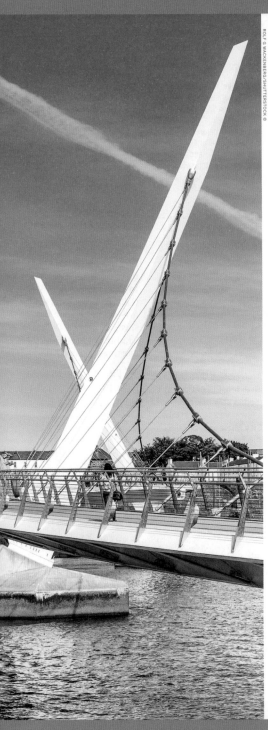

ROLF G WACKENBERG/SHUTTERSTOCK ©

Sligo County Museum
(☎071-911 1679; www.
sligoarts.ie; Stephen St;
⏱9.30am-12.30pm Tue-Sat,
plus 2-4.50pm Tue-Sat May-
Sep) showcases his manu-
scripts and letters, along
with sepia photos, a copy
of his 1923 Nobel Prize
medal and a complete
collection of his poetic
works.

✗ ⨼ p58, p72, p293,
p301, p351

The Drive » Take the N4
south then the N17 (signed
Galway). Soon the R293
meanders left through
Ballymote and a deeply
agricultural landscape. Make for
Gurteen (also spelt Gorteen),
32km from Sligo, following signs
for the Coleman Irish Music
Centre. It's the pink building
right beside the main village
crossroads.

----

❾ Gurteen

You've just explored
poetry, now for another
mainstay of Irish culture:
music. The **Coleman Irish
Music Centre** (☎071-918
2599; www.colemanirishmusic.
com; Gurteen; ⏱10am-
5.30pm Mon-Sat) champions
melody and culture,
south Sligo style, with
multimedia exhibits on
musical history, instru-
ments, famous musicians
and Irish dancing. The
centre also provides
tuition and sheet-music
sales, and stages perfor-
mances.

The Drive » Continue south
on the R293, an undulating
ribbon of a road that deposits
you in bustling Ballaghaderreen.

There pick up the N5 west (signed Westport) for an effortless cruise through lowlands that are grazed by cattle and dotted with rounded hills. Some 55km later, signs point right for the National Museum of Country Life.

⑩ Castlebar

Your discovery of Ireland's heritage continues, this time with a celebration of the ingenuity and self-sufficiency of the Irish people. The **National Museum of Country Life** (☎094-903 1755; www. museum.ie; off N5, Turlough Park; ☺10am-5pm Tue-Sat, 1-5pm Sun & Mon) explores everything from wickerwork to boat building, and herbal cures to traditional clothing. This historical one-stop shop is a comprehensive, absorbing depiction of rural traditions and skills between 1850 and 1950.

✗ p72

The Drive ≫ From the outskirts of Castlebar, the N84 heads south (signed Galway), bouncing beside scattered settlements before dog-legging through appealing Ballinrobe. This hummocky landscape of fields and dry-stone walls is replaced by bogs edged with peat stacks as you near Galway city (80km).

⑪ Galway City

The biggest reason to stop in Galway city is simply to revel in its hedonistic, culture-rich spirit. Narrow alleys lead from sight to sight beside strings of pubs overflowing with live music.

Start explorations at the quayside **Spanish Arch** (1584), thought to be an extension of Galway's medieval walls. Next walk a few paces to the **Galway City Museum** (☎091-532 460; www.galwaycitymuseum. ie; Spanish Pde; ☺10am-5pm Tue-Sat, plus noon-5pm Sun Easter-Sep), where exhibits trace daily life in the city through history. Highlights include the smelly medieval era and photos of President John F Kennedy's 1963 visit to Galway. Then stroll a few metres to the **Hall of the Red Earl** (www. galwaycivictrust.ie; Druid Lane; ☺9am-4.45pm Mon-Fri, 11am-3pm Sat), the artefact-rich archaeological remains of a 13th-century power base. You can't leave Galway without experiencing a music session, up Quay St and High St to Mainguard St and Tig Cóilí (p38), a gem of a fire-engine-red pub that stages two live *céilidh* (traditional music and dancing sessions) a day.

✗ ⌂ p44, p72, p93, p256, p268, p277

The Drive ≫ Join the M6 towards Dublin for the hour-long, smooth motorway cruise to Athlone. Follow signs to Athlone West/Town Centre. Soon the River Shannon, bobbing with houseboats and pleasure cruisers, eases into view. Park by Athlone Castle (80km), which appears straight ahead.

⑫ Athlone

The thriving riverside town of Athlone is an enchanting mix of stylish modern developments and ancient, twisting streets. **Viking Ship Cruises** (☎086 262 1136; www.vikingtoursireland.ie; The Quay; Lough Ree tour adult/

DETOUR: ATHENRY

Start: ⑪ Galway City

Most people sweep past Athenry, but it actually preserves one of Ireland's most intact collections of medieval architecture. This amiable town features a restored, box-like Norman **castle** (☎091-844 797; www. heritageireland.ie; adult/child €5/3; ☺9.30am-6pm Easter-Sep), the medieval **Parish Church of St Mary's**, a 13th-century **Dominican Priory** (with superb masonry) and an original market cross.
Athenry sits beside the M6, and is signed off it.

child €14/7, Clonmacnoise tour €20/10; ☺Easter-Oct) runs trips from beside Athlone Castle, cruising the River Shannon aboard a replica Viking longship sailed by costumed crew. The best trip goes south to the stunning ruins at Clonmacnoise.

 p72, p117

The Drive » Continue through Athlone, picking up the minor N62, which rises and dips past grazing livestock to Birr (45km). Soon a boggy landscape takes over; look for the swathes of exposed soil left by industrial-scale peat harvesting. At Birr follow signs to the imposing, crenellated gateway of the Birr Castle Demesne.

- - - - - - - - - - - - - - - - -

13 Birr

Feel-good Birr is one of the Midlands' most attractive towns, with elegant pastel Georgian buildings and a spirited nightlife buzzing with live music. It also features **Birr Castle** (☏057-912 0336; www.birrcastle.com; Rosse Row; gardens adult/child €9/5, gardens, exhibits & castle €18/10; ☺9am-6pm Mar-Oct, 9.30am-4pm Nov-Feb), where magnificent, 1000-species-strong gardens frame a large artificial lake. Don't miss the romantic Hornbeam cloister and the 12m-high box hedge, planted in the 1780s and now one of the world's tallest.

 p73, p109, p117

The Drive » The N62 loops south through Roscrea, with the Silvermine Mountains' dark

tops creeping up on the right. Then come Templemore's wide streets, before the N62 wiggles onto the M8 (head towards Cork); the Rock of Cashel (74km) is signed 13km later.

- - - - - - - - - - - - - - - - -

TRIP HIGHLIGHT

14 Rock of Cashel

The iconic and much-photographed **Rock of Cashel** (☏062-61437; www.heritageireland.ie; adult/child €8/4, incl Cormac's Chapel €11/7; ☺9am-7pm early Jun–mid-Sep, to 5.30pm mid-Mar–early Jun & mid-Sep–mid-Oct, to 4.30pm mid-Oct–mid-Mar; P) is one of Ireland's true highlights – Queen Elizabeth II included it on her historic 2011 visit. The 'rock' is a fortified hill, the defences of which shelter a clutch of historic religious monuments. The site has been a defensive one since the 4th century and its compelling features include the towering 13th-century Gothic cathedral, a 15th-century four-storey castle, an 11th-century round tower and a 12th-century Romanesque chapel.

It's a five-minute stroll along Bishop's Walk from the appealing market town of Cashel.

The Drive » As you head north up the M8 (signed Dublin) you'll notice rounded field-chequered hills, backed by a distant smudge of mountains. At Urlingford, take the R693 into central Kilkenny, 67km from Cashel.

- - - - - - - - - - - - - - - - -

TRIP HIGHLIGHT

15 Kilkenny

Kilkenny (Cill Chainnigh) is the Ireland of many people's imaginations, with its gracious medieval cathedral, tangle of 17th-century passageways, old-fashioned shopfronts and ancient live-music pubs. Make for **Kilkenny Castle** (☏056-770 4100; www.kilkennycastle.ie; The Parade; adult/child €8/4; ☺9am-5.30pm Jun-Aug, 9.30am-5.30pm Apr, May & Sep, 9.30am-5pm Mar, 9.30am-4.30pm Oct-Feb), a late-12th-century stone affair built by the son-in-law of Richard de Clare, the Anglo-Norman conqueror of Ireland (graced with the sobriquet 'Strongbow'). Guided tours focus on the Long Gallery, an impressive hall with high ceilings, vividly painted Celtic and Pre-Raphaelite motifs and ranks of po-faced portraits.

 p73, p141

LOCAL KNOWLEDGE: PAY YOUR WAY

The M6 heading east out of Galway is a sleek, effortless drive. But like all shiny new things it has to be paid for: have your €1.90 ready for the toll booth 20km east of Athenry.

Classic Trip

The Drive » Pick up the R700 southeast to New Ross. Hills feature again here, both in the rise and fall of the twisting road and in the blue-black ridge of the Blackstairs Mountains far ahead. At New Ross (42km) make for the quay and the three-masted sailing vessel.

16 New Ross

In Ireland's Great Famine of 1845–51 a staggering three million people died or emigrated, often to America and Australia. Many left in 'coffin ships', so called because of their appalling mortality rates. When you step aboard the replica **Dunbrody Famine Ship** (☏051-425 239; www.dunbrody. com; The Quay; adult/child €11/6; ☺9am-6pm) you 'become' a migrant: you're allocated a living space and rations, while actors around you vividly re-create life on board. Expect cramped conditions, authentic sounds and smells and often-harrowing tales.

The Drive » Head onto the N30 to Enniscorthy, a gentle, rural leg punctuated by the frequent treat of roadside stalls selling sweet Wexford strawberries. As you head towards central Enniscorthy (32km), the National Rebellion Centre is a sharp left, up the hill.

17 Enniscorthy

Enniscorthy's warren of steep streets descends from Augustus Pugin's cathedral to a riverside Norman castle. But the town is most famous for some of the fiercest fighting of the 1798 uprising against British rule, when rebels captured the town. That story is told in the **National 1798 Rebellion Centre** (☏053-923 7596; www.1798centre.ie; Parnell Rd; adult/child €7/3; ☺9am-5pm daily Jun-Sep, closed Sat & Sun Oct-May), where exhibits cover the French and American Revolutions that sparked Wexford's abortive revolt. It also chronicles what followed: the rebels' retreat and the massacre by English troops of hundreds of women and children.

📖 p73, p149

The Drive » Carry on through Enniscorthy, crossing the river to pick up the N11, south, to Wexford (22km). Then comes a long straight run, beside the River Slane and past more strawberry stalls, until the waters of Wexford Harbour glide into view.

18 Wexford Town

The sleepy port town of Wexford is a pleasing place to stroll through heritage-rich streets beside a wide estuary. Guided tours (€5) set out at 11am from Monday to Saturday (March to October) from the **tourist office** (☏053-912 3111; www. visitwexford.ie; Quay Front; ☺9am-5pm Mon-Sat; ☎) on the main Custom House Quay; it also provides maps. Or explore by yourself: head up Harper's Lane to North Main St and the 18th-century **St Iberius' Church** (where Oscar Wilde's forebears were rectors). A left up George St leads to Abbey St and **Selskar Abbey**

ROBINSONBECQUART/GETTY IMAGES ©

Kilkenny Castle

(Henry II did penance here after the murder of Thomas Becket); the 14th-century **Westgate** sits at the street's end.

✕ ⊨ p73

The Drive » Drive south along Wexford's boat-lined waterfront to join the R739, where you'll see more fruit stands and a gentle landscape of trees and rich pastures – it feels a world away from the harsh, high hills at your trip's start. Soon the thatched cottages of Kilmore Quay (23km) appear.

⑲ Kilmore Quay

This tiny, relaxed port is the perfect finish to your trans-Ireland trip. Seafood restaurants, fisher's pubs and B&Bs cluster around a boat-packed harbour. Just offshore, the **Saltee Islands** (www. salteeislands.info) overflow with gannets, guillemots, kittiwakes and puffins; **Declan Bates** (📞087 252 9736, 053-912 9684; Kilmore Quay Harbour; day trips €30)

runs boat trips (booking required). If the weather scuppers that plan, stroll west from the quay to the 9km-long, wildlife-rich dunes of Ballyteigue Burrow, passing a memorial garden for those lost at sea, before reaching the Cull, a 4km-long sliver of land sheltering a slender inlet teeming with widgeons, oystercatchers, curlews and more.

✕ ⊨ p73, p149

Eating & Sleeping

Derry ❶

✕ Walled City Brewery   Gastropub ££

(☎028-7134 3336; www.walledcitybrewery.
com; 70 Ebrington Sq; mains £14-25; ⊘kitchen
5-11pm Tue-Thu, 12.30-3pm & 5-11pm Fri & Sat,
2-8pm Sun; 🍴) Housed in the former army
barracks on Ebrington Sq, Walled City Brewery
is a craft brewery and restaurant run by master
brewer and Derry local James Huey. As well as
having 10 craft beers on tap, Walled City serves
top-notch grub, such as house-smoked pork
neck and tandoori chargrilled rump of lamb. It
also runs home-brewing courses.

🛏 Bishop's Gate Hotel   Hotel £££

(☎028-7114 0300; www.bishopsgatehotelderry.
com; 24 Bishop St; s/d/ste from £120/130/210)
The former Northern Counties gentleman's club
has been transformed into a stylish 30-room
hotel located within Derry's city walls. Rooms
combine period features with plush carpets and
contemporary furnishings in greys and yellows.
Leather armchairs, wood panelling and open
fires create a cosy atmosphere in the bar.

Dunlewey ❹

🛏 Glen Heights B&B   B&B €

(☎074-956 0844; www.glenheightsbb.com; s €50,
d €70-80; 🛜) The three rooms are bright and
inviting, and the Donegal charm is in full swing at
this fine choice run by Kathleen. Your breakfast
may well go cold on the plate in front of you as you
stare at the breathtaking views of Dunlewey Lake
and the Poisoned Glen from the conservatory.

Glencolumbcille ❻

✕ An Chistin   Cafe €€

(☎074-973 0213; R263; mains €12-16; ⊘10am-
8pm) This welcoming cafe is pretty much the
cooking hub of the village. The menu spans
seafood chowder (€8) and scampi to pizzas,
which can also be ordered to take away.

Sligo Town ❽

✕ Hargadons   Pub Food €€

(☎071-915 3709; www.hargadons.com;
4/5 O'Connell St; mains €10-25; ⊘food
noon-3.30pm & 4-9pm Mon-Sat) You'll have
a hard time leaving this superb 1868 inn with
its winning blend of Old World fittings and
gastropub style. The uneven floors, peat fire,
antique signage, snug corners and bowed
shelves laden down with ancient bottles lend it
a wonderful charm.

Castlebar ❿

✕ Rua Deli & Cafe   Irish €

(☎094-928 6072; www.caferua.com; Spencer
St; mains €9-12; ⊘8.30am-6pm Mon-Sat; 🍴)
Artisan, organic, local food packs the shelves
and tables of this gourmet deli-cafe. Picnic
goodies include Carrowholly cheese, Ballina
smoked salmon and luscious salads. Upstairs,
amid artfully mismatched furniture, Mayo
produce is teamed with global flavours such as
harrisa, pesto and toasted seeds.

Galway City ⓫

🛏 Heron's Rest   B&B €€

(☎091-539 574; www.theheronsrest.com;
16A Longwalk; d €179-199; 🛜) The thoughtful
hosts of this B&B in a lovely row of houses on
the banks of the Corrib provide binoculars and
deck chairs so you can sit outside and enjoy
the views.

Athlone ⓬

🛏 Bastion B&B   Guesthouse €

(☎090-649 4954; www.thebastion.net; 2
Bastion St; d without/with bathroom €55/65;
🛜) You can't miss Bastion's brightly coloured
facade near Athlone Castle. Inside, the white-
on-white interiors are a canvas for eclectic
artwork, Indian wall hangings and Buddhist

ornaments. The seven rooms (five with private bathroom) are crisp and clean, with dark wooden floors. Go for the spacious loft if you can. No breakfast but an adjacent cafe.

Birr ⑬

🛏 Walcot B&B
B&B €€

(📞057-912 1247; www.facebook.com/Walcotbandb; Rosse Row; s/d from €60/90; 🅿🛜) Set back from the road amid sprawling formal gardens across from Birr Castle, this Georgian townhouse is close to everything. The five large, antique-furnished bedrooms have period-style bathrooms with large tubs and showers.

Kilkenny ⑮

🍴 Foodworks
Bistro, Cafe €€

(📞056-777 7696; www.foodworks.ie; 7 Parliament St; mains €17.50-26.50, 3-course dinner menus €26-29; ⏱ noon-9pm Wed & Thu, to 9.30pm Fri & Sat, to 5pm Sun; 🛜♿) The owners of this cool and casual bistro keep their own pigs and grow their own salad leaves, so it would be churlish not to try their pork loin stuffed with black pudding, or pressed pig's trotter – and you'll be glad you did.

🛏 Rosquil House
Guesthouse €€

(📞056-772 1419; www.rosquilhouse.com; Castlecomer Rd; d/tr/f from €95/120/130, 2-person apt from €80; 🅿🛜) Rooms at this immaculately maintained guesthouse are decorated with dark-wood furniture and pretty paisley fabrics, while the guest lounge is similarly tasteful, with sink-into sofas, brass-framed mirrors and leafy plants.

🛏 Butler House
Hotel €€€

(📞056-772 2828; www.butler.ie; 16 Patrick St; d/ste from €200/275; 🅿🛜) You can't stay in Kilkenny Castle, but this 1786-built mansion is the next best thing. Once the home of the earls of Ormonde, the hotel today combines modern design with aristocratic trappings including sweeping staircases, marble fireplaces, an art collection and magnificent gardens.

Enniscorthy ⑰

🛏 Woodbrook House
Guesthouse €€

(📞053-925 5114; www.woodbrookhouse.ie; Killann; s/d from €105/170; ⏱Easter-Jun & Aug-

Sep; 🅿🛜) Rebuilt after sustaining damage in the 1798 Rising, this glorious Georgian country house has a superb setting beneath the Blackstairs Mountains. The lobby features a gravity-defying spiral staircase that still amazes, just as it did over 200 years ago.

Wexford Town ⑱

🍴 Greenacres
Bistro, Deli €€

(📞053-912 2975; www.greenacres.ie; 7 Selskar St; mains lunch €11.50-19.50, dinner €17.50-26.50; ⏱9am-10pm Mon-Sat; 🛜) Eating, shopping, culture...this place has it covered! Irish cheeses and local produce are beautifully displayed in the food hall, the wine selection is the best south of Dublin, and the gourmet bistro produces innovative dishes from premium ingredients such as wild pigeon, rock oysters and smoked rabbit.

🍴 La Côte
Seafood €€€

(📞053-912 2122; www.lacote.ie; Custom House Quay; mains €22.50-34, 3-course dinner menu €33; ⏱5.30-9.30pm Tue-Sat) 'The Coast' has raked in awards – notably Irish Seafood Restaurant of the Year – for its innovative takes on the finest of local seafood, such as turbot with oyster mousse, John Dory with squid ink bulgur (cracked wheat), or lemon sole with a Wexford mussel reduction.

Kilmore Quay ⑲

🍴 Silver Fox Seafood Restaurant
Seafood €€€

(📞053-912 9888; www.thesilverfox.ie; The Quay; mains €16-35; ⏱noon-9pm Easter-Oct, 5-8pm Fri, noon-8pm Sat & Sun Nov-Mar) The Silver Fox's fresh-from-the-ocean offerings include locally landed plaice, langoustines, crab and mussels, plus daily specials depending on what arrives at the quay.

🛏 Coast Kilmore Quay
Hotel €€

(📞053-914 8641; www.coastkilmorequay.com; R739; d/f from €125/159; 🅿🛜) An old roadside motel 500m north of the beach and village centre has been upcycled with storm-grey, driftwood-brown and bright white colour schemes while retaining the convenience of parking right outside your room. Its contemporary bar and quieter restaurant share an all-day menu.

Dublin & Eastern Ireland

A SPIDER'S WEB OF ROADS – from motorways to winding rural routes – spreads from Dublin's city centre and will lead you to multiple delights, all within easy reach of the capital. Within an hour's drive from Dublin you can find yourself on a lonely mountain pass with only the odd sheep for company, or be transported back 3500 years in time to explore a passage grave built before the pyramids were a twinkle in a pharaoh's eye.

You're now in the heartland of Ireland's Ancient East, Failte Ireland's second 'umbrella destination' (after the Wild Atlantic Way), that explores historic towns, castles, gardens and a wealth of monastic monuments that all serve to remind you of Ireland's breathtaking cultural heritage.

Thatched cottage, Kilmore Quay

Dublin & Eastern Ireland

4 **A Long Weekend Around Dublin 3 Days**
Seaside villages, monastic ruins and palatial Palladian mansions.

5 **East to West 7 Days**
Cut across central Ireland from the cosmopolitan capital to the wilds of Connemara.

6 **The Boyne Valley 2 Days**
A short trip that's long on history - from prehistoric monuments to bloody battlefields.

7 **Ancient Ireland 4 Days**
A four-day marathon to explore 4000 years of Irish history, right back to the beginning.

8 **Monasteries, Mountains & Mansions 3 Days**
A heritage trip that skirts on and off the beaten path

9 **Wicklow Mountains 3 Days**
Heritage and history along the spine of eastern Ireland's most scenic mountain range.

10 **Carlow Back Roads 3 Days**
Uncover the hidden delights of Ireland's second-smallest county

11 **Kilkenny's Treasures 3 Days**
The best of a medieval city and its pleasant surroundings.

12 **Wexford & Waterford 5 Days**
The sunny southeast revealed - from bustling harbour villages to moody monastic ruins.

13 **Blackwater Valley Drive 2 Days**
Follow the river from the sea and discover one of the country's most charming backwaters.

14 **Family Fun 3 Days**
Adventure, heritage and distractions for the whole family.

✔ DON'T MISS

Brú na Bóinne
Ireland's most important neolithic monument is a mesmerising experience. Let yourself be wowed on Trips **4** **6** **7** **14**

Dublin
Most visits to Ireland begin and end in the capital, so be a latter-day Dubliner on Trips **1** **2** **5** **14**

Monasterboice
Best experienced at sunset on a summer's day, when your only company are crowing ravens; contemplate the high crosses on Trip **6**

Clonegal
An arched stone bridge over a river populated by swans and a banked by buttercups? Visit a real fairytale village on Trip **7**

Ballysaggartmore Towers
A Gothic folly in the middle of a forest that is testimony to love's foolish ambition. Let yourself dream on Trip **13**

A Long Weekend Around Dublin

4

You don't have to venture far from the capital in any direction to find distractions, including cosy seaside towns, stunning monastic ruins and palatial 18th-century mansions.

TRIP HIGHLIGHTS

56 km

Brú na Bóinne
Fascinating pre-Celtic necropolis made up of a series of passage tombs

120 km

Castletown House
Magnificent Palladian pile of the 18th century's richest Irishman

START
Howth

FINISH ●Sandycove

● **Russborough House**

Powerscourt Estate
Georgian mansion, magnificent gardens and breathtaking views

● Glendalough

206 km

3 DAYS
230KM / 143 MILES

GREAT FOR...

BEST TIME TO GO
April to September sees big crowds, but the sun also shines the most then.

ESSENTIAL PHOTO
Sugarloaf Mountain, from the entrance drive to Powerscourt Estate.

BEST FOR CULTURE
Russborough House, a Palladian pile with a top-notch art collection.

A Long Weekend Around Dublin

4

You can plunge into the very depths of Irish history, be awestruck by some of Ireland's most beautiful buildings and lose yourself in stunning countryside without ever being more than 50km from Dublin. This trip explores the very best of what the capital's environs have to offer – from coastal breaks to mountain retreats and a rip-roaring trip through 3500 years of history.

❶ Howth

The pretty little port town of Howth is built on steep streets running down to its small but busy harbour, which has transformed itself from shipping port to yachting and fishing hub. Only 11km north of Dublin's city centre, it has long been a desirable residential suburb.

Howth is essentially a very large hill surrounded by cliffs, and the summit (171m) has excellent views across Dublin Bay right down to Wicklow. From the peak you can walk to the top of the Ben of Howth, which has a cairn said to mark a 2000-year-old

Celtic royal grave. The 1814 Baily Lighthouse, at the southeastern corner, is on the site of an old stone fort and can be reached by a dramatic clifftop walk. There was an earlier hilltop beacon here, in 1670.

Besides the views, the other draw is the busy weekend market and the collection of good seafood restaurants huddled around the harbour.

 p85

The Drive ❱❱ For the 56km trip, take the right at Sutton onto Harbour Rd (R105) towards Baldoyle; you'll have the Malahide estuary on your right and, on the spit of land beyond it, the famous Portmarnock Golf Links. Turn left onto Moyne Rd and take the M1 (tolled; €1.90) north, exiting at Junction 9 for Donore.

TRIP HIGHLIGHT

2 Brú na Bóinne

Pharaohs hadn't even conceived of the pyramids when the Neolithic pre-Celts built this vast necropolis on the banks of the River Boyne. Collectively known as Brú na Bóinne (the Boyne Palace), the passage tombs (and superb visitor centre) are one of the most extraordinary sites in Europe and shouldn't be missed.

p101

The Drive Take Staleen Rd for 6.8km to the N2/M2. After 37km, merge onto the M50, taking the exit at Junction 7 for the N4 and go west for 7km as far as Junction 6. Follow the R403 as far as Celbridge. The 63km trip should take between 45 minutes and an hour.

LINK YOUR TRIP

1 Iconic Ireland

Dublin is the starting point of this Classic Trip that delivers the country's five-star attractions.

2 The Long Way Round

From Dublin, take a couple of weeks to explore the country.

SCENICIRELAND.COM/CHRISTOPHER HILL PHOTOGRAPHIC/ALAMY STOCK PHOTO ©

TRIP HIGHLIGHT

❸ Celbridge

The magnificent **Castletown House** (☎01-628 8252; www.castletown.ie; Celbridge; house adult/child €8/3.50, with guided tour €10/5, grounds free; ⊙house 10am-6pm daily Mar-Oct, to 5.30pm Wed-Sun Nov–mid-Dec, grounds dawn-dusk year-round) simply has no equal. It is Ireland's largest and most imposing Georgian estate, and a testament to the vast wealth enjoyed by the Anglo-Irish gentry during the 18th century.

Built between 1722 and 1732, the house was commissioned by Speaker of the Irish House of Commons William Conolly (1662–1729), who wanted a house commensurate with his position as Ireland's richest man.

The original 16th-century Italian palazzo design of the house was created by the Italian architect Alessandro Galilei (1691–1737) in 1718. In 1724 the project was entrusted to Sir Edward Lovett Pearce (1699–1733).

The house is full of Palladian touches, including the terminating pavilions and the superb Long Gallery, full of family portraits and fancy stucco work by the Italian Francini brothers. Thomas Jefferson was such a fan of the style that much of Washington, DC is designed accordingly.

The Drive ≫ Drive southeast on the R409 for 1.6km. At the roundabout, take the first exit onto the R449. After 1.2km, take the R405 for 2.5km and take the Dublin Road south. After 22.2km turn right onto the N81. Russborough House is 3.9km away on your right. The whole drive is 34.4km.

DETOUR: POWERSCOURT WATERFALL

Start: ❻ Enniskerry

Signposted from the Powerscourt Estate is the 121m **Powerscourt Waterfall** (www.powerscourt.com/waterfall; Powerscourt Estate; adult/child €6/3.50; ⊙9.30am-7pm May-Aug, 10.30am-5.30pm Mar, Apr, Sep & Oct, 10.30am-4pm Nov-Feb). It's the highest waterfall in Britain and Ireland, and is most impressive after heavy rain. A nature trail has been laid out around the base of the waterfall, taking you past giant redwoods, ancient oaks, beech, birch and rowan trees. There are plenty of birds in the vicinity, including the chaffinch, cuckoo, and willow warbler. It's also a popular 7km walk to the waterfall.

❹ Blessington

Dominating the one-street town of Blessington (pubs, shops, a handful of 17th- and 18th-century townhouses) is magnificent **Russborough House** (☎045-865 239; www.russborough.ie; off N81; guided tour adult/child €12/6, parklands €5/free; ⊙10am-5pm Mar-Dec, parklands to 6pm Mar-Dec), one of Ireland's finest stately homes, built for Joseph Leeson (1705–83), later the first Earl of Milltown and, later still, Lord Russborough. The Palladian pleasure palace was built between 1741 and 1751 to the design of Richard

Castletown House, Celbridge

Cassels, who was at the height of his fame as an architect. Richard didn't live to see it finished, but the job was well executed by Francis Bindon. The house remained in the Leeson family until 1931. In 1952 it was sold to Sir Alfred Beit, the nephew of the cofounder of the de Beers diamond-mining company. Uncle Alfred was an obsessive art collector, and when he died, his impressive haul – which includes works by Velázquez, Vermeer, Goya and Rubens – was passed on to his nephew, who brought it to Russborough House.

The admission price includes a 45-minute tour of the house, which is decorated in typical Georgian style.

🛏 p85

The Drive » Follow the N81 south for 5.2km, take a left onto the R411 for 1.4km and then cut across the Wicklow Mountains on the R756 via the stunning Wicklow Gap. It's a 23.4km stretch to Laragh; Glendalough is only 3km further on.

- - - - - - - - - - - - - - - - -

⑤ Glendalough

Location, location, location. When St Kevin came to this spectacular glacial valley in the heart of the Wicklow Moun-

tains in 498 to found a small monastic settlement, did he realise that the settlement would grow into one of Ireland's most important centres of learning and, 15 centuries later, one of the country's most popular tourist attractions? Probably not.

🍴🛏 p85, p125

The Drive » Head northeast on the R755 for 21km, skirting the eastern edge of Wicklow Mountains National Park, then follow the road signs for Enniskerry. Overall distance 28.9km.

⑥ Enniskerry

Backing onto the pretty village of Enniskerry is the expanse of **Powerscourt Estate** (☎01-204 6000; www.powerscourt. com; Bray Rd; house free, gardens adult/child €10/5 Mar-Oct, €7.50/3.50 Nov-Feb; ☺9.30am-5.30pm Mar-Oct, to dusk Nov-Feb), which gives contemporary observers a true insight into the style of the 18th-century super-rich. The main entrance is 500m south of the village square.

The estate has existed more or less since 1300, when the LePoer (later anglicised to Power) family built themselves a castle here. The property changed Anglo-Norman hands a few times before coming into the possession of Richard Wingfield, newly appointed Marshall of Ireland, in 1603. His descendants were to live here for the next 350 years. A fire in 1974 gutted most of the house, so the biggest draws of the whole pile are the magnificent 20-hectare formal **gardens** and the breathtaking views that accompany them.

✗ 🛏 p85, p125

The Drive 》 Continue onto the M11 north and take the exit for Dun Laoghaire. The Wyatville Rd becomes Church Rd; keep going north and follow the road signs for Sandycove. It's 16.7km from Powerscourt to Sandycove.

RUSSBOROUGH HOUSE: THE TERRORISTS, THE THIEVES & THE ART LOVERS

In 1974 the IRA decided to get into the art business by stealing 16 paintings from Russborough House. They were eventually all recovered, but 10 years later the notorious Dublin criminal Martin Cahill (aka the General) masterminded another robbery from the Russborough House collection, this time for Loyalist paramilitaries. On this occasion, however, only some of the works were recovered and of those, several were damaged beyond repair – a good thief does not a gentle curator make. In 1988 the owner, Sir Albert Beit, decided to hand over the most valuable of the paintings to the National Gallery; in return, the gallery agreed to lend other paintings to the collection as temporary exhibits. The sorry story didn't conclude there. In 2001 two thieves drove a jeep through the front doors, making off with two paintings worth nearly €4 million, including a Gainsborough that had been stolen, and recovered, twice before. To add abuse to the insult already added to injury, the house was broken into again in 2002, with the thieves taking five more paintings, including two by Rubens. Thankfully, all of the paintings were recovered after both attempts, but where a succession of thieves couldn't succeed, the cost of the upkeep did: in 2015 the owners announced they were going to auction off 10 of the paintings, a decision that caused much consternation as the family had always maintained that the collection was to be held in trust for the Irish people.

⑦ Sandycove

The handsome seaside town of Sandycove is now just part of greater Dublin, but it is renowned for its excellent restaurants, pretty beach and a Martello tower – built by British forces to keep an eye out for a Napoleonic invasion – now housing the **James Joyce Tower & Museum** (☎01-280 9265; www.joycetower.ie; ☺10am-6pm May-Sep, to 4pm Oct-Apr; 🚉Sandycove & Glasthule). This is where the action begins in James Joyce's epic novel *Ulysses*. The museum was opened in 1962 by Sylvia Beach, the Paris-based publisher who first dared to put *Ulysses* into print, and has photographs, letters, documents, various editions of Joyce's work and two death masks of Joyce.

✗ p85

Eating & Sleeping

Howth ❶

🍴 Aqua   Seafood €€€

(📞01-832 0690; www.aqua.ie; 1 West Pier;
mains €29-37; ⏰12.30-3.30pm & 5.30-
9.30pm Tue-Thu, to 10pm Fri & Sat, noon-5pm
& 6-8.30pm Sun; 🚍31, 31A from Beresford
Pl, 🚇Howth) A contender for best seafood
restaurant in Howth, Aqua serves top-
quality fish dishes in its elegant dining room
overlooking the harbour.

🍴 House   Irish €€

(📞01-839 6388; www.thehouse-howth.ie;
4 Main St; mains €18-25; ⏰8.45am-9.30pm
Mon-Thu, to 10.30pm Fri, 10am-10.30pm Sat,
to 9.30pm Sun; 🚍31, 31A from Beresford Pl,
🚇Howth) A wonderful spot on the main street
leading away from the harbour where you can
feast on dishes such as squash and potato
gnocchi or wild Wicklow venison with smoked
black-pudding croquette, as well as a fine
selection of fish. The brunch is one of the best
you'll find on the north side of the city.

🛏 King Sitric   Boutique Hotel €€

(📞01-832 5235; www.kingsitric.ie; East Pier;
s/d from €125/160; 🚍31, 31A from Beresford
Pl, 🚇Howth) This handsome boutique hotel
above the long-established restaurant (two/
three-course menu €39/45) has eight rooms
with views of the port. The nautical theme is
everywhere and each room is named after an
Irish lighthouse.

Blessington ❹

🛏 Rathsallagh House & Country Club   Hotel €€€

(📞045-403 112; www.rathsallagh.com; Dunlavin;
s/d from €150/200; 🅿️🛜) This fabulous
country manor was converted from Queen Anne
stables after the main house was burned down
during the 1798 Rising. Luxury reigns here,
with 29 splendidly appointed rooms, exquisite
country-house dining (five-course dinner menu
€40) and a par-72 golf course designed by Peter
McEvoy and Christy O'Connor Jr. It's 23km
southwest of Blessington, off the R756.

Glendalough ❺

🛏 Heather House   B&B €€

(📞0404-45157; www.heatherhouse.ie;
Glendalough Rd, Laragh; d from €100; 🅿️🛜)
Understated country-style elegance radiates
from the luxurious bedrooms at this superb-
value B&B, around 2km east of Glendalough.
There's a lovely garden at the back with a view
along the wooded valley, and it's just next door
to the Wicklow Heather (p125) restaurant
(where you check in).

Enniskerry ❻

🍴 Johnnie Fox's   Seafood €€

(📞01-295 5647; www.johnniefoxs.com;
Glencullen; mains €15-26, seafood platters €28-
130, 3-course Hooley menu €59.50; ⏰kitchen
12.30-9.30pm, bar 11am-11.30pm Mon-Thu, to
12.30am Fri & Sat, noon-11pm Sun; 🛜🍴🎵)
Just over the County Dublin border, 5.5km
northwest of Enniskerry, traditional 19th-
century pub Johnnie Fox's fills with busloads
of tourists for its knees-up Hooley Show of Irish
music and dancing.

🛏 Powerscourt Hotel & Spa   Luxury Hotel €€€

(📞01-274 8888; www.powerscourthotel.com;
Powerscourt Estate; d/ste from €244/333;
🅿️🛜🏊) Wicklow's most luxurious hotel is
this 200-room stunner on the grounds of the
Powerscourt Estate . Inside this Marriott-
managed property, the decor is a thoroughly
contemporary version of the estate's Georgian
style. Rooms are massive; some have balconies.

Sandycove ❼

🍴 Caviston's Food Emporium   Seafood €€

(📞01-280 9245; www.cavistons.com; Glasthule
Rd; mains €20-26; ⏰noon-5pm Tue-Sat &
6-10pm Thu-Sat; 🚇Sandycove & Glasthule) This
is an excellent seafood restaurant with a long-
standing reputation. From tuna loin to seared
scallops, everything is fresh and beautifully
presented. Menus change twice weekly.

East to West

Music, landscape and history are the keys to this trip, which transports you across Ireland's midriff from the bustling capital to the pastoral splendour of the west.

TRIP HIGHLIGHTS

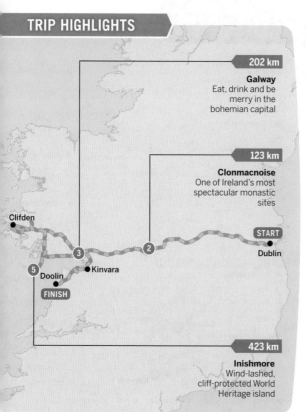

202 km

Galway
Eat, drink and be merry in the bohemian capital

123 km

Clonmacnoise
One of Ireland's most spectacular monastic sites

Clifden

START
Dublin

Kinvara

Doolin

FINISH

423 km

Inishmore
Wind-lashed, cliff-protected World Heritage island

7 DAYS
435KM / 270 MILES

GREAT FOR...

BEST TIME TO GO

The warmer months (April to September) are festival time in Galway.

ESSENTIAL PHOTO

Dun Aengus just before sunset.

BEST TWO DAYS

From the Aran Islands back to Connemara and down to County Clare and the Burren.

Inishmore Dun Aengus fort and sea cliffs

5 East to West

Go West! As you quit Dublin's suburban sprawl the landscape continues to soften and before you know it you're in Galway, gateway to beautiful, brooding Connemara, where the mountainous landscape is punctuated by brown bog and shimmering lakes. Explore one of the country's most magnificent spots before looping south into the Burren of County Clare, the spiritual home of Irish traditional music.

1 Dublin

A day in the capital should give you enough time to take a walk (p168) and check out the city's big-ticket items. Culture buffs should definitely take a stroll through the archaeology and history branch of the **National Museum of Ireland** (www.museum.ie; Kildare St; ⊕10am-5pm Tue-Sat, from 1pm Sun; ⊡ all city centre) – don't miss the Treasury's golden hoard of artefacts from the Bronze and Iron Ages as well as its eerily

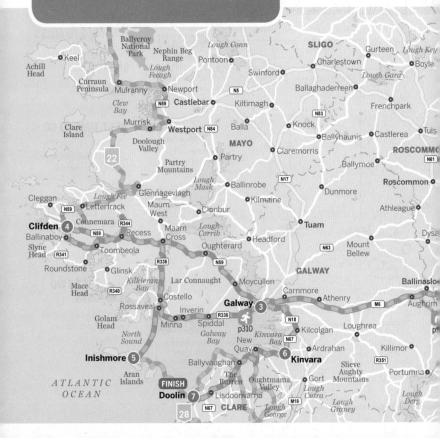

fascinating collection of preserved 'bog bodies'.

✕ ⛱ p44, p58, p93, p165

The Drive » The 123km drive to Clonmacnoise is largely uneventful, courtesy of the convenient M4/M6 tolled motorway, from which you see fields and little else. Take exit 7 towards Moate and get on the R444 – Clonmacnoise is signposted as you go.

TRIP HIGHLIGHT

② Clonmacnoise

Straddling a hill overlooking a bend in the Shannon, **Clonmacnoise**

(www.heritageireland.ie; R444; adult/child €8/4; 🕘9am-6.30pm Jun-Aug, 10am-6pm mid-Mar–May, Sep & Oct, 10am-5.30pm Nov–mid-Mar) is one of the main reasons Ireland got the moniker of 'land of saints and scholars'.

LINK YOUR TRIP

Best of the West
22 In Galway you can connect with this trip, which brings you from Sligo south to County Kerry.

County Clare
28 Explore the rest of lyrical County Clare by travelling the 40km from Doolin to Ennis.

The Drive » From Clonmacnoise, take the R357 for 18km towards Ballinasloe, Galway's county town and the first town you'll come to as you enter the county across the River Suck. Here you can rejoin the M6; it's 63km to Galway city.

TRIP HIGHLIGHT

③ Galway City

Galway is the long-established, self-proclaimed and generally accepted capital of bohemian Ireland, with a long-standing tradition of attracting artists, musicians and other creative types to its pub- and cafe-lined streets (p310).

✕ ⊨ p44, p72, p93, p256, p268, p277

The Drive » The N59 cuts through the heart of the region – in the distance you'll see Connemara's mountain ranges, the Maumturks and the Twelve Bens. After about 58km, just before Recess, take a 5km detour north along the R344 and take in the majesty of the Lough Inagh Valley before rejoining the road and continuing towards Clifden, 28km further on.

④ Clifden

Connemara's principal town is a genteel Victorian-era fishing port that makes a good stopover, especially during the summer months, when it casts off its wintry covers and offers visitors a nice taster of what drew 19th-century tourists to it. You can amble about its narrow streets or stare at the sea from the head of the narrow bay into which falls the River Owenglin.

✕ ⊨ p44, p93

The Drive » The R341 coast road goes to Roundstone, but cut through the Roundstone Bog from Ballinaboy for some fine scenery. Rejoin the R341 at Toombeola and turn left onto the N59 before turning right onto the R340 for the ferry to Inishmore from Rossaveal or a flight from Minna. From Clifden, it's 57km to Rossaveal, 64km to Minna.

**DETOUR:
THE MAN WHO REALLY
FOUND AMERICA?**

Start: ② Clonmacnoise

About 21km southeast of Ballinasloe along the R355 is the 12th-century **Clonfert Cathedral**, built on the site of a monastery said to have been founded in 563 by St Brendan 'the Navigator', who is believed to be buried here. Although the jury is out on whether St Brendan reached America's shores in a tiny *currach* rowing boat, there are carvings of Old Irish Ogham (the earliest form of writing in Ireland) in West Virginia that date from as early as the 6th century, suggesting an Irish presence in America well before Columbus set foot there. The marvellous six-arch Romanesque doorway, adorned with surreal human heads, is reason enough to visit.

TRIP HIGHLIGHT

⑤ Inishmore

Do not doubt that the effort you made to get here wasn't worth it, for a visit to the largest of the Aran Islands (indeed, any of the three) is one of the more memorable things you'll do in Ireland. The big draw is the spectacular Stone Age fort of **Dun Aengus** (Dún Aonghasa; ☎099-61008; www.heritage-ireland.ie; adult/child €5/3; ⊙9.30am-6pm Apr-Oct, to 4pm Nov-Mar), but don't forget to explore some of the island's other ruins, scattered about the place

Street musician, Galway City

like so much historical detritus. There's also a lovely beach at **Kilmurvey** (west of Kilronan), while up to 50 grey seals sun themselves and feed in the shallows of **Port Chorrúch**.

🍴 🛏 p59, p93, p269, p309

The Drive » You'll have to go back to Minna or Rossaveal to pick up your car. On your way back along the R336 to Galway, stop off in Spiddal, in the heart of Connemara's Gaeltacht (Irish-speaking) heartland. Beyond Galway city, turn off the N18 and go 10km along the N67 to Kinvara.

6 Kinvara

The small stone harbour of Kinvara (sometimes spelt Kinvarra) sits smugly at the southeastern corner of Galway Bay, which accounts for its Irish name, Cinn Mhara (Head of the Sea). It's a posh little village, the kind of place where all the jeans have creases in them. It makes a good pit stop between Galway and Clare.

THE BURREN

Stretching across northern Clare, from the Atlantic coast to Kinvara in County Galway, the Burren is a unique striated limestone landscape that was shaped beneath ancient seas, then forced high and dry by a great geological cataclysm. In the Burren, land and sea seem to merge into one vast, moody, rocky and at times fearsome space beneath huge skies, accented with ancient burial chambers and medieval ruins.

CLARINBRIDGE OYSTER FESTIVAL

South of Galway, Clarinbridge (Droichead an Chláirín) and Kilcolgan (Cill Cholgáin) are at their busiest during the **Clarenbridge Oyster Festival** (www.clarenbridge.com), held during the second weekend of September. However, the oysters are actually at their best from May through the summer.

Oysters are celebrated year-round at **Paddy Burkes Oyster Inn** (☏091-796 226; www.paddyburkesgalway.com; N67, Clarinbridge; mains €8-26; ⊙10am-12.30am Mon-Sat, noon-11pm Sun), a thatched inn by the bridge dishing up heaped servings in a roadside location.

Moran's Oyster Cottage (☏091-796 113; www.moransoystercottage.com; The Weir, Kilcolgan; mains €14-29, half-dozen oysters €13-16; ⊙noon-9.30pm Sun-Thu, to 10pm Fri & Sat; 👶) is a thatched pub and restaurant with a facade as plain as the inside of an oyster shell. Find a seat on the terrace overlooking Dunbulcaun Bay, where the oysters are reared before they arrive on your plate. It's a well-marked 2km west of the noxious N18, in a cove near Kilcolgan.

Dominating one end of the harbour is the chess-piece-style **Dunguaire Castle** (www.shannonheritage.com; off N67; adult/child €7/4; ⊙10am-5pm Apr–mid-Sep), erected around 1520 by the O'Hynes clan and in excellent condition following extensive restoration. It is widely believed that the castle occupies the former site of the 6th-century royal palace of Guaire Aidhne, the king of Connaught.

Dunguaire's past owners have included Oliver St John Gogarty (1878–1957) – poet, writer, surgeon and inspiration for James Joyce's fictional Buck Mulligan, one of the cast of *Ulysses*.

The least authentic way to visit the castle is to attend a medieval banquet. Stage shows and shtick provide diversions while you plough through a big group meal.

The Drive ≫ The N67 from Kinvara skirts along the western edge of the Burren; this particularly desolate-looking (but no less beautiful) landscape is in evidence beyond Ballyvaughan, about 20km on. Doolin is a further 23km away; just past Lisdoonvarna, take a right onto the R476.

- - - - - - - - - - - - - - - - - - -

❼ Doolin

Only 6km north of the Cliffs of Moher is Doolin; its reputation as a terrific spot to spend a couple of days isn't just down to its proximity to one of the bone fide stars of the Irish tourist trail. It helps, sure, but Doolin's popularity is largely due to its pubs, or, rather, to the musicians that play in them: the area is full of talented performers whose exquisite abilities can be enjoyed almost every night. There are lots of pubs to choose from, but if we had to pick one, it'd be **McGann's** (☏065-707 4133; www.mcgannspubdoolin.com; Roadford; ⊙10am-11.30pm Mon-Wed, to 12.30am Thu-Sat, to 11pm Sun; 👶), complete with turf fires, dartboard and great grub.

🛏 p93, p268

Eating & Sleeping

Dublin ❶

✗ Jerusalem Restaurant
Middle Eastern €€

(📞01-424 4001; www.jerusalemrestaurant.ie; 77 Lower Camden St; mains €15-20; ⊘noon-10pm Mon-Wed, to 10.30pm Thu, to midnight Fri, 1pm-midnight Sat, 1-10pm Sun; 📶; 🚌14, 15, 65, 83) A candidate for best ethnic cuisine in town, this friendly spot serves a mix of Lebanese and Palestinian dishes that range from the familiar (hummus, felafel, lamb shwarma) to the exotic – how about *dajaj musahab* (deboned chicken with Palestinian spices)?

🛏 Conrad Dublin
Hotel €€€

(📞01-602 8900; www.conradhotels.com; Earlsfort Tce; r from €350; 🅿 @ 📶; 🚌all city centre) A €13-million refit has transformed this standard business hotel into an exceptional five-star property. The style is contemporary chic – marble bathrooms, wonderfully comfortable beds and a clutter-free aesthetic that doesn't skimp on mod cons.

Galway City ❸

✗ Ard Bia at Nimmo's
Irish €€

(📞091-561 114; www.ardbia.com; Spanish Arch, Longwalk; cafe dishes €7-12, dinner mains €20-28; ⊘cafe 10am-3.30pm Mon-Fri, to 3pm Sat & Sun, restaurant 6-9pm; 🍴) Casually hip Ard Bia ('High Food' in Irish) is decorated with works by local artists and upcycled vintage furniture. Organic, local, seasonal produce (some foraged) features firmly – you might sample Cork monkfish, Burren smoked haddock or Galway goat's yogurt.

🛏 Kinlay Hostel
Hostel €

(📞091-565 244; www.kinlaygalway.ie; Merchants Rd; dm/d/q €33/98/845; @ 📶) The central location, cosy lounge, mellow vibe, pool table and smart kitchen and eating area make this large, brightly lit hostel a winner. Dorms vary in size but all the beds have individual curtains, lights and power and USB sockets. Tuesday night brings a pub crawl.

Clifden ❹

🛏 Dolphin Beach
B&B €€

(📞095-21204; www.dolphinbeachhouse.com; Lower Sky Rd; r from €110; 🅿 📶) The Atlantic views are superb from this stylish B&B tucked away off the Lower Sky Rd 5km west of Clifden, especially from the front terrace and atrium dining room. High-ceilinged rooms have chic, countrified furnishings. Organic vegetables from its own gardens are used at breakfast.

Inishmore ❺

✗ Bayview Restaurant
International €€

(📞086 792 9925; mains lunch €8-15, dinner €19-35; ⊘noon-9pm; 📶 👤) At Bayview there's local art on the walls, and a deal of artistry on the plates. Beautifully presented dishes might feature Aran goat's cheese with baked mushroom tapenade, whole lobster, chargrilled steaks or the day's catch with bursts of coriander or lime.

🛏 Kilmurvey House
B&B €€

(📞099-61218; www.aranislands.ie/kilmurvey-house; Kilmurvey; s/d from €60/95; ⊘Apr–mid-Oct; 📶) There's a dash of grandeur about Kilmurvey House, where 12 spacious rooms sit in an imposing, 18th-century stone mansion. Breakfasts are convivial affairs, with homemade granola, porridge with whiskey-and-baked scones.

Doolin ❼

🛏 O'Connors Guesthouse & Riverside Camping
Inn €

(📞065-707 4498; www.oconnorsdoolin.com; Doolin; s €55-70, d €70-100, campsites per 2 adults €16-20; ⊘late Feb-Nov; 🅿 📶) On a bend in the River Aille, this working farm has an L-shaped barn-style guesthouse with 10 spick-and-span rooms, two of which are equipped for visitors with limited mobility. Next door, tent pitches, and caravan and campervan sites, some right by the river, are available at its campground, along with glamping yurts, tepees and cool retro caravans (€80 to €100).

The Boyne Valley

6

A trip through the cradle of Irish history, from prehistoric tombs to bloody battlefields, with monasteries and old castles thrown in for good measure.

TRIP HIGHLIGHTS

76 km

Monasterboice
Monastic ruins with fine Celtic crosses and a round tower

7 FINISH

Mellifont Abbey

Millmount Museum

Brú na Bóinne

START
1

Hill of Tara

Trim Castle
One of Ireland's best-preserved Anglo-Norman castles

0 km

54 km

Battle of the Boyne Site
Learn about the most decisive battle in Irish history

---

2 DAYS
76KM / 47 MILES

GREAT FOR...

BEST TIME TO GO

The sun doesn't set until after 10pm between June and July, but September often gets the best weather.

ESSENTIAL PHOTO

The round tower at Monasterboice at sunset.

BEST FOR CULTURE

The magnificent Neolithic passage tombs at Brú na Bóinne.

6 The Boyne Valley

Only 112km long, the River Boyne isn't especially impressive, but its valley can lay claim to being Ireland's most significant historical stage. The breathtaking prehistoric passage tomb complex of Brú na Bóinne is the main highlight, but the remnants of Celtic forts, Norman castles and atmospheric monasteries are but the most obvious clues of the area's rich and long-standing legacy.

TRIP HIGHLIGHT

1 Trim

Remarkably preserved **Trim Castle** (King John's Castle; www.heritageireland.ie; Castle St; adult/child €5/3; ⏰10am-5pm mid-Mar–Sep, 9.30am-4.30pm mid-Feb–mid-Mar & Oct, 9am-4pm Sat & Sun Nov–mid-Feb) was Ireland's largest Anglo-Norman fortification and is proof of Trim's medieval importance. Hugh de Lacy founded Trim Castle in 1173, but Rory O'Connor, said to have been the last high king of Ireland,

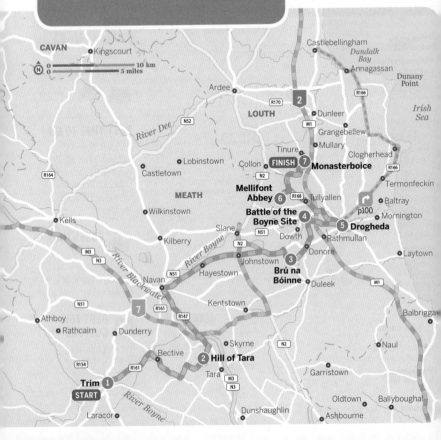

destroyed this motte-and-bailey within a year. The building you see today was begun around 1200 and has hardly been modified since, although it was badly damaged by Cromwellian forces when they took the town in 1649.

 p101, p165

The Drive » It's only 15km from Trim to Tara. Located 7.3km northeast of Trim, along the R161, is 12th-century Bective Abbey, built in the lush farmland still in evidence today on both sides of the road as you drive.

---

❷ Hill of Tara

The Hill of Tara is Ireland's most sacred stretch of turf, an entrance to the underworld, occupying a place at the heart of Irish history, legend and folklore. It was the home of the mystical druids, the priest-rulers of ancient Ireland, who practised their particular form of Celtic paganism under the watchful gaze of the all-powerful goddess Maeve (Medbh). Later it was the ceremonial capital of the high kings – 142 of them in all – who ruled until the arrival of Christianity in the 6th century. It is also one of the most important ancient sites in Europe, with a Stone Age passage tomb and prehistoric burial mounds that date back up to 5000 years. Although little remains other than humps and mounds of earth on the hill, its historic and folkloristic significance is immense.

The **Tara Visitor Centre** (📞046-902 5903; www.heritageireland.ie; adult/child €5/3; 🕐visitor centre 10am-6pm late Apr–mid-Sep, site open 24hr year-round) is housed within a former Protestant church (with a window by artist Evie Hone) and screens a 20-minute audiovisual presentation about the site.

The Drive » From Tara, the 31km drive to Brú na Bóinne takes you through the county town of Navan, the crossroads of the busy Dublin road (M3/N3) and the Drogheda–Westmeath road (N51). If you stop here, Trimgate St is lined with restaurants and pubs. Two kilometres south of the centre is the relatively intact 16th-century Athlumney Castle.

---

❸ Brú na Bóinne

The vast Neolithic necropolis known as Brú na Bóinne (the Boyne Palace) is one of the most extraordinary sites in Europe and shouldn't be missed. A thousand years older than Stonehenge, it's a powerful and evocative testament to the mind-boggling achievements of prehistoric humans.

The area consists of many different sites; the three principal ones are Newgrange, Knowth and Dowth, but only the first two are open to visitors, and then only as part of an organised tour, which departs from the **Brú na Bóinne Visitor Centre** (📞041-988 0300; www.world heritageireland.ie; Donore; adult/child visitor centre €4/3, visitor centre & Newgrange €7/4, visitor centre & Knowth €6/4, all 3 sites €13/8; 🕐9am-7pm Jun–mid-Sep, 9am-6.30pm May & mid-Sep–early Oct, 9.30am-5.30pm Feb-Apr & early Oct-early Nov, 9am-5pm early Nov-Jan), from where a bus will take you to the tombs. The centre houses an extraordinary series of interactive exhibits on prehistoric Ireland and its passage tombs, and has an excellent book and souvenir shop.

 p101

The Drive » The 7km drive from Brú na Bóinne is along a

LINK YOUR TRIP

7 **Ancient Ireland**
Connect to this trip from Brú na Bóinne and continue time travelling through Ireland's historic past.

2 **The Long Way Round**
From Monasterboice, head north on the M1 to Belfast and this hugely rewarding two-week trip.

tiny rural road that takes you through the village of Donore. The battle site is 5km north of Donore, on the southern bank of the River Boyne.

TRIP HIGHLIGHT

❹ Battle of the Boyne Site

More than 60,000 soldiers of the armies of King James II and King William III fought on this patch of farmland on the border of Counties Meath and Louth in 1690. In the end, William prevailed and James sailed off to France.

Today, the **battle site** (☎041-980 9950; www.battleoftheboyne.ie; Drybridge; adult/child €5/3; ⊗9am-5pm May-Sep, to 4pm Oct-Apr) is part of the Oldbridge Estate farm. At the visitor centre you can watch a short show about the battle, see original and replica weaponry of the time, and explore a laser battlefield model.

The Drive » It's only 5km to Drogheda; almost immediately you'll find yourself driving from fecund landscape into suburban sprawl as you approach Drogheda's outlying expanse.

❺ Drogheda

Across the river from the main town of Drogheda is Millmount, which may have once been a prehistoric burial ground but is now home to a Martello tower and army barracks.

Part of the barracks is now the **Millmount Museum** (☎041-983 3097; www.millmount.net; off Duleek St, Millmount; adult/child €6/3; ⊗10am-5.30pm Mon-Sat, 2-5pm Sun), which has interesting displays about the town and its history. Exhibits include three wonderful late-18th-century guild banners, perhaps the last in the country. There's also a room devoted to Cromwell's brutal siege of Drogheda and the Battle of the Boyne. Across the courtyard, the **Governor's House** opens for temporary exhibitions.

✕ ⊨ p101, p165

The Drive » The rich pastureland that drew the early Irish here has largely disappeared beneath the suburban sprawl, but, after 2km, as you go left off the N1 onto the N51, you'll get a better sense of classic Irish farmland (even though you'll drive over the M1 motorway!). As you get to the Boyne, go right onto the Glen Rd until you get to Mellifont. The whole drive is 9.5km long.

CROMWELL'S DROGHEDA INVASION

Oliver Cromwell (1599–1658) may be lauded as England's first democrat and protector of the people, but he didn't have much love for the Irish, dismissing them as a dirty race of papists who had sided with Charles I during the Civil War. So when 'God's own Englishman' landed his 12,000 troops in Dublin in August 1649, he set out for Drogheda, determined to set a brutal example to any other town that might resist his armies.

Over a period of hours, an estimated 3000 people were massacred, mostly royalist soldiers but also priests, women and children. The defenders' leader, Englishman and royalist Sir Arthur Aston, was bludgeoned to death with his own wooden leg. Of the survivors, many were captured and sold into indentured servitude in the Caribbean.

Cromwell defended his action as God's righteous punishment of treacherous Catholics, and was quick to point out that he had never ordered the killing of non-combatants: it was the 17th century's version of 'collateral damage'.

❻ Mellifont Abbey

In its Anglo-Norman prime, this **abbey** (☎041-982 6459; www.heritageireland.ie; Tullyallen; site admission free, visitor centre adult/student €5/3; ⊗site 24hr year-round, visitor centre 10am-6pm Jun-early Sep) was the Cistercians' first and most magnificent centre in the country. Although

Trim Castle, County Meath

DETOUR:
DROGHEDA TO CASTLEBELLINGHAM
VIA THE COAST ROAD

Start: ❺ **Drogheda**

Most people just zip north along the M1 motorway, but if you want to meander along the coast and see a little of rural Ireland, opt for the R166 from Drogheda north along the coast.

The picturesque little village of **Termonfeckin** was, until 1656, the seat and castle of the primate of Armagh. The 15th-century **castle** (📞086 079 1484; off Strand Rd, Termonfeckin; key deposit €50; ⏰10am-6pm), or tower house, is tiny and worth a five-minute stop.

About 2km further north is the busy seaside and fishing centre of **Clogherhead**, with a good, shallow Blue Flag beach at Lurganboy. Squint to ignore the caravan parks and take in the lovely views of the Cooley and Mourne Mountains instead.

The 33km route comes to an end in **Castlebellingham**. The village grew up around an 18th-century crenellated mansion, and generations of mud farmers served the landlord within. From here you can come back on the M1; it's only 29km from Castlebellingham to Drogheda.

the ruins are highly evocative and well worth exploring, they still don't do real justice to the site's former splendour.

Mellifont's most recognisable building, and one of the finest pieces of Cistercian architecture in Ireland, is the lavabo, an octagonal washing house for the monks. It was built in the early 13th century and used lead pipes to bring water from the river. A number of other buildings would have surrounded this main part of the abbey.

The visitor centre describes monastic life in detail. The ruins themselves are always open and there's good picnicking next to the rushing stream. The abbey is about 1.5km off the main Drogheda–Collon road (R168).

The Drive » The easiest way to get to Monasterboice from Mellifont Abbey is to take the Old Mellifont Rd; after 1.6km turn left onto the R168; after 1.5km, turn right onto Drogheda Rd. Follow it for 1.6km and turn left at the signpost for Monasterboice, from where it's a further 1.7km. The total distance is just 6.4km.

TRIP HIGHLIGHT

❼ Monasterboice

Crowing ravens lend an eerie atmosphere to **Monasterboice** (⏰sunrise-sunset), an intriguing monastic site containing a cemetery, two ancient church ruins, one of the finest and tallest round towers in Ireland, and two of the best high crosses.

The high crosses of Monasterboice are superb examples of Celtic art. The crosses had an important didactic use, bringing the gospels alive for the uneducated, and they were probably brightly painted originally, although all traces of colour have long disappeared.

Come early or late in the day to avoid the crowds.

Eating & Sleeping

Trim ❶

✕ StockHouse Steak €€

(☎046-943 7388; www.stockhouserestaurant.
ie; Emmet House, Finnegan's Way; mains €16-
30; ⏰5-9pm Mon-Thu, 4.30-10pm Fri & Sat,
1-8.30pm Sun) Cooked-to-order dry-aged steaks
from local abattoir-butcher Coogan's are the
stock-in-trade of this always-packed restaurant,
but noncarnivores can choose from vegetarian
dishes including sizzling fajitas.

⌂ Trim Castle Hotel Hotel €€

(☎046-948 3000; www.trimcastlehotel.com;
Castle St; s/d/f from €85/115/135; P @ 🅐)
Acres of glossy marble in the foyer set the
scene at this contemporary hotel opposite Trim
Castle. Some of its stylish rooms come with
balconies (try for sprawling corner room 225).
Its rooftop sun terrace overlooks Trim Castle,
and dining – whether at breakfast, the bar's
carvery, or upmarket Jules Restaurant (Friday
and Saturday evenings and Sunday lunch only)
– is top-notch.

Brú na Bóinne ❸

⌂ Newgrange Lodge Lodge €

(☎041-988 2478; www.newgrangelodge.
com; Staleen Rd, Donore; dm/s/d/f from
€22/65/75/119; P 🅐) Footsteps east of the
Brú na Bóinne Visitor Centre, this converted
farmhouse has 23 rooms ranging from dorms
with four to 10 beds to hotel-standard doubles
with private bathroom. Superb facilities include
a self-catering kitchen, two outdoor patios,
a lounge with an open fire, board games and
books, and free bikes. Rates include continental
breakfast with homemade scones.

Drogheda ❺

✕ Kitchen Mediterranean €€

(☎041-983 4630; www.facebook.com/
thekitchenrestaurantdrogheda; 2 South Quay;
mains lunch €13-17, dinner €19-27; ⏰11am-9pm
Wed, to 10pm Thu-Sat, noon-9pm Sun Mar-Oct,
noon-7pm Wed & Sun, from 11am Thu, 11am-9pm
Fri & Sat Nov-Feb; 🅐) Fronted by a sage-green
facade, Drogheda's best restaurant is aptly
named for its shiny open kitchen. Organic local
produce is used along with worldly ingredients
such as Cypriot halloumi and Serrano ham.
Breads are made on-site and there's an
excellent choice of wine by the glass. Don't miss
the salted-caramel baked Alaska for dessert.

✕ D'vine Bistro €€

(☎041-980 0440; www.dvine.ie; Dyer St; mains
lunch €8-12, dinner €13.50-27.50, tapas €3.50-9;
⏰noon-3pm & 5-11pm Wed & Thu, noon-11pm Fri
& Sat, from 1pm Sun) Hidden down a small flight
of steps and opening to a sunny courtyard, this
convivial cellar bistro has a great selection of
Mediterranean tapas dishes, elaborate salads,
and steak, seafood and gourmet burgers, plus
a long wine list. Service is faultless. Live music
performs on Sunday at 7pm.

⌂ Scholars Townhouse Hotel Hotel €€

(☎041-983 5410; www.scholarshotel.com; King
St; s/d/f from €79/135/139; P 🅐) This former
monastery dates from 1867 and was revamped
as a family-owned hotel and restaurant. Despite
the 16 rooms being on the small side, some
have four-poster beds and there's nothing
monastic about the facilities, which include an
atmospheric bar and a superb restaurant (mains
€18 to €32; bookings recommended). The
central location is ideal for exploring the town.

Ancient Ireland

Go time travelling through middle Ireland's collection of ancient tombs, Celtic sites and monastic cities, and cover 3000 years in four days.

7

TRIP HIGHLIGHTS

0 km

Brú na Bóinne
One of the world's most important Neolithic monuments

Hill of Slane

Loughcrew Cairns

1 START

Hill of Tara

219 km

6

Clonmacnoise
Spectacular monastic site on the banks of the Shannon

FINISH

7

Jerpoint Abbey

333 km

Rock of Cashel
Wonderful monastic city crowning a large hill

4 DAYS
529KM / 329 MILES

GREAT FOR...

BEST TIME TO GO
April to September for the long days and best weather.

ESSENTIAL PHOTO

The Rock of Cashel from the ruins of Hore Abbey.

BEST FOR CULTURE

The passage graves at Brú na Bóinne.

7 Ancient Ireland

This trip transports you from the Neolithic era to the last days of the first millennium, via the signposts of Ireland's astonishing history: the prehistoric treasure trove of Cruachan Aí; the ancient passage graves of Brú na Bóinne and Loughcrew; the ancient Celtic capital atop the Hill of Tara; and the rich monastic settlements of Clonmacnoise, Glendalough and Cashel – some of the most important early medieval universities in Europe.

TRIP HIGHLIGHT

❶ Brú na Bóinne

A thousand years older than Stonehenge, the extensive Neolithic necropolis known as Brú na Bóinne (the Boyne Palace) is simply breathtaking, even if at first glance it just looks like a handful of raised mounds in the fecund fields of County Meath.

The largest artificial structures in Ireland until the construction of the Anglo-Norman castles 4000 years later,

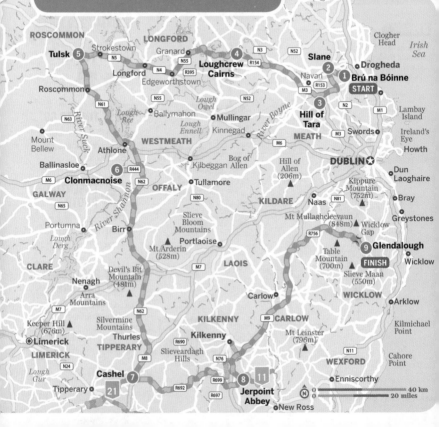

the necropolis was built to house VIP corpses. Only two of the passage graves are open to visitors (Newgrange and Knowth) and they can only be visited as part of a carefully controlled organised tour departing from the Brú na Bóinne Visitor Centre (p97).

The Drive » Follow the signposts for Slane and the N2 as you wend your way across the Meath countryside for 8km or so; the Hill of Slane is 1km north of the village.

🛏 p101

─────────────────────
❷ Slane

The fairly plain-looking **Hill of Slane** stands out only for its association with a thick slice of Celto-Christian mythology. According to legend, St Patrick lit a paschal (Easter) fire here in 433 to proclaim Christianity throughout the land.

LINK YOUR TRIP

11 **Kilkenny's Treasures**

It's 20km from Jerpoint Abbey to Kilkenny, the first stop in the trip dedicated to the county.

21 **The Holy Glen**

In Cashel you can connect to this trip exploring the very best of County Tipperary.

It was also here that Patrick supposedly plucked a shamrock from the ground, using its three leaves to explain the paradox of the Holy Trinity – the union of the Father, the Son and the Holy Spirit in one.

The Drive » Go south on the N2 for 11km and turn right onto the R153. After 2km, take the left fork and keep going for 7.5km before turning left on the R147. After 2km, turn right and drive 1.3km to the Hill of Tara (23.7km all up).

─────────────────────
❸ Hill of Tara

The Hill of Tara (Teamhair) has occupied a special place in Irish legend and folklore for millennia, although it's not known exactly when people first settled on this gently sloping hill with its commanding views over the plains of Meath. Tara's remains are not visually impressive. Only mounds and depressions in the grass mark where the Iron Age hill fort and surrounding ringforts once stood, but it remains an evocative, somewhat moving place, especially on a warm summer's evening. To make sense of it all, stop by the Tara Visitor Centre (p97).

The Drive » Head north and take the M3, which becomes the N3 at Kells. Keep going for 3.7km and at the roundabout take the first exit onto the R163. Follow it for 8km; it eventually

morphs into the R154. The cairns are along here, just west of Oldcastle. The drive is 44km altogether.

─────────────────────
❹ Loughcrew Cairns

There are 30-odd tombs here but they're hard to reach and relatively few people ever bother, which means you can enjoy this moody and evocative place in peace.

Like Brú na Bóinne, the graves were all built around 3000 BC, but unlike their better-known and better-excavated peers, the Loughcrew tombs were used at least until 750 BC. As at Newgrange, larger stones in some of the graves are decorated with spiral patterns. Some of the graves look like large piles of stones, while others are less obvious, their cairn having been removed.

Nearby is the **Loughcrew Megalithic Centre** (📞086 736 1948; www.lough crewmegalithiccentre.com; Summerbank, Oldcastle; ⏰11am-5pm), with a small but absorbing museum.

The Drive » The 87km between Loughcrew and Tulsk takes you through the heart of middle Ireland, past small glacial lakes and low-lying hills. Head 28km west and turn left onto the N55 at Granard to Edgeworthstown and take the N4 to Longford. Take the N5 as far as handsome Strokestown, where you should stop for an amble; Tulsk is 10km west along the same road.

A NIGHT IN BIRR

Feel-good Birr, County Offaly, is one of the most attractive towns in the Midlands, with elegant pastel Georgian buildings lining its streets, a magnificent old castle, an excellent choice of accommodation and spirited nightlife with great live music. Despite its appeal, Birr remains off the beaten track and you can enjoy its delights without jostling with the crowds.

CORENTIN/SHUTTERSTOCK ©

⑤ Tulsk

Anyone with an interest in Celtic mythology will be enthralled by the area around the village of Tulsk in County Roscommon, which contains 60 ancient national monuments including standing stones, barrows, cairns and fortresses, making it the most important Celtic royal site in Europe.

The **Cruachan Aí Visitor Centre (Rathcroghan)** (☏071-963 9268; www.rathcroghan.ie; Tulsk; adult/child museum €5/3, incl site tour €14/6; ☺museum & visitor centre 9am-5pm Mon-Sat year-round, plus noon-4pm Sun May-Aug) has audiovisual displays and informative panels and maps that explain the significance of the sites.

According to the legend of Táin Bó Cúailnge (Cattle Raid of Cooley), Queen Maeve (Medbh) had her palace at Cruachan Aí. The Oweynagat Cave (Cave of the Cats), believed to be the entrance to the Celtic other world, is also nearby.

The Drive » As you drive the 73km south to Clonmacnoise along the N61, you'll have Lough Ree on your left for much of the drive. Many of the lake's 50-plus islands were once inhabited by monks and their ecclesiastical treasures. These days, it's mostly anglers, sailors and birdwatchers who frequent it.

TRIP HIGHLIGHT

⑥ Clonmacnoise

Ancient Ireland is sometimes referred to as the 'land of saints and scholars', and one of the reasons why was the monastic city of Clonmacnoise (p89), one of Europe's most important centres of study between the 7th and 12th centuries. It was a top university *before* Oxford was a glint in the scholar's eye.

Founded in 548 by St Ciarán, the monastery (whose name in Irish is *Cluain Mhic Nóis,* which means 'Meadow of the Sons of Nós') that became a bustling city is in remarkably good condition: enclosed within a walled field above a bend in the River Shannon are a superb collection of early churches, high crosses, round towers and graves, including those of the high kings of Ireland.

🛏 p109

The Drive » It's 107km along the N62 to Cashel; overnighting in handsome Birr (which has great accommodation and nightlife) is recommended.

High crosses and church ruins, Clonmacnoise

TRIP HIGHLIGHT

7 Cashel

Straddling a green hill above the town, the **Rock of Cashel** (☎062-61437; www.heritageireland.ie; adult/child €8/4, incl Cormac's Chapel €11/7; ⏰9am-7pm early Jun–mid-Sep, to 5.30pm mid-Mar–early Jun & mid-Sep–mid-Oct, to 4.30pm mid-Oct–mid-Mar; [P]) is one of Ireland's most important archaeological sites and one of the most evocative of all ancient monuments. It had been a prominent Celtic power base since the 4th century; most of what remains today dates from when it was gifted to the Church in 1101. Over the next 400 years, various bishops ordered the construction of the 13th-century cathedral, a wonderfully complete **round tower**, the finest **Romanesque chapel** (1127) in the country and the sturdy walls that surround it all. Although it's a collection of religious buildings, the rock here was heavily fortified; the word 'cashel' is an Anglicisation of the Irish word *caiseal,* which means 'fortress'.

LOCAL KNOWLEDGE: THE CASHEL SHOT

Cashel looks good from pretty much every angle, but the most atmospheric photo is from the ruins of **Hore Abbey** (⊙dawn-dusk), set in flat farmland less than 1km west of Cashel.

Scattered throughout are monuments, panels from 16th-century altar tombs and coats of arms. If you have binoculars, look for the numerous stone heads on capitals and corbels high above the ground.

✖️🛏️ p109, p239, p277

The Drive » Tipperary and western Kilkenny are classic examples of good Irish farmland; as you wend your way east along the R692 and R690, you'll pass stud farms and cattle ranches. Ten kilometres northeast of Cottrellstown via the R697 is the 29m-high Kilree round tower and, next to it, a 9th-century high cross. The drive to Jerpoint Abbey from Cashel is 60km.

- - - - - - - - - - - - - - - - -

⑧ Jerpoint Abbey

One of Ireland's finest Cistercian ruins, **Jerpoint Abbey** (☎056-772 4623; www.heritageireland. ie; R448; adult/child €5/3;

⊙9am-5.30pm Mar-Sep, to 5pm Oct, 9.30am-4pm Nov) near Thomastown was established in the 12th century and has been partially restored. The tower and cloister date from the late 14th or early 15th century. The 45-minute tours are worthwhile, as the guides flesh out the abbey's fascinating history.

The Drive » As you come off the M9 and take the R756 east towards Glendalough, you'll climb into the wildest parts of the Wicklow Mountains, eastern Ireland's most scenic spectacle. Just before Glendalough you'll drive through the Wicklow Gap, between Mt Tonelagee (816m) to the north and Table Mountain (700m) to the southwest. Total distance to Glendalough: 117km.

- - - - - - - - - - - - - - - - -

⑨ Glendalough

Of all Ireland's monastic cities, none has the secluded beauty and isolated majesty of Glendalough, whose impressive ruins are more than rivalled by their setting: two dark glacial lakes at the foot of a forested valley that remain, despite the immense popularity of a visit, a profoundly peaceful and spiritual place.

In 498 the solitude-seeking St Kevin went to live in a Bronze Age tomb on the south side of the Upper Lake, but most of what you see dates from the 9th century onwards, when Kevin's settlement rivalled Clonmacnoise as one of Ireland's premier universities: huddled around the eastern end of the Lower Lake are Glendalough's most fascinating buildings, including a roofless cathedral, a couple of churches, a gatehouse and a round tower.

The **Glendalough Visitor Centre** (☎0404-45352; www.heritageireland.ie; adult/child €5/3; ⊙9.30am-6pm mid-Mar–mid-Oct, to 5pm mid-Oct–mid-Mar) has a 20-minute audiovisual presentation called *Ireland of the Monasteries*.

Eating & Sleeping

Clonmacnoise ⑥

🛏 Kajon House B&B €€

(📞090-967 4191; www.kajonhouse.ie; R444, Creevagh; s/d from €60/80; 🕙Mar-Oct; 🅿🛜) If you want to stay near the ruins, this is your best option, just 1.7km southwest. It has cosy rooms, comfy beds (warmed by electric blankets), a spacious garden (with a picnic table) and a warm welcome even by Irish standards, with scones and tea or coffee on arrival. Breakfast includes homemade pancakes and compotes.

Birr ⑥

🍴 Thatch Irish €€

(📞057-912 0682; www.thethatchcrinkill.com; Military Rd, Crinkill; lunch mains €12.50-27, 2-/3-course dinner menus €26/32; 🕙kitchen 4-7.30pm Mon, to 9pm Tue-Thu, 12.30am-9pm Fri & Sat, to 7.30pm Sun, bar to 10pm; 🛜🍴) This 200-year-old traditional thatched pub 2.2km southeast of Birr is a great place to sip a pint or enjoy a meal at lunch (à la carte) or dinner (fixed-price menus only) in its brick-and-stone interior warmed by open fires. Alongside traditional roasts, specialities include black-pudding–stuffed duck.

🛏 Walcot B&B B&B €€

(📞057-912 1247; www.facebook.com/Walcotbandb; Rosse Row; s/d from €60/90; 🅿🛜) Set back from the road amid sprawling formal gardens across from Birr Castle, this Georgian townhouse is close to everything. The five large, antique-furnished bedrooms have period-style bathrooms with large tubs and showers.

🛏 Maltings Guesthouse Guesthouse €

(📞057-912 1345; www.themaltingsbirr.com; Castle St; s/d from €50/80; 🛜) Based in an 1810 malt storehouse once used by Guinness, this guesthouse has a serene location by the River Camcor near the castle. The large, pine-

furnished rooms have a lilac-and-green colour scheme; all overlook the water, as does the breakfast room, which is framed by floor-to-ceiling glass and opens to a terrace. Kids aged under 12 pay half price.

Cashel ⑦

🍴 Mikey Ryan's Gastropub €€

(📞062-62007; www.mikeyryans.ie; 76 Main St; mains lunch €9-16, dinner €17-30; 🕙food served noon-3pm & 6-9.30pm; 🛜🍴) This long-established bar has been given a glitzy gastropub makeover, with a bright, sun-drenched dining room at the back, and a gorgeous garden complete with barbecue and horse-box bar. The delicious farmhouse-style food is sourced from local farmers and artisan producers, and Cashel Blue cheese makes several appearances on the menu – in pesto, on pizza and topping a burger.

🍴 Cafe Hans Cafe €€

(📞062-63660; Dominic St; mains €15-26; 🕙noon-5.30pm Tue-Sat; 🍴) Competition for the 32 seats is fierce at this gourmet cafe run by the same family as **Chez Hans** (p239) along the street. There are fantastic salads, open sandwiches (including succulent prawns with tangy Marie Rose sauce) and filling fish, shellfish, lamb and vegetarian dishes, accompanied by a discerning wine selection and mouth-watering desserts. No credit cards. Enter via Moor Lane. Arrive before or after the lunchtime rush or plan on waiting for a table.

🛏 Cashel Lodge & Camping Park B&B, Campground €€

(📞062-61003; www.cashel-lodge.com; Dundrum Rd; camping per person €10, s/d from €45/85; 🅿🛜) This converted 200-year-old coach house northwest of Cashel on the R505 (follow the signs for Dundrum) is a friendly and superb-value place with exposed stone-and-timber-beam interiors and terrific views of the Rock and Hore Abbey. As well as the B&B, there's a small campground.

Monasteries, Mountains & Mansions

From mountains and monastic ruins to stately homes and historic whiskey distilleries, there's nothing fictional about this trip through middle Ireland.

8

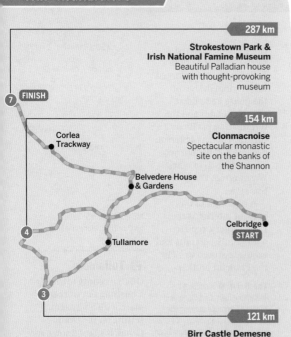

287 km

Strokestown Park & Irish National Famine Museum
Beautiful Palladian house with thought-provoking museum

FINISH ⑦

154 km

Corlea Trackway

Clonmacnoise
Spectacular monastic site on the banks of the Shannon

Belvedere House & Gardens

Celbridge ●
START

④

● Tullamore

③

121 km

Birr Castle Demesne
A magnificent telescope, fabulous gardens and one of the world's tallest box hedges

3 DAYS
278KM / 172 MILES

GREAT FOR...

BEST TIME TO GO
Late spring and early autumn are ideal: smaller crowds and good weather.

 ESSENTIAL PHOTO
Immortalise the gardens of Birr Castle demesne.

 BEST FOR CULTURE
Explore Ireland's tormented history at Strokestown Park.

8 Monasteries, Mountains & Mansions

This is a journey through Irish heritage, much of it overlapping with Ireland's Ancient East: handsome towns like Birr and Strokestown may not attract star billing but are all the better for it, while better-known attractions like Clonmacnoise and Castletown House are outstanding examples of monastic splendour and Georgian extravagance, respectively. And did we mention whiskey? How about a visit to the home of the smoothest Irish whiskey of all?

1 Celbridge

Celbridge, County Kildare, is now a satellite town serving Dublin, only 20km to the east, but in the 18th century it was known as the location for Ireland's most magnificent Georgian pile, Castletown House (p82), which simply has no peer.

The house was built between the years 1722 and 1732 for William Conolly (1662–1729), speaker of the Irish House of Commons and, at the time, Ireland's richest man.

The job of building a palace fit for a prince was entrusted to Sir Edward Lovett Pearce

(1699–1733). Inspired by the work of Andrea Palladio, Pearce enlarged the original design of the house and added the colonnades and the terminating pavilions. In the US, Thomas Jefferson became a Palladian acolyte and much of official Washington, DC, is in this style.

A highlight of the opulent interior is the Long Gallery, replete with family portraits and exquisite stucco work by the Francini brothers.

The Drive » It's 85km to Tullamore from Celbridge, and most of the route is along the painless and featureless M4 and M6 motorways; at Junction 11 on the M4, be sure to take the left-hand fork onto the M6 towards Galway and Athlone. Exit the

M6 at Junction 5; Tullamore is a further 11km along the N52.

2 Tullamore

Offaly's county town is a bustling but workaday place with a pleasant setting on the Grand Canal. It's best known for Tullamore Dew Whiskey, which was distilled in the

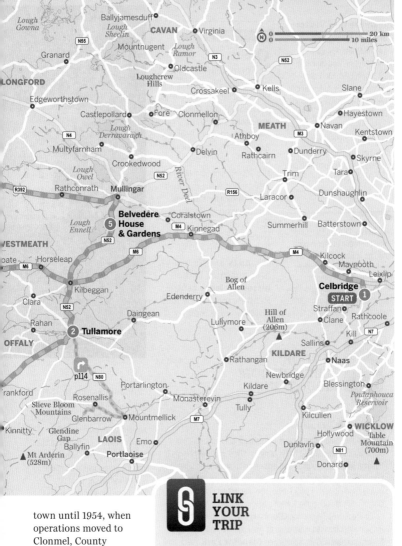

town until 1954, when operations moved to Clonmel, County Tipperary.

In 2014 this all changed again, when the distillery opened a new factory on the edge of town. You can't visit it, but you can explore the town's distilling history in the refurbished

LINK YOUR TRIP

32 Northwest on Adrenaline
Explore the northwest's heart-racing activities with an easy 61km drive from Strokestown to Sligo.

22 Best of the West
At trip's end, head west to Westport and pick up this western extravaganza.

Tullamore Dew Visitor Centre (☎057-932 5015; www.tullamoredew.com; Bury Quay; guided tour €16; ⏱9.30am-6pm Mon-Sat, 11.30am-5pm Sun), located in a 19th-century canal-side warehouse. At the end of the tour you'll get to sample some produce and, inevitably, be encouraged to buy it for friends and family.

 p117

The Drive ≫ It's only 36km from Tullamore to Birr. As you drive the N52 south towards Birr, you'll skirt the northern edge of the Slieve Bloom Mountains, which rise suddenly from the great plain of middle Ireland.

TRIP HIGHLIGHT

❸ Birr

The main reason to visit handsome Birr is to explore the attractions and gardens of **Birr Castle demesne** (☎057-912 0336; www.birrcastle.com; Rosse Row; adult/child gardens €9/5, gardens, exhibits & castle €18/10; ⏱9am-6pm Mar-Oct, 9.30am-4pm Nov-Feb), built in 1620 by the Parsons family, who still own it to this day. The Parsons were a remarkable family of pioneering Irish scientists, and their work is documented in the **historic science centre**. Exhibits include the massive telescope built by

SCENICIRELAND.COM/CHRISTOPHER HILL PHOTOGRAPHIC/ALAMY STOCK PHOTO ©

William Parsons in 1845, for 75 years the largest in the world. It was used to make innumerable discoveries, including the spiral galaxies, and to map the moon's surface.

Otherwise, the 50-hectare castle grounds are famous for their magnificent **gardens** set around a large artificial lake. They hold over 1000 species of plants from all over the world; something always seems to be in bloom. Look for one of the world's tallest box hedges, planted in the 1780s and now standing 12m high, and the Hornbeam cloister.

↪ DETOUR: SLIEVE BLOOM MOUNTAINS

Start: ❷ Tullamore

Although the Slieve Bloom Mountains aren't as spectacular as some Irish ranges, their sudden rise from a great plain and the absence of visitors make them highly attractive. You'll get a real sense of being away from it all as you tread the deserted blanket bogs, moorland, pine forests and isolated valleys.

For leisurely walking, **Glenbarrow**, southwest of Rosenallis, has an interesting trail by the cascading River Barrow. Other spots are **Glendine Park**, near the Glendine Gap, and the **Cut mountain pass**.

For something more challenging, you could try the **Slieve Bloom Way**, a 77km signposted trail that does a complete circuit of the mountains, taking in most major points of interest. The recommended starting point is the car park at Glenbarrow, 5km from Rosenallis, from where the trail follows tracks, forest firebreaks and old roads around the mountains. The trail's highest point is at Glendine Gap (460m).

Palladian House and gardens, Strokestown Park

🍴 🛏 p109, p117

The Drive » You'll see mostly fields of cows as you drive the 33km to Clonmacnoise along the N62; at Cloghan, turn left onto the slightly narrower and lonelier R357. You'll have the River Shannon on your left-hand-side when you turn onto the R444 for the last 7.5km, via Shannonbridge's 16-arch limestone bridge dating from 1757.

TRIP HIGHLIGHT

④ Clonmacnoise

One of the most important monastic sites in Ireland, the marvellous monastic ruins of Clonmacnoise (p89) are also one of the most popular tourist attractions in the country, so be prepared to share your visit with other awestruck tourists and busloads of curious schoolkids.

🍴 🛏 p109, p117

The Drive » Rejoin the M6 19km north of Clonmacnoise. At Junction 4, take the N52 north towards Mullingar; on your left, keep an eye out for Lough Ennell: the far side is home to Lilliput House, which was frequently used by Jonathan Swift and gave him the name he used in *Gulliver's Travels*. In total, the drive is 62km long. Detour to Athlone, 25km from Clonmacnoise for a Thai meal.

⑤ Belvedere House & Gardens

About 5.5km south of Mullingar, overlooking Lough Ennell, is **Belvedere House** (☎044-933 8960; www.belvedere-house. ie; off N52; adult/child €8/4; ⏱ house 9.30am-5pm Mar-Oct, to 4pm Nov-Feb, gardens 9.30am-8pm May-Aug, to 7pm Apr & Sep, to 6pm Mar & Oct, to 4.30pm Nov-Feb), an immense 18th-century hunting lodge set in 65 hectares of gardens. More than a few skeletons have come out of Belvedere's closets: the first earl, Lord Belfield, accused his wife and younger brother Arthur of adultery. His wife was placed under house arrest here for 30 years, and Arthur was jailed in London for the rest of his life. Meanwhile, the earl lived a life of decadence and debauchery. On his death, his wife emerged dressed in the fashion of three decades earlier, still protesting her innocence.

✗ ⊨ p117

The Drive >> Mullingar, just north, has a couple of good hotels and restaurants. From there, drive northwest into County Longford, whose low hills have few tourist sights but are a haven for anglers who come for the superb fishing around Lough Ree and Lanesborough. From Belvedere House, the drive to Corlea along the R392 is 42km.

- - - - - - - - - - - - - - - - -

6 Corlea Trackway

Longford's main attraction is the magnificent **Corlea Trackway** (☎043-332 2386; www.heritageireland.ie; off R392, Keenagh;

⊘10am-6pm Easter-Sep), an Iron Age bog road near Keenagh that was built in 148 BC. An 18m stretch of the historic track has now been preserved in a humidified hall at the visitor centre, where you can join a guided tour that details the bog's unique flora and fauna, and fills you in on how the track was discovered and the methods used to preserve it. Wear a windproof jacket as the bog land can be blowy.

The Drive >> Strokestown is 29km northwest of Corlea along the R392 as far as Lanesborough, after which you'll cut through the green, lush countryside along the R371. After 11km, take a left onto the N5, which will take you right into Strokestown, 4.5km further on.

- - - - - - - - - - - - - - - - -

TRIP HIGHLIGHT

7 Strokestown

Roscommon's most handsome town is, for nonresidents, all about **Strokestown Park and the Irish National Famine**

Museum (☎071-963 3013; www.strokestownpark.ie; off N5; house & Famine Museum adult/child €14/6, gardens free; ⊘10.30am-5.30pm mid-Mar–Oct, to 4pm Nov–mid-Mar, tours noon, 2.30pm, 4pm mid-Mar–Oct, 2pm Nov–mid-Mar, gardens dawn-dusk), the entrance to which is through the three Gothic arches at the end of Strokestown's main avenue.

Admission to the beautifully preserved **Palladian house** is by a 50-minute guided tour, taking in a galleried kitchen with state-of-the-art clockwork machinery, and a child's bedroom complete with 19th-century toys and fun-house mirrors.

In direct and deliberate contrast to the splendour of the house and its grounds is the harrowing **Irish National Famine Museum**, which sheds light on the devastating 1840s potato blight. There's a huge amount of information to take in, but you'll emerge with an unblinking insight into the starvation of the poor, and the ignorance, callousness and cruelty of those who were in a position to help. Allow at least half a day to see the house, museum and gardens.

**DETOUR:
ONE OF IRELAND'S BEST TRADITIONAL PUBS**

Start: 6 Corlea Trackway

About 10km east of Lanesborough is the tiny hamlet of Killashee, which is home to **Magan's**, a delightful old bar, grocery and hardware store that seems stuck in aspic, completely oblivious to the pull and push of modern life. It's well off the beaten track, and is rarely frequented by anyone other than locals, which makes it an even better destination for a pint.

Eating & Sleeping

Tullamore ❷

✖ Sirocco's   Italian €€

(☎057-935 2839; www.siroccos.net; Patrick
St; mains €15-27, pizzas €12-14; ⏰5-10pm
Mon-Thu, noon-3pm & 5-10pm Fri, 1-10.30pm
Sat, 1-9.30pm Sun; 🚸) Italian-Irish owned, this
popular town-centre bistro has a wide selection
of pasta dishes and pizzas named for famous
Italian names (eg Versace, with tiger prawns,
mussels and crab), as well as more substantial
mains (veal escalope with Marsala cream
sauce; mushroom- and Gorgonzola-stuffed
chicken breast; salt-baked cod with parsley).
Reservations are recommended; alternatively,
takeaway is available.

Birr ❸

✖ Spinners on Castle St   Irish €€

(☎057-912 3779; www.spinnersbirr.com; Castle
St; bar mains €12-18, restaurant mains €14-27;
⏰restaurant 6-9pm Fri & Sat, 12.30-3.30pm
Sun, bar 5-9pm Wed & Thu, 12.30-9pm Fri &
Sat, 12.30-7pm Sun; 🛜) By the castle wall,
Spinners is part of a complex spanning five
restored Georgian houses. The whitewashed
wine-cocktail bar is the perfect place for a
cheeseboard or burger with black pudding
and homemade relish, while the elegant
restaurant's seasonal menu might feature
Burren Smokehouse mackerel and potato
salad followed by baked brill with red lentil
broth. Service is excellent. Tables set up in the
tree-shaded enclosed courtyard in fine weather;
occasional live music plays in the bar.

🛏 Brendan House   B&B €€

(☎057-912 1818; www.tinjugstudio.com;
Brendan St; s/d without bathroom from €55/80;
🛜) Packed with knick-knacks, books, rugs,
art and antiques, this Georgian townhouse is
a bohemian delight. The three rooms share a
bathroom (allegedly one of Birr's oldest), but
the four-poster beds, period charm, superb
breakfast and artistic style are the real draws.
The owners arrange mountain walks, castle and
art tours, holistic treatments and art classes.

Shannonbridge ❸

✖ Killeens Village Tavern   Pub Food €

(☎090-967 4112; www.killeens.ie; Main St;
mains €10; ⏰kitchen noon-8.30pm, bar 10am-
11.30pm) Old-world pub and shop Killeens is
renowned for its lively traditional music six
nights a week from March to September and at
weekends the rest of the year. Traditional pub
grub spans steak sandwiches to fish and chips.

Athlone ❹

✖ Kin Khao   Thai €€

(☎090-649 8805; www.kinkhaothai.ie; Abbey
Lane; mains €10-19; ⏰5.30-10pm Mon & Tue,
12.30-2.30pm & 5.30-10pm Wed-Sat, 1-4pm
& 5.30-10pm Sun; 🍴🚸) Fronted by a bright
yellow facade, Kin Khao is renowned for its
extensive menu of authentic northern Thai
dishes, such as *larb gai* (minced chicken salad),
gaeng phed ped yang (red duck curry with
pineapple) and *pad gra* (prawn, Thai basil and
chilli stir fry). There's also a takeaway menu..

Mullingar ❺

✖ Oscar's Restaurant   International €€

(☎044-934 4909; www.oscarsmullingar.
com; 21 Oliver Plunkett St; mains €15.50-28;
⏰5.30-9.30pm Mon-Fri, to 10pm Sat, 12.30-
2.30pm & 5.30-8.30pm Sun; 🛜🚸) Perennially
popular, Oscar's is the place to go for upmarket
comfort food (steaks, stir fries, barbecued
rubs, smoky chicken wings, burgers et al) and
a lively atmosphere in a cavernous dining room
with exposed stone walls and a timber-beamed
ceiling. Sunday roasts are a local event.

🛏 Annebrook House Hotel   Hotel €€

(☎044-935 3300; www.annebrook.ie; Austin
Friars St; d/apt from €99/160; 🅿🛜) Right
in the town centre, the hub of this hotel is
a lovely early-19th-century stone house.
Accommodation is in an annex with 26
contemporary rooms in shades of creams and
yellows; apartments come with two bedrooms
and open-plan living rooms with cherry-wood
kitchens..

Wicklow Mountains

9

Eastern Ireland's most forbidding mountain range is as magnificent as it is desolate, with narrow roads cutting through the gorse- and bracken-covered hilltops.

TRIP HIGHLIGHTS

41 km

Glendalough
A monastic gem cradled at the foot of a romantic glacial valley

● Glencree

1 START

● The Featherbed

0 km

Powerscourt Estate
Georgian mansion, magnificent gardens and breathtaking views

● Glenmacnass Valley

4

70 km

Avondale House
Historic home of Charles Stewart Parnell

6 FINISH

3 DAYS
70KM / 43 MILES

GREAT FOR...

BEST TIME TO GO

From late August to September, the crowds thin out and the heather is in bloom.

ESSENTIAL PHOTO

Looking down on Lough Tay and Luggala from the Sally Gap.

BEST FOR CULTURE

Glendalough: 1500 years of monastic history beautifully nestled in a glacial valley.

---

ough Tay Dramatic lake in the Wicklow Mountains

9 Wicklow Mountains

This drive takes you down the spine of the Wicklow Mountains, whose dramatic scenery and weather-whipped bleakness make up for what they lack in height. Along the way you'll visit fine Palladian mansions and a beautiful monastic site nestled at the foot of a glacial valley – be prepared to pull over and gawp at the scenery that unfolds.

TRIP HIGHLIGHT

① Enniskerry

If you're coming from Dublin, Enniskerry is a handsome village at the top of the R117, aka the '21 Bends', but its pretty shops and cafes are merely a prelude to a visit to the superb 64-sq-km Powerscourt Estate (p85), whose workers' domestic needs were the very reason Enniskerry was built in the first place.

Due to a fire, you can't visit the Palladian mansion save the ground-floor cafe and outlet of the popular Avoca handicrafts store, but it's the gardens that will have you in thrall. Laid out (mostly) in the 19th century, they are a magnificent blend of landscaped gardens, sweeping terraces, statuary, ornamental lakes, secret hollows, rambling walks and walled enclosures replete with more than 200 types of trees and shrubs, all beneath the stunning natural backdrop of the Great Sugarloaf Mountain to the southeast.

✖ ⌂ p85, p125

The Drive ›› The narrow, twisting L1011 cuts 9.7km through the northern edge of the mountains, with only a hint of what's to come further on. As you approach Glencree you'll pass through mostly forest.

② Glencree

Glencree is a leafy hamlet set into the side of the valley of the same name, which opens east to give a magnificent view down to Great Sugarloaf Mountain and the sea.

The valley floor is home to the Glencree Oak Project, an ambitious

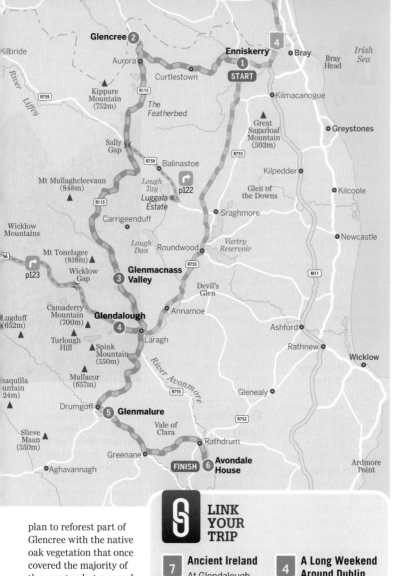

plan to reforest part of Glencree with the native oak vegetation that once covered the majority of the country, but now only covers 1% of Ireland's land mass.

The village, such as it is, has a tiny shop and a hostel but no pub. There's a poignant German

LINK YOUR TRIP

7 Ancient Ireland

At Glendalough you can start this trip through Ireland's ancient heritage...in reverse.

4 A Long Weekend Around Dublin

From Enniskerry, hook up with this trip exploring the best of Dublin's surrounds.

DETOUR: LUGGALA

Start: ❷ Glencree

If you turn right (east) at the Sally Gap crossroads onto the R759, you'll be on the Sally Gap, one of the two main east–west passes across the Wicklow Mountains and a stretch of road surrounded by some spectacular countryside. About 5km on, the narrow road passes above the dark and dramatic Lough Tay, whose scree slopes slide into Luggala (Fancy Mountain). This almost-fairy-tale estate is owned by one Garech de Brún, member of the Guinness family and founder of Claddagh Records, a leading producer of Irish traditional and folk music. You can't visit the estate itself, but there's a popular looped walk that circles it from a height. The small River Cloghoge links Lough Tay with Lough Dan just to the south. You can continue on the R759 for another 3km or so, turning right onto the R755 for Roundwood, or double-back onto the Old Military Rd and make your way south via Glenmacnass.

cemetery, **Deutscher Soldatenfriedhof** (German Military Cemetery; Glencree; ☉ dawn–dusk), dedicated to the 134 German servicemen who died in Ireland during WWI and WWII. Just south of the village, the former military barracks are a retreat house and reconciliation centre for people of different religions from the Republic and the North.

The Drive » At Glencree you'll join Wicklow's loveliest, loneliest road, the Old Military Rd (R115), which cuts through a desolate valley of gorse and brown bog and gets more desolate as you go south. After 8.4km, you'll reach the Sally Gap crossroads; turn right onto the R759 for the gap itself or

continue for another 5km to the Glenmacnass Valley.

---

❸ Glenmacnass Valley

Desolate and utterly deserted, the Glenmacnass Valley, a stretch of wild bogland between the Sally Gap crossroads and Laragh, is one of the most beautiful parts of the mountains, although the sense of isolation is quite dramatic.

The highest mountain to the west is Mt Mullaghcleevaun (848m), and the River Glenmacnass flows south and tumbles over the edge of the mountain plateau in a great foaming cascade.

There's a car park near the top of the **Glenmacnass Waterfall**. Be careful when walking on rocks near the waterfall, as a few people have slipped to their deaths. There are fine walks up Mt Mullaghcleevaun or in the hills to the east of the car park.

The Drive » Beyond the Glenmacnass Valley, the Old Military Rd descends for 13km into Laragh, a busy crossroads village that serves as a supply point for nearby Glendalough. It's a good spot to stop and eat or buy provisions. Glendalough is 2km west of here.

Round tower at Glendalough, County Wicklow

TRIP HIGHLIGHT

4 Glendalough

Wicklow's most visited attraction and one of the country's most important historic sites is the collection of ruined churches, buildings, shelters and a round tower that make up the ancient monastic city of Glendalough, founded in 498 by St Kevin, who came to the (then) desolate valley looking for a spot of contemplative tranquillity. The ruins are certainly evocative, but it's their setting that makes them

DETOUR:
THE WICKLOW GAP

Start: 4 Glendalough

Between Mt Tonelagee (816m) to the north and Table Mountain (700m) to the southwest, the Wicklow Gap (R756) is the second major pass over the mountains. The eastern end of the road begins just to the north of Glendalough and climbs through some lovely scenery northwestwards up along the Glendassan Valley. It passes the remains of some old lead and zinc workings before meeting a side road that leads south and up Turlough Hill, the location of Ireland's only pumped-storage power station. You can walk up the hill for a look over the Upper Lake. The western end of the gap meets the N81, from which it's only a few kilometres north to Blessington and Russborough House.

GLENDALOUGH VALLEY WALKS

The Glendalough Valley is all about walking and clambering. There are nine marked walkways in the valley, the longest of which is about 10km, or about four hours' walking. Before you set off, drop by the **National Park Information Office** (☎0404-45425; www.wicklowmountainsnationalpark.ie; Bolger's Cottage, Upper Lake car park; ☺10am-5.30pm May-Sep, to dusk Sat & Sun Oct-Apr) and pick up the relevant leaflet and trail map (all around €0.50). A word of warning: don't be fooled by the relative gentleness of the surrounding countryside or the fact that the Wicklow Mountains are really no taller than big hills. The weather can be merciless here, so be sure to take the usual precautions, have the right equipment and tell someone where you're going and when you should be back. For Mountain Rescue call 999.

special: two dark and mysterious lakes tucked into a deep valley covered in forest.

You could spend a day exploring the ruins and taking in the local scenery, but whatever you do, your exploration should start with a visit to the Glendalough Visitor Centre (p108), which has a decent 20-minute audiovisual presentation called *Ireland of the Monasteries*.

✘ ⊨ p85, p125

The Drive ›› As you go deeper into the mountains southwest of Glendalough along the R755, near the southern end of the Military Rd, everything gets a bit wilder and more remote. It's an 11km drive to Glenmalure.

❺ Glenmalure

Beneath the western slopes of Wicklow's highest peak, Lugna-quilla Mountain (924m), is Glenmalure, a dark and sombre blind valley flanked by scree slopes of loose boulders. After coming over the mountains into Glenmalure, you turn northwest at the Drumgoff bridge. From there it's about 6km up the road beside the River Avonbeg to a car park where trails lead off in various directions.

✘ ⊨ p125

The Drive ›› The tiny rural road to Rathdrum is called Riverside; it takes you down out of the mountains through some lush forest for 12km into Rathdrum for Avondale House.

TRIP HIGHLIGHT

❻ Avondale House

The quiet village of Rathdrum at the foot of the Vale of Clara comprises little more than a few old houses and shops, however, it's not what's in the town that's of interest to visitors, but what's just outside it.

Avondale House (☎0404-46111; www.heritage-island.com; Avondale Forest Park) is a fine Palladian mansion surrounded by a marvellous 209-hectare estate, which was the birthplace and Irish home of the 'uncrowned king of Ireland', Charles Stewart Parnell (1846–91), the champion of the struggle for Home Rule and one of the key figures of the Irish independence movement. Designed by James Wyatt in 1779, the house has many highlights, including a stunning vermilion-hued library and beautiful dining room.

Surrounding the house, running through the forest and parkland (managed by the Irish Forestry Service, Coillte), are many walking trails. You can visit the park during daylight hours year-round.

Eating & Sleeping

Enniskerry ❶

✖ Emilia's Ristorante   Italian €€

(📞01-276 1834; www.emilias.ie; The Square; mains €11-24; 🕐5-9pm Tue-Sat) A lovely 1st-floor dining room is the backdrop for Italian dishes such as Tuscan-wine-simmered cod, house-made Puglian pasta with clams and chicken breast in lemon sauce, as well as crispy thin-crust pizzas – try the Nettuno, with prawns, artichokes and black olives.

🛏 Coolakay House   B&B €€

(📞01-286 2423; www.coolakayhouse.ie; Waterfall Rd, Coolakay; s/d from €60/80; 🅿🛜) A great option for walkers along the Wicklow Way, this modern working farm is 4km south of Enniskerry off the R760. The light, airy bedrooms are well appointed and comfortable, the views are terrific and the breakfast sensational. March and April is lambing season and guests are encouraged to observe – and even name – a newborn lamb. Cash only.

Glendalough ❹

✖ Wicklow Heather   International €€

(📞0404-45157; www.wicklowheather.ie; Glendalough Rd, Laragh; mains €13-29; 🕐8am-9.30pm Mon-Thu, to 10pm Fri & Sat, to 9pm Sun) This long-established rustic family restaurant serves breakfast through to dinner amid the honeyed glow of polished wood. The globe-trotting menu ranges from Wicklow lamb, wild venison, Irish beef and fish (including excellent trout) to satay dishes, Cajun chicken,

and tomato and basil arancini. Its Writers Room houses a display of Irish literary memorabilia; there's also a well-stocked whiskey bar.

Glenmalure ❺

🛏 Glenmalure Hostel   Hostel €

(📞01-830 4555; www.anoige.ie; Baravore; dm from €20; 🕐daily Jun-Aug, Sat only Sep-May) No telephone (the listed number is An Óige head office), no electricity (lighting is by gas) and no running water, just a rustic two-storey former hunting lodge with 19 beds, a gas stove, water from the stream, and an open log fire. And a top literary connection – this place was the setting for JM Synge's play *The Shadow of a Gunman*. You can take a car to the hostel if the river is low enough to drive across; if not, it's a 750m walk northwest from the parking area by the bridge. Otherwise, you can hike here from Laragh, following the Wicklow Way south over the hills to the Glenmalure Lodge Hotel, then continuing up the valley (14km in total).

✖ Glenmalure Lodge   Pub Food €

(📞0404-46188; www.glenmalurelodge.ie; mains €9-15.50; 🕐 kitchen 7.30-10am & noon-9pm, bar 10am-11pm; 🛜) Hearty all-day pub food at Glenmalure Lodge includes steak and Guinness pie, lamb stew, leek and potato soup and a ploughman's lunch. Breakfast is available for guests and nonguests; hikers can also get packed lunches (€6.50) with sandwiches, fruit, chocolate and bottled water. Trad music often plays in the bar; upstairs are 14 simple but comfortable guest rooms (double/triple €60/90).

Carlow Back Roads

A jaunt through Ireland undisturbed by mass tourism, this trip reveals one of the country's most delightful, unexplored counties.

10

TRIP HIGHLIGHTS

Delta Sensory Gardens
Duckett's Grove

1
START

0 km

Carlow
Unspoilt country town with rich historical background

Leighlinbridge
FINISH

Altamont Gardens

Bagenalstown

6

63 km

7

Borris
Beautiful Georgian village with stunning mountain backdrop

St Mullins

Clonegal
Idyllic village straight out of a nursery rhyme

33 km

3 DAYS
118KM / 73 MILES

GREAT FOR...

BEST TIME TO GO

Carlow's flower festivals take place throughout July and September.

ESSENTIAL PHOTO

Immortalise the Black Castle from the banks of the Barrow.

BEST FOR GARDENS

The Altamont Gardens are the most spectacular of Carlow's beautiful gardens.

10 Carlow Back Roads

Strings of quietly picturesque villages wind through Carlow, Ireland's second-smallest county. The scenic Blackstairs Mountains dominate the southeast, while the region's most dramatic chunk of history is Europe's biggest dolmen, just outside quiet Carlow town. A ruined Gothic mansion and a reputedly haunted castle form the backdrop to two of the county's best flower-filled gardens.

TRIP HIGHLIGHT

① Carlow Town

Carlow town's narrow streets and lanes are quiet these days, a far cry from 25 May 1789, when several hundred Irish insurgents were ambushed and executed by British troops during a ferocious battle in the middle of town. The dead were buried in gravel pits on the far side of the River Barrow, at Graiguecullen.

Built by William de Marshall on the site of an earlier Norman motte-and-bailey fort, the 13-century **castle** (Mill Lane) survived Cromwell's attentions but was later converted into a lunatic asylum. The evocative portion that survives is a part of the keep flanked by two towers.

Other notable sights include the 19th-century **Cathedral of the Assumption** (☎059-916 4021; www.carlowcathedral. ie; College St; ◷9am-5pm Mon-Sat, to 7pm Sun) and the **Carlow County Museum** (☎059-913 1554; www.carlow museum.ie; cnr College & Tullow Sts; ◷10am-5pm Mon-Sat, 2-4.30pm Sun Jun-Aug, 10am-4.30pm Mon-Sat Sep-May).

✗ ⊨ p133

The Drive » Take the Athy road (R417) north for 2km; the Delta Sensory Gardens are on your left.

➋ Delta Sensory Gardens

Located in an incongruous industrial estate on the northern edge of Carlow town are these remarkable **gardens** (☎059-914 3527; www.deltasensorygardens.com; Cannery Rd, Strawhall Estate; adult/child €5/free; ☺9am-5.30pm Mon-Fri, 11am-5.30pm Sat & Sun, closed weekends Jan, Feb & Nov). Some 16 interconnecting, themed gardens cover 1 hectare and span the five senses – from a sculpture garden to a formal rose garden, a water and woodland garden, a willow garden and a musical garden with mechanical fountains. Admission proceeds benefit the adjoining Delta Centre, which provides services and respite for adults with learning disabilities.

 LINK YOUR TRIP

11 **Kilkenny's Treasures**

From Borris, it's only 10km to Graiguenamanagh, from where you can explore County Kilkenny.

3 **Tip to Toe**

Travel 14km from St Mullins south to New Ross, where you can join the north-to-south Classic Trip.

The Drive ›› Take the N80 for 2.2km, then the R726 for 2.4km heading east from Carlow town. You'll have to park the car and walk 300m to the dolmen field.

③ Browne's Hill Dolmen

Ireland's largest portal dolmen (tomb chamber) sits in a field and, from the road, doesn't look that impressive. But as you get closer you'll begin to appreciate the enormity of this 5000-year-old monster. The entrance to the chamber is flanked by two large upright stones (known as orthostats or megaliths) topped by a granite capstone that alone weighs well over 100 tonnes.

It's unclear how the stones got here in the first place, but experts have narrowed it down to two possibilities: they were deposited here during the Ice Age, or Stone Age men ate a hell of a lot of spinach and figured out a way of carrying them to the field.

The Drive ›› It's 6km to Duckett's Grove. Continue southeast on the R726 for 700m before turning left on the L1009. The house is 5km ahead on your right (pass over the M9 en route).

④ Duckett's Grove

Until the main building burnt in 1933, the Gothic fantasy that was **Duckett's Grove** (☎085 113 6075; ☺dawn-dusk) was Carlow's most impressive building, the centrepiece of an estate that once spread across five counties.

The house, which dates from the late 17th century, was transformed into a Gothic mansion in 1830 and was used as a training camp for the IRA during the War of Independence. The ruins are still impressive, and surrounding them are the original high brick garden walls that frame two sprawling, interconnected formal gardens.

The Drive ›› Start the 18km drive by heading southeast on the R418 to Tullow before continuing south along the N81. After 7km, take a right for the Altamont estate.

⑤ Altamont Gardens

Generally considered to be the jewel in the Irish gardening crown, **Altamont Gardens** (☎059-915 9444; www.heritageireland.ie; The Pottle, Altamont; ☺9am-6.30pm Apr-Sep, to 5pm Mar & Oct, to 4.30pm Feb & Nov, to 4pm Dec & Jan) covers 16 hectares and is made up of informal and formal gardens, including a walled garden with carefully selected plantings arranged in naturalistic, idealised settings.

The estate's main avenue is lined with trees, including imported species such as red oak and swamp cypresses, and it leads down to an artificial lake.

The Drive ›› Take the N80 south for 3.5km and then the signposted left for Clonegal.

**DETOUR:
MT LEINSTER
SCENIC DRIVE**

Start: ⑦ **Borris**

The highest peak in the Blackstairs Mountains, Mt Leinster (796m) has magnificent views of counties Waterford, Carlow, Kilkenny and Wicklow from the top. From Borris, drive south along the R702 and almost immediately take the signposted left for Mt Leinster. Keep going and take the left for Bunclody at the T-junction. Continue around, keeping the mountain on your right; you'll arrive at the car park at Corribut Gap. The ground falls away steeply, offering stunning views of the Coolasnaghta valley to the north. This is also the spot favoured by those taking advantage of Ireland's best hang-gliding spot – if you fancy taking off from the mountain, contact the **Irish Hang Gliding & Paragliding Association** (www. ihpa.ie) for further information.

Cottage in Clonegal, County Carlow

TRIP HIGHLIGHT

6 Clonegal

The idyllic village of Clonegal has a tiny little centre out of a nursery rhyme, with an arched stone bridge over a river that boasts swans and water flowers.

Huntington Castle
(☎053-937 7160; www. huntingtoncastle.com; house tours & gardens adult/child €10/5, gardens only €6/2.50; ☺house tours hourly 2-5pm May-Sep, gardens 10am-5pm May-Sep) is a spooky, dusty old keep built in 1625 by the Durdin-Robertson family, who still own it and live here today. The family conduct guided tours of the property, which, they claim, is haunted by two ghosts. The gardens combine the formal with rural fantasy. There's also a B&B and tearoom here.

✕ p133

The Drive » The R724 cuts across southern County Carlow; Borris is 29km away.

TRIP HIGHLIGHT

7 Borris

Handsome Borris is a seemingly untouched Georgian village, strung

---

ARTISANAL GLASS

About 3km east of Kells, in the neighbouring county of Kilkenny, is the small village of Stonyford. The local highlight, the nationally renowned **Jerpoint Glass Studio** (www.jerpointglass.com; Glenmore, Stoneyford; ☺10am-5.30pm Mon-Sat, noon-5pm Sun Apr-Sep, 10am-5pm Mon-Sat Oct-Mar), is housed in a rural stone-walled farm building 1km south of town, where you can watch workers craft molten glass into exquisite artistic and practical items.

DETOUR:
KILGRANEY HOUSE
HERB GARDENS

Start: ⑦ Borris

Herbs as you've never seen them grow in orderly profusion in **Kilgraney House Herb Gardens** (☎059-977 5283; www.kilgraneyhouse.com; Borris Rd, Kilgraney; €5; ⊙by appointment 2-6pm Sat & Sun May-Aug), which boasts a heady cocktail of medicinal and kitchen plants and also serves as a source of food for the inn and restaurant here. The recreated medieval monastic herb garden is a favourite. It's off the R705 halfway between Borris and Bagenalstown.

out like a string bean down the side of a hill, with a dramatic mountain backdrop. That's Mt Leinster, site of an excellent scenic drive.

✕ ⊨ p133

The Drive ❯❯ It's 15km from Borris to St Mullins, mostly along the R729 with the Blackstairs Mountains to your east.

- - - - - - - - - - - - - - - - - -

⑧ St Mullins

Tranquil little St Mullins sits 6km downstream from Graiguenamanagh, which is in County Kilkenny. The village is the maternal home of Michael Flatley of Riverdance fame. Sure enough, the river snakes through here in the shadow of Brandon Hill, as does the River Barrow towpath from Borris. From the river, a trail winds uphill to the ruined hulk of an old **monastery** surrounded by the graves of 1798 rebels. A 9th-century Celtic cross, badly worn down over the centuries, still stands beside the monastery. Nearby, **St Moling's Well** is a holy well that seems to attract spare change.

✕ ⊨ p133

The Drive ❯❯ It's 27km from St Mullins to Bagenalstown via Borris. The 12km stretch of the R705 from Borris to Bagenalstown follows the scenic River Barrow Valley, one of the nicest bits of road in all of Carlow.

- - - - - - - - - - - - - - - - - -

⑨ Bagenalstown

About 12km north of Borris is Bagenalstown, which isn't quite as handsome, but is home to the **Carlow Brewing Company** (☎059-972 0509; www.carlowbrewing.com; Royal Oak Rd; tours €10.50; ⊙tours 2pm Fri), a microbrewery that offers tours of its O'Hara's-brand beers. Its award-winning Irish stout bursts with flavour and certainly holds its own against that *other* Irish stout.

The Drive ❯❯ Leighlinbridge is 4km on along the R705.

- - - - - - - - - - - - - - - - - -

⑩ Leighlinbridge

Leighlinbridge would be just another Carlow town if it weren't for the ominous ruins of the **Black Castle** on the banks of the Barrow. Dating from 1181, this was one of the first Norman castles built in Ireland and was bequeathed to John de Claville by Henry II's lieutenant, Hugh de Lacy. The present castle was built by Sir Edward Bellingham in 1547, but was demolished by Cromwell's army in 1650.

CARLOW IN BLOOM

County Carlow is renowned for its gardens, 21 of which form part of Ireland's first dedicated **garden trail** (www.carlowgardentrail.com):

Delta Sensory Gardens (p129)

Huntington Castle's Gardens (p131)

Duckett's Grove (p130)

Kilgraney House Herb Gardens (p132)

Altamont Gardens (p130)

Eating & Sleeping

Carlow Town ❶

✖ Lennons
Cafe, Bistro €€

(📞059-917 9245; www.lennons.ie; Old Dublin Rd; mains lunch €8-13.50, dinner €19-28.50; ⏰10.30am-5pm Mon-Wed, 10.30am-5pm & 5.45-9.30pm Thu-Sat, noon-4pm Sun; 📶) Carlow's best dining is amid the arty surrounds of the **Visual Centre for Contemporary Art** (📞059-917 2400; www.visualcarlow.ie; ⏰11am-5.30pm Tue-Sat, 2-5pm Sun). It's a sleek and stylish space with a patio bordering the grassy grounds of St Patrick's College. Lunch features creative sandwiches, salads and hot specials, while dinner is more refined, with a seasonal menu that showcases local artisan produce. Book a table at weekends.

🛏 Red Setter Guest House
B&B €€

(📞059-914 1848; www.redsetterbandb.ie; 14 Dublin St; s/d/tr from €50/75/105; 🅿📶) A great attention to detail, with simply furnished but comfortable rooms, and extra touches such as fresh flowers, make this humble town-centre B&B a solid choice.

Clonegal ❻

✖ Sha-Roe Bistro
Irish €€

(📞053-937 5636; www.sha-roe.ie; Main St; mains €19-26; ⏰7-8.30pm Thu-Sat, 12.30-2.30pm Sun Feb-Dec) Tucked inside an 18th-century building, award-winning chef Henry Stone's restaurant has a huge open fireplace and a pretty courtyard at the back, providing a rustic setting for contemporary cuisine based on produce from the surrounding orchards and farms. Offerings include Carlow Farmhouse cheese soufflé, wild garlic risotto, and Blessington lamb shoulder with local herbs. Book at least two weeks ahead.

Borris ❼

✖ Step House Hotel
Irish €€

(📞059-977 3209; www.stephousehotel.ie; 66 Main St; brasserie mains €11-24, restaurant mains €20-29; ⏰brasserie & restaurant noon-9pm Wed-Sat, 4-9pm Sun; 📶) The Step House Hotel's handsome 1808 Brasserie & Bar, all polished mahogany, red-leather benches and green-glass lampshades, is an elegant yet relaxed place to enjoy sophisticated pub classics such as traditional seafood chowder and a house burger with honey-cured bacon and smoked paprika aioli. Its more upmarket Cellar Restaurant serves refined dishes such as cured mackerel with cucumber chutney and black-sesame-seed wafer.

St Mullins ❽

🛏 Old Grainstore
Cottage €€

(📞051-424 440; www.oldgrainstorecottages. ie; The Quay; cottages per 3 nights/week from €300/500; 🅿📶) Martin and Emer O'Brien eschewed corporate life to convert this former grain warehouse on the River Barrow into four self-catering cottages sleeping two to five people. Stylish yet cosy interiors have book-filled shelves and wood-burning stoves (gas and electricity are charged according to meter readings). Minimum stay is three nights.

🛏 Mulvarra House
B&B €€

(📞051-424 936; www.mulvarra.com; d/tr/f from €75/95/115; 🅿📶) Most of the bedrooms in this modern, comfortable B&B on a hillside above the village have balconies with glorious views over the River Barrow, which offers lovely evening walks along its banks. You can also indulge in body treatments such as hot stone massages, and yoga, meditation and traditional arts and crafts workshops. Mostly organic breakfasts use produce grown on-site.

Kilkenny's Treasures

Its namesake city is its marvellous centrepiece, but County Kilkenny, with its rolling hills dotted with relics of Irish history, will have you running out of adjectives for 'green'.

11

TRIP HIGHLIGHTS

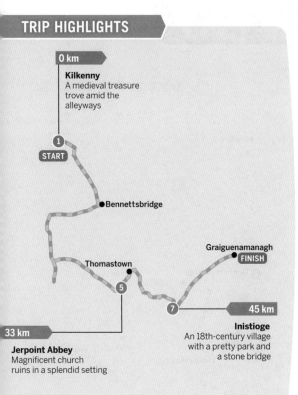

0 km

Kilkenny
A medieval treasure trove amid the alleyways

1
START

●Bennettsbridge

Graiguenamanagh
FINISH

Thomastown

5

7

45 km

Inistioge
An 18th-century village with a pretty park and a stone bridge

33 km

Jerpoint Abbey
Magnificent church ruins in a splendid setting

3 DAYS
54KM / 34 MILES

GREAT FOR...

BEST TIME TO GO
Spring and autumn are ideal: the weather's good but there are fewer visitors.

 ESSENTIAL PHOTO

Kells Priory at dusk.

✓ **BEST FOR CRAFTS**

The exquisitely made artisanal crafts at the Nicholas Mosse Irish Country Shop.

11 Kilkenny's Treasures

The enduring gift of the Normans, Kilkenny mesmerises visitors with its medieval alleys and castle, ruined abbeys and outstanding nightlife. Beyond the city limits, tiny roads navigate the beautiful valleys past the mementos of 800 years of Irish history, picture-postcard villages and a dynamic contemporary craft industry whose reputation is admired countrywide.

TRIP HIGHLIGHT

❶ Kilkenny

Kilkenny (Cill Chainnigh; p166) is the Ireland of many visitors' imaginations. Its majestic riverside castle, tangle of 17th-century passageways, rows of colourful, old-fashioned shopfronts and centuries-old pubs with traditional live music all have a timeless appeal, as does its splendid medieval cathedral.

Kilkenny's architectural charm owes a huge debt to the Middle Ages,

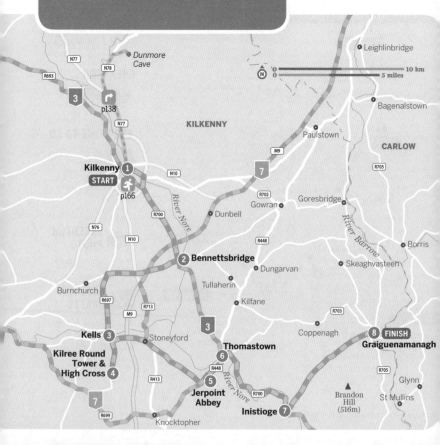

when the city was a seat of political power. It's also sometimes called the 'marble city' because of the local black limestone, used on floors and in decorative trim all over town.

You can cover pretty much everything on foot in half a day but sampling its many delights will take much longer.

✗ 📖 p73, p141

The Drive » Drive southeast with the castle and the Nore on your immediate left along the Bennettsbridge Rd, which becomes the R700. It's only a short 8km drive to Bennettsbridge.

---

② Bennettsbridge

Bennettsbridge is an arts-and-crafts treasure chest, although these treasures are scattered throughout the town,

LINK YOUR TRIP

7 **Ancient Ireland**
From Kilree or Jerpoint Abbey you can connect to this trip that visits some of ancient Ireland's most important sites.

3 **Tip to Toe**
Kilkenny is one of the main stops on the classic Tip to Toe trip, which explores Ireland from north to south.

rather than within a concentrated area.

In the big mill by the river west of town, the **Nicholas Mosse Irish Country Shop** (📞056-772 7505; www.nicholasmosse. com; Annamult Rd; ⊙10am-6pm Mon-Sat, 1.30-5pm Sun) specialises in handmade spongeware – ceramics decorated with sponged patterns – which is exported worldwide to retail outlets such as Tiffany's. Short audiovisual displays explain the manufacturing process. The cafe here is renowned for its scones, and is the best choice locally for lunch.

Established in 1999, the workshop **Moth to a Flame** (📞056-772 7826; www.mothtoaflame.ie; Kilkenny Rd; ⊙9am-6pm Mon-Sat) creates beautifully coloured and textured candles of all sizes, from bedside-table to church-altar scale.

The Drive » The 12km drive to Kells takes you across the flat, luscious green plain of central Kilkenny. Follow the Annamult Rd, cross over the N10, then turn left on the R697.

---

③ Kells

Kells (not to be confused with Kells in County Meath) is a mere hamlet with a fine stone bridge on a tributary of the Nore. However, in **Kells Priory**, the village has one of Ireland's most impressive and romantic monastic sites. This is the best sort of ruin,

where visitors can amble about whenever they like, with no tour guides, tours, set hours or fees. At dusk on a vaguely sunny day, the old priory is simply beautiful. Most days you stand a chance of exploring the site alone (apart from bleating and pooping sheep).

The ruins are 500m east of Kells on the Stonyford road.

The Drive » Kilree is only 2.5km south of Kells along a small country road.

---

④ Kilree Round Tower & High Cross

Standing in an overgrown graveyard is a 29m-high round tower that has lost its cap. It was built sometime between the 8th and 11th centuries, and served as a bell tower, although it was also a handy place of refuge for locals looking to escape the unwelcome attention of invaders.

Next to it, standing more than 2m tall, is a simple early high cross that was long believed to be the grave of a 9th-century Irish high king, Niall Caille, who drowned in the nearby river in 847 while attempting the rescue of a servant or soldier, even though experts now reckon the cross is older than that. Still, Niall's resting place lies beyond the church grounds because he wasn't a Christian.

TEEING OFF IN THOMASTOWN

Just 6km from Thomastown heading southwest, high-flyers can tee off at the Jack Nicklaus–blessed golf course **Mount Juliet** (☎056-777 3071; www. mountjuliet.ie; Mount Juliet Estate, Jerpoint; green fees €55-100). Set over 600 wooded hectares, the estate also has its own equestrian centre, a gym and spa, two restaurants, wine masterclasses, and posh rooms catering to every whim, right down to the pillow menu (accommodation from €120).

The Drive ›› The 11km drive will have you doubling back towards Kells, but then taking a right on the Stonyford road, past Kells Priory. You'll pass Mt Juliet on your left. Turn left on the R448, and Jerpoint Abbey is a further 700m on your right.

- - - - - - - - - - - - - - - - - -

TRIP HIGHLIGHT

⑤ Jerpoint Abbey

Ireland has an abundance of church ruins, but few are quite as magnificent as those of Jerpoint Abbey (p108), a fine exemplar of Cistercian power and church-building. The abbey was first established in the 12th century, with the tower and cloister added sometime in the late 14th or early 15th century. The excellent 45-minute tours happen throughout the day. Set yourself apart in the remains of the cloisters and see if you can hear the faint echo of a chant.

According to local legend, St Nicholas (or Santa Claus) is buried near the abbey. While retreating in the Crusades, the knights of Jerpoint removed his body from Myra in modern-day Turkey and reburied him in the **Church of St Nicholas** to the west of the abbey. The grave is marked by a broken slab decorated with a carving of a monk.

The Drive ›› Thomastown is only a quick 2.5km northeast of Jerpoint on the R448.

- - - - - - - - - - - - - - - - - -

⑥ Thomastown

Named after Welsh mercenary Thomas de Cantwell, Thomastown has some fragments of a medieval wall and the partly ruined 13th-century **Church of St Mary**. Down by the bridge, **Mullin's Castle** is the sole survivor of the 14 castles once here.

Like the rest of Kilkenny, the area has a vibrant craft scene. Look out for **Clay Creations** (☎087 257 0735; www.bridlyonsceramics. com; Low St; ☺10am-5.30pm Wed, Thu & Sat, 10am-1pm & 3.30-5.30pm Fri, by appointment Tue), displaying the quixotic ceramics and sculptures of local artist Brid Lyons.

✕ p141

DETOUR: DUNMORE CAVE

Start: ① **Kilkenny**

Just 6km north of Kilkenny on the Castlecomer road (N78) are the striking calcite formations of **Dunmore Cave** (☎056-776 7726; www.heritageireland.ie; Ballyfoyle; adult/child €5/3; ☺9.30am-6pm Jun-Aug, to 5pm Mar-May, Sep & Oct, to 5pm Wed-Sun Nov-Feb). In 928 marauding Vikings killed 1000 people at two ring forts near here. When survivors hid in the caverns, the Vikings tried to smoke them out by lighting fires at the entrance. It's thought that they then dragged off the men as slaves and left the women and children to suffocate. Excavations in 1973 uncovered the skeletons of at least 44 people, mostly women and children. They also found coins dating from the 10th century.

Admission to the cave is via a compulsory but highly worthwhile guided tour. Although well lit and spacious, the cave is damp and cold; bring warm clothes.

Jerpoint Abbey, County Kilkenny

TOWN OF BOOKS

Graiguenamanagh's narrow streets spill over with booksellers, authors and bibliophiles during the three-day **Town of Books Festival** (www.graiguenam anaghtownofbooks.com; ☺late Aug). There are a couple of good used and antiquarian bookshops open year-round as well.

The Drive >> The 8.5km drive south to Inistioge along the R700 is a splendidly scenic one through the valley of the River Nore; keep an eye out for the views of the ruined 13th-century Grennan Castle on your right as you go.

- - - - - - - - - - - - - - - -

TRIP HIGHLIGHT

⑦ Inistioge

The little village of Inistioge (*in*-ish-teeg) is a picture. Its 18th-century, 10-arch **stone bridge** spans the River Nore and vintage shops face its tranquil square.

About 500m south of the village is the heavily forested **Woodstock Gardens** (☎056-779 4373; www. woodstock.ie; €4; ☺9am-7pm Apr-Sep, 10am-4pm Oct-Mar), a beauty of a park with expansive 19th-century gardens, picnic areas and

trails. The panorama of the valley and village below is spectacular. Coming from town, follow the signs for Woodstock Estate and enter the large gates (despite appearances, it's a public road), then continue along the road for about 1.5km until you reach the car park (parking costs €4 in coins).

🛏 p141

The Drive >> It's 11km from Inistioge to Graiguenamanagh on the Graigue road, aka the L4209, so narrow that you'll wonder if there's room for oncoming traffic (there is).

- - - - - - - - - - - - - - - -

⑧ Graiguenamanagh

Graiguenamanagh (greg-*na*-muh-na; known locally simply as Graigue) is the kind of place where

you could easily find yourself staying longer than planned. Spanning the Barrow, an ancient six-arch stone bridge is illuminated at night and connects the village with the smaller township of Tinnahinch on the County Carlow side of the river (look for the darker stones on the Carlow side – a legacy from being blown up during the 1798 rebellion).

The big attraction in town is the Cistercian **Duiske Abbey** (☎059-972 4238; Main St; ☺9am-6pm May-Sep, to 5pm Oct-Apr), once Ireland's largest and still very much a working parish church (thanks to 800 years of changes and additions). To the right of the entrance look for the **Knight of Duiske**, a 14th-century, high-relief carving of a knight in chain mail who's reaching for his sword. On the floor nearby, a glass panel reveals some of the original 13th-century floor tiles, now 2m below the present floor level.

🛏 p141

Eating & Sleeping

Kilkenny ❶

✕ Campagne — Gastronomy €€€

(☎056-777 2858; www.campagne.ie; 5 Gashouse Lane; 3-course lunch & early bird menu €38, 3-course dinner menu €60; ⏰6-10pm Wed & Thu, 12.30-2.30pm & 6-10pm Fri & Sat, 12.30-2.30pm Sun, closed late Jun-early Jul & mid-Jan–early Feb) Chef Garrett Byrne was awarded a Michelin star for this bold, stylish restaurant in his native Kilkenny. He's passionate about supporting local and artisan producers, and adds a French accent to memorable culinary creations such as black-pudding-stuffed pigs trotters or rhubarb-crumble soufflé. The early bird menu (to 9pm Wednesday to Friday, to 6pm Saturday) is a serious bargain.

✕ Zuni — Irish €€

(☎056-772 3999; www.zuni.ie; 26 Patrick St; mains breakfast & lunch €8-15, dinner €19.50-28.50; ⏰8am-11.15am, 12.30-2.30pm & 6-9.30pm; 📶) Among Kilkenny's most stylish and busiest restaurants, Zuni is sophisticated yet informal, with a kitchen that elevates humble comfort food such as black pudding scotch eggs, confit duck terrine, spinach-wrapped cod and parsnip parcels and savoury beetroot cheesecake.

🛏 Butler House — Hotel €€€

(☎056-772 2828; www.butler.ie; 16 Patrick St; d/ste from €200/275; 🅿📶) You can't stay in Kilkenny Castle, but this 1786-built mansion is the next best thing. Once the home of the earls of Ormonde, the hotel today combines modern design with aristocratic trappings including sweeping staircases, marble fireplaces, an art collection and magnificent gardens. The generous rooms are individually decorated, and, to remind you that you're staying amid history, the floors creak.

Thomastown ❻

✕ Blackberry Cafe — Cafe €

(www.theblackberrycafe.ie; Market St; dishes €5.50-9; ⏰9.30am-5.30pm Mon-Sat year-round, plus 10am-5pm Sun Jun-Aug; 👶) Warming soups come with pumpkin-seed-speckled soda bread at this bright cafe, whose menu highlights also include breakfast baps with dry-cured bacon and sausage, superb thick-cut sandwiches, gourmet sausage rolls and quiches (with goat's cheese and pine nuts or sundried tomato and ham). Much is organic; tarts and cakes are baked daily. For €4.75, kids can get a half sandwich, a chocolate florentine and locally made apple juice. Between noon and 2pm, it gets packed to bursting.

Inistioge ❼

🛏 Woodstock Arms — Pub €€

(☎056-775 8440; www.woodstockarms.ie; The Square; s/d/tr from €50/85/100; 📶) This picturesque pub has tables on the square and seven basic bedrooms that are squeaky clean; the triples are particularly spacious. Breakfast is served in a pretty little room out the back with wooden tables and traditional local china.

Graiguenamanagh ❽

🛏 Waterside — Guesthouse €€

(☎059-972 4246; www.watersideguesthouse.com; The Quay; s/d from €65/98; 📶) Overlooking the boats tied up along the River Barrow, this inviting guesthouse occupies a converted 19th-century grain store. Its 10 renovated bedrooms have exposed timber beams, and the cafe/restaurant (mains €17 to €24.50; open March to October only) is well regarded for its interesting modern Irish menu and its regular 'After Dinner Live' music acts featuring anything from jazz to bluegrass.

Wexford & Waterford

Ireland's favourite beach destinations are dotted along the coastlines of Counties Wexford and Waterford, but there's far more to the region than just buckets and spades.

12

TRIP HIGHLIGHTS

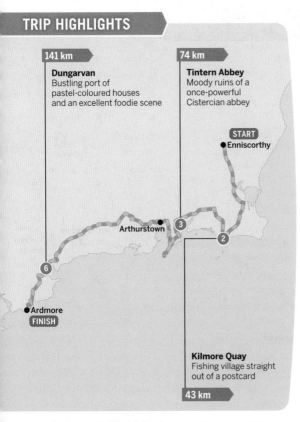

141 km

Dungarvan
Bustling port of pastel-coloured houses and an excellent foodie scene

74 km

Tintern Abbey
Moody ruins of a once-powerful Cistercian abbey

START
● Enniscorthy

Arthurstown ● ③

②

⑥

● Ardmore
FINISH

Kilmore Quay
Fishing village straight out of a postcard

43 km

---

5 DAYS
164KM / 102 MILES

GREAT FOR...

BEST TIME TO GO
April to September for the long days and best weather.

 ESSENTIAL PHOTO

Look down on Ardmore's bay from St Declan's Church.

 BEST FOR CULTURE

Learn about bloody Irish history at the National 1798 Rebellion Centre.

---

rdmore View of Ardmore Bay from St Declan's Church

12 Wexford & Waterford

Collectively labelled the 'sunny southeast', Wexford and Waterford get less rainfall and more sunshine than anywhere else in Ireland, but the southeastern counties are about more than resort towns and pretty beaches. There's history aplenty round here, some stunning inland scenery and a vibrant foodie scene that mightn't be as well known as that in neighbouring Cork but is just as good.

❶ Enniscorthy

Busy Enniscorthy (Inis Coirthaidh) is an attractive hilly town on the banks of the Slaney in the heart of County Wexford, 20km north of Wexford town. For the Irish, its name is forever linked to some of the fiercest fighting of the 1798 Rising, when rebels captured the town and castle and set up camp nearby at **Vinegar Hill** (www.vinegarhill.ie; ☉ dawn-dusk).

Before climbing the hill (a 2km drive east of

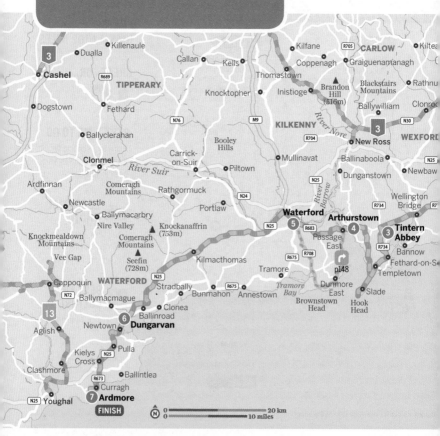

town), acquaint yourself with the story of the rebellion with a visit to the **National 1798 Rebellion Centre** (☎053-923 7596; www.1798centre.ie; Parnell Rd; adult/child €7/3; ⏰9am-5pm daily Jun-Sep, closed Sat & Sun Oct-May), which tells the tale of Wexford's abortive uprising against British rule in all its gory, fascinating detail. The rebels were inspired by the French and American revolutions, but were beaten back by English troops, who then massacred hundreds of women and children as reprisal for the uprising.

If you want to walk up Vinegar Hill, from Abbey Sq head out of town along Mill Park Rd or south along the river.

🛏 p149

The Drive » It's 43km to Kilmore Quay. You'll skirt around Wexford town on your way south along the N11; beyond the town, follow the directions for Rosslare and take the N25. Turn right onto the R739 to Kilmore Quay. The last stretch of road is the most scenic, as the countryside opens up in front of you.

TRIP HIGHLIGHT

❷ Kilmore Quay

Straight out of a postcard, peaceful Kilmore Quay is a small village on the eastern side of Ballyteige Bay, noted for its lobsters and deep-sea fishing. Lining the attractive main street up from the harbour are a series of pretty whitewashed thatched cottages. The harbour is the jumping-off point for the Saltee Islands, home to Ireland's largest bird sanctuary, clearly visible out to sea.

The four-day **Seafood Festival** (www.kilmorequayseafoodfestival.com) in the second week of July involves all types of seafood tastings, music and dancing.

🍴 🛏 p73, p149

The Drive » It's 31km from Kilmore Quay to the ruins of Tintern Abbey along the narrow R733. The promontory east of the Hook Peninsula, signposted as the Bannow Drive, is littered with Norman ruins, while Bannow Bay is a wildfowl sanctuary. As you cross Wellington Bridge onto the Hook Peninsula, keep an eye out for the remains of medieval Clonmines to the southwest.

TRIP HIGHLIGHT

❸ Tintern Abbey

In better structural condition than its Welsh counterpart, from where its first monks hailed, Ireland's moody **Tintern Abbey** (☎051-562 650; www.heritageireland.ie; Saltmills; adult/child €5/3, with Colclough Walled Garden €9/5; ⏰10am-5.30pm Jun-Aug, 9.30am-5pm Apr, May, Sep & Oct) is secluded amid 40 hectares of woodland. William Marshal, Earl of

LINK YOUR TRIP

13 Blackwater Valley Drive

It's only 5km from Ardmore to Youghal and the start of the Blackwater Valley Drive.

3 Tip to Toe

You can hook up to this long country-length trip in Kilmore Quay.

Pembroke, founded the Cistercian abbey in the early 13th century after he nearly perished at sea and swore to establish a church if he made it ashore.

The abbey is 1.5km from the town of Saltmills, among wooded trails, lakes and idyllic streams. The grounds are always open, and a walk here is worth the trip at any time.

The Drive » The 10km route across the Hook Peninsula along the R733 is the quickest way to Arthurstown, but the most scenic route is the 35km circumference of the peninsula, passing villages like Slade, where the most activity is in the swirl of seagulls above

the ruined castle and harbour. Beaches include the wonderfully secluded Dollar Bay and Booley Bay, just beyond Templetown. Don't forget to spot the world's oldest working lighthouse, right at Hook Head.

----

4 Arthurstown

Chef Kevin Dundon is a familiar face on Irish TV, and the author of cookbooks *Full On Irish* and *Great Family Food*. His **Dunbrody Country House Hotel** (📞051-389 600; www.dunbrodyhouse. com; Arthurstown; d/ste from €250/420; **P** 🛜), in a period-decorated 1830s Georgian manor on 120-hectare grounds, is the stuff of foodies'

fantasies, with a gourmet restaurant and cookery school (one-day courses from €175).

Beside the R733, some 6km north of Dundon's pile, the ruined **Dunbrody Abbey** (📞086 275 9149; www.dunbrodyabbey. com; Campile; abbey ruin adult/child €4/1, maze & museum €7/4; ⊙11am-6pm Jul & Aug, to 5.30pm May, Jun & Sep) is a remarkably intact Cistercian abbey founded by Strongbow in 1170 and completed in 1220. A combined ticket includes a **museum** with a huge doll's house, minigolf, and a very fun yew-hedge

DETOUR: SALTEE ISLANDS

Start: 2 Kilmore Quay

Just 4km offshore and accessible from Kilmore Quay via local boat (depending on the weather), the **Saltee Islands** (www.salteeislands.info) constitute one of Europe's most important bird sanctuaries, home to over 220 recorded species, principally the gannet, guillemot, cormorant, kittiwake, puffin and the Manx shearwater. It's a noisier but more peaceful existence than its past as the favoured haunt of privateers and smugglers. The islands are also where you'll find some of the oldest rocks in Europe, dating back 2000 million years or more; findings also suggest that the islands were inhabited by the pre-Celts as long ago as 3500 to 2000 BC.

The best time to visit is the spring and early-summer nesting season. The birds leave once the chicks can fly; by early August it's eerily quiet. To get here, try **Declan Bates** (📞087 252 9736, 053-912 9684; Kilmore Quay Harbour; day trips €30), but be sure to book in advance. You can park your car in town.

Kilmore Quay harbour, County Wexford

maze made up of over 1500 trees.

The Drive » Instead of going the long way around, cut out a lengthy detour around Waterford Harbour and the River Barrow by taking the five-minute car ferry between Ballyhack in County Wexford and Passage East in County Waterford. Then follow the R683 to Waterford city. This way is only 12km long.

- - - - - - - - - - - - - - - - - -

❺ Waterford City

Inhabited since AD 914, Waterford (Port Láirge) is Ireland's oldest city, and much of the centre's street plan has retained its medieval feel.

Waterford's 1000-year history is told in wonderful fashion in a trio of museums collectively known as the **Waterford Museum of Treasures** (www.waterfordtreasures.com) and include **Reginald's Tower** (☎0761 102 501; The Quay; adult/child €5/3; ☺9.30am-5.30pm late Mar-late Dec, to 5pm early Jan-late Mar), the oldest complete building in Ireland; the **Bishop's Palace** (☎0761 102 501; The Mall; adult/child €7/free, with Medieval Museum €10/free; ☺9.15am-6pm Mon-Fri, 9.30am-6pm Sat, 11am-5pm Sun Jun-Aug, 9.15am-5pm Mon-Fri, 10am-5pm Sat, 11am-

5pm Sun Sep-May), home to a superb interactive museum; and the superb **Medieval Museum** (Cathedral Sq; adult/child €7/free, with Bishop's Palace €10/free; ☺9.15am-6pm Mon-Fri, 9.30am-6pm Sat, 11am-5pm Sun Jun-Aug, 9.15am-5pm Mon-Fri, 10am-5pm Sat, 11am-5pm Sun Sep-May), which tells the story of Waterford life before 1700.

Since 1783 the city has been famous for its production of high-quality crystal. However, the factory closed in 2009 and all that's left is the **House of Waterford Crystal** (☎051-317 000; www.waterfordvisitorcentre.com;

DETOUR:
PASSAGE COAST ROAD

Start: ④ Arthurstown

A little-travelled 11km-long coast road wiggles south between Passage East and Dunmore East to the south. At times single-vehicle-width and steep, it offers mesmerising views of the ocean and undulating fields that you won't see from the main thoroughfares. Follow the R708 north to Waterford city.

The Drive » It's an easy 23km drive along the N25 to the turn-off for Ardmore, which then becomes the very rural R673 as you move south to the coast. This is rural Ireland at its most pristine, with farmhouses the only interruption to a stretch of undulating fields and stone walls.

The Mall; adult/child €13/6.50; ☺9am-4.15pm Mon-Sat, 9.30am-4.15pm Sun Apr-Oct, shorter hrs Nov-Mar), a flashy showroom where you can see some pieces of crystal being blown, but most of the stuff you buy in the shop is made in Eastern Europe.

✗ ⊨ p149

The Drive » Follow the southern bank of the River Suir and take the N25 to get to Dungarvan, 45km away. Or travel south and take the R675 coastal route along the stunning Copper Coast, where you'll meet cerulean skies, azure waters, impossibly green hills and ebony cliff faces along the way.

---

⑥ Dungarvan

It isn't enough that Dungarvan has the looks: pastel-coloured houses huddled around a boat-filled port at the mouth of the River Colligan make it one of the south-

east's prettiest towns. It now has the charm, in the form of a foodie reputation that makes it a must-stop destination for anyone looking to get the best of Irish cuisine.

At the heart of the town is the Norman **castle** (☎058-48144; www.heritageireland.ie; Castle St; ☺10am-6pm late May-late Sep), which is slowly being restored to its once impregnable glory. But the real draws are culinary: Paul Flynn's **Tannery Cookery School** (☎058-45420; www.tannery.ie; 6 Church St; courses from €75), adjoining a fruit, veg and herb garden, is one of Ireland's best. The annual **West Waterford Festival of Food** (www.westwaterfordfestivaloffood.com; ☺late Apr) celebrates the area's abundant fresh produce.

✗ ⊨ p149

⑦ Ardmore

The enticing seaside village of Ardmore may look quiet these days, but it's claimed that St Declan set up shop here between 350 and 420. This brought Christianity to southeast Ireland long before St Patrick arrived from Britain.

In a striking position on a hill above town, the ruins of **St Declan's Church** stand on the site of St Declan's original monastery alongside an impressive cone-roofed, 29m-high, 12th-century **round tower**, one of the best examples of these structures in Ireland.

If you're looking for a bit of beautiful seclusion, you'll find it on **Ballyquin beach**, home to tide pools, fascinating rocks and sheltered sand. It's 1km off the R673, 4km northeast of Ardmore. Look for the small sign.

⊨ p149

Eating & Sleeping

Enniscorthy ❶

🛏 Woodbrook House   Guesthouse €€

(📞053-925 5114; www.woodbrookhouse.ie; Killann; s/d from €105/170; ⊗Easter-Jun & Aug-Sep; P🛜) Rebuilt after sustaining damage in the 1798 Rising, this glorious Georgian country house has a superb setting beneath the Blackstairs Mountains. The lobby features a gravity-defying spiral staircase that still amazes, just as it did over 200 years ago.

Kilmore Quay ❷

✕ Silver Fox Seafood Restaurant   Seafood €€€

(📞053-912 9888; www.thesilverfox.ie; The Quay; mains €16-35; ⊗noon-9pm Easter-Oct, 5-8pm Fri, noon-8pm Sat & Sun Nov-Mar) The Silver Fox's fresh-from-the-ocean offerings include locally landed plaice, langoustines, crab and mussels, plus daily specials depending on what arrives at the quay.

✕ Mary Barry's   Seafood €€

(📞053-913 5982; www.marybarrys.ie; R739; mains €15-25; ⊗kitchen noon-8.30pm Mon-Thu, to 9.30pm Fri & Sat, to 9pm Sun, bar to 11pm Mon-Thu, to midnight Fri-Sun; 🛜) Cosy pub Mary Barry's, with low ceilings, timber panelling, burgundy paintwork, ships wheels and crackling fireplaces, is 4.5km northeast of Kilmore Quay. Dishes incorporate locally caught seafood (scallops with black pudding crumb; tiger prawn and smoked haddock gratin), with a live tank of lobsters and oysters in season.

Waterford City ❺

✕ La Bohème   French €€€

(📞051-875 645; www.labohemerestaurant.ie; 2 George's St; mains €22-32.50; ⊗5.30-11pm Tue-Thu & Sat, noon-3pm & 5.30-11pm Fri) In the kitchen basement of a Georgian townhouse, La Bohème's intimate dining rooms have barrel-vault roofs and arches. The kitchen combines French flair with fresh Irish produce, resulting in dishes like Waterford crab brûlée, Cappoquin guinea fowl with artichoke and tarragon

mousseline, and Irish Breakfast tea–poached pears with Wexford strawberry sorbet.

🛏 Waterford Castle   Castle €€€

(📞051-878 203; www.waterfordcastleresort. com; The Island, Ballinakill; d/lodge from €278/300; P🛜) Getting away from it all is an understatement at this turreted mid-19th-century castle set on its own private island (a free car ferry at Ballinakill on the eastern edge of town provides round-the-clock access). All 19 castle rooms have hand-painted tiles and claw-foot baths, and some have four-poster beds.

Dungarvan ❻

🛏 Tannery Townhouse   Guesthouse €€

(📞058-45420; www.tannery.ie; 2 Church St; d from €120; P🛜) Under the same management as the Tannery restaurant (p149), this boutique guesthouse spans two buildings just across the street. Its 14 rooms are modern and stylish, and have fridges stacked with juices, fruit and muffins so you can enjoy a continental breakfast in your own time.

✕ Tannery   Modern Irish €€€

(📞058-45420; www.tannery.ie; 10 Quay St; 2-/3-course menu lunch €26/33, dinner €45.50/58.50; ⊗5.30-9.30pm Tue-Thu, 12.30-2.30pm & 5.30-9.30pm Fri & Sat, 12.30-3pm Sun, plus 5.30-9.30pm Sun Jul & Aug) At this old tannery building, lauded chef Paul Flynn creates seasonally changing dishes that focus on just a few flavours, such as charred trout with lemon-and-fennel arancini or crab crème brûlée.

Ardmore ❼

🛏 Cliff House Hotel   Luxury Hotel €€€

(📞024-87800; www.cliffhousehotel.ie; Cliff Rd; d/ste from €350/490; P🛜⊛) All the bedrooms at this cutting-edge hotel, built into the hillside, overlook Ardmore Bay. Some suites even have two-person floor-to-ceiling glass showers so you don't miss a second of those sea views. More sea views extend from the indoor swimming pool, the outdoor Jacuzzi and spa, the bar and summer terrace serving lunch, dinner and snacks, and Michelin-starred The House Restaurant .

Blackwater Valley Drive

13

Great things come in short drives: the Blackwater Valley trip is only 65km long, but packed with history, culture, stunning views and great places to stay – all off the beaten track.

TRIP HIGHLIGHTS

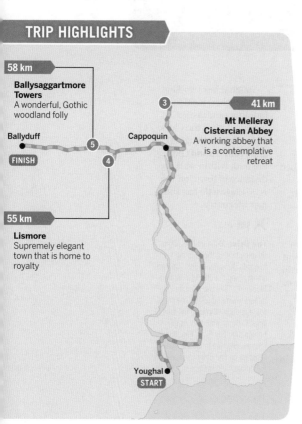

58 km

Ballysaggartmore Towers
A wonderful, Gothic woodland folly

Ballyduff

FINISH

Cappoquin

41 km

Mt Melleray Cistercian Abbey
A working abbey that is a contemplative retreat

55 km

Lismore
Supremely elegant town that is home to royalty

Youghal
START

2 DAYS
65KM / 40 MILES

GREAT FOR...

BEST TIME TO GO

July and August for traditional music.

ESSENTIAL PHOTO

The architectural folly at Ballysaggartmore Towers.

BEST FOR FOODIES

Aherne's Seafood Bar & Restaurant in Youghal.

13 Blackwater Valley Drive

This short drive takes you through one of the most scenic and historic stretches of southern Ireland. From the mouth of the River Blackwater in Youghal (where you can take to the river by boat), explore the river valley northwards as far as historic Lismore before turning west with the river to find traditional villages, beautiful mountain passes and one of the country's best centres for traditional music and dancing.

❶ Youghal

The ancient seaport of Youghal (Eochaill; pronounced yawl), at the mouth of the River Blackwater, was a hotbed of rebellion against the English in the 16th century. Youghal was granted to Sir Walter Raleigh during the Elizabethan Plantation of Munster, and he spent brief spells living here in his house, Myrtle Grove. Oliver Cromwell spent the winter here in 1649.

Award-winning Aherne's Seafood Bar & Restaurant (p157) is a great choice for a meal in town, where seafood is the star.

Youghal has two Blue Flag beaches, ideal for building sandcastles modelled after the Clock Gate. **Claycastle** (2km) and **Front Strand** (1km) are both within walking distance of town, off the N25. Claycastle has summer lifeguards.

🗙 🛏 p157

The Drive » Start the 33km drive by taking the N25 east towards Dungarvan and then go north along the R671 (direction Clonmel). Take the turn for Villierstown and follow the route to Cappoquin through the tree-lined Dromana Woods. At the bridge over the River Finisk is a remarkable Hindu-Gothic gate, inspired by the Brighton Pavilion in England and unique to Ireland.

----

❷ Cappoquin

With the picturesque Blackwater Valley to the west, the small market town of Cappoquin sits neatly on a steep hillside at the foot of the rounded, heathery Knockmealdown Mountains.

Cappoquin House & Gardens (www.cappoquin-houseandgardens.com; garden €5; ⊙ garden 10am-4pm Mon-Sat) is a magnificent 1779-built Georgian mansion and 2 hectares of formal gardens overlooking the River Blackwater. The entrance to the house is just north of the centre of Cappoquin; look for a set of huge black iron gates.

Cappoquin is also a good spot for anglers, as the town is right at the head of the Blackwater estuary, where there's some of the best game and coarse fishing in

LINK YOUR TRIP

12 **Wexford & Waterford**

From Youghal its only 5km to Ardmore, from which you can explore the sunny southeast.

21 **The Holy Glen**

Head 42km north from Lismore to Clonmel and explore some of Ireland's most important monastic sites.

the country. The fishing season runs from the beginning of February to the end of September; in order to fish for salmon you'll have to purchase a state licence (one day/21 days €20/40) and a day permit (€20 to €50); you can buy both at the **Titelines Tackle & Gift Shop** (058-54152; 19 Main St; 9am-1pm & 2-5.30pm Mon-Fri, 9am-1pm Sat).

 p157

The Drive » It's only 8km to Mt Melleray. Just right off the R669 to Mt Melleray is a signpost for Glenshelane Park, which has lovely forest walks and picnic spots that are popular with locals.

TRIP HIGHLIGHT

③ Mt Melleray Cistercian Abbey

A fully functioning monastery that is home to two dozen Trappist monks, the beautiful 19th-century **Mt Melleray Cistercian Abbey** (www. mountmellerayabbey.org; 7am-7pm) in the Knockmealdown foothills welcomes visitors looking for quiet contemplation. There are tearooms (closed Monday) and a heritage centre. In 1954 six of the monks departed for New Zealand, where they founded the Abbey of Our Lady of the Southern Star in a remote location near Takapau, on the North Island.

DETOUR: ARDMORE

Start: ① Youghal

Just 5km east of Youghal and south off the N25 is the beautifully isolated seaside village of Ardmore, whose setting and heritage are unmatched – St Declan brought Christianity here a good century before St Patrick showed up. The ruins of St Declan's Church stand on the site of the original **St Declan's Monastery** (Tower Hill; 24hr), next to one of Ireland's best examples of a 12th-century round tower. Ardmore is also home to one of the country's best hotels, the **Cliff House Hotel** (p149), which has a Michelin-starred restaurant (menus from €65). From the hotel, there's a lovely, 5km-circular **walk** that takes you past St Declan's Well, Ireland's oldest Christian ruin; the wreck of a crane ship that blew ashore in 1987; and a WWII lookout post.

The Drive » You'll have to double-back to Cappoquin (8km) and then take the N72 west for 6km to Lismore. The Blackwater River will be on your left as you go.

TRIP HIGHLIGHT

④ Lismore

Over the centuries, statesmen and luminaries have streamed through quiet, elegant Lismore, the location of a great monastic university founded by St Carthage in the 7th century. King Alfred of Wessex attended the university, Henry II visited the papal legate Bishop

St Carthage's Cathedral, Lismore

Christian O'Conarchy here in 1171, and even Fred Astaire dropped by when his sister Adele married into the Cavendish family, who own the huge, 19th-century **castle** (☎058-54061; www.lismorecastlegardens.com; Castle St; adult/child €8/6.50; ☻10.30am-5.30pm mid-Mar–mid-Oct, last entry 4.30pm). You can't visit inside (unless you rent it for an event) but you can access the 3 hectares of ornate and manicured **gardens**, thought to be the oldest in Ireland. There's a splendid yew walk where Edmund Spenser is said

to have written *The Faerie Queen*.

Otherwise, pop into **St Carthage's Cathedral** (1679), deemed by William Thackeray to be one of the prettiest edifices he'd ever seen,

and that was *before* the addition of the gorgeous Pre-Raphaelite Edward Burne-Jones stained-glass window.

✕ ⍩ p157

BLACKWATER CRUISE

If you want to explore the Blackwater River from the water, the jetty in Youghal is where you'll find the *Maeve*, which does 90-minute **tours** (☎087 988 9076; www.blackwatercruises.com; The Quays; adult/child €20/10; ☻Apr-Nov) of the river north to the remains of Templemichael Castle, about 8km north of Youghal. Captain Tony Gallagher is one of Youghal's best-known characters, as is his first mate, a dog called Pharaoh.

DETOUR: THE VEE GAP

Start: ❹ Lismore

The R668 north of Lismore cuts through the Knockmealdown Mountains and crosses the border into southern Tipperary. The road rises sharply through lush wooded countryside for 8km before emerging onto a beautiful upland plateau. A further 6km on, to your left, is Bay Lough, which makes for a nice amble. Beyond it is the Vee Gap, which cuts through the highest point of the mountains and offers superb views over three counties: Tipperary, Waterford and Limerick. Beyond the gap is the village of Clogheen, from where you can keep going to Clonmel.

The Drive ❯❯ Take the R666 Lismore–Fermoy road, signposted left over the bridge past Lismore Castle. The scenic drive overlooks the Blackwater; the 'towers' are signposted 3.5km out of Lismore on your right.

`TRIP HIGHLIGHT`

❺ Ballysaggartmore Towers

One of the more breathtaking bits of architectural folly in southern Ireland, the Ballysaggartmore Towers are just off the R666 road to Fermoy, in the heart of a woodland that was once the demesne of Arthur Kiely-Ussher, an Anglo-Irish landlord with a reputation for harshness, ordering evictions of famine-stricken tenants for nonpayment of rent.

But he had a soft spot for his wife, who in 1834 demanded that he build her an estate to match that of her sister-in-law's, so he ordered the construction of two Gothic-style gate **lodges** (one of which serves as a bridge) as a prelude to a huge mansion. But Kiely-Ussher ran out of money and the house was never built, a bit of hubris that, given his treatment of his tenants, left locals to delight in his misfortune. The lodges are free to visit at any time.

The Drive ❯❯ Continue west on the R666 to Ballyduff, with the River Blackwater on your left, a total distance of just 6km.

❻ Ballyduff

This rural village (not to be confused with another Ballyduff in County Waterford) is a slice of traditional heaven: beautifully positioned on the Blackwater (the views are stunning), it goes about its business largely unperturbed by the demands of modern tourism.

During the summer, the big draw is the **Booley House** (☎058-60456; www.thebooleyhouse.com; St Michael's Hall, Ballyduff; adult/child €15/10; ⊗8.15pm Wed late Jul-Aug), which since 1991 has been showcasing traditional Irish music, dancing and storytelling in its weekly show. The **Lismore Heritage Centre** (☎0761 102 157; www.discoverlismore.com; Main St; adult/child €5/3.50; ⊗9am-5.30pm Mon-Fri, 10am-5pm Sat, noon-5pm Sun Mar-Nov, weekdays only Dec-Feb) has details of upcoming shows.

The village's artistic tradition extends to amateur drama: companies from all over the country descend on St Michael's Hall for the annual **West Waterford Drama Festival** (www.adci.ie), which runs for 10 days in March.

Eating & Sleeping

Youghal ❶

✗ Aherne's Seafood
Bar & Restaurant   Seafood €€

(📞024-92424; www.ahernes.net; 163 North
Main St; bar meals €14-25, restaurant mains
€29-34; 🕐 bar meals noon-9.30pm, restaurant
6.30-9.30pm; 🛜 📶) Three generations of
the same family have run the award-winning
Aherne's. Seafood is the star, but there are also
plenty of meat and poultry dishes. Besides
the upmarket restaurant there's a cosy bar, all
mahogany and polished brass, where you can
enjoy fresh local seafood with wine by the glass.
Kids menu available.

🛏 Roseville   B&B €€

(📞087 294 7178; www.rosevilleyoughal.com;
New Catherine St; d from €118; 🛜) Despite being
right in the middle of town, this B&B feels like
a secret hideaway with its two luxurious guest
suites beautifully furnished in modern style with
country farmhouse touches, and opening onto
a private walled garden. Sumptuous breakfasts
include eggs all ways, and fruit and vegetable
smoothies.

Cappoquin ❷

✗ Barron's Bakery   Bakery €

(📞058-54045; www.barronsbakery.ie; The
Square; dishes €4-8.50; 🕐8.30am-5.30pm
Mon-Sat) This famous local bakery has used
the same brick Scotch ovens since 1887.
Sandwiches, light meals and a mouth-watering
selection of cakes and buns baked on the
premises are available in the cafe, while its
handmade breads are renowned throughout
the area.

🛏 Richmond House   Guesthouse €€

(📞058-54278; www.richmondhouse.net;
Carigeen; s/d from €70/120; 🅿 🛜) Dating from
1704, Richmond House is set in 6 hectares of
parkland, yet its 10 guest rooms – furnished

with countrified plaids, prints and mahogany
– are cosy rather than imposing, and service is
genuinely friendly. Nonguests are welcome at
its restaurant (dinner €58 per person; Sunday
lunch €33), where produce from its own
gardens features alongside local specialities
such as West Waterford lamb.

Lismore ❹

✗ Lismore Farmers Market   Market €

(www.facebook.com/lismoremarket; Castle
Ave; 🕐11am-4pm Sun Apr-Sep) The upmarket
surrounds on the approach to Lismore Castle
attract a fab collection of vendors to this
market, with stalls selling artisan food and local
arts and crafts. You can enjoy freshly prepared
sandwiches, barbecued sausages and other
goodies in the park or at tables set up on the
gravel path.

✗ Foley's on the Mall   Pub Food €€

(📞058-72511; www.foleysonthemall.ie; Main St;
mains lunch €8-13, dinner €14-28; 🕐 kitchen
12.30-8.30pm, bar 3-11pm; 🛜) At the heart of
Lismore, this inviting Victorian pub – complete
with decorative wallpaper, leather-backed
benches, an open fire, and a beer garden out
the back – serves staples such as chargrilled
steaks, burgers and fish and chips. Kids are
warmly welcomed.

🛏 Ballyrafter Country
House Hotel   Hotel €€

(📞058-54002; www.ballyrafterhouse.com;
Ballyrafter; s/d/tr from €90/110/140; 🅿 🛜)
Built for the Duke of Devonshire in the early 19th
century, this country-house hotel 1km across
the river from Lismore has grand views of the
town's castle. Rooms are traditionally furnished
and there's an in-house restaurant (open daily
March to November, Saturday evenings only
from December to February). The owners
can arrange salmon fishing on nearby River
Blackwater (including licences, equipment
and guides).

Family Fun

Want to keep everybody in the car happy, distracted and entertained? From pet farms to adventure centres, this trip is one for the whole family.

14

TRIP HIGHLIGHTS

154 km

Carlingford
Beautiful village with a top-class adventure centre

6 FINISH

Millmount Museum

Brú na Bóinne Visitor Centre

Trim

2

27 km

Tayto Park
Amusement park adjacent to the popular potato-chips company

Dublin Zoo
Lions and tigers and bears, oh my!

0 km

1 START

3 DAYS
154KM / 96 MILES

GREAT FOR...

BEST TIME TO GO
April to September for the long days and best weather.

ESSENTIAL PHOTO
The medieval Trim Castle – memorable and impressive.

BEST FOR FAMILIES
The revamped Dublin Zoo has something for everyone.

blin Zoo Bornean orangutan

159

14 Family Fun

Within an hour's drive of Dublin is a wealth of child-friendly activities and distractions. The big draws are the interactive exhibits of Brú na Bóinne and the superb adventure centre in Carlingford, but there's plenty more in-between, including a popular farm, where kids get to play with the animals, a potato crisp factory with tours, plus a fantastic amusement park.

❶ Dublin

A bit of interesting Dublin (p168) trivia: the original lion that roars at the beginning of all MGM films was Slats, born in the 28-hectare **Dublin Zoo** (www.dublinzoo.ie; Phoenix Park; adult/child/family €19.50/14/53; ⏰9.30am-6pm Mar-Sep, to dusk Oct-Feb; ♿; 🚌10 from O'Connell St, 25, 26 from Middle Abbey St) in 1919. The zoo's other claim to fame is that it's one of the world's oldest, established in 1831. The lion-breeding programme, begun in 1857, is another highlight, and you can see these tough cats – from a distance – on the recently established 'African Plains', part of an expansion that saw the zoo double in size; other areas include 'World of Primates' and 'Fringes of the Arctic'.

Meet the Keeper is a big hit with kids, especially as they get a chance to feed the animals and participate in other activities. The City Farm is also excellent: it brings you within touching distance of chickens, cows, goats and pigs. There's also a zoo train and a nursery for infants.

✕ 🛏 p44, p58, p93, p165

The Drive » The 29km drive to Tayto Park will take

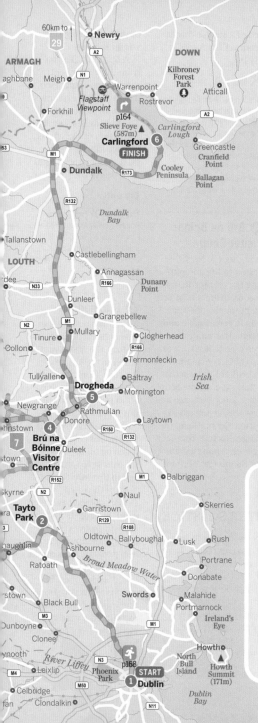

you northwest along the N2 to Ashbourne, where signs direct you left along the L50161 for the last 3.5km.

TRIP HIGHLIGHT

② Tayto Park

An Irish icon, Tayto has been producing much-loved potato crisps since 1954. Alongside the factory, its **amusement park** (☎01-835 1999; www.taytopark.ie; Kilbrew, Ashbourne; €15.50, incl day pass €31.50; ☉9.30am-7pm Jul & Aug, shorter hours Apr-Jun & Sep-Dec) has attractions including Europe's largest wooden inverted roller coaster, a 5D cinema (yes, 5D), a high-speed spinning Rotator and the stomach-churning Air Race ride. There's also a zoo, rock climbing, a zip line and a fantastic playground.

Admission includes a self-guided crisps-factory tour and zoo and playground entry; the

🔗 LINK YOUR TRIP

29 The North in a Nutshell

From Carlingford, it's only 80km along the A1 to Belfast and the beginning of this trip.

7 Ancient Ireland

You can connect to this trip through time at Brú na Bóinne.

wristband day pass is the most economical option for the rides.

The Drive » Head southwest on the R125 for 12km, crossing over the M3 before turning right on the R154 for the remaining 15km to Trim (27km in all).

---

❸ Trim

If you've watched the film *Braveheart,* Mel Gibson's 1995 epic about Scots rebel William Wallace, then you may recognise the remarkably preserved Trim Castle (p96), which made a very acceptable stand-in for the castle at York.

Founded in 1173 by Hugh de Lacy, this was Ireland's largest Anglo-Norman fortification, but the original was destroyed by Rory O'Connor, Ireland's last high king, within a year of its construction: what you see here is the reconstruction, dating from 1200, and it's hardly changed since (even though it was given one

hell of a shellacking by Cromwellian forces in 1649).

🍴 🛏 p101, p165

The Drive » Halfway along the 32km drive to Brú na Bóinne you'll hit the county town of Navan, which is pretty unremarkable except for the traffic – expect delays. Past Navan, the R147 is a classic rural road, with nothing but fields on either side and private houses.

---

❹ Brú na Bóinne Visitor Centre

Bringing the Neolithic period to life and putting the extraordinary accomplishments of Brú na Bóinne's constructors in remarkable and fascinating context is this excellent visitor centre (p97). It explains in brilliant, interactive detail exactly how people lived 3500 years ago and how they managed to garner the mathematical genius to construct a passage tomb that allows for the precise alignment

of the sun during the winter solstice.

A bus will take you from the visitor centre to the passage tomb itself, where a guide explains how it all came about. The tour finishes with a recreation of the winter solstice illumination: even with artificial light it's a pretty cool moment.

🛏 p101

The Drive » From Brú na Bóinne, you'll pass through farmland and the village of Donore, then the industrial outskirts of Drogheda, an 8km trip in all.

---

❺ Drogheda

If the younger kids can stomach a little more history, the Millmount Museum (p98), across the river from the main town of Drogheda, has 9000 years of it to tell. But it does so in an engaging, interactive way: the various collections touch on all aspects of the area's past, from geology to Cromwell's brutal siege of the town.

The cobbled basement is full of gadgets and utensils from bygone times, including a cast-iron pressure cooker and an early model of a sofa bed. A series of craft studios allow you to see the work of craftspeople working in a variety of mediums, from ceramics to silk.

🍴 🛏 p101, p165

NEWGRANGE WINTER SOLSTICE

From the Brú na Bóinne Visitor Centre take the bus to Newgrange where there lies the finest Stone Age passage tomb in Ireland. From here, at 8.20am on the winter solstice (between 18 and 23 December), the rising sun's rays shine through the roof box above the entrance, creep slowly down the long passage and illuminate the tomb chamber for 17 minutes. There is little doubt that this is one of the country's most memorable, even mystical, experiences (access is by lottery). There's a simulated winter sunrise for every group taken into the mound.

Tayto Park, Kilbrew

NEWGRANGE FARM

One for the kids. A few hundred metres down the hill to the west of Newgrange tomb is a 135-hectare working farm. The truly hands-on, family-run **Newgrange Farm** (☏041-982 4119; www.newgrangefarm.com; Newgrange; per person €9, tractor ride €3, family pass 2/4/6 people €15/28/42; ⊗10am-6pm mid-Mar–Aug; ⊞) allows visitors to feed the ducks and lambs, and tour the exotic bird aviaries. Charming Farmer Bill keeps things interesting, and demonstrations of threshing, sheepdog work and shoeing a horse are absorbing. Sunday at 3pm is a very special time when the 'sheep derby' is run. Finding jockeys small enough isn't easy, so teddy bears are tied to the animals' backs. Visiting children are made owners of their own sheep for the race.

The Drive 》 Carlingford is 60km north of Drogheda along the M1 and, for the last 19km, the R173. Alternatively, you can take the longer, but much more scenic coastal R166, which wends its way through the lovely villages of Termonfeckin and Clogherhead before rejoining the main road at Castlebellingham.

TRIP HIGHLIGHT

⑥ Carlingford

Amid the medieval ruins and whitewashed houses, this vibrant little village buzzes with great pubs, chic restaurants and upmarket boutiques, spirited festivals and gorgeous views of the mountains and across Carlingford Lough to Northern Ireland.

Besides the medieval ruins, attractions include a pretty interesting **heritage centre** on the town's history, and the beginning of the 40km **Táin Trail**, which makes a circuit of the Cooley Peninsula through the Cooley Mountains. The route is a mixture of surfaced roads, forest tracks and green paths.

We strongly recommend you check out the **Carlingford Adventure Centre** (☏042-937 3100; www.carlingfordadventure. com; Tholsel St), which runs a wide range of activities including sailing, kayaking, windsurfing, rock climbing and archery.

If you're here in mid-August, the **Carlingford Oyster Festival** (www. carlingford.ie) celebrates Carlingford's famous oysters with an oyster treasure hunt, fishing competition, music, food markets and a regatta on Carlingford Lough.

✗ ⌂ p165

DETOUR: FLAGSTAFF VIEWPOINT

Start: ⑥ Carlingford

Travelling along the Cooley Peninsula from Carlingford to Newry in Northern Ireland, a quick 3km detour rewards you with sweeping views of Carlingford Lough, framed by rugged, forested mountains, green fields and the glittering blue Irish Sea beyond. Flagstaff Viewpoint lies *just* over the border in County Armagh. Heading northwest along the coast road (the R173), follow the signs to your left onto Ferryhill Rd, then turn right up to the viewpoint's car park. The quickest way to reach Newry from here is to retrace your steps and rejoin the R173.

Eating & Sleeping

Dublin ❶

🛏 Morgan Hotel   Boutique Hotel €€€

(📞01-643 7000; www.themorgan.com; 10 Fleet St; r from €280; @ 🛜; 🖥 all city centre) Fresh out of a €15m redesign in 2018, the Morgan is one of the sleekest hotels in town. The rooms are contemporary and calming, with a pale grey decor and slick marble bathrooms. The restaurant, 10 Fleet Street, is exceptional, as are the cocktails whizzed up with smoke and pizazz.

Trim ❷

✕ Harvest Home Bakery   Bakery €

(18 Market St; dishes €4-11; 🕑9am-5pm Mon-Wed, to 5.30pm Thu-Sat) This little gem sells delicious breads, cakes, pies and biscuits (including sugar- and gluten-free options), as well as homemade soups and full-to-bursting sandwiches. There are outside tables in fine weather.

Drogheda ❺

✕ Black Bull   Irish €€

(📞041-983 7139; www.blackbullinn.ie; Dublin Rd; mains €10.50-28; 🕑kitchen 9.30am-10pm Mon-Sat, to 8pm Sun, bar 9.30am-11.30pm Mon-Thu, to 12.30am Fri & Sat, to 11pm Sun; 🛜) Topped by a gleaming golden (not black) bull, this cosy pub has low ceilings, candlelit corners and a centrepiece glass table filled with illuminated liqueur bottles. The modern extension houses a spacious restaurant serving solidly good pub standards such as char-grilled steaks, burgers, and fish and chips. Afterwards, have a pint in the ingeniously named beer garden, the China Shop.

🛏 D Hotel   Hotel €€

(📞041-987 7700; www.thedhotel.com; Scotch Hall, Marsh Rd; d/tr from €115/175; P 🛜) Minimalist rooms at this slick riverside hotel are bathed in light and decked out with designer furniture and cool gadgets. There's a stylish bar and a restaurant, a mini-gym and fantastic views over the skyline. The hotel is popular for hen and stag parties: beware of pounding music (and higher prices) on weekends.

Carlingford ❻

✕ Ghan House   Irish €€€

(📞042-937 3682; www.ghanhouse.com; Old Quay Lane; tasting menus €45-52.50, 3-course Sun lunch €35; 🕑6-9.30pm Mon-Sat, 1-3pm Sun) The restaurant at boutique hotel Ghan House is renowned for its classic multicourse menus (no à la carte) incorporating its own breads, stocks, ice creams and sauces, and herbs and vegetables from its garden. Dishes might include chestnut dumplings with mushroom fricassée or Mourne mountain lamb with nettle and blackberry jus. Be sure to book.

🛏 Carlingford House   B&B €€

(📞042-937 3118; www.carlingfordhouse.com; Dundalk St; d from €110; P 🛜) In the village centre, but set back from the road in manicured grounds, this stately 1844 manor house (once the local doctor's house) is especially stunning in warmer months when it's enveloped by vines. Welcoming hosts Peter and Irene achieve the perfect balance of old-world character and contemporary comfort. Exceptional breakfasts are included in the rate from mid-March to September. Rates drop the rest of the year, when breakfast isn't served.

STRETCH YOUR LEGS
KILKENNY

Start/Finish: Kilkenny Castle

Distance: 1.7km

Duration: 2 hours

Kilkenny's medieval centre is conveniently compact, with most of the major sights collected between the castle to the south and the cathedral to the north.

Take this walk on Trips

Kilkenny Castle

Rising above the Nore, **Kilkenny Castle** (☎056-770 4100; www.kilkennycastle.ie; The Parade; adult/child €8/4; ☺9am-5.30pm Jun-Aug, 9.30am-5.30pm Apr, May & Sep, 9.30am-5pm Mar, 9.30am-4.30pm Oct-Feb) is one of Ireland's most visited heritage sites. Regular 40-minute guided tours focus on the **Long Gallery**, in the wing of the castle nearest the river. The gallery, which showcases stuffy portraits of the Butler family members over the centuries, is an impressive hall with high ceilings vividly painted with Celtic and Pre-Raphaelite motifs.

The Walk ›› Cross Castle Rd; the design centre is adjacent to the castle.

National Design & Craft Gallery & Design Centre

Contemporary Irish crafts are showcased at this imaginative **gallery** (☎056-779 6147; www.ndcg.ie; Castle Yard; ☺10am-5.30pm Tue-Sat, from 11am Sun) in the former castle stables that also house the shops of the Kilkenny Design Centre. Ceramics dominate, but exhibits often feature furniture, jewellery and weaving from the members of the Crafts Council of Ireland.

The Walk ›› Turn left and walk north onto High St until you reach the Tholsel on your right.

Tholsel

The Tholsel (City Hall) on High St was built in 1761 on the spot where Dame Alice Kyteler's maid Petronella was burned at the stake in 1324 for witchcraft (even if it was actually Dame Alice who was most likely the guilty party).

The Walk ›› The Butter Slip is a narrow alley to the right after the Tholsel.

Butter Slip

With its arched entry and stone steps, Butter Slip, a narrow and dark walkway connecting High St with St Kieran's St (previously called Low Lane), is the most picturesque of Kilkenny's many narrow medieval corridors.

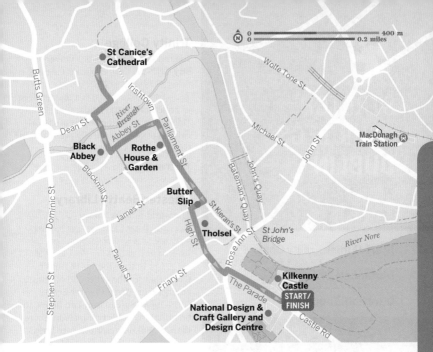

The Walk » Turn left on St Kieran's St and rejoin High St; Rothe House is on your left.

Rothe House & Garden

Ireland's best surviving example of a 16th-century merchant's house is the Tudor Rothe House. Built around a series of courtyards, it now houses a **museum** (☎056-772 2893; www.rothehouse. com; 16 Parliament St; house & garden adult/ child €7.50/4.50, garden only €4/2; ☺10.30am-5pm Mon-Sat, noon-5pm Sun) with local artefacts including a well-used Viking sword found nearby and a grinning head sculpted by a Celtic artist. Recent changes include new exhibits about the Rothe family and ongoing restorations of the urban gardens out the back.

The Walk » Turn left on Parliament St and after 80m take a left on Abbey St.

Black Abbey

This Dominican **abbey** (www.dominicans. ie; Abbey St; ☺7.30am-7pm Mon-Sat, 9am-7pm Sun Apr-Sep, 7.30am-5.30pm Mon-Sat, 9am-5.30pm Sun Oct-Mar) was founded in 1225 by William Marshall and takes its name from the monks' black habits. In 1543, six years after Henry VIII's dissolution of the monasteries, it was turned into a courthouse. Much of what survives dates from the 18th and 19th centuries, but remnants of more ancient archways are evident within the newer stonework.

The Walk » Continue north through the lane and take a right on Dean St, then a left onto Coach St into the cathedral grounds.

St Canice's Cathedral

Soaring over the north end of the centre is Ireland's second-largest medieval **cathedral** (☎056-776 4971; www.stcanices-cathedral.ie; Coach Rd; cathedral/round tower/combined adult €4.50/4/7, child €3.50/4/6.50; ☺9am-6pm Mon-Sat, 1-6pm Sun Jun-Aug, shorter hours Sep-May) after St Patrick's in Dublin. Legend has it that the first monastery was built here in the 6th century by St Canice, Kilkenny's patron saint.

The Walk » Go back down Parliament St to the castle, stopping in a pub or two along the way.

STRETCH YOUR LEGS
DUBLIN

Start/Finish Trinity College

Distance 4.9km

Duration 3 hours

Dublin's most important attractions are concentrated on the south side of the Liffey, split between the older medieval town dominated by the castle and the two cathedrals, and the handsome 18th-century city that is a showcase of exquisite Georgian aesthetic.

Take this walk on Trips

Trinity College

Ireland's most prestigious **university** (📞01-896 1000; www.tcd.ie; College Green; ⏰8am-10pm; 🚌all city centre, 🚊Westmoreland or Trinity) is a masterpiece of architecture and landscaping, and Dublin's most attractive bit of historical real estate, beautifully preserved in Georgian and Victorian style.

The Walk » From Trinity College, walk west along Dame St and turn into Dublin Castle.

Chester Beatty Library

The world-famous **library** (📞01-407 0750; www.cbl.ie; Dublin Castle; ⏰10am-5pm Mon-Fri, from 11am Sat & Sun Mar-Oct, from 10am-5pm Tue-Fri, from 11am Sat & Sun Nov-Feb; 🚌all city centre), in the grounds of Dublin Castle, houses the collection of mining engineer Sir Alfred Chester Beatty (1875–1968). Spread over two floors, the breathtaking collection includes more than 20,000 manuscripts, rare books, miniature paintings, clay tablets, costumes and other objects of historical and aesthetic importance.

The Walk » Exit the castle and walk west; you'll see Christ Church directly in front of you.

Christ Church Cathedral

Its hilltop location and eye-catching flying buttresses make this the most photogenic by far of Dublin's three **cathedrals** (Church of the Holy Trinity; www.christchurchcathedral.ie; Christ Church Pl; adult/student/child €7/5.50/2.50, with Dublinia €15/12.50/7.50; ⏰9.30am-5pm Mon-Sat, from 12.30pm Sun year-round, longer hours Mar-Oct; 🚌50, 50A, 56A from Aston Quay, 54, 54A from Burgh Quay) as well as one of the capital's most recognisable symbols. It was founded in 1030 on what was then the southern edge of Dublin's Viking settlement. The Normans rebuilt the lot in stone from 1172.

The Walk » Go south along Nicholas St (which becomes News St); St Patrick's is 400m along.

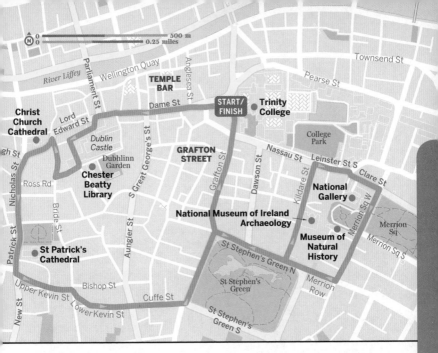

St Patrick's Cathedral

It was at this **cathedral** (☏01-453 9472;
www.stpatrickscathedral.ie; St Patrick's Close;
adult/student €8/7; ⏰9.30am-5pm Mon-Fri,
9am-6pm Sat, 9-10.30am, 12.30-2.30pm & 4.30-
6pm Sun Mar-Oct, 9.30am-5pm Mon-Fri, from
9am Sat, 9-10.30am & 12.30-2.30pm Sun Nov-
Feb; 🚌50, 50A, 56A from Aston Quay, 54, 54A
from Burgh Quay), reputedly, that St Paddy
himself dunked the Irish heathens into
the waters of a well. Although there's
been a church here since the 5th century, the present building dates from
1190 or 1225 (opinions differ).

The Walk ›› Just south of St Patrick's, turn left
onto Kevin St and keep going until you reach St
Stephen's Green; turn onto Kildare St.

National Museum of Ireland – Archaeology

The star attraction of this branch
of the National Museum of Ireland
(p88) is the Treasury, home to the
finest collection of Bronze Age and
Iron Age gold artefacts in the world,
and the world's most complete collection of medieval Celtic metalwork.

The Walk ›› Walk north on Kildare St and turn
right on Nassau St, then stay right on Clare St.

National Museum of Ireland – Natural History

Dusty, weird and utterly compelling,
and a window into Victorian times, this
museum (www.museum.ie; Upper Merrion St;
⏰10am-5pm Tue-Sat, from 1pm Sun; 🚌7, 44
from city centre) has barely changed since
Scottish explorer Dr David Livingstone
opened it in 1857 – before disappearing
into the African jungle for a meeting
with Henry Stanley.

The Walk ›› Turn right onto Merrion Row, skirt
St Stephen's Green and go right into Grafton St to
head back to Trinity College.

Cork & Southwest Ireland

THE SOUTHWEST CONTAINS SOME OF IRELAND'S MOST ICONIC SCENERY: crenulated coastlines, green fields criss-crossed by tumbledown stone walls, and mist-shrouded mountain peaks and bogs.

This idyllic area claims the country's top three peninsula drives – the Ring of Kerry, Dingle Peninsula and Ring of Beara – as well as a shoal of charming fishing towns and villages that have helped establish the southwest as a gourmet heartland, fanning out from the country's spirited second-largest city, Cork.

The region's exquisite beauty makes it one of Ireland's most popular tourist destinations, but there's always an isolated cove or untrodden trail to discover along its roads.

Ring of Kerry Coastal views, County Kerry
JORG GREUEL/GETTY IMAGES ©

Classic Trip

15 **Ring of Kerry 4 Days**
Weave your way past jaw-dropping scenery as you circumnavigate the Iveragh Peninsula.

16 **Dingle Peninsula 3–4 Days**
Dingle's ancient landscape is ringed by quaint fishing villages and spectacular beaches.

17 **Southwest Blitz 4 Days**
Blitz the best of southwest Ireland's coast, countryside and cosmopolitan city life.

18 **Southwestern Pantry 5 Days**
Sample some of the country's finest seafood, artisan produce and sociable markets.

19 **West Cork Villages 7 Days**
Colourful villages burst with life in West Cork, including its picturesque peninsulas.

20 **Shannon River Route 4 Days**
Meander alongside Ireland's mightiest river and get out on the water too.

21 **The Holy Glen 2–3 Days**
Awe-inspiring mountain vistas and sacred sites including the extraordinary Rock of Cashel.

 DON'T MISS

Hunt Museum
Limerick's true treasure hunt – open drawers and poke around its collections on Trip **20**

Garinish Island (Ilnacullin)
Sail from Glengarriff past islands and seal colonies to Garinish's subtropical gardens on Trip **19**

Killarney Jaunting Cars
Clip-clop in a traditional horse-drawn jaunting car on Trips **15** **16** **17**

Cork City Gaol
Models of suffering prisoners bring home the harshness of the 19th-century penal system on Trip **17**

Rough Point Diving
Dive crystal-clear waters and spot whales and dolphins on Trip **16**

Durrus Farmhouse Cheese
Taste Durrus' famous cheese at its farm on Trip **18**

Seals, Garinish Island

Classic Trip

Ring of Kerry

Circumnavigating the Iveragh Peninsula, the Ring of Kerry is the most diverse of Ireland's prized peninsula drives, combining jaw-dropping coastal scenery with soaring mountains.

15

4 DAYS
202KM / 125 MILES

GREAT FOR...

BEST TIME TO GO
Late spring and early autumn for temperate weather free of summer crowds.

 ESSENTIAL PHOTO
Ross Castle as you row a boat to Inisfallen.

BEST FOR WILDLIFE
Killarney National Park, home to Ireland's only wild herd of native red deer.

Classic Trip

15 Ring of Kerry

You can drive the Ring of Kerry in a day, but the longer you spend, the more you'll enjoy it. The circuit winds past pristine beaches, medieval ruins, mountains, loughs (lakes) and the island-dotted Atlantic, with the coastline at its most rugged between Waterville and Caherdaniel in the peninsula's southwest. You'll also find plenty of opportunities for serene, starkly beautiful detours, such as the Skellig Ring and the Cromane Peninsula.

1 Killarney

A town that's been in the business of welcoming visitors for more than 250 years, Killarney is a well-oiled tourism machine fuelled by the sublime scenery of its namesake national park, with competition helping keep standards high. Killarney nights are lively and most pubs put on live music.

Killarney and its surrounds have likely been inhabited since the Neolithic period, but it wasn't until the 17th century that Viscount Kenmare developed the region as an Irish version of England's Lake District; among its notable 19th-century tourists were Queen Victoria and Romantic poet Percy Bysshe Shelley. The town itself lacks major attractions, but the landscaped grounds of nearby Killarney House and Muckross House frame photo-worthy panoramas of lake and mountain, while former carriage drives around these aristocratic estates now serve as scenic hiking and biking trails open to all.

The town can easily be explored on foot in an hour or two, or you can get around by horse-drawn jaunting car.

✕ ⛏ p45, p185, p195

The Drive » From Killarney, head 22km west to Killorglin

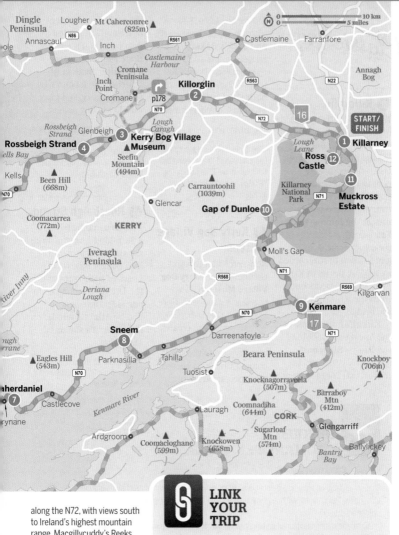

along the N72, with views south to Ireland's highest mountain range, Macgillycuddy's Reeks. The mountains' elegant forms were carved by glaciers, with summits buttressed by ridges of purplish rock. The name derives from the ancient Mac Gilla Muchudas clan; *reek* means 'pointed hill'. In Irish, they're known as Na Crucha Dubha (the Black Tops).

LINK YOUR TRIP

 16 Dingle Peninsula

Another of Ireland's iconic peninsula drives, the picturesque Dingle Peninsula, is on Killarney's doorstep.

 17 Southwest Blitz

Kick off from Killarney along the Ring of Kerry's coastline and continue into captivating County Cork.

Classic Trip

② Killorglin

Killorglin (Cill Orglan) is quieter than the waters of the River Laune that lap against its 1885-built eight-arched bridge – except in mid-August, when there's an explosion of time-honoured ceremonies at the famous **Puck Fair** (Aonach an Phuic; www.puckfair.ie; ⊙mid-Aug), a pagan festival first recorded in 1603. A statue of King Puck (a goat) peers out from the Killarney end of the bridge.

Killorglin has some of the finest eateries along the Ring – **Bianconi** (🖀066-976 1146; www.bianconi.ie; Lower Bridge St; mains €10-28; ⊙kitchen 11.30am-10pm Mon-Sat, 6-9pm Sun; 🛜) and **Jack's Bakery** (Lower Bridge St; dishes €2.50-8; ⊙8am-6.45pm Mon-Fri, to 6pm Sat, 9am-2pm Sun) are both good spots for a late breakfast or early lunch.

🍴 p185, p207

The Drive » Killorglin sits at the junction of the N72 and the N70; continue 13km along the N70 to the Kerry Bog Village Museum.

③ Kerry Bog Village Museum

Between Killorglin and Glenbeigh, the **Kerry Bog Village Museum** (www.kerrybogvillage.ie; Ballincleave, Glenbeigh; adult/child €6.50/4.50; ⊙9am-6pm; P) re-creates a 19th-century settlement typical of the small communities that carved out a precarious living in the harsh environment of Ireland's ubiquitous peat bogs. You'll see the thatched homes of the turf cutter, blacksmith, thatcher and labourer, as well as a dairy, and meet rare Kerry Bog ponies.

The Drive » It's less than 1km from the museum to the village of Glenbeigh; turn off here and drive 2km west to unique Rossbeigh Strand.

④ Rossbeigh Strand

This unusual beach is a 3km-long finger of shingle and sand protruding into Dingle Bay, with views of Inch Point and the Dingle Peninsula. On one side, the sea is ruffled by Atlantic winds; on the other, it's sheltered and calm.

The Drive » Rejoin the N70 and continue 25km southwest to Cahersiveen.

DETOUR: CROMANE PENINSULA

Start: ② Killorglin

Open fields give way to spectacular water vistas and multihued sunsets on the Cromane Peninsula, with its tiny namesake village sitting at the base of a narrow shingle spit.

Cromane's exceptional eating place, **Jack's Coastguard Restaurant** (p207), is a local secret and justifies the trip. Entering this 1866-built coastguard station feels like arriving at a low-key village pub, but a narrow doorway at the back of the bar leads to a striking, whitewashed contemporary space with lights glittering from midnight-blue ceiling panels, stained glass and metallic fish sculptures, and huge picture windows looking out across the water. Seafood is the standout, but there's also steak, roast lamb and a veggie dish of the day.

Cromane is 9km from Killorglin. Heading southwest from Killorglin along the N70, take the second right and continue straight ahead until you get to the crossroads. Turn right; Jack's Coastguard Restaurant is on your left.

⑤ Cahersiveen

Cahersiveen's population – over 30,000 in 1841 – was decimated by the Great Famine and emigration to the New World. A sleepy outpost remains, overshadowed by the 688m peak of **Knocknadobar**. It looks rather dour compared with the peninsula's other settlements, but the atmospheric remains of 16th-century **Ballycarbery Castle**, 2.4km along the road to White Strand Beach from the town centre, are well worth a visit.

Along the same road are two stone ring forts. The larger, **Cahergall**, dates from the 10th century and has stairways on the inside walls, a *clochán* (circular stone building shaped like an old-fashioned beehive) and the remains of a house. The smaller, 9th-century **Leacanabuile** has an entrance to an underground passage. Their inner walls and chambers give a strong sense of what life was like in a ring fort. Leave your car in the parking area next to a stone wall and walk up the footpaths.

The Drive » From Cahersiveen you can continue 17km along the classic Ring of Kerry on the N70 to Waterville, or take the ultrascenic route via Valentia Island and the Skellig Ring, and rejoin the N70 at Waterville.

DETOUR:
VALENTIA ISLAND & THE SKELLIG RING

Start: ⑤ Cahersiveen

Crowned by Geokaun Mountain, 11km-long Valentia Island (Oileán Dairbhre) makes an ideal driving loop, with some lonely ruins that are worth exploring. Knightstown, the only town, has pubs, food and walks.

The **Skellig Experience** (☎066-947 6306; www.skelligexperience.com; adult/child €5/3, incl cruise €35/20; ☻10am-7pm Jul & Aug, to 6pm May, Jun & Sep, to 4.30pm Fri-Wed Mar, Apr, Oct & Nov; ⓟ) heritage centre, in a distinctive building with turf-covered barrel roofs, has informative exhibits on the offshore Skellig Islands. From April to September, it also runs two-hour cruises around the Skelligs (no landing; adult/child €35/20, including museum entry).

If you're here between April and October, and you're detouring via Valentia Island and the Skellig Ring, a ferry service from Reenard Point, 5km southwest of Cahersiveen, provides a handy shortcut to Valentia Island. The five-minute crossing departs every 10 minutes. Alternatively, there's a bridge between **Portmagee** and the far end of the island.

Immediately across the bridge on the mainland, Portmagee's single street is a rainbow of colourful houses. On summer mornings the small pier comes to life with boats embarking on the choppy crossing to the Skellig Islands.

Portmagee holds **set-dancing workshops** over the May bank holiday weekend, with plenty of stomping practice sessions in the town's **Bridge Bar** (☎066-947 7108; www.moorings.ie; mains €13-18; ☻8am-11.30pm Mon-Sat, to 11pm Sun, kitchen to 9pm; ⛟), a friendly local gathering point that's also good for impromptu music year-round and more formal sessions in summer.

The wild and beautiful, 18km-long Skellig Ring road links Portmagee and Waterville via a Gaeltacht (Irish-speaking) area centred on Ballinskelligs (Baile an Sceilg), with the ragged outline of Skellig Michael never far from view.

Classic Trip

WHY THIS IS A CLASSIC TRIP
NEIL WILSON, WRITER

In a land criss-crossed with classic drives, the Ring of Kerry is perhaps the most classic of all. Now a key stretch of the Wild Atlantic Way, this trip showcases Ireland's most spectacular coastal scenery, its ancient and recent history, traditional pubs with crackling turf fires and spontaneous, high-spirited trad-music sessions, and the Emerald Isle's most engaging asset: its welcoming, warm-hearted locals.

Above: Derrynanae Beach, along the Ring of Kerry
Left: Muckross House, Killarney National Park
Right: Stone bridge at the Gap of Dunloe, Killarney National Park

APROTT/GETTY IMAGES ©

❻ Waterville

A line of colourful houses on the N70 between Lough Currane and Ballinskelligs Bay, Waterville is charm-challenged in the way of many mass-consumption beach resorts. A statue of its most famous guest, Charlie Chaplin, beams from the seafront. The **Charlie Chaplin Comedy Film Festival** (www.chaplinfilmfestival.com) is held in August.

Waterville is home to a world-renowned **links golf course**. At the north end of Lough Currane, **Church Island** has the ruins of a medieval church and beehive cell reputedly founded as a monastic settlement by St Finian in the 6th century.

🛏 p185

The Drive » Squiggle your way for 14km along the Ring's most tortuous stretch, past plunging cliffs, craggy hills and stunning views, to Caherdaniel.

TRIP HIGHLIGHT

❼ Caherdaniel

The scattered hamlet of Caherdaniel counts two of the Ring of Kerry's highlights: Derrynane National Historic Park, the childhood home of the 19th-century hero of Catholic emancipation, Daniel O'Connell; and what is plausibly claimed as 'Ireland's finest view' over rugged cliffs and

181

Classic Trip

islands, as you crest the hill at Beenarourke (there's a large car park here).

Most activity here centres on the Blue Flag beach. **Derrynane Sea Sports** (☎087 908 1208; www.derrynaneseasports.com; Derrynane Beach) organises sailing, canoeing, surfing, windsurfing and waterskiing (from €40 per person), as well as equipment hire (around €15 per hour). **Eagle Rock Equestrian Centre** (☎066-947 5145; www.eaglerockcentre.com; Ballycarnahan; horse riding per hour €40) offers beach, mountain and woodland horse treks for all levels.

The Drive » Wind your way east along the N70 for 21km to Sneem.

---

⑧ Sneem

Sneem's Irish name, An tSnaidhm, translates as 'the knot', which is thought to refer to the River Sneem that twists and turns, knot-like, into nearby Kenmare Bay.

Take a gander at the town's two cute squares, then pop into the **Blue Bull** (☎064-664 5382; South Sq; mains €9-15, dinner €14-24; ✆ kitchen noon-2pm & 6-9.30pm, bar 11.30am-midnight), a perfect little old stone pub, for a pint.

🛏 p185

The Drive » Along the 27km drive to Kenmare, the N70 drifts away from the water to take in views towards the Kerry mountains.

---

⑨ Kenmare

The copper-covered limestone spire of Holy Cross Church, drawing the eye to the wooded hills above town, may make you forget for a split second that Kenmare is a seaside town. With rivers named Finnihy, Roughty and Sheen emptying into Kenmare Bay, you couldn't be anywhere other than southwest Ireland.

In the 18th century Kenmare was laid out on an X-shaped plan, with a triangular market square in the centre. Today the inverted V to the south is the focus. Kenmare River (actually an inlet of the sea) stretches out to the southwest, and there are glorious mountain views.

Signposted southwest of the square is an early Bronze Age **stone circle**, one of the biggest in southwest Ireland. Fifteen stones ring a boulder dolmen, a burial monument rarely found outside this part of the country.

🍴 🛏 p45, p59, p185, p207

The Drive » The coastal scenery might be finished but, if anything, the next 23km are even more stunning as you head north from Kenmare to the Gap of Dunloe on the narrow, vista-crazy N71, winding between crag and lake, with plenty of lay-bys to stop and admire the views (and recover from the switchback bends).

TRIP HIGHLIGHT

⑩ Gap of Dunloe

Just west of Killarney National Park, the Gap of Dunloe is ruggedly beautiful. In the winter it's an awe-inspiring mountain pass, squeezed between

---

✓ **TOP TIP:**
AROUND (AND ACROSS) THE RING

Tour buses travel anticlockwise around the Ring, and authorities generally encourage visitors to drive in the same direction to avoid traffic congestion and accidents. If you travel clockwise, watch out on blind corners, especially on the section between Moll's Gap and Killarney. There's little traffic on the Ballaghbeama Gap, which cuts across the peninsula's central highlands, with some spectacular views.

Purple Mountain and Macgillycuddy's Reeks. In high summer it's a magnet for the tourist trade, with buses ferrying countless visitors here for horse-and-trap rides through the Gap.

On the southern side, surrounded by lush, green pastures, is **Lord Brandon's Cottage** (Gearhameen; dishes €3-8; ⊗8am-3pm Apr-Oct), accessed by turning left at Moll's Gap on the R568, then taking the first right, another right at the bottom of the hill, then right again at the crossroads (about 13km from the N71 all up). A simple 19th-century hunting lodge, it has an open-air cafe and a dock for boats from Ross Castle near Killarney. From here a (very) narrow road weaves up the hill to the Gap – theoretically you can drive this 8km route to the 19th-century pub **Kate Kearney's Cottage** (☎064-664 4146; mains €10-24; ⊗ kitchen noon-9pm, bar to 11.30pm Mon-Thu, to 12.30am Fri & Sat, to 11pm Sun; P ⊕) and back *but* only outside summer. Even then walkers and cyclists have right of way and the precipitous hairpin bends are nerve-testing. It's worth walking or taking a jaunting car (or, if you're carrying two wheels, cycling) through the Gap: the scenery is a fantasy of rocky bridges over clear mountain streams and lakes. Alternatively, there are various options for exploring the Gap from Killarney.

The Drive ⟩⟩ Continue on the N71 north through Killarney National Park to Muckross Estate (32km).

TRIP HIGHLIGHT

⑪ Muckross Estate

The core of Killarney National Park is Muckross Estate, donated to the state by Arthur Bourn Vincent in 1932. **Muckross House** (☎064-667 0144; www.muckross-house.ie; adult/child €9.25/6.25, incl Muckross Traditional Farms

---

KILLARNEY NATIONAL PARK

Designated a Unesco Biosphere Reserve in 1982, **Killarney National Park** (www.killarneynationalpark.ie) is among the finest of Ireland's national parks. And while its proximity to one of the southwest's largest and liveliest urban centres (including pedestrian entrances right in Killarney's town centre) encourages high visitor numbers, it's an important conservation area for many rare species. Within its 102 sq km is Ireland's only wild herd of native red deer, which has lived here continuously for 12,000 years, as well as the country's largest area of ancient oak woods and views of most of its major mountains.

Glacier-gouged Lough Leane (the Lower Lake or 'Lake of Learning'), Muckross Lake and the Upper Lake make up about a quarter of the park. Their crystal waters are as rich in wildlife as the surrounding land: great crested grebes and tufted ducks cruise the lake margins, deer swim out to graze on islands, and salmon, trout and perch prosper in a pike-free environment.

With a bit of luck, you might see white-tailed sea eagles, with their 2.5m wingspan, soaring overhead. The eagles were reintroduced here in 2007 after an absence of more than 100 years. There are now more than 50 in the park and they're starting to settle in Ireland's rivers, lakes and coastal regions. And like Killarney itself, the park is also home to plenty of summer visitors, including migratory cuckoos, swallows and swifts.

Keep your eyes peeled, too, for the park's smallest residents – its insects, including the northern emerald dragonfly, which isn't normally found this far south in Europe and is believed to have been marooned here after the last ice age.

€15.50/10.50; ⊘9am-7pm Jul & Aug, to 6pm Apr-Jun, Sep & Oct, to 5pm Nov-Mar; [P]) is a 19th-century mansion, restored to its former glory and packed with period fittings. Entrance is by guided tour.

The beautiful **gardens** slope down, and a building behind the house contains a restaurant, craft shop and studios where you can see potters, weavers and bookbinders at work. Jaunting cars wait to run you through deer parks and woodland to **Torc Waterfall** and **Muckross Abbey** (about €20 each, return; haggling can reap discounts). The visitor centre has an excellent cafe.

Adjacent to Muckross House are the **Muckross Traditional Farms** (adult/ child €9.25/6.25, incl Muckross House €15.50/10.50; ⊘10am-6pm Jun-Aug, from 1pm Apr, May & Sep, from 1pm Sat & Sun Mar & Oct). These reproductions of 1930s Kerry farms, complete with chickens, pigs, cattle and horses, re-create farming and living conditions when people had to live off the land.

The Drive ⟫ Continuing a further 2km north through the national park brings you to historic Ross Castle.

---

⑫ Ross Castle

Restored **Ross Castle** (☎064-663 5851; www.heritageireland.ie; Ross Rd; adult/ child €5/3; ⊘9.30am-5.45pm early Mar–Oct; [P]) dates back to the 15th century, when it was a residence of the O'Donoghues. It was the last place in Munster to succumb to Cromwell's forces, thanks partly to its cunning spiral staircase, every step of which is a different height in order to break an attacker's stride. Access is by guided tour only.

You can take a motorboat trip (around €10 per person) from Ross Castle to **Inisfallen**, the largest of Killarney National Park's 26 islands. The first monastery on Inisfallen is said to have been founded by St Finian the Leper in the 7th century. The island's fame dates from the early 13th century when the Annals of Inisfallen were written here. Now in the Bodleian Library at Oxford, they remain a vital source of information on early Munster history. Inisfallen shelters the ruins of a 12th-century oratory with a carved Romanesque doorway and a monastery on the site of St Finian's original.

The Drive ⟫ It's just 3km north from Ross Castle back to Killarney.

Eating & Sleeping

Killarney ❶

✕ Celtic Whiskey Bar & Larder
Gastropub €€

(☎064-663 5700; www.celticwhiskeybar.com; 93 New St; mains €9-27; ⊙ food served noon-9.45pm; 🛜) This buzzing gastropub serves some of the tastiest food in town, with menu highlights ranging from cheese and charcuterie platters and aged fillet steaks to brioche sliders and steamed Glenbeigh mussels.

🛏 Cahernane House Hotel
Heritage Hotel €€€

(☎064-663 1895; www.cahernane.com; Muckross Rd, Muckross; d/ste from €230/310, 4-course dinner menu €60; P 🛜) A tree-lined driveway leads to this magnificent manor 2km south of town, dating from 1877. A dozen of its 38 antique-furnished rooms (some with claw-foot bath or Jacuzzi) are in the original house; garden-wing rooms have balcony or patio. Fishing is possible in the River Flesk, which flows through the grounds.

Killorglin ❷

✕ Giovannelli
Italian €€€

(☎087 123 1353; www.giovannellirestaurant. com; Lower Bridge St; mains €19-34; ⊙6.30-9pm Mon-Sat) Northern Italian native Daniele Giovannelli makes all his pasta by hand at this simple but intimate little restaurant. Highlights of the blackboard menu might include seafood linguine with mussels in the shell and beef ravioli in sage butter. Wonderful wines are available by the bottle and glass.

Waterville ❻

🛏 Butler Arms Hotel
Historic Hotel €€

(☎066-9474156; www.butlerarms.com; New Line Rd; s/d from €145/160; P 🛜) The castellated towers of the Butler Arms have dominated the north end of the village since 1884, and the hotel has provided accommodation for many famous guests through the years – Walt Disney in the 1940s,

Charlie Chaplin in the 1960s, Mark Hamill and Daisy Ridley (Star Wars) in 2014 and 2015.

Sneem ❽

🛏 Parknasilla Resort & Spa
Hotel €€€

(☎064-667 5600; www.parknasillaresort. com; Parknasilla; d/f/ste from €169/195/325; P @ 🛜 ⛵) On the tree-fringed shores of the Kenmare River with views to the Beara Peninsula, this hotel has been wowing guests (including George Bernard Shaw) since 1895.

Kenmare ❾

✕ Boathouse Bistro
Bistro €€

(☎064-664 2889; www.dromquinnamanor.com; Dromquinna Manor, Sneem Rd; mains €15-28; ⊙12.30-9pm daily mid-Mar–Sep, Fri-Sun only Oct–mid-Mar; P) At the water's edge, this blue-and-white 1870s boathouse 4.5km west of Kenmare, has been stunningly converted to a beach-house-style bistro specialising in local seafood delivered daily to its own wharf. Expertly cooked dishes (Kenmare Bay crab claws in chilli and garlic butter, beer-battered fish and chips) are accompanied by a great selection of by-the-glass wines and craft gins.

✕ Tom Crean Fish & Wine
Irish €€

(☎064-664 1589; www.tomcrean.ie; Main St; mains €17-31; ⊙5-9.30pm Thu-Mon Sep-Jun, daily Jul & Aug; 🛜) Named for Kerry's pioneering Antarctic explorer, and run by his granddaughter, this venerable restaurant uses only the best of local organic produce, cheeses and fresh seafood. Sneem lobster is available in season, the oysters au naturel capture the scent of the sea, and the seafood gratin served in a scallop shell is divine.

🛏 Dromquinna Manor
Tented Camp €€

(☎064-664 2888; www.dromquinnamanor.com; Sneem Rd; d/f €160/190; ⊙May-Aug; P) This country estate on the shores of Kenmare River, 4.5km west of Kenmare, has 14 sturdy safari-style tents, luxuriously outfitted with plush double beds and antique furniture (but shared showers and toilets), on a gorgeous landscaped site sloping down to the sea.

Dingle Peninsula

16

Driving around this history-infused headland, you'll encounter churches, castles, neolithic monuments, captivating scenery and artistic little Dingle, the peninsula's delightful 'capital'.

TRIP HIGHLIGHTS

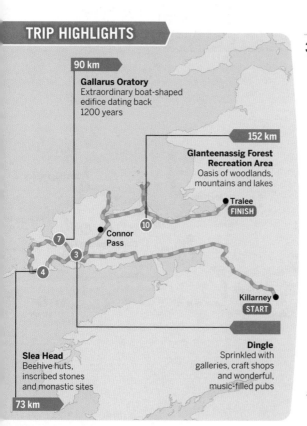

90 km

Gallarus Oratory
Extraordinary boat-shaped edifice dating back 1200 years

152 km

Glanteenassig Forest Recreation Area
Oasis of woodlands, mountains and lakes

● Tralee
FINISH

10

● Connor Pass

7

3

4

Killarney ●
START

Slea Head
Beehive huts, inscribed stones and monastic sites

73 km

Dingle
Sprinkled with galleries, craft shops and wonderful, music-filled pubs

---

3–4 DAYS
185KM / 115 MILES

GREAT FOR...

BEST TIME TO GO

June to August offer the best beach weather.

ESSENTIAL PHOTO

Snap a perfect panorama from Clogher Head viewpoint.

BEST FOR HISTORY

Slea Head's astonishing concentration of ancient sites.

---

16 Dingle Peninsula

As you twist and turn along this figure-of-eight drive, the coastline is the star of the show. The opal-blue waters surrounding the Dingle Peninsula provide a wealth of aquatic adventures and superbly fresh seafood, and you'll find that where the promontory meets the ocean — at wave-pounded rocks, secluded coves and wide, golden-sand beaches — Dingle's beauty is at its most unforgettable.

1 Killarney

The lively tourist town of Killarney is an ideal place to kick off your trip, with a plethora of places to eat, drink and sleep. If you have time, the 102-sq-km **Killarney National Park** (p183), immediately to its south, and the **Gap of Dunloe** (p182), with its rocky terrain, babbling brooks and alpine lakes, are well worth exploring. On a tight schedule, however, you can still get a good overview of the area – and entertaining

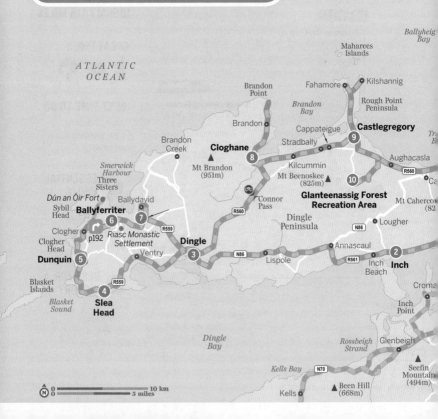

commentary, too – aboard a horse-drawn jaunting car, also known as a trap, which comes with a driver called a jarvey. The pick-up point, nicknamed 'the Ha Ha' or 'the Block', is on Kenmare Pl. Trips cost €40 to €80, depending on distance; traps officially carry up to four people.

✗ 🛏 p45, p185, p195

The Drive » The quickest route from Killarney to the peninsula is via the R563 to Milltown and Castlemaine. Turn west here onto the R561; you'll soon meet the coast before coming to the vast beach at Inch (41km).

② Inch

Inch's 5km-long sand spit was a location for the movies *Ryan's Daughter* and *Playboy of the Western World*. Sarah Miles, a star of the former film, described her stay here as 'brief but bonny'.

The dunes are certainly bonny, a great spot for windswept walks, birdwatching and bathing. The west-facing Blue Flag beach (lifeguarded in summer) is also a hot surfing spot; waves average 1m to 3m. You can learn to ride them with **Offshore Surf School** (📞087 294 6519; www.offshoresurfschool.ie; lessons adult/child per 2hr from €25/20, board & wetsuit hire per 2hr €15; ⊙9am-6pm Apr–mid-Oct).

Cars are allowed on the beach, but don't end up providing others with laughs by getting stuck.

Sammy's (📞066-915 8118; www.facebook.com/sammysinchbeach; mains €7-15; ⊙10am-6pm Mon-Thu, to 9pm Fri-Sun, shorter hours Oct-Easter; 🛜🚻), at the entrance to the beach, is the nerve centre of the village. In addition to its beach-facing bar and restaurant, there's a shop, tourist information and trad music sessions during the summer.

The Drive » Shadowing the coast, about 7km west of Inch, Annascaul (Abhainn an Scáil; also spelled Anascaul) is home to a cracking pub,

🔗 LINK YOUR TRIP

15 **Ring of Kerry**
From Tralee it's a quick 22km zip along the N22 to pick up Ireland's most famous driving loop in Killarney.

17 **Southwest Blitz**
Killarney is also the jumping-off point for another classic Irish road trip along the Ring of Kerry and a stunning swathe of County Cork.

the South Pole Inn, formerly run by Antarctic explorer Tom Crean in his retirement and now something of a Crean museum. Continuing 18km west of Annascaul brings you into Dingle town.

TRIP HIGHLIGHT

❸ Dingle Town

Fanned around its fishing port, the peninsula's charming little capital is quaint without even trying. Dingle is one of Ireland's largest Gaeltacht (Irish-speaking) towns (although locals have voted to retain the name Dingle rather than go with the officially sanctioned Gaelic version An Daingean) and has long drawn runaways from across the world, making it a surprisingly cosmopolitan, creative place.

This is one of those towns whose very fabric is its attraction. Wander the higgledy-piggledy streets, shop for handcrafted jewellery, arts, crafts and artisan food and pop into old-school pubs. Two untouched examples are **Foxy John's** (Main St; ⏰10am-11pm; 🛜) and **Curran's** (Main St; ⏰10am-11pm), which respectively have old stock of hardware and outdoor clothing on display.

Dingle's most famous 'resident' is Fungie the dolphin. Boats leave Dingle's pier daily for one-hour **dolphin-spotting trips** (📞066-915

2626; www.dingledolphin.com; The Pier; adult/child €16/8).

On land, the **Dingle Oceanworld** (📞066-915 2111; www.dingle-oceanworld.ie; The Wood; adult/child/family €15.50/10.75/47; ⏰10am-7pm Jul & Aug, to 6pm Sep-Jun) aquarium has a walk-through tunnel and a touch pool.

Don't leave Dingle without catching traditional live music at pubs such as the **An Droichead Beag** (Small Bridge Bar; www.androicheadbeag.com; Lower Main St; ⏰3pm-2.30am Mon-Thu, from noon Fri & Sat, to 1.30am Sun), where sessions kick off at 9.30pm nightly, and standout seafood at its restaurants.

🍴 🏠 p45, p59, p195, p257

The Drive » West of Dingle, along the R559, the signposted Slea Head Drive runs around the tip of the Dingle Peninsula. Driving clockwise offers the best views and although it's a mere 47km in length, doing this stretch justice requires a full day, at least.

TRIP HIGHLIGHT

❹ Slea Head

Overlooking the mouth of Dingle Bay, Mt Eagle and Ireland's most westerly islands, the Blaskets, Slea Head has fine beaches and superbly preserved structures from Dingle's ancient past, including beehive huts, forts, inscribed stones and monastic sites.

The nearby village of **Ventry** (Ceann Trá), 6km west of Dingle town, is idyllically set next to a wide sandy bay. Full-day boat trips to the Blasket Islands with **Blasket Islands Eco Marine Tours** (📞086 335 3805; www.marinetours.ie; Ventry Pier, Ventry; full-/half-day tour €70/55; ⏰Apr-Oct) depart from Ventry Harbour, with three hours ashore on Great Blasket; shorter trips are available. The **Celtic & Prehistoric Museum** (📞087 770 3280; Kilvicadownig, Ventry; €5; ⏰10am-5.30pm mid-Mar–Oct; 🅿), 4km southwest of the village, squeezes in

An Droichead Beag pub, Dingle Town

an incredible collection of Celtic and prehistoric artefacts.

About 4.5km further west, the **Fahan beehive huts** (Fahan; adult/child €3/ free; ☺8am-7pm Easter-Sep, shorter hours Oct-Easter) sit on the on the inland side of the road. Fahan once had some 48 drystone *clochán* beehive huts dating from AD 500, although the exact dates are unknown. Today five structures remain, including two that are fully intact. The huts are on the slope of Mt Eagle (516m), which still has an estimated 400-plus huts in various states of preservation.

The Drive » Continuing north from Slea Head for just over 2km brings you to Dunmore Head, the westernmost point on the Irish mainland and the site of tiny but pretty Coumeenoole beach. From here it's around 3km to Dunquin.

- - - - - - - - - - - - - - - -

⑤ Dunquin

Yet another pause on a road of scenic pauses, Dunquin is a scattered village beneath Mt Eagle and Croaghmarhin.

The Blasket Islands (now uninhabited) are visible offshore. Dunquin's **Blasket Centre** (Ionad an Bhlascaoid Mhóir; ☎066-915 6444; www.blasket. ie; adult/child €5/3; ☺10am-6pm Easter-Oct; Ⓟ) is a wonderful interpretive centre with a floor-to-ceiling window overlooking the islands. Great Blasket Island's past community of storytellers and musicians is profiled, along with its literary visitors such as John Millington Synge, writer of *Playboy of the Western World*. The practicalities of island life are covered by exhibits on shipbuilding and fishing. There's a cafe with Blasket views and a bookshop.

The Drive >> North from Dunquin is Clogher Head; a short walk takes you out to the head, with stunning views to Sybil Head and the Three Sisters. Follow the road another 500m around to the crossroads, where a narrow paved track leads to Clogher beach. Back on the loop road, head inland towards Ballyferriter (about 9km in all).

 Ballyferriter

Housed in the 19th-century schoolhouse in the village of Ballyferriter (Baile an Fheirtearaigh), the **Dingle Peninsula Museum** (Músaem Chorca Dhuibhne; ☎066-915 6333; www.westkerrymuseum.com; Ballyferriter; admission by donation; ⏰10am-5pm Easter & Jun–mid-Sep, by appointment rest of year; P) has displays on the peninsula's archaeology and ecology. Across the street

there's a lonely, lichen-covered church.

The remains of the 5th- or 6th-century **Riasc Monastic Settlement** are an impressive, haunting sight, particularly the pillar with beautiful Celtic designs. Excavations have also revealed the foundations of an oratory first built with wood and later stone, a kiln for drying corn and a cemetery. The ruins are signposted as 'Mainistir Riaisc' along a narrow lane off the R559, about 2km east of Ballyferriter.

The Drive >> The landscape around Ballyferriter is a rocky patchwork of varying shades of green, stitched by miles and miles of ancient stone walls. Wind your way along the R559 some 2km east of the Riasc Monastic Settlement turn-off to reach an amazing dry-stone oratory.

TRIP HIGHLIGHT

7 Gallarus Oratory

The dry-stone **Gallarus Oratory** (www.heritageireland.ie; P) is quite a sight, standing in its lonely spot beneath the brown hills as it has done for some 1200 years. It has withstood the elements perfectly, apart from a slight sagging in the roof. Traces of mortar suggest that the interior and exterior walls may have been plastered. Shaped like an upturned boat, it has a doorway on the western side and a round-headed window on the east. Inside the doorway are two projecting stones with holes that once supported the door.

The Drive >> Pass back through Dingle town before cutting across the scenic Connor Pass to reach the northern side of the peninsula. About 6km before you reach Kilcummin, a narrow road leads north to the quiet villages of Cloghane (23km) and Brandon, and finally to Brandon Point overlooking Brandon Bay.

---

8 Cloghane

Cloghane (An Clochán) is another little piece of peninsula beauty. The village's friendly pubs nestle between Mt Brandon and Brandon Bay, with views across the water to the Stradbally Mountains. For many, the main goal is scaling 951m-high **Mt Brandon**

DETOUR: DÚN AN ÓIR FORT

Start: ⑤ **Dunquin**

En route between Dunquin and Ballyferriter, turn north 1km east of Clogher, from where narrow roads run to the east of the Dingle Golf Links course to **Dún an Óir Fort** (Fort of Gold), the scene of a hideous massacre during the 1580 Irish rebellion against English rule. All that remains is a network of grassy ridges, but it's a pretty spot overlooking sheltered Smerwick Harbour.

The fort is about 6km from Clogher. Return on the same road to just south of the golf course and turn east to rejoin the R559 and continue to Ballyferriter.

(Cnoc Bhréannain), Ireland's eighth-highest peak. If that sounds too energetic, there are plenty of coastal strolls.

The 5km drive from Cloghane out to **Brandon Point** follows ever-narrower single-track roads wandered by sheep, culminating in cliffs with fantastic views south and east.

On the last weekend in July, Cloghane celebrates the ancient Celtic harvest festival **Lughnasa** with events – especially bonfires – both in the village and atop Mt Brandon. The **Brandon Regatta**, a traditional *currach* (rowing boat race), takes place in late August.

The Drive » Retrace your route to Cloghane and head east to Kilcummin (7km) and continue a further 7km east to Castlegregory, the Dingle Peninsula's water-sports playground.

of Ireland's best diving areas, where you can glimpse pilot whales, orcas, sunfish and dolphins. Professional dive shop **Waterworld** (☑066-713 9292; www. waterworld.ie; Harbour House, Scraggane Pier; ☺9am-6pm year-round) is based at Harbour House in Fahamore. **Jamie Knox Watersports** (☑066-713 9411; www.jamieknox.com; Sandy Bay; equipment rental per hour €5-15; ☺lessons Apr-Oct, shop year-round) offers surf, windsurf, kitesurf, canoe and pedalo hire and lessons.

 p195

The Drive » Continue east on the R560 for 4km then turn right and follow signs to one of the Dingle Peninsula's least-known gems, the Glanteenassig Forest Recreation Area.

⑩ Glanteenassig Forest Recreation Area

Encompassing 450 hectares of forest, mountains, lakes and bog, **Glanteenassig Forest Recreation Area** (www. coillte.ie/site/glanteenassig; ☺8am-10pm May-Aug, to 6pm Sep-Apr) is a magical, little-visited treasure. There are two lakes; you can drive right up to the higher lake, which is encircled by a plank boardwalk, though it's too narrow for wheelchairs or prams.

The Drive » From Glanteenassig Forest Recreation Area, return to the main road and head east through the village of Aughacasla – home to the wonderful Seven Hogs inn – on the coast road (R560), which links up with the N86 to Blennerville (27km in total).

----

⑨ Castlegregory

A highlight of the quiet village of Castlegregory (Caislean an Ghriare) is the vista to the rugged hills to the south (a lowlight is the sprawl of philistine holiday homes).

However, things change when you drive up the sand-strewn road along the **Rough Point Peninsula**, the broad spit of land between Tralee Bay and Brandon Bay. Great underwater visibility makes this one

CONNOR PASS

At 456m, Connor (or Conor) Pass is Ireland's highest motor road. On a foggy day you'll see nothing but the road just in front of you, but in fine weather it offers phenomenal views of Dingle Harbour to the south and Mt Brandon to the north. The road is in good shape, despite being very narrow and *very* steep on the north side (large signs portend doom for buses and trucks).

The car park at the pass yields views down to a scatter of lakes in the rock-strewn valley below, plus the remains of walls and huts where people once lived impossibly hard lives. When visibility is good, the 10-minute climb west to the summit of An Bhinn Dubh (478m) is well worthwhile for the kind of vistas that inspire mountain climbers.

⑪ Blennerville

Blennerville, just over 1km southwest of Tralee on the N86, used to be the city's chief port, though the harbour has long since silted up. A 19th-century **windmill** (☎066-712 1064; www.blennerville-windmill.ie; Blennerville; adult/child €7/3; ⏰9am-6pm Jun-Aug, 9.30am-5.30pm Apr, May, Sep & Oct; **P**) here has been restored and is the largest working flour mill in Ireland and Britain. Its modern visitor centre houses an exhibition on grain milling and on the thousands of emigrants who boarded 'coffin ships' from what was then Kerry's largest embarkation point. Admission includes a 30-minute guided windmill tour.

The Drive » Staying on the N86 brings you into the heart of Tralee.

⑫ Tralee

Although Tralee is Kerry's county town, it's more engaged with the business of everyday life than the tourist trade. Elegant Denny St and Day Pl are the oldest parts of town, with 18th-century buildings, while the Square, just south of the Mall, is a pleasant, open contemporary space hosting **farmers markets** (liveliest on Saturday).

A 15-minute nature-safari boat ride is the highlight of a visit to Tralee's **wetlands centre** (☎066-712 6700; www.traleebaywetlands.org; Ballyard Rd; adult/child €5/2, guided tour €10/5; ⏰10am-7pm Jul & Aug, to 5pm Sep, Oct & Mar-Jun, 11am-4pm Nov-Feb; **P** 🚻). You can also get a good overview of Tralee Bay Nature Reserve's 3000 hectares, encompassing saltwater and freshwater habitats, from the 20m-high viewing tower (accessible by lift/elevator), and spot wildlife from bird hides.

In Ireland and beyond, Tralee is synonymous with the **Rose of Tralee** (www.roseoftralee.ie) beauty pageant, open to Irish women and women of Irish descent from around the world (the 'roses'). It takes place amid five days of celebrations in August.

An absolute treat is the **Kerry County Museum** (☎066-712 7777; www.kerrymuseum.ie; 18 Denny St; adult/child €5/free; ⏰9.30am-5.30pm Jun-Aug, to 5pm Tue-Sat Sep-May), with excellent interpretive displays on Irish historical events and trends. The Medieval Experience recreates life (smells and all) in Tralee in 1450.

Ingeniously converted from a terrace house, **Roundy's** (5 Broguemakers Lane; ⏰6pm-midnight Thu-Sun) is Tralee's hippest little bar, spinning old-school funk, while **Baily's Corner** (30 Lower Castle St; ⏰9am-11.30pm Mon-Thu, to 12.30am Fri & Sat, 4-11pm Sun; 🎵) is deservedly popular for its traditional sessions.

🛏 p195

Eating & Sleeping

Killarney ①

✖ Treyvaud's Irish €€

(📞064-663 3062; www.treyvaudsrestaurant. com; 62 High St; mains €10-30; ⊗5-10pm Mon, from noon Tue-Thu & Sun, to 10.30pm Fri & Sat) Mustard-fronted Treyvaud's has a strong reputation for subtle dishes that merge trad Irish with European influences. The seafood chowder – a velvet stew of mussels, prawns and Irish salmon – makes a filling lunch; dinner mains incorporating local ingredients include roast cod with horseradish mash and tomato-and-caper salsa, and a hearty beef and Guinness stew.

🛏 Fairview Guesthouse €€€

(📞064-663 4164; www.fairviewkillarney. com; College St; s/d/f from €199/229/239; 🅿@🛜) Reflected in polished wooden floors, the individually decorated rooms (some with classical printed wallpaper, some with contemporary sofas and glass) at this boutique guesthouse offer more bang for your buck than bigger, less personal places.

Dingle Town ③

✖ John Benny's Pub Food €€

(📞066-915 1215; www.johnbennyspub.com; Strand St; mains €13-20; ⊗noon-11pm, kitchen to 9.30pm) A toasty cast-iron wood stove, stone slab floor, memorabilia on the walls, great staff and no intrusive TV make this one of Dingle's most enjoyable traditional pubs. Glenbeigh oysters and Cromane mussels are highlights of its excellent pub menu. Local musos pour in most nights for trad sessions.

✖ Out of the Blue Seafood €€€

(📞066-915 0811; www.outoftheblue.ie; The Wood; mains €19-39; ⊗5-9.30pm Mon-Sat, 12.30-3pm & 5-9.30pm Sun) Occupying a bright blue-and-yellow waterfront fishing shack, this rustic spot is one of Dingle's top restaurants, with an intense devotion to fresh local seafood (and only seafood). If staff don't like the catch, they don't open, and they resolutely don't serve chips. Highlights might include Dingle Bay prawn bisque with lobster or chargrilled whole sea bass flambéed in cognac.

🛏 An Capall Dubh B&B €€

(📞066-915 1105; www.ancapalldubh.com; Green St; d/tw/f €130/130/180; 🅿🛜) Entered via a 19th-century coaching gateway leading into a cobbled courtyard where breakfast is served in fine weather, this airy B&B has five simple rooms furnished with light timbers and checked fabrics.

🛏 Pax House B&B €€€

(📞066-915 1518; www.pax-house.com; Upper John St; d €130-230; ⊗Mar-Dec; 🅿🛜) From its highly individual decor (including contemporary paintings) to the outstanding views over the estuary from the glass-framed terrace and balconies opening from some rooms, Pax House is a treat. Breakfast incorporates produce grown in its own garden; families can be accommodated with fold-out beds.

Castlegregory ⑨

✖ Gregory's Garden Irish €€

(📞087 213 0866; Main St, Castlegregory; mains €16-26; ⊗5.30-9pm Wed-Sun May-Sep) This cute cottage restaurant in the middle of Castlegregory village takes the claims of 'locally sourced produce' very seriously indeed, pairing the likes of Dingle-whiskey-cured salmon, Kerry lamb and Brandon Bay crab with vegetables, herbs and salad leaves plucked from the chef's very own kitchen garden.

Tralee ⑫

🛏 Meadowlands Hotel Hotel €€

(📞066-718 0444; www.meadowlandshotel. com; Oakpark Rd; s/d/f from €95/125/178; 🅿🛜) Strolling distance from town but far enough away to be quiet, Meadowlands is an unexpectedly romantic four-star hotel with stunning vintage-meets-designer public areas. Rooms have autumnal hues and service is spot-on. Its beamed-ceilinged bar (mains €13 to €29), serving top-notch seafood (the owners have their own fishing fleet), is popular with locals and visitors.

Classic Trip

Southwest Blitz

17

Catch the very best of Ireland's southwest along this classic route as it curls from Killarney around the Ring of Kerry coast and across County Cork's lush countryside to charming Dungarvan.

TRIP HIGHLIGHTS

139 km

Kenmare
Board a seal-spotting cruise accompanied by sea shanties

265 km

Cork
Thriving, cultured metropolis made glorious by its location

Killorglin

START
Killarney

FINISH
Dungarvan

Youghal

Cobh

183 km

Bantry
Visit Bantry House gardens' enormous 'stairway to the sky'

Caherdaniel
Lush gardens at Derrynane's historic park

92 km

4 DAYS
369KM / 229 MILES

GREAT FOR...

BEST TIME TO GO
Late spring and early autumn for the best weather and manageable crowds.

ESSENTIAL PHOTO
The view from Beenarourke across rocky coastline and scattered islands.

BEST FOR FAMILIES
Ride the train or stroll around animal-filled Fota Wildlife Park.

17 Southwest Blitz

This drive around the country's stunning southwest conjures up iconic impressions of Ireland: soaring stone castles, dizzying sea cliffs, wide, sandy beaches, crystal-clear lakes, dense woodlands and boat-filled harbours. Villages you'll encounter en route spill over with brightly painted buildings, vibrant markets and cosy pubs with toe-tapping live music, perfectly poured pints and fantastic craic.

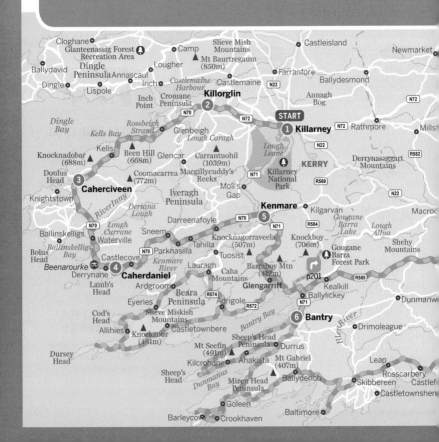

❶ Killarney

Killarney's biggest attraction, in every sense, is Killarney National Park (p188), with magnificent Muckross Estate at its heart. If you're not doing the classic Ring of Kerry route that brings you through the park, you should definitely consider a detour here. Right in town, there are pedestrian entrances to the park opposite **St Mary's Cathedral** (www.killarneyparish.com; Cathedral Pl; ⏲8am-6.30pm), a superb example of neo-Gothic revival architecture, built between 1842 and 1855.

Also worth a visit in the town centre is the 1860s **Franciscan Friary** (www.franciscans. ie; Fair Hill; ⏲8am-8pm), with an ornate Flemish-style altarpiece, some impressive tilework and, most notably, stained-glass windows by Harry Clarke. The Dublin artist's organic style was influenced by art nouveau, art deco and symbolism.

Plunkett and College Sts are lined with pubs;

LINK YOUR TRIP

13 **Blackwater Valley Drive**

Youghal is the starting point for a glorious drive through the Blackwater Valley.

19 **West Cork Villages**

From Cork city, it's a quick 27km trip south to Kinsale to wind your way around West Cork's picturesque peninsulas.

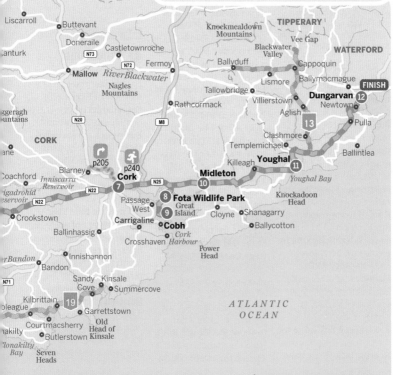

behind leaded-glass doors, tiny traditional **O'Connor's** (www.oconnors traditionalpub.ie; 7 High St; ⊙ noon-11.30pm Sun-Thu, to 12.30am Fri & Sat; 🔊) is one of Killarney's most popular haunts, with live music every night.

🍴 🛏 p45, p185, p195

The Drive » It's 22km west to Killorglin on the N72. To visit the too-gorgeous-for-words Gap of Dunloe, after 5km turn south onto Gap Rd and follow it for 3km to Kate Kearney's Cottage, where many drivers park in order to walk up to the Gap. You can also hire ponies and jaunting cars here (bring cash).

- - - - - - - - - - - - - - - -

❷ Killorglin

Unless you're here during mid-August's ancient Puck Fair (p178), the main reason to pause at the pretty riverside town of Killorglin (Cill Orglan) is its excellent selection of eateries. These become rather more scarce on the Ring of Kerry coast road until you get to Kenmare, so considering picking up picnic fare here, too.

At smokery **KRD Fisheries** (📞066-976 1106; www.krdfisheries.com; Tralee Rd; ⊙9am-1pm & 2-5pm Mon-Fri, to 1pm Sat, to 11am Sun) you can buy salmon direct from the premises. Nearby, Jack Healy bakes

amazing breads and also makes pâté and beautiful sandwiches at Jack's Bakery (p178).

🍴 p185, p207

The Drive » It's 40km from Killorglin to Cahersiveen. En route, you'll pass the turn-off to the little-known Cromane Peninsula, with a truly exceptional restaurant, as well as the quaint and insightful Kerry Bog Village Museum and the turn-off to Rossbeigh Strand, with dazzling views north to the Dingle Peninsula.

- - - - - - - - - - - - - - - -

❸ Cahersiveen

The ruined cottage on the eastern bank of the Carhan River, on the left as you cross the bridge to Cahersiveen, is the humble birthplace of Daniel O'Connell (1775–1847). On the opposite bank there's a stolid bust of the man. Known as 'the Great Liberator', O'Connell was elected to the British Parliament in 1828, but as a Catholic he couldn't take his seat. The government was forced to pass the 1829 Act of Catholic Emancipation, allowing some well-off Catholics voting rights and the right to be elected as MPs. Learn more about it at the **Old Barracks Heritage Centre** (📞066-401 0430; www.theoldbarracks cahersiveen.com; Bridge St; adult/child €4/2; ⊙10am-5pm Mon-Sat, 11am-4pm Sun Mar-Nov; 🅿), housed in a tower of the former Royal Irish Constabulary (RIC). The barracks were burnt

down in 1922 by anti-Treaty forces.

Ballycarbery Castle and ring forts are located here; Cahersiveen is also a jumping-off point for exploring Valentia Island and the Skellig Ring.

The Drive » Continue from Cahersiveen for 17km along the N70 to Waterville. From Waterville the rugged, rocky coastline is at its most dramatic as the road twists, turns and twists again along the 12km stretch to Caherdaniel. At Beenarourke, the highest point of the road, you can stop to enjoy what is plausibly claimed to be 'Ireland's finest view', looking across the rocky coastline and scattered islands to Kenmare River, Bantry Bay and the rugged hills of the Beara Peninsula.

- - - - - - - - - - - - - - - -

TRIP HIGHLIGHT

❹ Caherdaniel

Hiding between Derrynane Bay and the foothills of Eagles Hill, Caherdaniel barely qualifies as a tiny hamlet. Businesses are scattered about the undergrowth like smugglers, which is fitting since this was once a haven for the same.

There's a Blue Flag **beach**, plenty of activities, good hikes and pubs where you may be tempted to break into pirate talk.

Sublime **Derrynane National Historic Park** (📞066-947 5113; www.derry nanehouse.ie; Derrynane; adult/child €5/3; ⊙10.30am-6pm mid-Mar–Sep, 10am-5pm

Oct, to 4pm Sat & Sun Nov–early-Dec; **P**) incorporates **Derrynane House**, the ancestral home of Daniel O'Connell, whose family made money smuggling from their base by the dunes Its **gardens** are astonishing, warmed by the Gulf Stream, with palms, 4m-high tree ferns, gunnera ('giant rhubarb') and other South American species. A **walking track** through the gardens leads to wetlands, beaches and cliff tops.

The Drive >> The N70 zigzags for 21km northeast to the quaint, colourful little village of Sneem. This area is home to one of the finest castle hotels in the country, the Parknasilla Resort and Spa. It's a further 27km drive along the N70 to Kenmare.

TRIP HIGHLIGHT

5 Kenmare

Set around its triangular market square, the sophisticated town of Kenmare is stunningly situated by Kenmare Bay.

Reached through the tourist office, the **Kenmare Heritage Centre** (☎064-664 1233; The Square; ⌚10am-5.30pm Mon-Sat Apr-Oct, by appointment Nov-Mar) tells the history of the town from its founding as Neidín by the swashbuckling Sir William Petty in 1670. The centre also relates the story of the Poor Clare Convent, founded in 1861, which is still standing behind Holy Cross Church.

Local women were taught needlepoint lacemaking at the convent and their lacework catapulted Kenmare to international fame. Upstairs from the Heritage Centre, the **Kenmare Lace and Design Centre** has displays, including designs for 'the most important piece of lace ever made in Ireland' (in a 19th-century critic's opinion).

Star Outdoors (☎064-664 1222; www.staroutdoors.ie; Dauros) offers activities such as dinghy sailing (from €65 per hour for up to six people; you'll need some prior experience), sea kayaking (single/double per hour €22/38) and hill walking for all levels.

Warm yourself with tea, coffee, rum and the captain's sea shanties on

DETOUR:
GOUGANE BARRA FOREST PARK

Start: 6 Bantry

Almost alpine in feel, **Gougane Barra** (www.gouganebarra.com) is a truly magical part of inland County Cork, with spectacular vistas of craggy mountains, silver streams and pine forests sweeping down to a mountain lake that is the source of the River Lee. St Finbarre, the founder of Cork, established a monastery here in the 6th century. He had a hermitage on the island in Gougane Barra Lake (Lough an Ghugain), which is now approached by a short causeway. The small chapel on the island has fine stained-glass representations of obscure Celtic saints. A loop road runs through the park, with plenty of opportunities to walk the well-marked network of paths and nature trails through the forest.

The only place to air your hiking boots is the **Gougane Barra Hotel** (☎026-47069; www.gouganebarrahotel.com; s/d from €79/122; ⌚Apr-Oct; **P 🛜**). There's an on-site restaurant (daytime snacks €6 to €10, two-/three-course dinner menus €26.50/33.50), a cafe and a pub next door.

To reach the forest park, turn off the N71 onto the R584 about 6km north of Bantry and follow it northeast for 23km. Retrace your route to the N71 to continue back to Bantry and on to Cork City.

WHY THIS IS A CLASSIC TRIP
NEIL WILSON, WRITER

Journeying from Killarney to Dungarvan, this trip not only incorporates all of Ireland's definitive elements but also plenty of unexpected ones, from the *Titanic*'s fateful final port to exotic animals roaming free in an island-set zoo to a spine-tingling 9th-century prison – as well as countless opportunities for serendipitous detours (because, of course, serendipity is what makes a road trip a true classic).

Above: Bantry House, County Cork
Left: Giraffes, Fota Wildlife Park, County Cork
Right: Cork City Gaol

an entertaining two-hour voyage with **Seafari** (☎064-664 2059; www.sea fariireland.com; Kenmare Pier; adult/child €25/12.50; ☺Apr-Oct; 👪) to spot Ireland's biggest seal colony and other marine life. Binoculars (and lollipops!) are provided.

✕ 🛏 p45, p59, p207

The Drive » Leave the Ring of Kerry at Kenmare and take the steep and winding N71 south for 44km to Bantry. For an even more scenic alternative, consider driving via the Ring of Beara, encircling the Beara Peninsula. If you don't have time to do the entire Ring, a shorter option is to cut across the Beara's spectacular Healy Pass Rd (R574).

- - - - - - - - - - - - - - -

TRIP HIGHLIGHT

6 Bantry

Framed by the craggy Caha Mountains, sweeping Bantry Bay is an idyllic inlet famed for its oysters and mussels. One kilometre southwest of the centre of bustling market town Bantry is **Bantry House** (☎027-50047; www.bantryhouse.com; Bantry Bay; house & garden adult/child €11/3, garden only €6/free; ☺10am-5pm daily Jun-Aug, Tue-Sun mid-Apr–May, Sep & Oct; P), the former home of Richard White, who earned his place in history when in 1798 he warned authorities of the imminent landing of patriot Wolfe Tone and his French fleet to join the countrywide rebellion of the

Classic Trip

United Irishmen. Storms prevented the fleet from landing, altering the course of Irish history. The house's **gardens** and the panoramic 'stairway to the sky' are its great glory, and it hosts the week-long **West Cork Chamber Music Festival** (www.westcorkmusic. ie) in June/July, when it closes to the public (the garden, craft shop and tearoom remain open).

🍴 p207, 223

The Drive » Head north on the N71 to Ballylickey and take the R584 and R585 to Crookstown, then the N22 through rugged terrain softening to patchwork farmland along the 86km journey to Cork city.

TRIP HIGHLIGHT

⑦ Cork City

Ireland's second city is first in every important respect, at least according to the locals, who cheerfully refer to it as the 'real capital of Ireland'.

A flurry of urban renewal has resulted in new buildings, bars and arts centres and tidied-up thoroughfares. The best of the city is still happily traditional, though – snug pubs with regular live-music sessions, excellent local produce in an ever-expanding list of restaurants and a genuinely proud welcome from the locals.

Cork swings during the **Guinness Jazz Festival** (www.facebook. com/corkjazzfestival), with an all-star line-up in venues across town in late October. An eclectic week-long program of international films screens in October/November during the **Cork Film Festival** (www.corkfilm-fest.org).

About 2km west of the city centre, faint-hearted souls may find the imposing former prison, **Cork City Gaol** (☏021-430 5022; www.corkcitygaol. com; Convent Ave; adult/ child €10/6; ☺9.30am-5pm Apr-Sep, 10am-4pm Oct-Mar), grim but it's actually very moving, bringing home the harshness of the 19th-century penal system. An audio tour guides you around the restored cells, with models of suffering prisoners and sadistic-looking guards. The most common crime was simply poverty, with many of the inmates sentenced to hard labour for stealing loaves of bread. The prison closed in 1923, reopening in 1927 as a radio station – the Governor's House has been converted into a Radio Museum (€2).

🍴 🛏 p59, p207, p215, p257

The Drive » Head east of central Cork via the N8 and N25, and take the turn-off to Cobh to cross the bridge to Fota Island and reach Fota Wildlife Park (18km).

---

⑧ Fota Wildlife Park

Kangaroos bound, monkeys and gibbons leap and scream on wooded islands, and cheetahs run without a cage or fence in sight at the huge outdoor **Fota Wildlife Park** (☏021-481 2678; www.fotawildlife. ie; Carrigtwohill, Fota Island; adult/child €16.70/11.20, parking €3; ☺10am-6pm; P ♿).

A tour train (one way/ return €1/2) runs a circuit round the park every 15 minutes in high season, but the 2km circular walk offers a more close-up experience.

From the wildlife park, you can stroll to the Regency-style **Fota House** (☏021-481 5543; www.fota-house.com; house tours adult/ child €9/3.50, house & gardens €13.50/6; ☺10am-5pm daily Mar-Sep, Sat & Sun Feb & Oct-Dec; P). The mostly barren interior contains a fine kitchen and ornate plasterwork ceilings; interactive displays bring the rooms to life.

Attached to the house is the 150-year-old **arboretum**, which has a Victorian fernery, a magnolia walk and some beautiful trees, including giant redwoods and a Chinese ghost tree.

The Drive » From Fota Wildlife Park, head south for 5km to Cobh.

---

9 Cobh

For many years Cobh (pronounced 'cove') was the port of Cork. During the Famine, some 2.5 million people left Ireland through the glistening estuary. In 1838 the *Sirius,* the first steamship to cross the Atlantic, sailed from Cobh, and the *Titanic* made its final stop here in 1912.

The original White Star Line offices, where 123 passengers embarked on the *Titanic's* final voyage now houses the unmissable **Titanic Experience Cobh** (📞021-481 4412; www.titanicexperience cobh.ie; 20 Casement Sq; adult/child €10/7; ⏰9am-6pm Apr-Sep, 10am-5.30pm Oct-Mar; 🚻). Admission is by tour, which is partly guided and partly interactive, with holograms, audiovisual presentations and exhibits.

Standing dramatically above Cobh, the massive French Gothic **St Colman's Cathedral** (📞021-481 3222; www.cobh-cathedralparish.ie; Cathedral Pl; admission by donation; ⏰8am-6pm May-Oct, to 5pm Nov-Apr) is out of all proportion to the town. Its 47-bell carillon, the largest in Ireland, weighs a stonking 3440kg.

In 1849 Cobh was renamed Queenstown after Queen Victoria paid a visit; the name lasted until Irish independence in 1921. Housed in the old train station, **Cobh, The Queenstown Story** (📞021-481 3591; www.cobh-heritage.com; Lower Rd; adult/child €10/6; ⏰9.30am-6pm mid-Apr–mid-Oct, 9.30am-5pm Mon-Sat & 11am-5pm Sun mid-Oct–mid-Apr) has exhibits evoking the Famine tragedy, a genealogy centre and a cafe.

🛏 p207

The Drive » Travel north on the R624 then east on the N25 to Midleton (18km in total).

---

10 Midleton

The number-one attraction in Midleton is the

DETOUR:
BLARNEY CASTLE

Start: 7 Cork City

If you need proof of the power of a good yarn, join the queue to get into the 15th-century **Blarney Castle** (📞021-438 5252; www.blarneycastle.ie; Blarney; adult/child €18/8; ⏰9am-7pm Mon-Sat, to 6pm Sun Jun-Aug, shorter hours Sep-May; 🅿), one of Ireland's most inexplicably popular tourist attractions. Queen Elizabeth I is said to have invented the term 'to talk blarney' out of exasperation with Lord Blarney's ability to talk endlessly without ever actually agreeing to her demands.

The clichéd **Blarney Stone** is perched at the top of a steep climb up a slippery spiral staircases. On the battlements, you bend backwards over a long, long drop (with safety grill and attendant to prevent tragedy) to kiss the stone (an act which is said to confer on you the gift of eloquence). Once you're upright, don't forget to admire the stunning views before descending.

If the throngs get too much, vanish into the Rock Close, part of the beautiful and often ignored gardens.

Head out of central Cork via Merchant's Quay and the N20; Blarney is about 10km northwest of the city.

former whiskey distillery now housing the **Jameson Experience** (☎021-461 3594; www.jamesonwhiskey.com; Old Distillery Walk; tours adult/child €22/11; ⏰ shop 10am-6pm; Ⓟ), where you can learn how Irish whiskey is made. Attractive cafes, restaurants and a great farmers market (p214) make it worth stopping for a while.

The Drive » Continue east on the N25 for the 28km drive to Youghal.

⑪ Youghal

The ancient seaport of Youghal (Eochaill; pronounced 'yawl'), at the mouth of the River Blackwater, was a hotbed of rebellion against the English in the 16th century. Oliver Cromwell wintered here in 1649 as he sought to drum up support for his war in England and quell insurgence from the Irish. Youghal was granted to Sir Walter Raleigh during the Elizabethan Plantation of Munster.

The curious **Clock Gate** was built in 1777 and served as a clock tower and jail concur-rently; several prisoners taken in the 1798 Rising were hanged from its windows.

Main St has an interesting curve that follows the original shore; many of the shopfronts are from the 19th century. Further up the street are six almshouses built by Englishman Richard Boyle, who bought Raleigh's Irish estates and became the first earl of Cork in 1616 in recognition of his work in creating 'a very excellent colony'. Across the road is the 15th-century tower house, **Tynte's Castle**, which originally had a defensive riverfront position before the River Blackwater silted up and changed course.

Built in 1220, **St Mary's Collegiate Church** incorporates elements of an earlier Danish church dating back to the 11th century. The churchyard is bounded by a fine stretch of the 13th-century town wall and one of the remaining turrets.

Beside the church, **Myrtle Grove** (not open to the public) is the former home of Sir Walter Raleigh, and a rare Irish example of a late medieval Tudor-style house.

✕ ⌷ p157

The Drive » Rejoin the N25 and cross the River Blackwater.

Continue following the N25 northeast for the final run to Dungarvan, a 31km trip in all.

⑫ Dungarvan

One of Ireland's most enchanting coastal towns, pastel-shaded Dungarvan is best known by its foodie reputation, but there are some intriguing sights, too. On the waterfront, **Dungarvan Castle** (☎058-48144; www.heritageireland.ie; Castle St; ⏰10am-6pm late May-late Sep) dates back to the 12th century. Admission is by (free) guided tour only.

Housed in a handsome building dating from the 17th century, the **Old Market House Arts Centre** (☎058-48944; www.facebook.com/oldmarkethouse; Lower Main/Parnell St; ⏰11am-1.30pm & 2.30-5pm Tue-Fri, 1-5pm Sat, hours can vary) showcases contemporary art by local artists.

The **Waterford County Museum** (☎058-45960; www.waterfordmuseum.ie; 2 St Augustine St; ⏰10am-5pm Mon-Fri) covers maritime heritage (with relics from shipwrecks), Famine history, local personalities and various other titbits, all displayed in an 18th-century grain store.

Eating & Sleeping

Killorglin ②

✕ Jacks' Coastguard Restaurant
Seafood €€€

(☏066-976 9102; www.jackscromane.com; Cromane; mains €19-36, 5-course tasting menu €65, 3-course Sun lunch €29; ☺6-9pm Thu-Sun, 1-3pm Sun, hours can vary; P 🖴) A door at the back of this village pub, housed in an 1886 coastguard station, leads to a striking contemporary restaurant with picture windows looking out across Castlemaine harbour to the Dingle hills. Seafood, such as steamed Cromane mussels, or Cajun-spiced monkfish, is the standout.

Kenmare ⑤

🛏 Sheen Falls Lodge
Historic Hotel €€€

(☏064-664 1600; www.sheenfallslodge.ie; Knockduragh; d/ste from €370/650; ☺Feb-Dec; P @ 🛜 🏊) The Marquis of Landsdowne's former summer residence still feels like an aristocrats' playground, with a fine-dining modern Irish restaurant, cocktail bar, spa, and 66 rooms and sumptuous suites with Italian-marble bathrooms.

Bantry ⑥

✕ Manning's Emporium
Cafe €

(☏027-50456; www.manningsemporium.ie; N71, Ballylickey; mains €8-13; ☺10am-5pm Sun-Thu, to 9pm Fri & Sat; P 🛜) This gourmet deli and cafe is an Aladdin's cave of West Cork's finest food. Grab a menu, choose a table, and order at the counter – tasting plates are the best way to sample the local artisan produce and farmhouse cheeses on offer. Foodie events take place regularly. It's on the N71 in Ballylickey (on the right approaching from Bantry).

Cork City ⑦

✕ Nash 19
International €€

(☏021-427 0880; www.nash19.com; Princes St; mains €12-22; ☺7.30am-4pm Mon-Fri, from 8.30am Sat) A superb bistro and deli where locally sourced food is honoured at breakfast and lunch, either sit-in or take away. Fresh scones draw crowds early; daily lunch specials (soups, salads, desserts etc), free-range chicken pie and platters of smoked fish from Belvelly Smokehouse (p214) keep them coming for lunch.

✕ Market Lane
Irish €€

(☏021-427 4710; www.marketlane.ie; 5 Oliver Plunkett St; mains €14-25; ☺noon-9.30pm Mon-Wed, to 10pm Thu, to 10.30pm Fri & Sat, 1-9.30pm Sun; 🛜 🖴) It's always hopping at this bright corner bistro. The menu is broad and hearty, changing to reflect what's fresh at the English Market: perhaps roast hake with wild garlic velouté, or beetroot, walnut and feta cakes?

🛏 Auburn House
B&B €€

(☏021-450 8555; www.auburnguesthouse.com; 3 Garfield Tce, Wellington Rd; s/d €58/90; P 🛜) There's a warm family welcome at this neat B&B, which has smallish but well-kept rooms brightened by window boxes. Try to bag one of the back rooms, which are quieter and have sweeping views over the city. Breakfast includes vegetarian choices, and the location near the fun of MacCurtain St is a plus.

🛏 River Lee Hotel
Hotel €€€

(☏021-425 2700; www.doylecollection.com; Western Rd; r from €269; P 🛜 🏊) This modern riverside hotel brings a touch of luxury to the city centre. It has gorgeous public areas with huge sofas, a designer fireplace, a stunning five-storey glass-walled atrium and superb service. There are well-equipped bedrooms (nice and quiet at the back, but request a corner room for extra space) and possibly the best breakfast buffet in Ireland.

Cobh ⑨

🛏 Commodore Hotel
Hotel €€

(☏021-481 1277; www.commodorehotel.ie; 4 Westbourne Pl; s/d from €87/120; 🛜 🏊) A classic seaside hotel with soaring chandeliered hallways and 42 well-appointed rooms (it's worth paying extra for one with a sea view).

Southwestern Pantry

18

County Cork has earned itself a reputation as the gourmet capital of Ireland. Graze your way around the county on this foodie's fantasy while also feasting on its sumptuous scenery.

139 km

Belvelly
Sublime smoked salmon at Ireland's oldest smokehouse

126 km

Cork City
Cork's 1788-established English Market showcases the county's fare

START
Durrus

FINISH
Midleton

58 km

Clonakilty
Home to the country's most famous black pudding

Kinsale
Sensational seafood, food festivals and gourmet purveyors galore

100 km

5 DAYS
165KM / 103 MILES

GREAT FOR...

BEST TIME TO GO
Produce is at its most abundant from spring onwards.

ESSENTIAL PHOTO
Kinsale's boat-filled harbour is a picture.

☑ BEST FOR FOODIES
The English Market in Cork city showcases the county's tantalising bounty.

nsale Lobster thermidore at Fish Fishy

18 Southwestern Pantry

Farmers markets, farmhouse cheeses, fishing fleets hauling in fresh seafood, the country's oldest smokehouse and its most famous black pudding, as well as icons such as Cork's mouth-watering English Market, Jameson's old whiskey distillery, the wonderful Ballymaloe House and its prestigious cookery school, and some of the nation's finest eateries are among the treats awaiting in Ireland's southwestern pantry. *Bain taitneamh as do bhéil* (bon appétit)!

① Durrus

This little crossroads at the head of Dunmanus Bay has become something of a gourmet hotspot in recent years and earned an international reputation for the cheese produced by **Durrus Farmhouse** (☏027-61100; www.durruscheese.com; Coomkeen; ☺ by appointment 9am-1pm Mon-Fri). Its produce is sold all over Ireland and as far afield as America. You can visit by prior arrangement, and watch the cheese-making process through

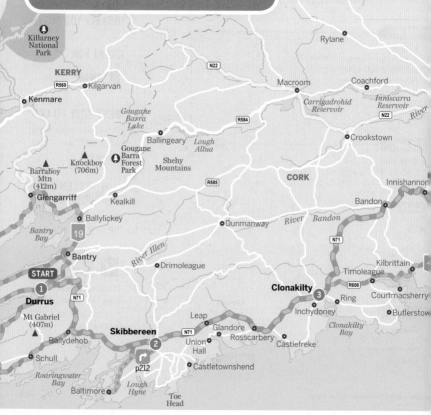

a viewing panel. To reach the farm, drive 900m out of Durrus along the Ahakista road, turn right at St James' Church and continue for 3km until you see the sign for the farm on the left.

The Drive » From Durrus, zigzag 30km southeast through wooded hills on the N71 to Skibbereen.

---

② Skibbereen

Try to time your journey through the busy market town of Skibbereen (Sciobairín) to catch the **farmers market** (www. skibbereenmarket.com; The Fairfield, Bridge St; ⊙9.30am-2pm Sat). If you're in town in mid-September, don't miss the **Taste of West Cork Food Festival** (www.atasteofwestcork. com), with a lively market and events at local restaurants.

Popular one-day courses at **Good Things Cookery School** (www. goodthings.ie) include Whole Food and Vegan (€150), and Cooking the Basics (€200) for those whose kitchen skills extend no further than the microwave.

The Drive » It's 33km along the N71 from Skibbereen to Clonakilty; there are also slower but more scenic alternatives along the coast.

TRIP HIGHLIGHT

③ Clonakilty

Clonakilty is legendary as the birthplace of Michael Collins, commander-in-chief of the army of the Irish Free State that won independence from Britain in 1922. It's also home to the most famous black pudding in the country. The best place to buy the town's renowned blood sausage is **Edward Twomey** (☎023-883 4835; www.clonakilty blackpudding.ie; 16 Pearse St; ⊙9am-6pm Mon-Sat), with different varieties based on the original 1880s recipe. Look out for it too at Clonakilty's weekly **farmers market** (☎087 135 6848; www.facebook.com/ clonmarket; Pearse St; ⊙9am-3pm Fri).

LINK YOUR TRIP

13 **Blackwater Valley Drive**
Head 26km east along the N25 for more glorious food over the border in County Waterford.

19 **West Cork Villages**
Return to Kinsale to discover Cork's picturesque peninsulas.

The state-of-the-art **Clonakilty Distillery** (023-884 0635; www.clonakiltydistillery.ie; The Waterfront; tours from €15; ⊙noon-5.30pm Sun-Tue, 11am-6.30pm Wed-Sat; P 👫) opened its doors to the public in 2019, producing triple-distilled single pot still Irish whiskey made with grain grown on the owners' family farm nearby.

🍴 🛏 p215

The Drive ›› Continue 42km northeast along the N71 through farming country interspersed with towns and villages to Kinsale (alternatively you can take the slower and more scenic coastal R600 road for 35km).

❹ Kinsale

Harbour-set Kinsale (Cionn tSáile) is revered for its fine seafood restaurants thanks in large part to its busy fishing fleet. Tastings, meals and harbour cruises take place during Kinsale's two-day **Gourmet Festival** (www.kinsalerestaurants.com) in early October.

A weekly **farmers market** (📞085 722 0259; www.facebook.com/kinsale-farmersmarket; Short Quay; ⊙10am-2pm Wed) takes place in Short Quay. Handmade chocolates and crystallised orange and ginger are among the enticing wares at artisan chocolatier **Koko Kinsale** (📞087 611 0209; www.kokokinsale.com; Pier Rd; ⊙9am-5pm Mon-Sat, noon-5pm Sun).

Kinsale's roots in the wine trade are on display at the early-16th-century **Desmond Castle** (📞021-477 4855; www.heritageireland.ie; Cork St; adult/child €5/3; ⊙10am-6pm Apr-Sep), which houses a small **wine museum**.

🍴 🛏 p215

The Drive ›› Head north for 27km on the R600 through patchwork farmland to Ireland's second-largest city.

DETOUR: BALTIMORE

Start: ❷ Skibbereen

Not only does Baltimore, 13km south of Skibbereen on the R595, have aquatic activities galore, but its seafood is sublime.

Over the last full weekend of May, Baltimore's **Seafood Festival** (www.baltimore.ie/event/seafood-festival) sees jazz bands perform, wooden boats parade and pubs bring out free mussels and prawns.

The Lookout (Chez Youen; 📞028-20600; www.waterfrontbaltimore.ie; The Quay; mains €20-40; ⊙6.30-9.30pm Wed-Mon Aug, Wed-Sat Jun, Jul & Sep, Fri & Sat May) restaurant, upstairs at the Waterfront hotel, enjoys elevated sea views and serves luscious shellfish platters containing lobsters, prawns, brown crabs, velvet crabs, shrimps and oysters. Check opening times online.

The beautiful gardens at the **Glebe Gardens & Café** (📞028-20579; www.glebegardens.com; Skibbereen Rd; admission €5; mains €10-16; ⊙10am-5pm Wed-Sun Easter-Oct, Sat & Sun only Nov-Easter; P 📶) are an attraction in themselves. If you're dining, lavender and herbs add fragrant aromas that waft over the tables inside and out. Food is simple and fresh, and is sourced from the gardens and a list of local purveyors.

English Market, Cork City

5 Cork City

Cork's food scene is reason enough to visit. It sometimes seems you can't walk 100m through the city streets without bumping into a boutique coffee roaster, a farmhouse cheesemaker or an artisan baker.

Cork's **English Market** (www.englishmarket.ie; main entrance Princes St; ☺8am-6pm Mon-Sat) is a local – no, make that national – treasure. It could just as easily be called the Victorian Market for its ornate vaulted ceilings and columns. Scores of vendors sell some of the very best local produce, meats, cheeses and takeaway food in the region. Favourites include **On the Pig's Back** (☎021-427 0232; www.onthepigsback.ie; Unit 11, English Market; ☺8am-5.30pm Mon-Sat), serving house-made sausages and incredible cheeses.

On a mezzanine overlooking part of the market is one of Cork's best eateries. **Farmgate Café** (☎021-427 8134; www.farmgatecork.ie; mains €8-14; ☺8.30am-5pm Mon-Sat) is an unmissable experience. Everything from the rock oysters to the ingredients for Irish stew and raspberry crumble is sourced from the market below. The best seats are at the balcony counter overlooking the passing parade of shoppers. On fine days, picnic in nearby **Bishop Lucey Park**.

The narrow, pedestrianised streets in Cork's **Huguenot Quarter** north of St Patrick's St throng with cafes and restaurants with outside tables; many serve till late.

Don't leave Cork without sampling the heavenly Chocolatier's Hot Chocolate at confectioners **O'Connaill** (☎021-437 3407; www.oconaillchocolate.ie; 16B French Church St; ☺8.30am-7pm; 🔊).

✕ 🛏 p59, p207, p215, p257

The Drive » Some 19km east of Cork on the R624 towards Cobh is the feted Belvelly smokehouse.

- - - - - - - - - - - - - - - - -

TRIP HIGHLIGHT

❻ Belvelly

No trip to County Cork is complete without a visit to an artisan food producer, and the effervescent Frank Hederman is more than happy to show you around **Belvelly** (📋021-481 1089; www. frankhederman.com; Belvelly; free for individuals, charge for groups; ⏰ by reservation 10am-5pm Mon-Fri), the oldest natural smokehouse in Ireland. Seafood and cheese are smoked here, but the speciality is fish – in particular, salmon. In a traditional process that takes 24 hours from start to finish, the fish is filleted and cured before being hung in the tiny smokehouse over beech woodchips. Phone or email Frank to arrange your visit.

The Drive » It's just 14km from Belvelly to Midleton.

- - - - - - - - - - - - - - - - -

❼ Midleton

Aficionados of fine Irish whiskey will know the main reason to linger in this bustling market town is to visit the restored 200-year-old building housing the Jameson Experience (p206)... and purchase bottles of it, of course. Exhibits and tours explain the process of taking barley and creating whiskey (Jameson is today made in a modern factory in Cork).

Midleton's **farmers market** (Main St; ⏰9am-1pm Sat), behind the courthouse, is one of Cork's best markets, with bushels of local produce and producers who are happy to chat.

The original and sister establishment to Cork's Farmgate Café, **Farmgate Restaurant** (📋021-463 2771; www.farmgate.ie; Broderick St; mains lunch €13-20, dinner €20-30; ⏰9am-5pm Tue-Sat, 5.30-9.30pm Thu-Sat) also has a shop selling amazing baked goods and local, often organic, produce, cheeses and preserves.

DETOUR:
BALLYMALOE HOUSE & COOKERY SCHOOL

Start: ❼ **Midleton**

Drawing up at wisteria-clad **Ballymaloe House** (📋021-465 2531; www.ballymaloe. ie; Shanagarry; r from €280; 🅿🛜🏊🐾), 12km southeast of Midleton on the R629, you know you've arrived somewhere special. Rooms are period furnished and the beautiful grounds include a tennis court, swimming pool and shop. The menu at its celebrated restaurant is drawn up daily according to the produce available from Ballymaloe's extensive farms and other local sources. It also runs wine and gardening weekends.

Just over 3km further east (go through the village of Shanagarry and turn left opposite the church), TV personality Darina Allen runs the famous **Ballymaloe Cookery School** (📋021-464 6785; www.ballymaloecookeryschool.com; Shanagarry). Book lessons, starting from half-day sessions (€95 to €145), well in advance. There are pretty cottages for overnight students around the 40-hectare organic farm.

Eating & Sleeping

Clonakilty ❸

✗ Scannells — Modern Irish €€

(☎023-883 4116; www.scannellsbar.com; Connolly St; mains €12-16; ⏱food served noon-4pm Mon-Sat; 🛜) The sheltered, flower-filled garden at this gastropub is absolutely hopping, rain or shine, thanks to an ambitious menu that ranges from superb West Cork steak sandwich with hand-cut chips (or salad), to trad seafood chowder and organic salads with halloumi, chia seeds and toasted almonds.

⛱ Bay View House — B&B €€

(☎023-883 3539; www.bayviewclonakilty.com; Old Timoleague Rd; s/d from €55/90; 🅿🛜) This spacious modern villa offers immaculate B&B accommodation, a genial welcome and great breakfasts. Rooms 5 and 6 and the cosy landing lounge offer fantastic views over fields that slope down to Clonakilty Bay. It is 300m east of the town centre, just off the main N71 roundabout into town.

Kinsale ❹

✗ Finn's Table — Modern Irish €€€

(☎021-470 9636; www.finnstable.com; 6 Main St; mains €30-40; ⏱6-10pm Mon, Tue & Thu-Sat) Owning a gourmet restaurant in Kinsale means plenty of competition, but John and Julie Finn's venture is more than up to the challenge. Elegant but unstuffy, Finn's Table offers a warm welcome, and its menu of seasonal, locally sourced produce rarely fails to please. Seafood (including lobster when in season) is from West Cork, while meat is from the Finn family's butchers.

✗ Bastion — Modern Irish €€€

(☎021-470 9696; www.bastionkinsale.com; cnr Main & Market Sts; mains €18-35; ⏱5-10pm Wed-Sun; 🍽) Holder of a Michelin Bib Gourmand since 2016, this place offers diners a relaxed and informal entry into the world of haute cuisine. Waitstaff will guide you through the concise à la carte menu of local oysters, beef, fish and venison, but it's best to go for the seven-course tasting menu (€78) or the five-course early-bird menu (pre-6pm; €58).

✗ Fishy Fishy Cafe — Seafood €€€

(☎021-470 0415; www.fishyfishy.ie; Crowley's Quay; mains €20-28; ⏱noon-9pm Mar-Oct, shorter hours rest of year) One of the most famous seafood restaurants in the country, Fishy Fishy has a wonderful setting with stark white walls splashed with bright artwork and striking steel fish sculptures, and a terrific decked terrace at the front. All the fish is caught locally, and dishes include lobster thermidor, gourmet fish pie, and a surf'n'turf tapas menu.

⛱ Pier House — B&B €€

(☎021-477 4169; www.pierhousekinsale.com; Pier Rd; d €100-140; 🅿🛜) Set back from the road in a sheltered garden, this is a lovely place to rest your head. Pristine rooms, decorated with shell-and-driftwood sculptures, have black-granite bathrooms with power showers and underfloor heating; four open to balconies with garden and harbour views.

Cork City ❺

✗ Paradiso — Vegetarian €€

(☎021-427 7939; www.paradiso.restaurant; 16 Lancaster Quay; 2-/3-course menus €39/47; ⏱5.30-10pm Mon-Sat; 🍽) A contender for best restaurant in town of any genre, Paradiso serves contemporary vegetarian dishes, including vegan fare: how about corn pancakes filled with leek, parsnip and Dunmanus cheese with fennel-caper salsa and smoked tomato? Reservations are essential.

Rates for dinner, bed and breakfast, staying in the funky upstairs rooms, start from €180/220 per single/double.

⛱ Garnish House — B&B €€

(☎021-427 5111; www.garnish.ie; 18 Western Rd; d/f from €126/165; 🅿🛜) Attention is lavished on guests at this award-winning B&B where the legendary breakfast menu (30 choices) ranges from grilled kippers to French toast. Typical of the touches here is freshly cooked porridge, served with creamed honey and your choice of whiskey or Baileys; enjoy it out on the garden terrace. The 14 rooms are very comfortable; reception is open 24 hours.

West Cork Villages

19

West Cork claims some of Ireland's most scenic driving country, with three spectacular peninsulas and maritime villages filled with colourful shops and pubs alive with music.

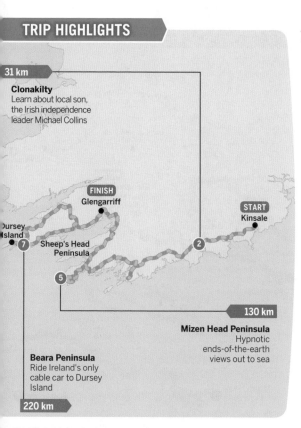

31 km

Clonakilty
Learn about local son, the Irish independence leader Michael Collins

FINISH
Glengarriff

START
Kinsale

Dursey Island

7

Sheep's Head Peninsula

5

2

130 km

Mizen Head Peninsula
Hypnotic ends-of-the-earth views out to sea

Beara Peninsula
Ride Ireland's only cable car to Dursey Island

220 km

7 DAYS
354KM / 220 MILES

GREAT FOR...

BEST TIME TO GO
West Cork's villages are liveliest between April and October.

 ESSENTIAL PHOTO
Staggering sea cliffs at the far-flung Mizen Head Signal Station.

 BEST AERIAL VIEWS
Take the cable car from the Beara Peninsula to tiny Dursey Island.

Mizen Head Peninsula Signal station at Mizen Head

19 West Cork Villages

This trip contains one of Ireland's trinity of top peninsula drives: the spellbinding Beara Peninsula, straddling Counties Cork and Kerry. Beara's southern side, along Bantry Bay, harbours working fishing villages, while on the rugged northern side craggy roads cut in and out of nooks and crannies and tiny coves are like pearls in a sea of rocks.

1 Kinsale

Narrow, winding streets lined with artsy shops and a harbour full of bobbing fishing boats and pleasure yachts make Kinsale (Cionn tSáile) one of Ireland's favourite midsized towns. Its superb foodie reputation is a bonus.

The peninsula of Scilly is barely a 10-minute walk southeast, from where a lovely walking path continues 3km east to Summercove and the vast 17th-century,

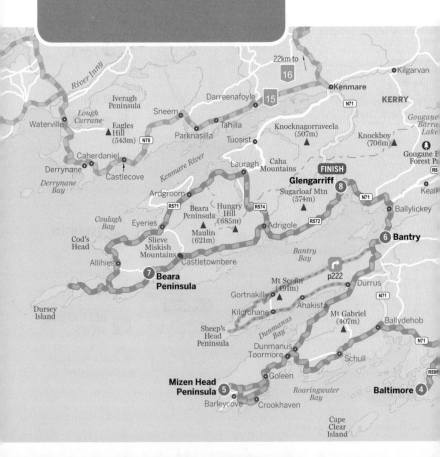

star-shaped **Charles Fort** (021-477 2263; www.herit ageireland.ie; Summercove; adult/child €5/3; ⊘10am-6pm mid-Mar–Oct, to 5pm Nov– mid-Mar; P).

The Drive » At times you'll meet the coast as you wind 35km west along the R600 to Clonakilty.

TRIP HIGHLIGHT

② Clonakilty

Cheerful Clonakilty is a bustling market town coursed by little water- ways. It serves as a hub for the scores of beguil- ing little coastal towns that surround it.

Superb miniature models of the main towns in West Cork star at the **West Cork Model Railway Village** (023-883 3224; www.modelvillage.ie; Inchy- doney Rd; adult/child incl road train tour €12/7.50; ⊘10am-

6pm Jul-Aug, 11am-5pm Sep- Jun; P ♿). A road train departs from the village on a 20-minute guided circuit of Clonakilty.

A visit to the **Michael Collins Centre** (023-884 6107; www.michaelcollinscen tre.com; Castleview; adult/child €5/3; ⊘10.30am-5pm Mon-Fri,

LINK YOUR TRIP

15 Ring of Kerry
Head 27km north from Glengarriff to pick up the Ring of Kerry in Kenmare.

16 Dingle Peninsula
Killarney, 60km north of Glengarriff, is the gateway to the charming Dingle Peninsula.

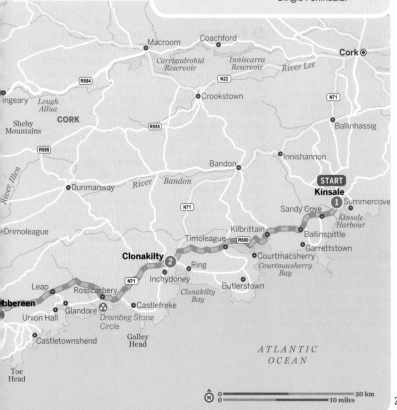

11am-2pm Sat mid-Jun–mid-Sep; P), signposted off the R600 between Timoleague and Clonakilty, is an excellent way to make sense of the life of Clonakilty's most famous son, Irish Free State commander-in-chief Michael Collins. The main negotiator of the 1921 Anglo-Irish Treaty, Collins was forced to make major concessions, including the partition of the country, famously declaring that he was signing his own death warrant. He was tragically correct, as Civil War broke out in the treaty's aftermath. A tour reveals photos, letters and a reconstruction of the 1920s country lane, complete with armoured vehicle, where Collins was killed.

✕ ⌂ p215

The Drive » It's 33km along the N71 from Clonakilty to Skibbereen but it's possible to freelance along the coast the entire way. As a taster, at Rosscarbery, you can turn left onto the R597, which takes you past the pretty villages of Glandore (Cuan Dor) and Union Hall, and the turn-off to the Drombeg Stone Circle, rejoining the N71 at Leap.

-----

❸ Skibbereen

Weekending swells and yachties from Dublin descend on the busy market town of Skibbereen (Sciobairín), which is as close to glitzy as West Cork gets. It's a far cry from the Famine, when Skibb was hit perhaps harder than any other town in Ireland, with huge numbers of the local population emigrating or dying of starvation or disease. The **Skibbereen Heritage Centre** (☎028-40900; www.skibbheritage.com; Upper Bridge St; adult/child €6/3; ⏰10am-6pm Mon-Sat May-Sep, Tue-Sat mid-Mar–Apr & Oct, closed Nov–mid-Mar; P) puts its history into harrowing perspective.

⌂ p223

The Drive » Islands are dotted offshore to the west as you drive 13km south on the R595 to Baltimore.

-----

❹ Baltimore

Crusty old sea dog Baltimore has a busy little port full of yachts and fishing trawlers. There's excellent **diving** on the reefs around Fastnet Rock (the waters are warmed by the Gulf Stream and a number of shipwrecks lie nearby) and a variety of island trips and **cruises**.

The Drive » Retrace your route north to the N71, which rolls west through Ballydehob, the gateway to the Mizen, and then on to the pretty village of Schull (pronounced 'skull'). Travelling on into the undulating countryside along the coastal road takes you through ever-smaller settlements to the village of Goleen. Baltimore to Goleen is 48km.

TRIP HIGHLIGHT

❺ Mizen Head Peninsula

The welcoming village of Goleen marks the start of the Mizen Head experience. Continue first to **Barleycove Beach**, with vast sand dunes hemmed in by two long bluffs dissolving into the surf. Then take the increasingly narrow roads to spectacular Mizen Head, Ireland's most southwesterly point. It's dominated by the **Mizen Head Signal Station** (☎028-35115; www.mizenhead.ie; adult/child €7.50/4.50; ⏰10am-6pm Jun-Aug, 10.30am-5pm mid-Mar–May, Sep & Oct, 11am-4pm Sat & Sun Nov–mid-Mar; P ♿), completed in 1909 to warn ships off rocks that appear in the water around here like crushed ice in cola. From the visitors centre, various pathways lead to the station, culminating in the crossing of a spectacular **arched bridge** that spans a vast gulf in the cliffs.

Pints in the sunshine are the reward for venturing on the crooked road to the outpost of **Crookhaven** (if it's raining, make that 'pints by the fireplace...'). In its heyday Crookhaven's natural harbour was an important anchorage, and mail from America was collected here.

Dursey Island cable car

Leaving Crookhaven, you'll spot the turn-off to the left, marked **Brow Head** – the Irish mainland's southernmost point. Park at the bottom of the hill – the track is very narrow and there's nowhere to pull over should you meet a tractor coming the other way. After 1km the road ends and a path continues to the head.

🛏 p223

The Drive » Bear north to join the scenic coast road that follows the edge of Dunmanus Bay for most of the way to Durrus. Continue north to Bantry, 60km north of Goleen.

⑥ Bantry

The pleasant town of Bantry offers the chance to refuel at one of its excellent eateries, and to get a feel for the life of the 18th-century Irish aristocracy with a visit to impressive Bantry House (p203) and its glorious gardens, 1km southwest of the town centre on the N71.

✕ 🛏 p207, p223

The Drive » Continue north on the N71 to Glengarriff and the Beara Peninsula. The contorted strata of the peninsula's underlying bedrock become evident as you drive west on the R572 towards Castletownbere,

50km from Bantry. On the highest hills – Sugarloaf Mountain and Hungry Hill – rock walls known as 'benches' snake backwards and forwards across the slopes.

TRIP HIGHLIGHT

⑦ Beara Peninsula

Encircling the Beara Peninsula, the Ring of Beara is, along with the Ring of Kerry and Dingle, one of Ireland's podium peninsula drives.

In the fishing town of **Castletownbere** (Baile Chais Bhéara), you might recognise the front-cover photo of the late Pete McCarthy's 1998 bestseller,

McCarthy's Bar, in three dimensions on Main St.

Tiny **Dursey Island**, at the end of the peninsula, is reached by Ireland's only **cable car** (☎028-21766; www.durseyisland.ie; adult/child return €10/5; ⏰9.30am-1pm & 1.30-5pm Mon-Thu, to 9.30pm Fri-Sun Jun-Aug, less frequently Sun & Sep-May), which sways 30m above Dursey Sound. After the thrill of the cable car ride, you can hike to the signal tower at the top of the island, and spot whales and dolphins in the surrounding waters.

It's 12km from the cable car to **Allihies** (Na hAilichí). From here the beautiful R575 coast road, with hedges of fuchsias and rhododendrons, twists and turns for about 12km

to **Eyeries**, a cluster of brightly coloured houses overlooking Coulagh Bay. From Eyeries you can forsake the R571 for the even smaller coast roads (lanes really) to the north and east, with views north to the Ring of Kerry.

At the crossroads of **Ardgroom** (Ard Dhór), heading east towards Lauragh, look for signs pointing to the Bronze Age **stone circle**.

🍴 🛏 p223

The Drive » Cut across the spectacular Healy Pass Rd (R574) to Adrigole and return on the R572 to Glengarriff (32km). Alternatively, leaving Lauragh, you can skip Glengarriff a second time and take the R573, which hugs the coast, rejoining the more no-nonsense R571 at Tuoist for the 16km run east to Kenmare in County Kerry.

- - - - - - - - - - - - - - - - - -

⑧ **Glengarriff**

Offshore from the village of Glengarriff, sub-tropical plants flourish in the rich soil and warm climate of the magical Italianate garden on **Garinish Island** (Ilnacullin; ☎027-63040; www.garinish island.ie; adult/child €5/3, plus ferry fare; ⏰9.30am-5.30pm Jul & Aug, shorter hours Apr-Jun, Sep & Oct, closed Nov-Mar). Ferry companies, including **Blue Pool Ferry** (☎027-63333; www.bluepoolferry.com; adult/child return €10/5; ⏰Apr-Nov), leave every 30 minutes for the 15-minute boat trip past islands and seal colonies when the garden is open; fares exclude garden entry.

🛏 p223, p257

DETOUR:
SHEEP'S HEAD PENINSULA

Start: ⑤ **Mizen Head Peninsula**

At Durrus, one road heads for Bantry; take the other, which turns west to circumnavigate Sheep's Head Peninsula.

The least visited of Cork's three peninsulas, Sheep's Head has a charm all its own – and plenty of sheep. There are good seascapes from along most of the loop road. Heading west from Durrus, the first hamlet you meet is **Ahakista** (Atha an Chiste), which consists of a couple of pubs and a few houses stretched along the R591. The peninsula's other village is **Kilcrohane**, 6km to the southwest, beside a fine beach. You can get pub food in both villages.

From Kilcrohane, the **Goat's Path** road runs north over the western flank of Mt Seefin to Gortnakilly and offers terrific views. Alternatively, keep heading southwest to the tip of Sheep's Head, from where an excellent one-hour walk leads from the road end at Tooreen to the **Sheep's Head Lighthouse**. Rejoin the N71 at Bantry. For more information, visit www.thesheepsheadway.ie.

Eating & Sleeping

Skibbereen ❸

🛏 Bridge House   B&B €€

(☎028-21273; www.bridgehouseskibbereen.com; 46 Bridge St; s/d from €55/85; 🛜) Mona Best has turned her entire house into a work of art, filling the rooms with fabulous Victorian tableaux and period memorabilia. The whole place bursts at the seams with cherished clutter, crazed carvings, dressed-up dummies and fragrant fresh flowers; personalised service extends to Champagne breakfasts for guests celebrating a birthday – not bad for a B&B!

Mizen Head Peninsula ❺

🛏 Heron's Cove   B&B €€

(☎028-35225; www.heronscove.com; Harbour Rd; s/d from €60/90; 🅿🛜) A delightful location on the shores of the tidal inlet of Goleen Harbour makes this fine restaurant and B&B a top choice. Rooms are brightly decorated and several have balconies overlooking the inlet.

Bantry ❻

✖ Fish Kitchen   Seafood €€

(☎027-56651; http://thefishkitchen.ie; New St; mains lunch €10-14, dinner €16-28; ⊗noon-3pm & 5.30-9pm Tue-Sat) This outstanding little restaurant above a fishmonger's shop does seafood to perfection, from the live-tank local oysters (served with lemon and Tabasco sauce) to Bantry Bay mussels in white wine.

✖ O'Connors Seafood Restaurant   Seafood €€

(☎027-55664; www.oconnorseafood.com; Wolfe Tone Sq; mains lunch €10-20, dinner €18-26; ⊗noon-3pm & 5.30-9pm, closed Tue & Wed Oct-Mar; ♿) West Cork scallops with black pudding and roasted parsnip purée; Union Hall hake pan-roasted and topped with lemon butter drizzle; Bantry Bay mussels done four ways: these are among the innovative dishes here that make the most of the area's renowned seafood.

🛏 Sea View House Hotel   Hotel €€

(☎027-50073; www.seaviewhousehotel.com; Ballylickey; s/d/f from €120/150/215; 🅿🛜)

You'll find everything you'd expect from an old country house hotel here: aristocratic ambience, tastefully decorated public rooms, expansive service and 25 cosy, smart bedrooms.

🛏 Bantry House   Historic Hotel €€€

(☎027-50047; www.bantryhouse.com; Bantry Bay; d from €189; ⊙Apr-Oct; 🅿🛜) The six guest rooms in this aristocratic mansion (p203) are decorated with antiques and contemporary furnishings – when you're not playing croquet, lawn tennis or billiards you can lounge in the library (once the doors of the historic house have closed to the public guests have free access to the house).

Beara Peninsula ❼

✖ Ocean Wild   Seafood €€

(☎027-71544; www.oceanwild.ie; West End; mains €19-30; ⊙6-10pm Thu-Mon Jun-Sep & Dec; 🅿) Opened in 2017 by local sisters Mairead and Eileen (one the chef, the other front of house), Ocean Wild has quickly established a reputation as the Beara's top seafood restaurant. Expect dishes such as pan-roasted hake with lemon, olives and capers, or monkfish in Thai red curry sauce, as well as perfectly grilled steak and slow-cooked lamb shank.

🛏 Berehaven Lodge   Cottage €€

(☎027-71464; www.berehavenlodge.com; Millcove; per 2 nights €375, per week from €750; 🅿🛜) This complex of cosy self-catering cottages occupies an enviable setting overlooking the sea 6km east of Castletownbere. Each 'lodge' has three bedrooms, a Jacuzzi, an outdoor deck and an open-plan living area with a log fire.

Glengarriff ❽

🛏 Casey's Hotel   Hotel €€

(☎027-63010; www.caseyshotelglengarriff.ie; Main St; r from €130; 🅿@🛜) Old-fashioned Casey's has been welcoming guests since 1884 (Eamon de Valera stayed here). The 19 rooms have been modernised a bit but are still small. It's got stacks of atmosphere, and the vast terrace is a treat.

Shannon River Route

20

Follow the majestic River Shannon as it wends from Lough Derg to the broad estuary at vibrant Limerick city, and take in the stupendous views at Loop Head.

TRIP HIGHLIGHTS

190 km

Loop Head
Awesome Atlantic views extend from this little-visited peninsula

114 km

Foynes
Atmospheric museum devoted to 1940s flying boats

START
Portumna

FINISH
Bunratty

3

Kilkee

9

Tarbert-Killimer Ferry Crossing

5

81 km

Limerick
Has a fabulous castle, gallery, museum and cathedral

4 DAYS
296KM / 184 MILES

GREAT FOR...

BEST TIME TO GO
Even in high summer there are plenty of crowd-free escapes.

ESSENTIAL PHOTO
The soaring cliffs on the aptly named 'Scenic Loop' road west of Kilkee.

BEST FOR DOLPHIN SPOTTING
Estuary-set Kilrush has a nature centre, dolphin trail and cruises.

op Head Spectacular cliffs at County Clare's southernmost point

20 Shannon River Route

Ireland's longest river provides a stunning backdrop to this route. It begins with gentle lake scenery around the boaters' paradise of Lough Derg, followed by fascinating historical sights in and around Limerick city. A visit to the world's only flying boat museum is followed by a short ferry trip across the Shannon estuary to take in the sweeping white-sand beaches of Kilkee and the dramatic seacliffs of Loop Head.

Lettermullen

North Sound

Kilronan

Aran Islands

ATLANTIC OCEAN

Cost

Car

Doc

Kilkee 8 Mo
N

Loop Head R487 Carrigaho
9 Kilbaha

Mouth of the Shannon Ballyb

Ballyduff

1 Portumna

In the far southeastern corner of County Galway, the lakeside town of Portumna is popular for boating and fishing.

Impressive **Portumna Castle & Gardens** (☏090-974 1658; www.heritageireland.ie; Castle Ave, Portumna; adult/child €5/3; ⏰9.30am-6pm Apr-Sep, to 5pm Oct) was built in the early 1600s by Richard de Burgo and boasts an elaborate, geometrical organic garden.

The Drive » From Portumna, cross the River Shannon – also the county border – into County Tipperary. Take the N65 south for 7km then turn right onto the R493, winding through farmland. Briefly rejoin the N52 at the Nenagh bypass, then turn west on the R494, following it to Ballina (52km in all).

2 Ballina & Killaloe

Facing each other across a narrow channel, Ballina and Killaloe (Cill Da Lúa) are really one destination, even if they have different personalities (and counties). A fine 1770 13-arch one-lane **bridge** spans the river, linking the pair. You can walk it in five minutes, or drive it in about 20 (a Byzantine system of lights controls traffic).

Ballina, in County Tipperary, has some of the better pubs and restaurants, while Killaloe typifies picturesque County Clare. It lies on the western banks of lower Loch Deirgeirt (the southern extension of Lough Derg), where it narrows at one of the principal crossings of the Shannon.

The Drive » Continue following the R494 then the M7 southwest to Limerick city (about 24km).

TRIP HIGHLIGHT

③ Limerick City

Limerick city straddles
the Shannon's broaden-
ing tidal stream, where
the river runs west to
meet the Shannon Estu-
ary. Despite some unex-
pected glitz and gloss, it
doesn't shy away from its

LINK YOUR TRIP

24 Mountains & Moors

Head 70km northwest
of Portumna to discover
County Galway's
romantic landscapes.

28 County Clare

It's just 25km
north from Bunratty
to Ennis for a tour
of County Clare's
cliff-framed coast, the
otherworldly Burren and
music-filled pubs.

tough past, as portrayed in Frank McCourt's 1996 memoir *Angela's Ashes*.

Limerick has an intriguing **castle** (☎061-711 222; www.kingjohnscastle. com; Nicholas St; adult/child €13/9.50; ⏰9.30am-6pm Apr-Sep, to 5pm Oct-Mar), built by King John of England between 1200 and 1212 on King's Island; the ancient **St Mary's Cathedral** (☎061-310 293; www.saint maryscathedral.ie; Bridge St; adult/child €5/free; ⏰9am-5pm Mon-Thu, to 4pm Fri & Sat, from 1.30pm Sun), founded in 1168 by Donal Mór O'Brien, king of Munster; and the fabulous **Hunt Museum** (www.huntmuseum. com; Custom House, Rutland St; adult/child €7.50/free, free on Sun; ⏰10am-5pm Mon-Sat, from 2pm Sun; ♿), with the finest collection of Bronze Age, Iron Age and medieval treasures outside Dublin.

The dynamic **Limerick City Gallery of Art** (www. gallery.limerick.ie; Carnegie Bldg, Pery Sq; ⏰10am-5.30pm Mon-Wed, Fri & Sat, to 8pm Thu, noon-5.30pm Sun) is set in the city's Georgian area. Limerick also has a contemporary cafe culture, and renowned nightlife to go with its uncompromised pubs – as well as locals who go out of their way to welcome you.

✕ ⌂ p231

The Drive » The narrow, peaceful N69 follows the Shannon Estuary west from Limerick; 27km along you come to Askeaton.

TRIP HIGHLIGHT

➍ Askeaton

Hidden just off the N69, evocative ruins in the pint-sized village of Askeaton include the mid-1300s **Desmond Castle** (⏰weekends by appointment May-Oct), a 1389-built **Franciscan friary**, and **St Mary's Church of Ireland** and **Knights Templar Tower**, built around 1829, as well as the 1740 **Hellfire** gentlemen's club. The ruins are undergoing a slow process of restoration that started in 2007. The town's **tourist office** (☎086 085 0174; askeaton-touristoffice@gmail.com; The Square; ⏰limited hours - call to check) has details of ruins that you can freely wander (depending on restoration works) and can arrange free **guided tours** lasting about one hour led by a passionate local historian.

The Drive » Stunning vistas of the wide Shannon Estuary come into view as you drive 12km to Foynes.

TRIP HIGHLIGHT

➎ Foynes

Foynes is an essential stop along the route to visit the fascinating **Foynes Flying Boat Museum** (☎069-65416; www. flyingboatmuseum.com; adult/child €12/6; ⏰9.30am-6pm Jun-Aug, to 5pm mid-Mar–Jun & Sep–mid-Nov; ℗). From 1939 to 1945 this was the landing place for the flying boats that linked North America with the British Isles. Big Pan Am clippers – there's a replica here – would set down in the estuary and refuel.

The Drive » The most scenic stretch of the N69 is the 20km from Foynes to Tarbert in northern County Kerry, which hugs the estuary's edge.

➏ Tarbert

The little town of Tarbert is where you'll hop on the car ferry to Killimer, in County Clare, saving yourself 137km of driving.

Foynes Flying Boat Museum

 **DETOUR:**
ADARE

Start: ❸ Limerick City

Frequently dubbed 'Ireland's prettiest village', Adare centres on its clutch of perfectly preserved thatched cottages built by the 19th-century English landlord, the Earl of Dunraven, for workers constructing Adare Manor (now a palatial hotel). Today the cottages house craft shops and some of the region's finest restaurants (p231).

In the middle of the village, **Adaire Heritage Centre** (📞061-396 666; Main St; ⊙9am-6pm) has entertaining exhibits on the history and the medieval context of the village's buildings and can point you to a number of fascinating religious sites. It also books tours of **Adare Castle** (Desmond Castle; www.heritageireland.ie; tours adult/child €10/8; ⊙tours hourly 11am-5pm Jul-Sep). Dating back to around 1200, this picturesque feudal ruin was wrecked by Cromwell's troops in 1657. Restoration work is ongoing; look for the ruined great hall with its early-13th-century windows. You can view the castle from the main road, the riverside footpath, or the grounds of the Augustinian priory.

From Limerick city, the fastest way to reach Adare is to take the M20 and N21 16km southwest to the village on the banks of the River Maigue. From Adare it's 9km northwest to rejoin the N69 at Kilcornan. Alternatively, you can take the less-travelled N69 from Limerick to Kilcornan and slip down to Adare.

Before you do so, though, it's worth visiting the renovated **Tarbert Bridewell Jail & Courthouse** (www.tarbertbridewell.com; adult/child €5/2.50; ⊙10am-6pm Apr-Sep, to 4pm Mon-Fri Oct-Mar), which has exhibits on the rough social and political conditions of the 19th century. From the jail, the 6.1km **John F Leslie Woodland Walk** runs along Tarbert Bay towards the river mouth.

The ferry dock is clearly signposted 2.2km west of Tarbert. Services are operated by **Shannon Ferry Limited** (☎068-905 3124; www.shannonferries.com; cars €20, motorcyclists, cyclists & pedestrians €5; ⊙7.30am-8.30pm Mon-Sat, from 9.30am Sun Apr-Sep, longer hours Jun-Aug, shorter hours Oct-Mar; ☏). Ferries depart hourly (every half-hour in high summer).

The Drive » The car-ferry crossing from Tarbert in County Kerry to Killimer in County Clare (from where it's an 8km drive west to Kilrush) takes just 20 minutes and, because the estuary is sheltered, you can usually look forward to smooth sailing.

----

❼ Kilrush

Some 170-plus bottlenose dolphins swim around in the Shannon; **Dolphin Discovery** (☎065-905 1327; www.discoverdolphins.ie; Kilrush Marina; adult/child €26/14; ⊙late May–mid-Oct) runs trips to see them out of Kilrush Marina. The atmospheric town also harbours the remarkable 'lost' **Vandeleur Walled Garden** (☎065-905 1760; www.vandeleurwalledgarden.ie; Killimer Rd; ⊙10am-5pm Tue-Sat), home to a 170-hectare forest with winding trails, a colourful array of plants and a beech maze.

The Drive » Continue 14km west along the N67 to the beach haven of Kilkee.

----

❽ Kilkee

The centrepiece of Kilkee (Cill Chaoi) is its wide, sheltered, crescent-shaped beach. The bay has high cliffs on the north end; to the south a coastal path leads to natural swimming pools known as the Pollock Holes. The waters are very tidal with sandy expanses replaced by waves in just a few hours.

Kilkee has plenty of guesthouses and B&Bs, though during high season, rates can soar and vacancies are scarce.

✖ p231

The Drive » The 26.5km drive from Kilkee south to Loop Head ends in cliffs plunging into the Atlantic.

TRIP HIGHLIGHT

❾ Loop Head

Capped by a working lighthouse, Loop Head (Ceann Léime) is County Clare's southernmost point, with breathtaking views as well as cycling, fishing and snorkelling opportunities.

The Drive » On the R487, follow the 'Scenic Loop' (an understatement): you'll be struck by one stunning vista of soaring coastal cliffs after another. At Kilkee pick up the N67 east to just after Killimer, before continuing northeast on the looping, coastal R473. Next hop on M18/N18 south to Bunratty (110km all up).

----

❿ Bunratty

Bunratty (Bun Raite) draws more tourists than any other place in the region. The namesake **castle** (☎061-711 222; www.bunrattycastle.ie; adult/child/family €16/12/45; ⊙9am-5.30pm) has stood over the area for centuries. In recent decades it's been spiffed up and swamped by attractions and gift shops. A theme park re-creates a clichéd – and sanitised – Irish village of old.

With all the hoopla, it's easy to overlook the actual village, at the back of the theme park, which has numerous leafy spots to eat and sleep.

Eating & Sleeping

Limerick City ③

✖ Milk Market
Market €

(www.milkmarketlimerick.ie; Cornmarket Row; ⏰10am-3pm Fri, from 8am Sat, from 11am Sun) Pick from organic produce and artisan foods including local fruits and vegetables, preserves, baked goods and farmhouse cheeses, browse the flower and craft stalls, or grab a bite at one of the hot-food tables at this busy market held in Limerick's old market buildings. There's usually traditional live music as well.

✖ Hook & Ladder
Cafe €€

(☎061-413 778; www.hookandladder.ie; 7 Sarsfield St; mains €11-15; ⏰8am-5pm Mon-Wed, to 6pm Thu-Sat, 9am-5pm Sun) A haven of understated style and a champion of local produce, this cafe set in a converted bank building epitomises Limerick's foodie scene. Exquisite sandwiches include Doonbeg crab with lemon mayo on honey and pumpkin-seed bread, while hot lunch dishes range from sausage and mash to falafel and hummus wrap. There are associated cookery schools in Limerick and Waterford.

⛏ No 1 Pery Square
Hotel €€

(☎061-402 402; www.oneperysquare.com; 1 Pery Sq; club/period r from €145/195; 🅿🛜) Treat yourself to a night in Georgian Limerick at this elegant hotel right on the corner of Pery Sq. Choose between very well-presented club rooms (each named after an Irish poet) in the modern extension and one of the four period rooms in the classic Georgian townhouse, each a feast of huge sash windows, high ceilings and capacious bathrooms.

⛏ George Boutique Hotel
Hotel €€

(☎061-460 400; www.georgelimerick.com; Shannon St; s/d/tr/f from €129/139/164/179; 🅿🛜) 'Boutique' might be overstating things a bit, but the rooms at this brisk, buzzing and centrally located hotel – with a decor of blond wood, caramels, browns, and the occasional splash of designer colour – are stylish and comfortable. It's frequently booked solid, so reserve well in advance.

Adare ③

✖ Restaurant
1826 Adare
Modern Irish €€

(☎061-396 004; www.1826adare.ie; Main St; mains €20-27; ⏰6-9.30pm Wed-Sat, 3-8pm Sun; 🚼) One of Ireland's most highly regarded chefs, Wade Murphy continues to wow diners at this art-lined 1826-built thatched cottage. His passion for local seasonal produce is an essential ingredient in dishes such as pan-seared halibut with Connemara clams and pickled samphire. A three-course early-bird menu (€36) is served daily until 7pm.

⛏ Dunraven Arms
Inn €€

(☎061-605 900; www.dunravenhotel.com; Main St; r from €165; 🛜🏊) This jewel of an inn, built in 1792, exudes old-fashioned charm, with cottage-style gardens, hanging baskets, open fires and a comfortable lobby. Smart bedrooms are decorated with antiques, high-thread-count linens and – for the choosy – four-poster beds. Service is warm and helpful, and there's a great **restaurant** (mains restaurant €16-28, bar €14-17; ⏰7-9.30pm daily, 12.30-2.30pm Sun).

Kilkee ⑧

✖ Diamond Rocks Cafe
Cafe €

(☎086 372 1063; www.diamondrockscafe.com; West End; dishes €6-14; ⏰10am-5pm) Before heading off on a cliff walk, fuel up at this contemporary cafe opening to a huge terrace at the water's edge. Food is well above the norm for places found in stunning spots, and encompasses daily changing specials such as asparagus and goat's cheese quiche, and Guinness beef stew. It's set at the far western end of the coast road that hugs Kilkee's shore.

The Holy Glen

21

This hallowed patch of County Tipperary shelters the Glen of Aherlow and the Rock of Cashel, crowned by historic buildings that seem like an ethereal extension of the landscape itself.

TRIP HIGHLIGHTS

71 km

Cashel
The extraordinary Rock of Cashel soars heavenwards above town

7

Slievenamuck Hills

5

Glen of Aherlow

Galtee Mountains

16 km

Cahir
Pretty riverside town centred on its moated, turreted castle

2

Clonmel

Newtown
Views extend across the glen from a hillside statue of Christ

42 km

2–3 DAYS
71KM / 45 MILES

GREAT FOR...

BEST TIME TO GO
Autumn brings glorious colours and a walking festival.

ESSENTIAL PHOTO

The awe-inspiring Rock of Cashel from inside the Hore Abbey ruins.

BEST CASTLE
Cahir Castle, like the quintessential beach sandcastle, with towers and moat.

---

21 The Holy Glen

The landscapes viewed from your car windows are sublime, and it's easy to get out and about among them. The Glen of Aherlow is renowned for its walking. You will encounter varying terrain, from lush riverbanks on the Aherlow to whispering pine forests and windswept, rocky mountains that seem to stretch on forever.

❶ Clonmel

County Tipperary's largest and busiest town, Clonmel (Cluain Meala; 'Meadows of Honey') sits on the northern bank of the River Suir. Its historic buildings include the beautifully restored **Main Guard** (📞052-612 7484; www.heritageireland.ie; Sarsfield St; ⏰9am-5pm Tue-Sun Apr-Sep, hours vary), a James Butler courthouse dating from 1675; the 1802-built **County Courthouse** (Nelson St), where the Young Irelanders of 1848 were tried and sentenced

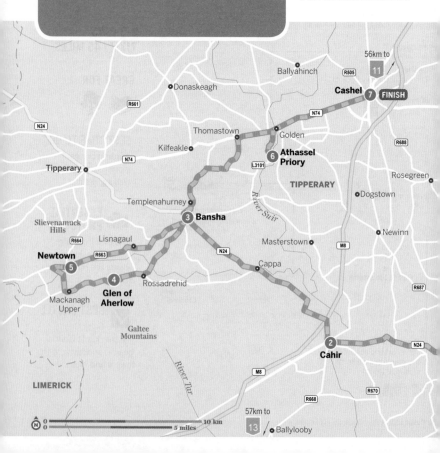

to transportation to Australia; and the **Franciscan Friary** (www.franciscans.ie/friaries/clonmel-co-tipperary; Mitchell St; ◷8am-6pm) – inside, near the door, a 1533 Butler-family tomb depicts a knight and his lady. There's some fine modern stained glass, especially in St Anthony's Chapel.

Informative displays on County Tipperary's history, from Neolithic times to the present, are covered at the well-put-together **South Tipperary County Museum** (www.tipperarycoco.ie/museum; Mick Delahunty Sq; ◷10am-4.45pm Tue-Sat), which also hosts changing exhibitions.

 p239

The Drive » It's a quick 17km trip along the N24 west to Cahir.

TRIP HIGHLIGHT

❷ Cahir

At the eastern tip of the Galtee Mountains, the compact town of Cahir (An Cathair; pronounced 'care') encircles the moated **Cahir Castle** (☎052-744 1011; www.heritageireland.ie; Castle St; adult/child €5/3; ◷9am-6.30pm mid-Jun–Aug, 9.30am-5.30pm Mar–mid-Jun & Sep–mid-Oct, to 4.30pm mid-Oct–Feb), a feudal fantasy of rocky foundations, massive walls, turrets and towers, defences and dungeons. Founded by Conor O'Brien in 1142, it passed to the Butler family in 1375. In 1599 the Earl of Essex used cannons to shatter its walls, and it was surrendered to Cromwell in 1650. Its future usefulness may have discouraged the typical Cromwellian 'deconstruction' and it remains one of Ireland's largest and most intact medieval castles.

Walking paths follow the banks of the **River Suir** – a pretty path from behind the castle car park meanders 2km south to the thatched **Swiss Cottage** (☎052-744 1144; www.heritageireland.ie; Cahir Park; adult/child €5/3; ◷10am-6pm mid-Mar–Oct), surrounded by roses, lavender and honeysuckle. A lavish example of Regency Picturesque, it's more a sizeable house. The compulsory 30-minute guided tours are thoroughly enjoyable.

The Drive » Drive northwest for 14km through farmland along the N24 (which, despite being a National Road, is narrow and twisting) to the village of Bansha, the jumping-off point for the Glen of Aherlow.

----

❸ Bansha

The tiny village of Bansha (An Bháinseach, meaning 'a grassy place') sits at the eastern end of the Glen of Aherlow.

 LINK YOUR TRIP

11 Kilkenny's Treasures

Head 60km northeast of Cashel along the M8 and R693 to discover the medieval treasures of County Kilkenny.

13 Blackwater Valley Drive

Travel 87km south from Cashel to Youghal (County Cork), via Lismore, for the beautiful Blackwater Valley.

Although Bansha itself has just a handful of facilities, it makes a good pit stop before embarking on the prettiest stretch of this trip.

The Drive » From Bansha the 11km drive southwest takes in the best of County Tipperary's verdant, mountainous landscapes. Leave Bansha on the R663 and, after 500m, take the left fork (signposted 'Rossadrehid') in the road. Keep your eyes peeled for walkers and cyclists as you drive.

PETER ZOELLER/DESIGN PICS/GETTY IMAGES ©

④ Glen of Aherlow

Cradled between the Slievenamuck Hills and the Galtee Mountains, this gorgeous valley is a scenic drive within a scenic drive. From Bansha you'll travel through a scattering of hamlets, including Booleen, Rossadrehid and Mackanagh Upper, with majestic mountain views.

The Drive » At Mackanagh Upper, turn north to reconnect with the R663, following it east (4.2km in total) to reach the glen's tourism hub, the tony hamlet of Newtown.

TRIP HIGHLIGHT

⑤ Newtown

The R663 from Bansha and the R664 south from Tipperary town converge at Newtown.

Hidden around the back of the pub, the enthusiastically staffed Glen of Aherlow **tourist office** (☎062-56331; www. aherlow.com; Coach Rd, New-town; ⊙9am-5pm Mon-Fri, 10am-4pm Sat May-Sep) is an excellent source of local information, including **walking festivals**.

For views of biblical proportions, head 1.6km north of Newtown on the R664 to its lofty **viewing point** and **Christ the King statue**, on the side of the Slievenamuck Hills facing the Galtee Mountains. The statue's raised hand is believed to bless those who pass by it and live beneath it. Initially erected in 1950, the original statue was damaged in 1975, but replaced soon after with an identical sculpture.

There's a good range of rural accommodation, including some bucolic campgrounds.

🛏 p239

Swiss Cottage, Cahir

The Drive » Continue along the scenic R663 to Bansha and turn briefly north on the N24, then turn northeast opposite the petrol station on the L4306 to connect with the N74 east to the village of Golden. From Golden, head 2km south along the narrow road signposted 'Athassel Priory' (23.5km all up).

----

6 Athassel Priory

The atmospheric – and, at dusk, delightfully creepy – ruins of Athassel Priory sit in the shallow and verdant River Suir valley. The original buildings date from 1205, and Athassel was once one of the richest and most important monasteries in Ireland. What survives is substantial: the gatehouse and portcullis gateway, the cloister and stretches of walled enclosure, as well as some medieval tomb effigies.

Roadside parking is limited and very tight. The priory is reached across often-muddy fields.

The Drive » Return to Golden and continue east along the N74 for 7km to the grand finale of the trip, Cashel, resplendently crowned by the Rock of Cashel.

237

TRIP HIGHLIGHT

❼ Cashel

Rising from a grassy plain on the edge of the town, the **Rock of Cashel** (📞062-61437; www.heritage-ireland.ie; adult/child €8/4, incl Cormac's Chapel €11/7; 🕙9am-7pm early Jun–mid-Sep, to 5.30pm mid-Mar–early Jun & mid-Sep–mid-Oct, to 4.30pm mid-Oct–mid-Mar; 🅿) is one of Ireland's most spectacular archaeological sites. The 'Rock' is a prominent green hill, banded with limestone outcrops, which bristles with ancient fortifications – the word 'cashel' is an Anglicised version of the Irish word *caiseal,* meaning 'fortress'. Sturdy walls circle an enclosure that contains a complete round tower, a 13th-century Gothic cathedral and the finest 12th-century Romanesque chapel in Ireland. For more than 1000 years the Rock of Cashel was a symbol of power and the seat of kings and churchmen who ruled over the region. It's a five-minute stroll from the town centre to the Rock; pretty paths include the **Bishop's Walk**. There are a couple of parking spaces for visitors with disabilities at the top of the approach road to the ticket office.

Just under 1km from the Rock, in flat farmland, is the formidable ruin of 13th-century **Hore Abbey** (🕙dawn-dusk). Originally Benedictine and settled by monks from Glastonbury in England at the end of the 12th century, it later became a Cistercian house.

Next to the car park below the Rock, heritage centre **Brú Ború** (📞062-61122; www.bruboru.ie; The Kiln; adult/child €5/3; 🕙9am-5pm Mon-Fri, longer hours Jul–mid-Aug) offers an absorbing insight into Irish traditional music, dance and song.

Town museums include the engaging **Cashel Folk Village** (📞087 915 1316; www.cashel-folkvillage.ie; St Dominic St; adult/child €7/4; 🕙10.15am-7.30pm Mon-Sat, 11am-5.30pm Sun mid-Mar–mid-Oct, by appointment mid-Oct–mid-Mar), exhibiting old buildings, shopfronts and memorabilia from around Cashel.

✕ 🛏 p109, p239 p277

THE GALTEE MOUNTAINS

Extending west from Cahir for 23km, the Galtees stand slightly aloof from the other mountain groups in Ireland's south. They rise comparatively gradually from the sprawling 'Tipperary Plain' and much more steeply from beautiful Glen of Aherlow to the north. The range's highest peak is Galtymore Mountain (919m), which towers over at least 12 other distinct summits. A prominent landmark far and wide, it stands proud of the rest of the range by almost 100m and is one of Ireland's 14 peaks or summits over 900m. Valleys bite deep into the main ridge, composed of purplish Devonian sandstone, so that the Galtees (pronounced with a short 'a' as in 'fact') are characterised by long spurs reaching out from the relatively narrow main ridge. Tors, created by frost-shattering during the last ice age, are scattered along the ridge, notably forming a heap of conglomerate boulders known as O'Loughnan's Castle. The north face of the range is punctuated by corries – relics of the ice age that hide Lough Muskry and Bohreen Lough, impounded by massed moraine. The uplands of the range are largely covered with blanket bog, and conifer plantations are widespread across the lower slopes. The Glen of Aherlow tourist office in Newtown has walking information.

Eating & Sleeping

Clonmel ❶

✕ Mani   Irish €€

(📞052-617 0007; www.mani.ie; 20 Parnell
St; mains €14-30; 🕑5-9.30pm Tue-Thu,
12.30-2.30pm & 5-10pm Fri & Sat, 12.30-8pm
Sun; 🛜) This relaxed yet stylish restaurant
places seasonal Irish produce front and centre
in dishes such as pan-fried hake (landed
at Kilmore Quay in County Wexford) with
garlic mash and star anise beurre blanc, and
chargrilled Tipperary beef sirloin with sweet-
onion confit and brandy and green-peppercorn
sauce.

🛏 Raheen House Hotel   Hotel €€

(📞052-612 2140; www.raheenhouse.ie; Raheen
Rd; r from €125; 🅿🛜) Grand but homely, this
gorgeous old country-house hotel offers high
ceilings, massive rooms, some fine four-poster
beds, wooden floors, a bar, a conservatory and
two huge gardens with maples, magnolias and
a vast cypress. There's also a walled garden,
roaring fires in winter and a self-catering lodge
(from €200).

Newtown ❺

🛏 Aherlow House Hotel   Hotel €€

(📞062-56153; www.aherlowhouse.ie; Newtown;
d/lodge from €75/149; 🅿🛜) Up a pine-
forested lane from the R663, a 1928 hunting
lodge has been turned into an atmospheric
woodland retreat. There are 29 rooms with
king-size beds and 15 contemporary countrified
self-catering lodges (minimum two-night stay).
There's a flowing bar, a fine restaurant and
glorious mountain views from the terrace.

🛏 Ballinacourty House
Camping Park & B&B   Campground €

(📞087 327 8573; www.camping.ie;
Ballinacourty; campsites €10, s/d €60/80;
🕑Apr-Sep; 🅿) Set against the spectacular

backdrop of the Galtee hills, this attractive
site is 10km west from Bansha. It has excellent
facilities, as well as a fine garden, a much-loved
restaurant serving classic Irish fare, a wine bar
and a tennis court. An old stone house has been
renovated and offers B&B accommodation.

Cashel ❼

✕ Mikey Ryan's   Gastropub €€

(📞062-62007; www.mikeyryans.ie; 76 Main
St; mains lunch €9-16, dinner €17-30; 🕑food
served noon-3pm & 6-9.30pm; 🛜🖥) This
long-established bar has been given a glitzy
gastropub makeover, with a bright, sun-
drenched dining room at the back, and a
gorgeous garden complete with barbecue and
horse-box bar. The delicious farmhouse-style
food is sourced from local farmers and artisan
producers, and Cashel Blue cheese makes
several appearances on the menu – in pesto, on
pizza and topping a burger.

✕ Chez Hans   Irish €€€

(📞062-61177; www.chezhans.net; Dominic
St; mains €28-39, 2-/3-course Sun lunch
€28/35; 🕑6-10pm Wed-Sat, 12.30-3.30pm
Sun) Since 1968 this former church has been
a place of worship for foodies from Ireland and
beyond. Still as fresh and inventive as ever, the
restaurant has a regularly changing menu and
gives its blessing to all manner of Irish produce,
including steamed Galway mussels, beetroot
risotto with deep-fried goat's cheese and
steamed halibut with fennel puree.
No credit cards.

🛏 Cashel Town B&B   B&B €

(📞062-62330; www.cashelbandb.com; 5
John St; d/q from €65/120; 🅿🛜) Within this
1808-built Georgian townhouse are seven
comfortable, homely rooms, and a cosy guest
lounge with a toasty open fire and a piano.
Breakfast is not included in room rates and
must be ordered at time of booking.

STRETCH YOUR LEGS
CORK
CITY

Start/Finish: Lewis Glucksman Gallery

Distance: 4.7km

Duration: 3 hours

The River Lee flows around Cork's central island of grand Georgian parades, 17th-century alleys and modern masterpieces. As you criss-cross between galleries and architecture, you'll discover that the single-best sight is the city itself.

Take this walk on Trips

Lewis Glucksman Gallery

Situated on the leafy campus of prestigious University College Cork (UCC), the award-winning limestone, steel and timber **Lewis Glucksman Gallery** (☏021-490 1844; www.glucksman.org; University College Cork, Western Rd; suggested donation €5; ◷10am-5pm Tue-Sat, 2-5pm Sun; ♿) displays the best in national and international contemporary art.

The Walk ≫ From UCC, head south on Donovan's Rd and then east on Connaught Rd and Gill Abbey St, to reach St Fin Barre's Cathedral.

St Fin Barre's Cathedral

Spires, gargoyles and sculpture adorn Cork's Protestant **St Fin Barre's Cathedral** (☏021-496 3387; www.cork-cathedral.webs.com; Bishop St; adult/child €6/3; ◷9.30am-5.30pm Mon-Sat year-round, 1-2.30pm & 4.30-5pm Sun Apr-Oct). Local legend says the golden angel on the eastern side will blow its horn when the Apocalypse is due to start...

The Walk ≫ Go east along Dean St and turn left on Barrack St to find the entrance to Elizabeth Fort.

Elizabeth Fort

Originally built in the 1620s, this small star-shaped artillery **fort** (☏021-497 5947; www.elizabethfort.ie; Barrack St; ◷10am-5pm Mon-Sat & noon-5pm Sun, closed Mon Oct-May) once formed an important part of the city's defences. Exhibits offer an insight into Cork's military history, and there are good views across the city from the ramparts. Free guided tours at 1pm provide additional context.

The Walk ≫ Head downhill to the riverside quays and turn right. Cross the bridge north at Mary St to reach the English Market.

English Market

Cork's ornate Victorian English Market (p213), crammed with colourful stalls selling fine foodstuffs from around the county, is a must-see. You're also spoiled for dining options, which range from gourmet sandwiches to the famous Farmgate Cafe (p213).

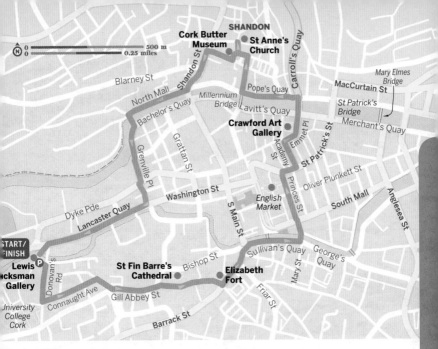

The Walk » Princes St meets St Patrick's St, the main shopping and commercial area. Turn left onto Academy St and right on Emmet Pl to the city's premier gallery.

Crawford Municipal Art Gallery

Highlights of the excellent permanent collection at Cork's public gallery, **Crawford Municipal Art Gallery** (☏021-480 5042; www.crawfordartgallery.ie; Emmet Pl; ◷10am-5pm Mon-Wed, Fri & Sat, to 8pm Thu, 11am-4pm Sun), **covering the 17th century to today, include works by Sir John Lavery, Jack B Yeats, Nathaniel Hone and a room devoted to Irish women artists, including Mainie Jellet and Evie Hone. The Sculpture Galleries contain plaster casts of Roman and Greek statues, given to King George IV by the pope in 1822.**

The Walk » Continue on Emmet Pl, passing Cork Opera House, cross the river and turn west to the hillside neighbourhood of Shandon, with galleries, antique shops and cafes along its old lanes and squares lined with tiny old row houses.

St Anne's Church

Shandon is dominated by the 1722 **St Anne's Church** (☏021-450 5906; www.shandonbells.ie; John Redmond St, Shandon; tower incl bells adult/child €5/2.50; ◷10am-5pm Mon-Sat, 11.30am-4.30pm Sun Jun-Sep, shorter hours Oct-May), **aka the 'Four-Faced Liar', so called as each of the tower's four clocks used to tell a different time. Ring the bells on the 1st floor and continue the 132 steps to the top for 360-degree views of the city.**

The Walk » It's a short walk south on Exchange St and right on John Redmond St to the Cork Butter Museum.

Cork Butter Museum

Cork's long tradition of butter manufacturing is related through displays and dioramas in the **Cork Butter Museum** (☏021-430 0600; www.corkbutter.museum; O'Connell Sq; adult/child €4/1.50; ◷10am-5pm Mar-Oct). **The square in front is dominated by the round Firkin Crane building, central to the old butter market and now housing a dance centre.**

Galway & the West of Ireland

LITTLE WONDER THE WEST OF IRELAND is top of most must-see lists – apart from the weather, it has it all. Routes through Mayo offer wild, romantic beauty, without the crowds. Road tripping in timeless Connemara reveals one of Europe's most stunning corners, replete with intriguing villages, white beaches and tawny bogs.

Westport and Galway deliver pit stops full of fun and frolic, as do the music-filled bars of County Clare – all provide perfect soundtracks for the mesmerising landscapes of The Burren and the Aran Islands.

Counties Kerry and Cork are iconic Ireland: crenulated coastlines, ancient sites and mist-shrouded peaks. And it's all bound together by the Wild Atlantic Way – a 2500km driving route snaking from Cork to Donegal.

The Burren, County Clare
PETER ZELEI IMAGES/GETTY IMAGES ©

Galway &
the West of
Ireland

Céide Fields, County Mayo

 DON'T MISS

Céide Fields
One of the world's major prehistoric sites still feels as undiscovered as it really was more than 50 years ago. Unearth it on Trip 22

Inisheer
A trip to the smallest of the Aran Islands will take you far from 21st-century living. Sail there on Trips 23 28

Ennistimon
This authentic market town in County Clare gives a genuine taste of country living. Savour its fine bars on Trips 23 28

Dingle Town
A colourful fishing village at the end of the earth (well, the Connor Pass) provides delightful eateries, dolphin- and people-watching. Dive in on Trip 22

Galway
You may find it hard to leave the City of Tribes. Go for its culture, conviviality and craic on Trips 22 23 24 25

Classic Trip

Best of the West

This is a rewarding foray through the west's ultimate stops, taking in mysterious megalithic remains, historic national parks and lively market towns, all in an epic coastal landscape.

22

TRIP HIGHLIGHTS

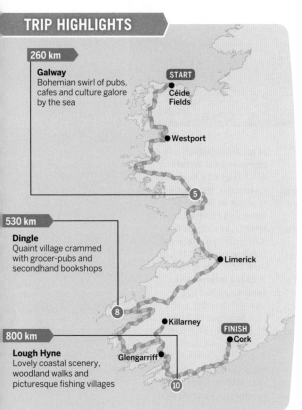

260 km

Galway
Bohemian swirl of pubs, cafes and culture galore by the sea

START
● Céide Fields

● Westport

—5—

530 km

Dingle
Quaint village crammed with grocer-pubs and secondhand bookshops

● Limerick

—8—

800 km

Lough Hyne
Lovely coastal scenery, woodland walks and picturesque fishing villages

● Killarney

FINISH
● Cork

Glengarriff ●

—10—

6 DAYS
890KM / 553 MILES

GREAT FOR...

BEST TIME TO GO
July for the best selection of summer festivals.

ESSENTIAL PHOTO
Clew Bay's many islands from the foot of Croagh Patrick.

BEST FOR DOLPHIN-WATCHING
Fungie the dolphin, in Dingle Bay, delivers thrills to young and old.

ew Bay View from Croagh Patrick

247

Classic Trip

22 Best of the West

The most westerly fringe of Europe is the wild, rugged and incredibly beautiful west of Ireland. It offers quintessential landscapes, which is why Irish tourism created the Wild Atlantic Way as its signature driving route. Here you'll discover the best beaches in Europe, the epic landscapes of Connemara, culture-packed Galway and Clare, and the kingdom of Kerry right round to West Cork's wonderful fishing villages.

ATLANTIC OCEAN

---

❶ Céide Fields

A famous wit once described archaeology as being all about 'a series of small walls'. But it's not often that said walls have experts hopping up and down with such excitement as at Céide Fields, 8km northwest of Ballycastle. During the 1930s, local man Patrick Caulfield was digging in the bog when he noticed piled-up stones buried beneath it. About 40 years later, his son Seamus, who had become an archaeologist on the basis of his father's discovery, uncovered the world's most extensive Stone Age monument, consisting of stone-walled fields, houses and megalithic tombs – as early as five millennia ago a thriving farming community had lived here. The award-winning **interpretive centre** (☎096-43325; www.heritageireland.ie; off R314; adult/child €5/3; ☺visitor centre 10am-6pm Jun-Sep, to 5pm Easter-May & Oct, last tour 1hr before closing) gives a fascinating glimpse into these times. However, it's a good idea

Annas
Dingle ❽
Dingle Bay Kel
Caherciveen
Waterville
Derrynane
Dursey Island

0 ———— 40 km
0 ———— 20 miles

to take a guided tour of the site itself, or it may seem nothing more than, well, a series of small walls.

The Drive » Head south to the hillside village of Mulranny – a prime vantage point for counting the 365 or so islands that grace Clew Bay. En route to the picturesque village of Newport look for signs to 15th-century Carrigahowley Castle (also called Rockfleet Castle). From there a wiggling 12km drive south leads to the atmospheric, pub-packed, heritage town of Westport.

② Westport

Bright and vibrant even in the depths of winter, Westport is a photogenic Georgian town with tree-lined streets, riverside walks and a great vibe. Matt Malloy, the fife player from the Chieftains, opened **Matt Molloy's** (☎098-27663; www.mattmol loy.com; Bridge St; ☺12.30-11.30pm Mon-Thu, to 12.30am

---

LINK YOUR TRIP

27 **Sligo Surrounds**
From Céide Fields continue northeast for a glimpse of Sligo's wild side.

12 **Wexford & Waterford**
When you hit Cork, keep going east through Ardmore to experience Ireland's sunny southeast.

Fri & Sat, to 11pm Sun; 🔊), an old-school pub, years ago and the good times haven't let up. Head to the back room around 9pm and you'll catch live *céilidh* (traditional music and dancing). Or perhaps a veteran musician will simply slide into a chair and croon a few classics.

Westport House
(📞098-27766; www.west porthouse.ie; Quay Rd; adult/child house only €14/7, house & pirate adventure park €25/20; 🕙10am-6pm Jun-Aug, to 4pm Mar-May & Sep-Nov, hours vary Dec-Feb; 🚼) is a charming Georgian mansion with gardens and an adventure playground that make a terrific day's outing for all ages.

🍴🛏️ p256, p293

The Drive » Just 15km southwest of town is Croagh Patrick, one of Ireland's most famous pilgrimage sites.

GALWAY HOOKERS

Obvious jokes aside, Galway hookers are the iconic small sailing boats that were the basis of local seafaring during the 19th century and part of the 20th century. Small, tough and highly manoeuvrable, these wooden boats are undergoing a resurgence thanks to weekend sailors and hobbyists. The hulls are jet black, due to the pitch used for waterproofing, while the sails flying from the single mast are a distinctive rust colour. Expect to see them all along the Galway coast.

❸ Croagh Patrick

St Patrick couldn't have picked a better spot for a pilgrimage than this conical mountain (also known as 'the Reek'). On a clear day the tough two-hour climb rewards with stunning views over Clew Bay and its sandy islets. It was on Croagh Patrick that Ireland's patron saint fasted for 40 days and nights, and it's where he reputedly banished venomous snakes. Climbing the 764m holy mountain is an act of penance for thousands of believers on the last Sunday of July (Reek Sunday). The truly contrite take the ancient 35km pilgrim's route, from Ballintubber Abbey, Tóchar Phádraig (Patrick's Causeway), and ascend the mountain barefoot. The 7km trail taken by the less repentant begins at a signed car park in the west end of the village of Murrisk.

The Drive » The scenic route along Doolough Valley on the R335 to Leenane is the site of a tragic Famine walk of 1849, when in icy weather many people died as they walked from Louisburgh to Delphi in vain search of aid from a landlord. The side roads to the north and west of the valley lead to glorious beaches.

❹ Leenane

The small village of Leenane (also spelt Leenaun) rests on the shore of dramatic **Killary Harbour**. Dotted with mussel rafts, the long, narrow harbour is Ireland's only fjord – maybe. Slicing 16km inland and more than 45m deep in the centre, it certainly looks like a fjord, although some scientific studies suggest it may not actually have been glaciated. **Mt Mweelrea** (814m) towers to its north.

Leenane has both stage and screen connections. It was the location for *The Field* (1989), a movie with Richard Harris based on John B Keane's play about a tenant farmer's ill-fated plans to pass on a rented piece of land to his son.

🛏️ p256

The Drive » From Leenane, an ultrascenic loop of Connemara via the N59 crosses the beauty spots of Kylemore Abbey and Connemara National Park and then on through the lively town of Clifden, where you continue east through Maam Cross into Galway city in under two hours.

5 Galway City

Galway city is a swirl of enticing old pubs that hum with trad music sessions throughout the year. More importantly, it has an overlaying vibe of fun and frolic that's addictive. Soak it up on a walk through the city's medieval centre (p310). Galway is often referred to as the 'most Irish' of Ireland's cities (and it's the only one where you're likely to hear Irish spoken in the streets, shops and pubs). **Tigh Neachtain** (www. tighneachtain.com; 17 Upper Cross St; ⏱11.30am-midnight Mon-Thu, to 1am Fri, 10.30am-1am Sat, 12.30-11.30pm Sun), a 19th-century pub known simply as Neachtain's (*nock*-tans) or

Naughtons and painted a bright cornflower blue, has a wraparound string of tables outside, many shaded by a large tree. It's a must-stop place where a polyglot mix of locals plop down and let the world pass them by. Nearby, the long-established and award-winning **Druid Theatre** (☎091-568 660; www.druid. ie; Druid Lane) is famed for staging experimental works by young Irish playwrights, as well as new adaptations of classics.

🍴 🛏 p44, p72, p93, p256, p268, p277

The Drive » Plenty of time to think about lunch on the busy 20km seaside route between Galway city and County Clare. Clarinbridge and Kilcolgan offer welcome pit stops, especially if you're into oysters.

6 Clarinbridge & Kilcolgan

Some 16km south of Galway, Clarinbridge (Droichead an Chláirin) and Kilcolgan (Cill Cholgáin) are at their busiest during the **Clarenbridge Oyster Festival** (www. clarinbridge.com), held during the second weekend of September. However, the oysters are actually at their best from May through the summer. Oysters are celebrated year-round at **Paddy Burkes Oyster Inn** (☎091-796 226; www. paddyburkesgalway.com; N67, Clarinbridge; mains €8-26; ⏱10am-12.30am Mon-Sat, noon-11pm Sun), a thatched pub by the bridge in Clarinbridge that dishes up heaped servings. In more scenic surroundings is another thatched inn –

FESTIVALS OF FUN

Galway's packed calendar of festivals turns the city and surrounding communities into what feels like one nonstop party – streets overflow with revellers, and pubs and restaurants often extend their opening hours. The following are highlights:

Cúirt International Festival of Literature (www.cuirt.ie) Top-name authors converge on Galway in April for one of Ireland's premier literary festivals.

Galway International Arts Festival (www.giaf.ie) A two-week extravaganza of theatre, music and comedy in mid-July.

Galway Film Fleadh (www.galwayfilmfleadh.com) One of Ireland's biggest film festivals, held in July.

Galway Race Week (www.galwayraces.com) Horse races in Ballybrit, 7km northeast of the city, are the centrepiece each July or August of Galway's biggest, most boisterous festival of all.

Galway International Oyster and Seafood Festival (www.galwayoysterfest.com) Oysters are washed down with plenty of pints in the last week in September.

Classic Trip

WHY THIS IS A CLASSIC TRIP
BELINDA DIXON,
WRITER

For many visitors, the best of the west is synonymous with the best of Ireland – the wild, rugged scenery is reason enough to do it, and that's before you meet the people, visit the pubs and eat the food. Six days is just about right to enjoy the experience, but you're just as likely to find a spot that you'll want to grow old in.

Above: Fungie the dolphin, Dingle Bay
Left: Lough Hyne, County Cork
Right: Tigh Neachtain pub, Galway City

BRICKLEY PIX/ALAMY STOCK PHOTO ©

waterside **Moran's Oyster Cottage** (☎091-796 113; www.moransoystercottage. com; The Weir, Kilcolgan; mains €14-29, half-dozen oysters €13-16; ⏰ noon-9.30pm Sun-Thu, to 10pm Fri & Sat; 🚻).

Find a seat on the terrace overlooking Dunbulcaun Bay, where the oysters are reared before they arrive on your plate. It's well signposted some 2km off the N18, in a cove near Kilcolgan, just south of Clarinbridge.

The Drive ≫ From the N67, it's a short jaunt to the sleepy harbour village of Kinvara. From Ballyvaughan the inspiring scenery along the R480 highlights the barren Burren and its scattered prehistoric stone structures at its best. Drive through Ennis and around the Limerick city bypass to the pretty village of Adare. It's just over two hours of driving in all.

❼ Adare

Often dubbed 'Ireland's prettiest village', Adare centres on its clutch of perfectly preserved thatched cottages built by the 19th-century English landlord the Earl of Dunraven for workers constructing Adare Manor. Today, the cottages house craft shops and some of the county's finest restaurants, with prestigious golf courses nearby. Unsurprisingly, tourists are drawn to the postcard-perfect village, on the River Maigue, by the busload. Dating back to around 1200, **Desmond Castle**

(Desmond Castle; 📞 tour bookings 061-396 666; www.heritageireland.ie; tours adult/child €10/8; ⏱ tours hourly 11am-5pm Jul-Sep), a picturesque feudal ruin, saw rough usage until it was finally wrecked for good by Cromwell's troops in 1657.

🍴 🛏 p231, p256

The Drive » It's about two hours' drive southwest to Dingle (128km). The scenery ramps up several notches as you head from Tralee on to the peninsula – where the roads are pretty twisty – and over the famously picturesque Connor Pass.

TRIP HIGHLIGHT

8 Dingle Town

If you've arrived via the dramatic mountain-top Connor Pass, the fishing town of Dingle can feel like an oasis at the end of the earth...and maybe that's just what it is.

Chocolate-box quaint, though grounded by a typical Kerry earthiness, its streets are crammed with brightly painted grocer-pubs and great restaurants, second-hand bookshops and, in summer, coachloads of visitors. Announced by stars in the pavement bearing the names of its celebrity customers, **Dick Mack's** (www.dickmackspub.com; Green St; ⏱ 11am-11.30pm Mon-Thu, to 12.30am Fri & Sat, noon-11pm Sun) has an irrepressible sense of self. Ancient wood and ancient snugs dominate the interior, which is lit like the inside of a whiskey bottle.

Dingle Bay's most famous resident (and maybe the most famous resident in the whole area) is Fungie, a bottlenose dolphin that's been a friendly presence since 1983. There are regular boat tours.

🍴 🛏 p45, p59, p195, p257

TOP TIP:
THAT'S A GAS

A word of caution for visitors driving the wilds of Connemara: they're not called wilds for nothin'. There are long distances between filling stations on those gorgeous swathes of uninhabited valley and sheep-dotted mountainside. What's more, the few stations there are are often closed by early evening, so make sure you have enough fuel to keep you going for at least 80km. Find stations at Recess, Clifden and Kylemore.

The Drive » Dragging yourself away from Dingle, take the peninsula's lower road (R561) back, passing the windswept 5km stretch of dune-backed Inch Beach, and veer south at Castlemaine round the jewel of the southwest, the Ring of Kerry, through Kenmare to the magnificent Killarney National Park. The scenery becomes a lot wilder at Glengarriff on the awe-inspiring Beara Peninsula.

9 Glengarriff

Hidden deep in the Bantry Bay area, Glengarriff (Gleann Garbh) is an attractive village that snares plenty of passersby. In the second half of the 19th century, Glengarriff became a popular retreat for prosperous Victorians, who sailed from England. The tropical Italianate garden on **Garinish Island** (📞 027-63040; www.garinishisland.ie; adult/child €5/3, plus ferry fare; ⏱ 9.30am-5.30pm Jul & Aug, shorter hours Apr-Jun, Sep & Oct, closed Nov-Mar) is the top sight in Glengarriff. Subtropical plants flourish in the rich soil and warm climate. The camellias, magnolias and rhododendrons especially provide a seasonal blaze of colour. This little miracle of a place was created in the early 20th century, when the island's owner commissioned the English architect Harold Peto to design him a garden on the then-barren outcrop.

🛏 p223, p257

The Drive ›› Wend your way down the N71 through Bantry and on to pretty Skibbereen, where you access the R595 and follow signs to Lough Hyne. Glengarriff to Lough Hyne is 55km.

TRIP HIGHLIGHT

⑩ Lough Hyne

This beautiful lough is one of Ireland's natural wonders, and in 1981 it became the country's first marine nature reserve. Its glacier-gouged depths were originally filled with fresh water until rising sea levels breached one end around 4000 years ago. It is now linked to the sea by a narrow tidal channel known as the Rapids, where the tide pours in and out twice a day in a rush of white water.

There are lovely walks around the lough and in the neighbouring Knockomagh Wood Nature Reserve. A waymarked nature trail leads up a steep hill through the forest; you're rewarded with stunning views at the top.

Atlantic Sea Kayaking (☎028-21058; www. atlanticseakayaking.com; Reen Pier; half-day from €50) offers guided sea-kayak tours of the lough, including superbly atmospheric 2½-hour 'starlight paddles' after dark.

The Drive ›› Back at the N71, it's less than 10km to the dual villages of Union Hall and Glandore at Glandore Harbour.

⑪ Union Hall & Glandore

The pretty waterside villages of Union Hall and Glandore (Cuan Dor) burst into life in summer when fleets of yachts tack into the shelter of the Glandore Harbour inlet. A tangle of back roads meanders across the area; you should, too. Accessible from Glandore via a long, narrow causeway over the estuary, Union Hall was named after the 1800 Act of Union, which abolished the separate Irish parliament. There's an ATM, a post office and a general store here.

The Drive ›› From here you can glide into Cork, 70km away, in about 1½ hours. Along the way, you'll drive through Clonakilty, where you can buy Ireland's most famous black (blood) pudding. Rather than follow the main N71 all the way, explore the picturesque R600 coastal road via Kinsale.

⑫ Cork City

Competing fiercely with Dublin for recognition, the south's largest city has arguably every bit as much to offer as the capital, yet on a smaller and even friendlier scale. The River Lee flows around the centre, an island packed with grand Georgian parades, cramped 17th-century alleys and modern masterpieces such as the opera house. Dotted around the compact centre are a host of historic buildings, cosmopolitan restaurants, local markets and cosy traditional bars. The award-winning **Lewis Glucksman Gallery** (☎021-490 1844; www.glucksman.org; University College Cork, Western Rd; suggested donation €5; ⊙10am-5pm Tue-Sat, 2-5pm Sun; ♿), in the grounds of University College Cork (UCC), is a startling limestone, steel and timber construction that displays the best in both national and international contemporary art and installation. It's always buzzing with people coming to attend lectures, view the artwork or procrastinate in the cafe.

✕ ⮕ p59, p207, p215, p257

Eating & Sleeping

Westport

✖ An Port Mór   Irish €€

(☎098-26730; www.anportmor.com; 1 Brewery Pl; mains €14-22, 5 courses €39; ☺5-9pm Sun-Thu, to 9.30pm Fri & Sat; 🛜) Proprietor-chef Frankie Mallon's little restaurant packs a big punch. It's an intimate place with a series of long narrow rooms and a menu featuring gutsy flavours, excellent meats and much-lauded seafood (try the excellent Clew Bay scallops). Just about everything is procured from the region. The two-course early-bird menu (€24), served nightly between 5pm and 6pm, is superb value.

🛏 St Anthony's Riverside B&B   B&B €€

(☎098-28887; www.st-anthonys.com; Distillery Rd; s from €90, d €100-115; 🅿🛜) It may be in the middle of Westport, but a tall hedge and thick, twisted vines give this genteel, 19th-century B&B a tucked-away feel. Rooms have clean lines and restful, light colours, some also have Jacuzzis. There's a large garden to relax in and breakfast is excellent.

Leenane ④

🛏 Delphi Lodge   Historic Hotel €€€

(☎095-42222; www.delphilodge.ie; off R335; s from €150, d €265-295, f €295, ste €295; 🅿@) Dwarfed by the mountainous backdrop, this wonderful 1830s Georgian mansion beside Fin Lough was built by the Marquis of Sligo. The 13-room country hotel features beautiful interiors, colossal 405-hectare grounds, delicious food (six-course dinner €65) and a serious lack of pretension. It's popular with fishers (half-day with fishing tutor €180) and those seeking relaxation and escape.

Galway City ⑤

✖ Aniar   Irish €€€

(☎091-535 947; www.aniarrestaurant.ie; 53 Lower Dominick St; 6/8/10 courses €72/89/99, with wine pairings €107-169; ☺6-9.30pm Tue-Thu, 5.30-9.30pm Fri & Sat) Terroir specialist Aniar is passionate about the flavours and food producers of Galway and west Ireland. Owner and chef JP McMahon's multicourse tasting menus have earned him a Michelin star, yet the casual spring-green dining space remains refreshingly down to earth. The wine list favours small producers. Reserve at least a couple of weeks in advance. To discover the secrets behind classic and contemporary Irish cuisine, book a course at the on-site **Aniar Boutique Cookery School** (day courses €225).

🛏 Heron's Rest   B&B €€

(☎091-539 574; www.theheronsrest.com; 16A Longwalk; d €179-199; 🛜) The thoughtful hosts of this B&B in a lovely row of houses on the banks of the Corrib provide binoculars and deck chairs so you can sit outside and enjoy the views – views also extend from all three snug but cute double-glazed rooms. Breakfasts incorporate organic local produce; other touches include complimentary decanters of port. Gourmet picnic baskets can be arranged on request.

Adare ⑦

✖ Restaurant 1826 Adare   Modern Irish €€

(☎061-396 004; www.1826adare.ie; Main St; mains €20-27; ☺6-9.30pm Wed-Sat, 3-8pm Sun; 🚹) One of Ireland's most highly regarded chefs, Wade Murphy continues to wow diners at this art-lined 1826-built thatched cottage. His passion for local seasonal produce is an essential ingredient in dishes such as pan-seared halibut with Connemara clams and pickled samphire. A three-course early-bird menu (€36) is served daily until 7pm.

🛏 Adare Manor
Hotel €€€

(📞061-605 200; www.adaremanor.com; Main St; r from €700; P @ 🛜 🏊) Built in the mid-19th century for the Earl of Dunraven, this magnificent manor house s now a luxury hotel. After extensive renovations in 2017 it sports a new bedroom wing and a huge ballroom to complement an already elegant property dripping in antique furniture and class. The manor's superb **Oakroom Restaurant** (afternoon tea €55, 3-course dinner €90; 🕑 afternoon tea 1.30-3.30pm, dinner 6-9.30pm) and lavish high tea are also open to nonguests.

Dingle Town ⑧

🍴 Chart House
Seafood €€€

(📞066-915 2255; www.thecharthousedingle. com; The Mall; mains €22-32; 🕑6-10pm Jun-Sep, hours vary Oct-Dec & mid-Feb–May) Window boxes frame this free-standing stone cottage, while inside dark-red walls, polished floorboards and flickering candles create an intimate atmosphere. Creative cooking uses Irish produce: Cromane mussels and Dingle Bay prawns, Annascaul black pudding and Brandon Bay crab, fillet of Kerry beef and Cashel blue cheese. Book up to several weeks ahead at busy times.

🛏 Dingle Benner's Hotel
Hotel €€€

(📞066-915 1638; www.dinglebenners.com; Main St; s/d/f from €129/199/259; P 🛜) A Dingle institution, melding old-world elegance, local charm and modern comforts in the quiet bedrooms, lounge, library, and (very popular) Mrs Benner's Bar. Family rooms sleep four. Rooms in the 300-year-old wing have the most character; those in the new parts are quieter and more spacious.

Glengarriff ⑨

🛏 Eccles Hotel
Historic Hotel €€

(📞027-63003; www.eccleshotel.com; Glengarriff Harbour; s/d from €80/120; 🕑 closed Nov-Mar; P 🛜) Just east of the centre, this grande dame of West Cork hotels has a long and distinguished history (since 1745), counting the British War Office, WM Thackeray, George Bernard Shaw and WB Yeats as former guests. The public areas retain some 19th-century grandeur, though some bedrooms are on the small side. Ask for a bayside room on the 2nd floor for the best views.

Cork City ⑫

🍴 Farmgate Cafe
Cafe €

(📞021-427 8134; www.farmgatecork.ie; Princes St, English Market; mains €8-14; 🕑8.30am-5pm Mon-Sat) An unmissable experience at the heart of the **English Market** (www.englishmarket. ie; main entrance Princes St; 🕑8am-6pm Mon-Sat), the Farmgate is perched on a balcony overlooking the food stalls below, the source of all that fresh local produce on your plate – everything from crab and oysters to the lamb in your Irish stew. Go up the stairs and turn left for table service, or right for counter service.

🍴 Paradiso
Vegetarian €€

(📞021-427 7939; www.paradiso.restaurant; 16 Lancaster Quay; 2-/3-course menus €39/47; 🕑5.30-10pm Mon-Sat; 🍴) A contender for best restaurant in town of any genre, Paradiso serves contemporary vegetarian dishes, including vegan fare: how about corn pancakes filled with leek, parsnip and Dunmanus cheese with fennel-caper salsa and smoked tomato? Reservations are essential. Rates for dinner, bed and breakfast, staying in the chic upstairs rooms, start from €180/220 per single/double.

🛏 River Lee Hotel
Hotel €€€

(📞021-425 2700; www.doylecollection.com; Western Rd; r from €269; P 🛜 🏊) This modern riverside hotel brings a touch of luxury to the city centre. It has gorgeous public areas with huge sofas, a designer fireplace, a stunning five-storey glass-walled atrium and superb service. There are well-equipped bedrooms (nice and quiet at the back, but request a corner room for extra space) and possibly the best breakfast buffet in Ireland.

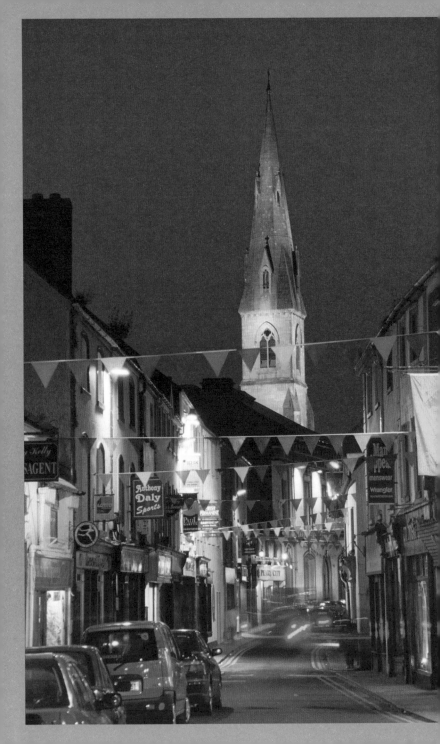

Classic Trip

Musical Landscapes

*From the busker-packed streets of Galway
city, this rip-roaring ride guides you around
County Clare and the Aran Islands to delight
in fine festivals and traditional-music pubs.*

23

TRIP HIGHLIGHTS

155 km

Inisheer
End-of-the-earth
landscape and
traditional drumming
festival

START
Galway

Inishmore

⑨
FINISH
Doolin **Lisdoonvarna**
Kilfenora
④

**Miltown
Malbay**
②

65 km

Ennistimon
Country village with
roaring Cascades and
music at every turn

Ennis
Medieval town simply
bursting with trad
sessions and fine pubs

110 km

**5 DAYS
155KM / 96 MILES**

GREAT FOR...

BEST TIME TO GO
The summer months
for outdoor *céilidh*
(traditional music and
dancing) and music
festivals.

 **ESSENTIAL
PHOTO**

Set-dancing at
the crossroads, in
Vaughan's of Kilfenora.

 **BEST FOR
TUNES**

Ennis, on summer
nights, where local
musicians showcase
their skills.

nis Historic town streetscape by night

259

23 Musical Landscapes

Prepare for an embarrassment of musical riches. Join the big bawdy get-togethers of Galway's always-on music scene and Ennis' rollicking urban boozers. Then take a seat at the atmospheric small pub sessions in crossroad villages like Kilfenora and Kilronan on the Aran Islands, where pretty much everyone joins in. Whatever way you like it, this region is undeniably one of Ireland's hottest for toe-tapping tunes.

Greatman's Bay

Gorumna Island Carrar

Lettermullen

Lettermullen Island

North Sound

Inishmore 8 Kilronan

Aran Islands Inishn

Inishr

ATLANTIC OCEAN

N 0 ————————— 10
    0 ————————— 5 miles

1 Galway City

Galway (Gaillimh) has a young student population and a largely creative community that give a palpable energy to the place. Walk its colourful medieval streets (p310), packed with heritage shops, streetside cafes and pubs, all ensuring there's never a dull moment. Galway's pub selection is second to none and some swing to tunes every night of the week. **Crane Bar** (☎091-587 419; www.thecranebar.

com; 2 Sea Rd; ☺10.30am-11.30pm Mon-Thu, to 1am Fri, 12.30pm-1am Sat, to 11.30pm Sun), an atmospheric old pub west of the River Corrib, is the best spot in Galway to catch an informal *céilidh* most nights. Or for something more contemporary, **Róisín Dubh** (☎091-586 540; www.roisindubh.net; 9 Upper Dominick St; ☺5pm-2am Sun-Thu, to 2.30am Fri & Sat) is *the* place to hear emerging international and local singer-songwriters.

✗ ⌂ p44, p72, p93, p256, p268, p277

The Drive ›› From Galway city centre, follow the coast road (R338) east out of town as far as the N18 and then cruise south to Ennis, where your great musical tour of Clare begins.

TRIP HIGHLIGHT

2 Ennis

Ennis (Inis), a medieval town in origin, is packed with pubs featuring trad

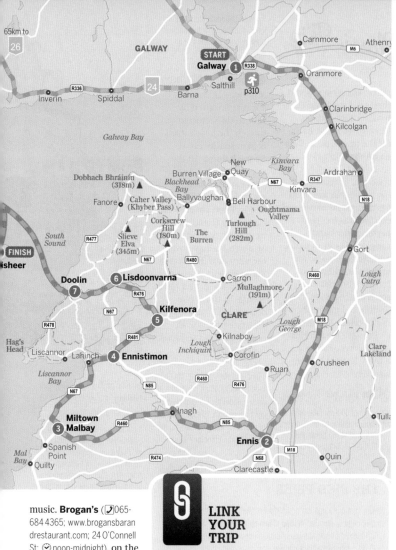

music. **Brogan's** (☎065-684 4365; www.brogansbaran drestaurant.com; 24 O'Connell St; ⊘noon-midnight), on the corner of Cook's Lane, sees a fine bunch of musicians rattling even the stone floors almost every night in summer, while the wood-panelled Poet's Corner Bar (p39) is a hideout for local

LINK YOUR TRIP

24 **Mountains & Moors**

From Galway take in some of Connemara's loveliest points.

26 **North Mayo & Sligo**

Cruise up to Westport to join this wondrous trail around the hidden gems of north Connaught.

ROBIN BUSH/GETTY IMAGES ©

Classic Trip

musicians serious about their trad sessions. The tourist office collates weekly live music listings for the town's pubs. **Cois na hAbhna** (☎065-682 4276; www.coisnahabhna. ie; Gort Rd; ☺opening hours vary), a pilgrimage point for traditional music and culture, has frequent performances and a full range of classes in dance and music; it's also an archive and library of Irish traditional music, song, dance and folklore. Traditional music aficionados might like to time a visit with **Fleadh Nua** (www.fleadhnua.com; ☺May), a lively festival held in late May.

✗▭ p45, p268, p309

The Drive » From the N85, which runs south of The Burren, you'll arrive at the blink-and-you'll-miss-it village of Inagh.

Swing right on to the smaller R460 for the run into Miltown Malbay – some 32km in all.

- - - - - - - - - - - - - - - - - -

③ Miltown Malbay

Miltown Malbay was a resort favoured by well-to-do Victorians, though the beach itself is 2km southwest at **Spanish Point**. To the north of the Point there are beautiful **walks** amid the low cliffs, coves and isolated beaches. A classically friendly place in the chatty Irish way, Miltown Malbay hosts the annual Willie Clancy Summer School, one of Ireland's great trad music events. In town, one of a couple of genuine old-style places with occasional trad sessions is **Friel's Bar** (Lynch's; ☎065-708 5883; Mullagh Rd; ☺6pm-midnight Mon-Thu, to 1am Fri & Sat, 2pm-midnight Sun) – don't be confused by the much bigger sign on the front proclaiming 'Lynch's'. Another top

music pub is the dapper **Hillery's** (☎065-708 4188; Main St; ☺3pm-1am).

The Drive » Hugging the coast, continue north on the N67 until you come to the small seaside resort of Lahinch. Just a few streets backing a wide beach, it's renowned for surfing. From here, it's only 4km up the road to the lovely heritage town of Ennistimon.

- - - - - - - - - - - - - - - - - -

TRIP HIGHLIGHT

④ Ennistimon

Ennistimon (Inis Díomáin) is one of those charming market towns where people go about their business barely noticing the characterful

THE PIED PIPER

Half the population of Miltown Malbay seems to be part of the annual **Willie Clancy Summer School** (☎065-708 4148; www.scoilsamhraidhwillieclancy.com; ☺Jul), a tribute to a native son and one of Ireland's greatest pipers. The eight-day **festival**, now in its fourth decade, begins on the first Saturday in July, when impromptu sessions occur day and night, the pubs are packed and Guinness is consumed by the barrel – up to 10,000 enthusiasts from around the globe turn up for the event. Specialist workshops and classes underpin the event; don't be surprised to attend a recital with 40 noted fiddlers.

Kilfenora Cathedral, County Clare

buildings lining Main St. Behind this bustling facade there's a surprise: the roaring **Cascades**, the stepped falls of the River Inagh. After heavy rain they surge, beer-brown and foaming, and you risk getting drenched on windy days in the flying drizzle. Not to be missed, **Eugene's** (📞065-707 1777; Main St; ⏲10.30am-11.30pm Mon-Thu, to 12.30am Fri & Sat, 12.30-11pm Sun) is intimate and cosy, and has a trademark collection of visiting cards covering its walls, alongside photographs of famous writers and musicians. The inspiring collection

of whiskey (Irish) and whisky (Scottish) will have you smoothly debating their relative merits. Another great trad pub is **Cooley's House** (📞065-707 1712; Main St; ⏲10.30am-11.30pm Mon-Thu, to 12.30am Fri & Sat, noon-11pm Sun), with music most nights in summer and several evenings a week in winter.

🍴 🛏 p268, p309

The Drive » Heading north through a patchwork of green fields and stony walls on the R481, you'll land at the tiny village of Kilfenora, some 9km later. Despite its diminutive size, the pulse of Clare's music scene beats strongly in this area.

----

⑤ Kilfenora

Underappreciated Kilfenora (Cill Fhionnúrach) lies on the southern fringe of The Burren. It's a small place, with a diminutive 12th-century **cathedral** (off Main St; ⏲9.30am-5.30pm Jun-Aug, 10am-5pm Mar-May, Sep & Oct), which is best known for its **high crosses**. The town has a strong music tradition that rivals that of Doolin but without the crowds. The celebrated **Kilfenora Céili Band** (www.kilfenoraceiliband. com) has been playing for more than a century. Its traditional music

WHY THIS IS A CLASSIC TRIP
BELINDA DIXON, WRITER

To witness a proper traditional session in one of the music houses of Clare or the fine old pubs of Galway can be a transcendent experience, especially if it's appropriately lubricated with a pint (or few) of stout. Sure, there'll be plenty of tourists about, but this is authentic, traditional Ireland at its most evocative.

Above: Traditional music session, Galway City
Left: Inisheer, County Galway
Right: Local pub, Ennistimon, County Clare

features fiddles, banjos, squeeze boxes and more and can be enjoyed most Wednesday evenings at **Linnane's Pub** (📞065-708 8157; Main St; ⏰10.30am-11.30pm, hours can vary).

A short stroll away, **Vaughan's** (📞065-708 8004; www.vaughanspub.ie; Main St; ⏰10.30am-11.30pm, hours can vary) has music in the bar every night during the summer and terrific set-dancing sessions in the neighbouring barn on Sunday nights.

The Drive » From Kilfenora the R476 meanders northwest 8km to Lisdoonvarna, home of the international matchmaking festival. Posh during Victorian times, the town is a little less classy today, but friendly, good-looking and far less overrun than Doolin.

6 Lisdoonvarna

Lisdoonvarna (Lios Dún Bhearna), often just called 'Lisdoon', is well known for its mineral springs. For centuries people have been visiting the local spa to swallow its waters. Down by the river at **Roadside Tavern** (📞065-707 4084; www.roadsidetavern.ie; Kincora Rd; ⏰noon-11.30pm Mon-Thu, to 12.30am Fri & Sat, to 11pm Sun Mar-Oct, shorter hours Nov-Feb), third-generation owner Peter Curtin knows every story worth telling. There are trad sessions nightly in summer and on Friday and Saturday evenings in winter. Look for a trail beside the pub that runs 400m down to two **wells** by the river. A few paces from the tavern, the **Burren Smokehouse** (☎065-707 4432; www.burrensmokehouse.ie; Kincora Rd; ⊙9am-6pm May-Aug, 10am-4pm Sep-Apr) is where you can learn about the ancient Irish art of oak-smoking salmon.

The Drive » Just under 10 minutes' drive west, via the R478/479, you'll reach the epicentre of Clare's trad music scene, Doolin. Also known for its setting – 6km north of the Cliffs of Moher – Doolin is really three small neighbouring villages. First comes Roadford, then 1km west sits Doolin itself, then another 1km west comes pretty Fisherstreet, nearest the water.

❼ Doolin

Doolin gets plenty of press as a centre of Irish traditional music, owing to a trio of pubs that have sessions through the year. **McGann's** (☎065-707 4133; www.mcgannspubdoolin.com; Roadford; ⊙10am-11.30pm Mon-Wed, to 12.30am Thu-Sat, to 11pm Sun; 🛜) has all the classic touches of a full-on Irish music pub; the action often spills out on to the street. Right on the water, **Gus O'Connor's** (☎065-707 4168; www.gusoconnors-doolin.com; Fisherstreet;

⊙9am-midnight Mon-Thu, to 2am Fri-Sun), a sprawling favourite, has a rollicking atmosphere. It easily gets the most crowded and has the highest tourist quotient. **McDermott's** (MacDiarmada's; ☎065-707 4328; www.mcdermottspub.com; Roadford; ⊙10am-11pm Sun-Wed, to 12.30am Thu-Sat) is a simple and sometimes rowdy old pub popular with locals.

🛏 p93, p269

The Drive » This 'drive' is really a sail – you'll need to leave your car at one of Doolin's many car parks to board the ferry to the Aran Islands.

- - - - - - - - - - - - - - - -

❽ Inishmore

The Aran Islands sing their own siren song to thousands of travellers each year, who find their desolate beauty beguiling. The largest and most accessible Aran, Inishmore (Inis Mór), is home to ancient fort **Dun Aengus** (Dún Aonghasa; ☎099-61008; www.heritageireland.ie; adult/child €5/3; ⊙9.30am-6pm Apr-Oct, to 4pm Nov-Mar), one of the oldest archaeological remains in Ireland, as well as some lively pubs and restaurants in the only town, Kilronan. Irish remains the local tongue, but most locals speak English with visitors. **Tí Joe Watty's Bar** (☎086 049 4509; www.joewattys.ie; Kilronan; ⊙noon-midnight Sun-Thu, 11.30am-12.30am Fri

& Sat Apr-Oct, 4pm-midnight Mon-Fri, noon-midnight Sat & Sun Nov-Mar) is the best pub in Kilronan, with traditional sessions most summer nights. Turf fires warm the air on the 50 weeks a year when this is needed. Informal music sessions, glowing fires and a broad terrace with harbour views make **Tí Joe Mac's** (Kilronan; ⊙11am-11pm Mon-Thu, 11am-12.30am Fri & Sat, noon-10pm Sun; 🛜) another local favourite, as is the **Bar** (☎099-61130; www.inismorbar.com; Kilronan; ⊙noon-11pm Sun-Thu, 11.30am-midnight Fri & Sat), which has nightly live music from May to mid-October, and weekends the rest of the year.

✕ 🛏 p59, p93, p269, p309

The Drive » In the summer passenger ferries run regularly between the Aran Islands. They cost €10 to €15; schedules can be a little complex – book in advance.

- - - - - - - - - - - - - - - -

TRIP HIGHLIGHT

❾ Inisheer

On Inisheer (Inis Oírr), the smallest of the Aran Islands, the breathtakingly beautiful end-of-the-earth landscape adds to the island's distinctly mystical aura. Steeped in mythology, traditional rituals are very much respected here. Locals still carry out a pilgrimage with potential

Gus O'connor's pub, Doolin, County Clare

healing powers, known as the *Turas,* to the Well of Enda, an ever-burbling spring in the southwest. For a week in late June the island reverberates to the thunder of traditional drums during **Craiceann Inis Oírr International Bodhrán Summer School** (www.craiceann.com; ☻ late Jun). Bodhrán masterclasses, workshops and pub sessions are held, as well as Irish dancing. Rory Conneely's atmospheric inn **Tigh Ruaírí** (Rory's; ☎099-75002; d €55-94; ☎) hosts live music sessions and, here since 1897, **Tigh Ned** (☎099-75004; www.tighned.com; dishes €7-15; ☻ kitchen noon-4pm Apr-Oct, bar 10am-11.30pm Apr-Oct) is a welcoming, unpretentious place, with harbour views and lively traditional music.

✖ 🛏 p269, p309

Eating & Sleeping

Galway City ❶

✖ Loam
Gastronomy €€€

(☎091-569 727; www.loamgalway.com; Fairgreen Rd; 2/3/7/9 courses €45/55/119/159; ⊙6-10pm Tue-Sat) Enda McEvoy is one of the most groundbreaking chefs in Ireland today (with a Michelin star to prove it), producing inspired flavour combinations from home-grown, locally sourced or foraged ingredients: dried hay, fresh moss, edible flowers, wild oats, forest gooseberries, Salthill sea vegetables and hand-cut peat (which McEvoy uses in his extraordinary peat-smoked ice cream). The on-site wine bar opens at 5pm and closes at 10pm Tuesday to Saturday.

🛏 Glenlo Abbey Hotel
Historic Hotel €€€

(☎091-519 600; www.glenloabbeyhotel.ie; Kentfield Bushy Park, off N59; d €357-448, ste €538-984; ☎) Set on the shores of Lough Corrib, 4km northwest of Galway, this 1740-built stone manor is the ancestral home of the Ffrench family, one of Galway's 14 tribes. Exceptionally preserved period architecture is combined with antique furnishings, sumptuous marble bathrooms, duck-down duvets and king-sized pillows. Breakfasts are lavish, while the hotel's fine-dining **Pullman Restaurant** (2/3 courses €61/69; ⊙6.30-10pm daily Mar-Oct, 6.30-9.30pm Fri & Sat Nov–early-Feb; 🍴) occupies original *Orient Express* train carriages. The vast grounds include a never-completed abbey with a walled garden, started by the family in 1790, as well as a nine-hole golf course (green fees €45) – the fourth hole sits on an island in the lough that's reached by a bridge. Booking a week in advance, online, brings 10% off the standard price.

🛏 Stop
B&B €€

(☎091-586 736; www.thestopbandb. com; 38 Father Griffin Rd; s/d/tr/f from €60/110/150/200; ☎) Done up with contemporary artworks, stripped floorboards and bold colours, this design-conscious B&B delivers snug rooms where aesthetically pleasing space-saving tricks include hangers instead of wardrobes and streamlined work desks. Gourmet breakfast includes freshly squeezed orange juice and there's a handy supermarket right across the street.

Ennis ❷

🛏 Rowan Tree Hostel
Hostel €

(☎065-686 8687; www.rowantreehostel.ie; Harmony Row; dm €25-29, d €79-89, f €125; ☎) Balconies overlooking the swift-flowing River Fergus; bright, airy dorms; and doubles with Egyptian linen add to the appeal at this town-centre hostel. It's set in a grand 1740-built former gentlemen's club, and fantastic facilities include a kitchen, a laundry and the excellent **Cafe Bar** (☎065-686 8669; www. rowantreecafebar.ie; mains €8-14; ⊙10.30am-11pm; 🍴) in the former ballroom.

Ennistimon ❹

✖ Cheese Press
Deli €

(☎085 760 7037; Main St) Everything you need for a riverside picnic or a packed lunch for a Burren hike is on offer at this enticing deli. Organic Irish cheeses include St Tola Irish Goat Cheese, Abbey Brie, Ballyhooly Blue, Burren Gold, Smoked Gubbeen and Bay Lough Cheddar. It also has smoked salmon and hams, relishes and house-baked bread, and the best coffee in town.

🛏 Falls Hotel   Hotel €€

(📞065-707 1004; www.fallshotel.ie; off N67; s/d/f/tr €100/150/190/225; 🅿 🛜 💺) Built on the ruins of an O'Brien castle on the western edge of town, the vast, Georgian Falls Hotel was once the family home of Caitlín MacNamara, who married Dylan Thomas. Today it houses a large indoor pool, a spa and 142 modern rooms overlooking the rushing River Inagh and 20 hectares of wooded grounds.

Self-catering apartments sleeping two people start at €235; cots and high chairs are available.

Doolin ⑦

🛏 Cullinan's Guesthouse   Inn €€

(📞065-707 4183; www.cullinansdoolin.com; Doolin; d €120-140; ⏱Mar-Nov; 🅿 🛜) Owned by well-known fiddle-playing James Cullinan, this mustard-coloured inn on the River Aille has eight spotless, comfortable, pine-furnished rooms. A couple of rooms are slightly smaller than the others, but have river views.

It has a lovely back terrace for enjoying the views and a well-regarded **restaurant** (mains €22-29; ⏱6-9pm Mon, Tue & Thu-Sat Easter–mid-Oct).

Inishmore ⑧

✖ Tí Joe Watty's Bar   Pub €€

(📞086 049 4509; www.joewattys.ie; Kilronan; mains €14 to €25; ⏱noon-midnight Sun-Thu, 11.30am-12.30am Fri & Sat Apr-Oct, 4pm-

midnight Mon-Fri, noon-midnight Sat & Sun Nov-Mar) Warmed by peat fires, the island's oldest and most popular pub has trad sessions every night in summer from 9pm or 10pm, and weekends the rest of the year. Wednesday's darts night is a local fixture. There's a large beer garden and an extensive list of Irish gins, craft beers and whiskeys. Its seafood-focused menu is excellent; book for dinner in summer.

🛏 Pier House Guest House   Inn €€

(📞099-61417; www.pierhousearan.com; Kilronan; d from €95; 🛜) You won't have time to lose your sea legs on the 50m walk from the ferry to this two-storey inn set on a small rise. The 12 rooms are decorated in rich shades of red, and come with tea- and coffee-making facilities. The sun terrace at the front is the perfect spot to watch harbour life go by.

Inisheer ⑨

🛏 South Aran House & Restaurant   B&B €€

(📞099-75073; www.southaran.com; s/d €65/84; ⏱Apr-Oct; 🛜) There's an idyllic feel to this rustic B&B; lavender grows outside windows framing broad Atlantic views, and the four bedrooms have underfloor heating and wrought iron beds. Breakfasts feature apple fritters with potato cakes and the evening restaurant (mains €17 to €25) showcases local seafood and organic produce; booking required. Guests must be over 18. Regular events include cookery and foraging courses (from €30 per person).

Mountains & Moors

A whirl around Connemara's end-of-the-earth landscape of valleys, secret strands and even a fjord will leave you pining for more so we've added cottages, abbeys and a gastro village.

24

TRIP HIGHLIGHTS

175 km

Kylemore Abbey
Crenellated neo-Gothic fantasy with Victorian walled gardens

Glassilaun

7

Clifden

Oughterard

5   4

START/ FINISH

Galway

Spiddal

115 km

Roundstone
Terraces and pubs overlooking the dark recess of Bertraghboy Bay

120 km

Gurteen Bay & Dog's Bay
A dog-bone-shaped peninsula lined with idyllic beaches

**6 DAYS
206KM / 128 MILES**

GREAT FOR...

BEST TIME TO GO
Winter, when the sea and landscape are at their wildest.

 ESSENTIAL PHOTO
Create your own historic movie still at the Quiet Man Bridge.

 BEST FOR DIVING
The turquoise water of Glassilaun Bay offers superb diving.

24 | Mountains & Moors

West of Galway the scenery behind the windscreen becomes increasingly wild and rugged. Crossing the Gaeltacht (Gaelic-speaking territory) beyond Spiddal, you'll take in the cottage of writer, poet and Easter Rising leader Pádraig Pearse, characterful Roundstone for exceptional food, and the impossibly blue waters of white-sand bays. A spin through Connemara's heartland to gothic Kylemore Abbey brings you to pretty Oughterard and back on to Galway.

1 Galway City

County Galway's namesake city is such a charmer you might not want to tear yourself away to the countryside. Arty, bohemian Galway city (Gaillimh) is renowned for its pleasures. Brightly painted pubs heave with live music, while cafes offer front-row seats for observing street performers, weekend hen parties run amok, lovers entwined and more. Steeped in history, the city nonetheless has a contemporary vibe.

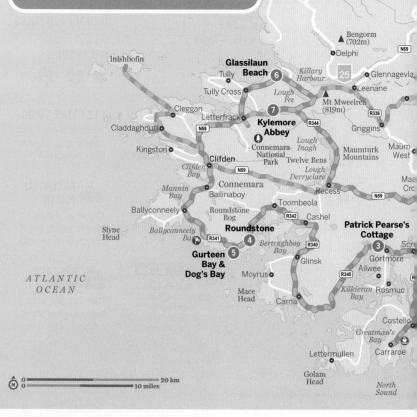

ATLANTIC OCEAN

Inishbofin
Bengorm (702m)
Delphi
N59
Glassilaun Beach 6
Tully
Killary Harbour
25
Glennagevla
Tully Cross
Lough Fee
Leenane
Cleggan
Letterfrack
Mt Mweelrea (819m)
Claddaghduff
N59
Kylemore Abbey 7
R344
Griggins
Kingston
Connemara National Park
Lough Inagh
R336
Clifden
N59
Twelve Bens
Maumturk Mountains
Maum West
Clifden Bay
Connemara
Lough Derryclare
Mannin Bay
Ballinaboy
Maa Cro
Ballyconneely
Roundstone Bog
Toombeola
Recess
N59
Slyne Head
Ballyconneely Bay
R341
Roundstone 4
R342
Cashel
Patrick Pearse's Cottage 3
Gurteen Bay & Dog's Bay 5
Bertraghboy Bay
R340
Scre
Glinsk
Gortmore
Moyrus
Ailwee
R340
Mace Head
Carna
Kilkieran Bay
Rosmuc
Costello
Greatman's Bay
Lettermullen
Carraroe
Golam Head
North Sound

0 — 20 km
0 — 10 miles

Walking the cobblestone streets (p310) you'll find remnants of the medieval town walls between shops selling Aran sweaters, handcrafted Claddagh rings, and stacks of secondhand and new books.

✕ ⌂ p44, p72, p93, p256, p268, p277

The Drive » The slow coastal route (R336) between Galway and Connemara takes you past pretty seascapes and villages. Opposite the popular Blue Flag beach Silver Strand, 4.8km west of Galway, are the Barna Woods, a dense, deep-green natural oak forest perfect for rambling and picnicking before hitting Spiddal.

----

② Spiddal

Spiddal (An Spidéal) is a refreshingly untouched little village, and the start of the Gaeltacht region. On your right as you approach the settlement is **Spiddal Craft Village** (Ceardlann an Spidéil; www.spiddalcrafts.com; off R336, Spiddal; ☺10am-6pm Easter-Sep, hours vary deOct-Easter), where you can watch woodworkers, leatherworkers, sculptors and weavers plying their crafts. Spiddal also makes an excellent foodie pit stop – for the top-notch coffee and fresh dishes of the craft village's own **Builín Blasta** (☎091-558 559; www.builinblasta.com; Spiddal Craft Village, Spiddal; dishes €5-16; ☺10am-5pm Mon-Fri, 11am-5pm Sat & Sun Easter-Sep, reduced hours Oct-Easter) cafe, or first-rate seafood at the acclaimed **O'Grady's on the Pier** (☎091-592 223; www.ogradysonthepier.ie; Seapoint, Barna; mains lunch €10-17, dinner €18-30, seafood platters €27; ☺12.30-3pm & 6-9.30pm).

⌂ p277

The Drive » West of Spiddal, the scenery becomes more dramatic, with fields crisscrossed by low stone walls rolling to a ragged shore. Carraroe (An Cheathrú Rua) has

LINK YOUR TRIP

23 **Musical Landscapes**

This rip-roaring ride takes you from Galway's music bars to the best trad sessions of Clare.

25 **Loughs of the West**

Cruise Galway's gorgeous inland waterways on this tour of its lakes and rivers. Pick it up at Delphi, near Leenane.

MAYO

Tourmakeady
'artry
untains

Curramore

N84

Lough Mask

Hollymount

Ballinrobe

25

Kilmaine

Neale

R332

Clonbur

Cong Cross

e's Country

Gortbrack

Lough Corrib

Clerhaun

Shrule

R345

R333

Headford

N84

Oughterard

8

ALWAY

N59

Lar Connaught

Cloonboo

Moycullen

River Clare

N17

START/ FINISH

Galway ①

p310

23

Inverin

②

R336

Salthill

Barna

Spiddal

Galway Bay

fine beaches, including the Coral Strand. Exploring the small roads surrounding Greatman's Bay reveals tiny inlets often watched over by local donkeys – the perfect scenic muse for a nationalist writer such as Pádraig Pearse.

❸ Patrick Pearse's Cottage

Writer, poet and teacher Pádraig Pearse (1879–1916) led the Easter Rising with James Connolly and others in 1916; after the revolt he was executed by the British. Pearse wrote some of his short stories and plays in this small thatched **cottage** (Ionad Cultúrtha an Phiarsaigh; www.heritage ireland.ie; R340, Ros Muc; adult/ child €5/3; ⊙9.30am-6pm Easter-Sep, to 4pm Oct-Easter) in a wonderfully picturesque location. Although the interior was burned out during the War of Independence, it has been restored and contains an interesting exhibition about Pearse's life.

🛏 p277

The Drive » The scenic R340 swings south along Kilkieran Bay, an intricate system of tidal marshes, basins and bogs containing an amazing diversity of wildlife. The R342 meanders past Cashel (An Caiseal), skirting Bertraghboy Bay. At Toombeola a short trip south on the R341 takes you to the picture-postcard village of Roundstone. A drive of some 28km in all.

TRIP HIGHLIGHT

❹ Roundstone

Clustered around a boat-filled harbour, Roundstone (Cloch na Rón) is one of Connemara's gems. Colourful terrace houses and inviting pubs overlook the dark recess of Bertraghboy Bay, which is home to lobster trawlers and traditional *currachs* (rowing boats with tarred canvas bottoms stretched over wicker frames). Wander the short **promenade** for views over the water to ribbons of eroded land. Malachy Kearns' **Roundstone Musical Instruments** (☑095-35808; www.bodhran.com; Monastery Rd; ⊙9.15am-7pm Jul-Sep, 10.30am-6pm Mon-Sat Oct-Jun) is just south of the village in the remains of an old Franciscan monastery. Kearns is Ireland's only full-time maker of traditional bodhráns (handheld goatskin drums). Watch him work and buy a tin whistle, harp or booklet filled with Irish ballads; there's also a small free folk museum and a cafe.

🍴 p277

The Drive » The R341 shadows the coast from Roundstone to Clifden. Beaches along here have such beautiful white sand and turquoise water that, if you added 10°C to the temperature, you could be in Antigua. Don't believe us? Feast your eyes on the azure waters and brilliant white-sand beaches

NORADOA/SHUTTERSTOCK ©

of Gurteen Bay and Dog's Bay ahead.

TRIP HIGHLIGHT

❺ Gurteen Bay & Dog's Bay

About 2.5km west of Roundstone, look for the turn to Gurteen Bay (sometimes spelt Gorteen Bay). After a further 800m there is a turn for Dog's Bay. Together, the pair form the two sides of a dog-bone-shaped peninsula lined with idyllic **beaches**. Park and enjoy a day strolling the grassy heads and frolicking on the hard-packed sand.

Kylemore Abbey, County Galway

The Drive » Dust the sand off for a 47km drive. Continue north on the R341 through the village of Ballyconneely to Clifden. There pick up the N59 for a scenic cruise north. At the Letterfrack crossroads turn left, signed Connemara Loop (also signed Scuba Dive West). Continue to follow those signs along bumpy, sometimes single-track, water-view lanes until you reach Glassilaun Beach.

❻ Glassilaun Beach

Although Connemara is a pearl necklace of sights, the north coast is diamond encrusted. Gorgeous beaches frame stark, raw mountain vistas and views out to the moody sea. Glassilaun Beach is arguably one of Connemara's best, offering a gorgeous, dune-backed crescent of sand. Islands dot the bay and tawny hills surge up behind. If you're drawn to the beauty of the underwater world, **Scuba Dive West** (☏095-43922; www.scubadivewest.com; Glassilaun Beach, Renvyle; shore/boat dives incl gear from €45/70, snorkelling per 2hr €35), based at Glassilaun Beach, runs highly recommended courses and dives. Beginners are welcome.

The Drive » Continue southeast along the final 5km stretch of road that runs along Lough Fee. In spring, when the gorse explodes in yellow bloom, the views here are, again, simply breathtaking. When you hit the N59 head right (southwest) until, suddenly, imposing Kylemore Abbey appears, backed by mountains and surrounded by water, on your right.

TRIP HIGHLIGHT

❼ Kylemore Abbey

Magnificently situated on the shores of a lake, the crenellated 19th-century neo-Gothic fantasy **Kylemore Abbey** (☏095-52001; www.kylemoreabbey.com; off N59; adult/child €13/free; ⏱9am-7pm Jul & Aug,

BRIDGING THE QUIET MAN

Whenever an American cable TV station needs a ratings boost, they invariably trot out the iconic 1952 film *The Quiet Man*. Starring John Wayne and filmed in lavish colour to capture the crimson locks of his costar Maureen O'Hara, the film regularly makes the top-10 lists of ageing romantic-comedy lovers for its portrayal of rural Irish life, replete with drinking and fighting, fighting and drinking etc. Director John Ford returned to his Irish roots and filmed the movie almost entirely on location in Connemara and the little village of Cong, just over the border in County Mayo. One of the most photogenic spots from the film, the eponymous **Quiet Man Bridge**, is just 7km west of Oughterard off the N59. Looking much as it did in the film, the picture-perfect arched span (whose original name was Leam Bridge) is a lovely spot. Purists will note, however, that the scene based here had close-ups done on a cheesy set back in Hollywood. That's showbiz. Hardcore fans will want to buy the superb *The Complete Guide to The Quiet Man*, by Des MacHale. It's sold in most tourist offices in the area.

9.30am-5.30pm Sep & Oct, 9am-6pm Apr-Jun, 10am-4.30pm Nov-Mar) was built for a wealthy English businessman, Mitchell Henry, who spent his honeymoon in Connemara. His wife died tragically young. Admission also covers the abbey's tranquil **Victorian walled gardens**. There's a cafe and a teahouse on the grounds, which also offer hikes and woodland walks. Prepare for large volumes of visitors in high summer, when it's best to arrive in the early morning for uncluttered views.

The Drive » The next 50km stretch, heading towards Galway via the R344 and N59, cruises through a kaleidoscopic tapestry of typical Connemara scenery. It feels like the end of the earth with colours changing from lime green, to mustard, to purple on the mountain side – views interrupted only by drystone walls, the odd derelict cottage or an oblivious sheep crossing your path.

----

8 Oughterard

The writer William Makepeace Thackeray sang the praises of the small town of Oughterard (Uachtar Árd), saying: 'A more beautiful village can scarcely be seen'. Even if those charms have faded a little over the years, shadows of its former Georgian glory remain. And it is one of Ireland's principal angling centres. If you see tourists wandering around, talking with a drawl, it's probably because they are here to relive the iconic American film *The Quiet Man*.

The Drive » Heading east again, stop close by for a great photo op at 16th-century Aughnanure Castle, 4km east of Oughterard, off the N59. From here it's a 27km run into Galway city for a well-deserved pint at Galway's finest, Tigh Neachtain.

Eating & Sleeping

Galway City ❶

🍴 Sheridans Cheesemongers   Deli €

(📞091-564 829; www.sheridanscheesemongers.
com; 14 Churchyard St; platters €9-18; ⊙ shop
10am-6pm Mon-Fri, 9am-6pm Sat, wine bar
1pm-midnight Wed-Fri, noon-midnight Sat,
5pm-midnight Tue & Sun) Heavenly aromas waft
from this fabulous cheesemongers filled with
superb local and international cheeses. But the
real secret is up a narrow flight of stairs at its
wonderfully convivial wine bar. Sample from
an Italian-influenced wine list while nibbling on
platters of cheeses and charcuterie.

🍴 John Keogh's   Gastropub €€

(📞091-449 431; www.johnkeoghs.iem; 22
Upper Dominick St; mains €11-24; ⊙ kitchen
5-9pm Mon-Fri, 1-9pm Sat & Sun) Dark-wood
panelling, snugs, stained glass, antique mirrors,
book-lined shelves and blazing open fires set
the scene for standout gastropub fare. John
Keogh's doesn't take reservations, so arrive
early to dine on mussels with home-baked soda
bread and garlic aioli, or Irish oysters with a
Guinness shot. End with a Roscommon-brewed
Sheep Stealer ale or rare whiskey at the bar.

🛏 Adare Guesthouse   Guesthouse €€

(📞091-582 638; www.adareguesthouse.ie; 9
Father Griffin Pl; s/d/f €75/130/150; 🅿🛜♿)
Overlooking a football pitch and children's
playground, this beautifully kept guesthouse
has generously sized rooms and service that
runs like clockwork. Sift through 16, often
organic, menu choices at breakfast including
French toast with caramelised plums, smoked
salmon and scrambled eggs, and buttermilk
pancakes with honeyed pears.Prices fall
dramatically, by as much as €60 per double,
from October to March.

Spiddal ❷

🛏 Cloch na Scíth   B&B €€

(📞091-553 364; www.thatchcottage.com;
Kellough, Spiddal; d/tr €80/96; 🅿🛜) Set in a
storybook garden where ducks and chickens
roam, this 18th-century thatched cottage
has cosy rooms with private bathrooms. The
wonderfully warm, friendly host, Nancy, cooks
bread in an iron pot over the peat fire (as her
grandmother taught her and as she'll teach
you), along with hearty breakfasts.

Cashel ❸

🛏 Cashel House Hotel   Hotel €€€

(📞095-31001; www.cashelhouse.ie; R342,
Cashel; d €190-210, ste from €225; ⊙ Easter-
Nov; 🅿🛜🐾) At the head of Cashel Bay, this
19th-century country mansion warmed by
open peat and log fires has 30 period rooms
surrounded by 17 hectares of woodland and
gardens. Nonguests are welcome for three-
course evening meals (€60) and afternoon tea
served in the conservatory, or on the lawns in
fine weather.

Roundstone ❹

🍴 O'Dowd's   Seafood €€

(📞095-35809; www.odowdsseafoodbar.com;
Main St; mains €14-29; ⊙ restaurant 5-9.30pm,
bar menu noon-9.30pm; 🛜) Roundstone
lobster, Aran Islands hake, plaice and sea bass,
local crab and mackerel smoked in-house
are sourced off the old stone dock directly
opposite this wonderfully authentic old pub
and restaurant, while produce comes from its
garden. There's a strong list of Irish craft beers
and ciders. Its neighbouring summertime **cafe**
(dishes €5.50-11.50; ⊙9am-6pm Mar-Oct; 🛜)
serves breakfast and lunch.

Loughs of the West

This trip takes you around beautiful, less-visited backwaters to see lakeside scenery at its most untarnished, visiting epic castles and intriguing islands en route.

25

TRIP HIGHLIGHTS

243 km

Inishbofin
Deserted lanes, green pastures and sandy beaches grace this sleepy island

128 km

Delphi
Striking mountains perfect for hiking or relaxing

Tourmakeady

Ballinrobe

10 FINISH

7

Leenane

3

58 km

Cong
Timeless Irish village immortalised by the classic film *The Quiet Man*

Galway
START

4–5 DAYS
243KM / 151 MILES

GREAT FOR...

BEST TIME TO GO
May for ultimate fishing and the Inishbofin Arts Festival.

 ESSENTIAL PHOTO
Cong, with the spectacular vista of Ashford Castle and the lake as backdrop.

 BEST FOR FISHING
Loughs Corrib and Mask are world-renowned for their brown trout.

25 Loughs of the West

Following the lay of the lakes, this panoramic waterside drive takes in the very best of Loughs Corrib and Mask. Pass the picture-postcard villages of Cong and Tourmakeady before crossing the barren beauty of Connemara to dramatic mountain-backed Delphi. Cruising Connemara's filigreed northern coast, you'll discover pretty strands and ancient remains both on the mainland and on the striking island retreat of Inishbofin.

Mt Knockm (46

Inishturk

FINISH
10 Inishbofin Re P

Inishshark

Clegg

Omey 9 Claddag
Strand

Clifd

Ballinabc

Ballyconneely o

Slyne *Ballycon*
Head *Bay*

ATLANTIC OCEAN

1 Galway City

Galway's Irish name, Gaillimh, originates from the Irish word *gaill,* meaning 'outsiders' or 'foreigners', and the term resonates throughout the city's history. Colourful and cosmopolitan – many dark-haired, olive-skinned Galwegians consider themselves descended from the Spanish Armada – this small city is best explored by strolling its medieval streets (p310). Bridges arc the salmon-filled River Corrib, and a long promenade leads to the seaside suburb of **Salthill**, on Galway Bay, the source of the area's famous oysters.

A favourite pastime for Galwegians and visitors alike is walking along the seaside **Prom**, running from the edge of the city along Salthill. Local tradition dictates 'kicking the wall' across from the diving boards before turning around. In and around Salthill are plenty of cosy pubs from where you can watch storms roll over the bay.

✕ 🛏 p44, p72, p93, p256, p68, p277

The Drive » From Galway take the inspiringly named Headford Rd north on to the N84 into, well, Headford, skirting Lough Corrib, the Republic's biggest lake, which virtually cuts off western Galway from the rest of the country. At the crossroads in the centre of Headford turn left, initially following brown tourist signs for Rinnaknock Pier, then later for Greenfields.

2 Lough Corrib

Just under 7km west of Headford, Greenfields pier juts out into Lough Corrib. Over 48km long and covering some 200 sq km, it encompasses

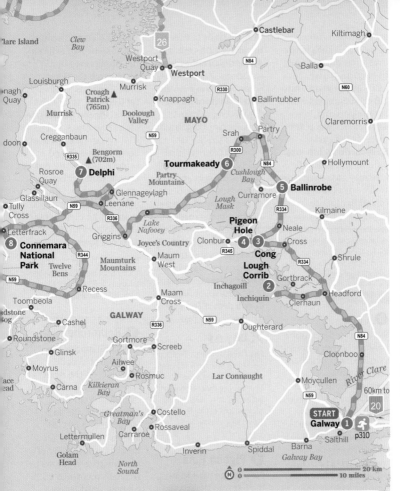

more than 360 islands, including **Inchagoill**, home to some 5th-century monastic remains, a simple graveyard and the Lugnaedon Pillar – a 6th-century inscribed stone. **Inchiquin** island can be accessed by a short, water-framed road from Greenfields pier. The lough is world-famous

LINK YOUR TRIP

20 **Shannon River Route**

From the waters to the wild, continue on the west's inland waterways at Portumna.

26 **North Mayo & Sligo**

Continue exploring the northwest's incredible coastline, joining the route at Westport.

for its salmon and wild brown trout, with the

highlight of the fishing calendar being mayfly

281

season, when zillions of the small bugs hatch over a few days (usually in May) and drive the fish – and anglers – into a frenzy. Salmon begin running around June. Upstream, signs point towards the curious **Ballycurrin Lighthouse**, built in 1772 when the lake may have seen more traffic – it's Europe's only inland lighthouse.

The Drive » From Headford, take the R334 north out of town as far as Cross, where you'll join the R346, which takes you into the outstanding village of Cong, some 16km later.

TRIP HIGHLIGHT

❸ Cong

Sitting on a sliver-thin isthmus between Lough Corrib and Lough Mask, Cong complies with romantic notions of a traditional Irish village. Time appears to have stood still ever since the evergreen American classic *The Quiet Man* was filmed here in 1951. Though popular on the tour-bus circuit, the wooded trails between the lovely 12th-century **Augustinian abbey** (Mainistir Chonga; ☎094-954 6542; Abbey St; ☺dawn-dusk) and stately **Ashford Castle** (☎094-954 6003; www.ashfordcastle.com; Cong; grounds adult/child €10/5; ☺grounds 9am-dusk) offer genuine quietude. First built in 1228 as the seat of the de Burgo family, one-time owner Arthur Guinness (of stout fame) turned the castle into a regal hunting and fishing lodge, which it remains today. A range of **cruises** (www.corribcruises.com; adult/child €20/10) on Lough Corrib depart from the Ashford Castle pier.

✕ 🛏 p285

The Drive » Next a 2km hop. From Cong take the R345 west out of town towards Cornamona. After you see the entrance for McGrath Quarry, take the first left then look out for the lay-by signed Pigeon Hole Wood.

❹ Pigeon Hole

Pick up the path leading left into the woods.

You're about to discover one of some half a dozen limestone caves that honeycomb the Cong area. Each has a colourful legend or story to its credit. **Pigeon Hole** is one of the best caves; steep, slippery, stone steps lead down towards it and subterranean water flows here in winter. Keep an eye out for the white trout of Cong, a mythical woman who turned into a fish to be with her drowned lover.

The Drive » After heading back into Cong, it's a 15-minute drive on the R345 and R334 north to Ballinrobe.

❺ Ballinrobe

The small market town of Ballinrobe (Baile an Roba), on the River Robe, is a good base for exploring trout-filled Lough Mask, the largest lake in the county. **St Mary's Church** has an impressive collection of stained-glass windows by Ireland's renowned 20th-century artist Harry

BOYCOTT BEGINNINGS

It was near the unassuming little village of Neale, near Cong, that the term 'boycott' first came into use. In 1880 the Irish Land League, in an effort to press for fair rents and improve the lot of workers, withdrew field hands from the estate of Lord Erne, who owned much of the land in the area. When Lord Erne's land agent, Captain Charles Cunningham Boycott, evicted the striking labourers, the surrounding community began a campaign to ostracise the agent. Not only did farmers refuse to work his land, people in the town refused to talk to him, provide services or sit next to him in church. The incident attracted attention from the London papers, and soon Boycott's name was synonymous with such organised, nonviolent protests. Within a few months, Boycott gave up and left Ireland.

Ashford Castle, Cong

Clarke. One depicts St Brendan 'the Navigator', with oar in hand, who reputedly sailed to America long before Columbus. You can access Lough Mask at **Cushlough Bay**, just 5km west of town. Take the Castlebar road north and immediately on the left you'll see signs for Cushlough. Follow these along winding lanes and eventually the road will open out into a wide car park with broad lough views. Here slender boats are pulled up on to the gravel and picnic tables dot the grass; it's a delightful place to pause and take in the views.

The Drive » Rejoin the N84 as it stretches north, before veering west at Partry. The landscape is made up of mostly small farm holdings, rusty bogland and tumbledown drystone walls. Follow the serene lakeside route (R300) before pit stopping to take in the lake around Tourmakeady.

----

6 Tourmakeady

With the Partry Mountains acting as a picturesque backdrop to its west, the small village of Tourmakeady, on the shore of Lough Mask, is part of an Irish-speaking community. Once a flax-growing area, its name is derived from Tuar Mhic Éadaigh, meaning

'Keady's field', referring to the field where the flax was once laid out to dry before spinning. Tourmakeady Woods, with a charming 58m-high **waterfall** at its centre, makes a wonderful spot for a picnic. Or head another 2km along R300 and refuel at the cosy **Paddy's Thatched Bar**, overlooking a shimmering expanse of water.

The Drive » Follow the swooping, curling lakeside road, pulling in at stunning Lake Nafooey, at the foot of Maumtrasna, to take in the view. Head north on the R336 through Leenane and around the harbour, passing Assleagh Falls to Delphi, a scenic 45km in all.

283

Delphi

Geographically just inside County Mayo, but administratively in County Galway, this swathe of mountainous moorland is miles from any significant population, allowing you to set about the serious business of relaxing. At the southern extent of the Doolough Valley, the area was named by its most famous resident, the second marquis of Sligo, who was convinced that it resembled the land around Delphi, Greece. If you can spot the resemblance, you've a better imagination than most, but in many ways it's even more striking than its Mediterranean namesake. At the beautiful Delphi Resort opt for a day's surfing, kayaking or rock climbing, followed by a stay and some pampering spa treatments.

✗ 🛏 p285

The Drive ≫ Return to Leenane and follow the N59 southwest to Letterfrack. Go through the town's crossroads and 400m later you'll see signs pointing left to the Connemara National Park Visitor Centre.

⑧ Connemara National Park

Spanning 2000 dramatic hectares of bog, mountain and heath, Connemara National Park encloses a number of the **Twelve Bens**, including Bencullagh, Benbrack and Benbaun. The heart of the park is **Gleann Mór** (Big Glen), through which the River Polladirk flows. There's fine walking up the glen and over the surrounding mountains. There are also short, self-guided walks and, if the Bens look too daunting, you can hike up **Diamond Hill** nearby. Various types of flora and fauna native to the area are explained, including the huge elephant hawkmoth, in the excellent **visitor centre** (☎076-100 2528; www.connemarana alpark.ie; off N59, Letterfrack; ⏰9am-5.30pm Mar-Oct).

🛏 p285

The Drive ≫ Zip back east on the N59 for 9km before joining the R344 south through the Lough Inagh Valley as it skirts the brooding Twelve Bens. The N59 then sweeps west to Clifden. A few killometres north signs point you towards Omey Island, a jagged coastal route that leads to tiny Claddaghduff (An Cladach Dubh).

⑨ Omey Strand

Omey Island (population 20) is a low islet of rock, grass, sand and a handful of houses. Between half tide and low tide you can walk to the island (or if you're brave, drive) across the sand at Omey Strand. Tide times are displayed on the noticeboard in the car park; the route is marked by blue road signs bearing white arrows. Don't be tempted to cross between half tide and high tide, or if there's water on the route.

The Drive ≫ Return to Claddaghduff and head north to Cleggan to park and take the 30-minute ferry to Inishbofin.

⑩ Inishbofin

By day sleepy Inishbofin is a haven of tranquillity. You can walk or bike its narrow, deserted lanes, green pastures and sandy beaches, with farm animals and seals for company. But with no *gardaí* (Irish Republic police) on the island to enforce closing times at the pub, by night – you guessed it – Inishbofin has wild craic. Situated 9km offshore, Inishbofin is only just under 6km long by 4km wide, and its highest point is a mere 86m above sea level. Inishbofin's pristine waters offer superb scuba diving, sandy beaches and alluring trails that encourage exploring. The island well and truly wakes up during the **Inishbofin Arts Festival** (www.inishbofin.com) in May, which includes accordion workshops, archaeological walks, art exhibitions and concerts. Ferries from Cleggan to Inishbofin are run by **Island Discovery** (☎095-45819; www.inishbofinisland discovery.com; adult/child return €20/10).

🛏 p285

Eating & Sleeping

Cong ③

✖ Hungry Monk Cafe €

(📞094-954 5842; Abbey St; mains €6-14;
🕙10am-5pm Mon-Sat Mar-Nov; 🛜) With
the warmest of welcomes, this simple cafe
with bright colours and artfully mismatched,
distressed furniture is a perfect refuge on a
misty day. Locally sourced ingredients make up
the excellent sandwiches, soups and salads, the
luscious cakes are homemade and the coffee is
excellent.

🛏 Lodge at Ashford Castle Hotel €€€

(📞094-954 5400; www.thelodgeac.com;
Quay Rd; d from €289-323, ste €395-540; 🛜)
Built in the 1820s by the owners of nearby,
prestigious **Ashford Castle** (📞094-954
6003; www.ashfordcastle.com; Cong; d €675-
950, ste €1725-5000; 🛜), the lodge has rich,
contemporary colours, plush furnishings,
hand-made toiletries and dreamy lake views.
The suites are magnificent: some boast private
terraces and mini-balconies; others have rain
showers and range over two floors. The lodge's
renowned eatery, **Wilde's at the Lodge**
(5 courses €65; 🕙6.30-9pm Thu-Sun plus
1-3.30pm Sun; 🛜), delivers fine dining at
its best.

Delphi ⑦

✖ Wild Atlantic Cafe Cafe €

(📞095-42208; www.delphiadventureresort.
com; Delphi Resort, off the R335; mains from €7;
🕙9.30am-5.30pm; 🛜) Within the swish Delphi
Resort, this friendly and bright cafe doubles
as a craft shop to promote local artists and
craftspeople, and serves fine food and decent
coffee.

🛏 Delphi Resort Lodge €€

(📞095-42208; www.delphiadventureresort.
com; off R335; dm €15-17, d €129, ste €199-229;
P @ 🛜) There's a bed for most budgets at
the modern, multipurpose Delphi Resort, from

standard guest rooms, loft rooms and larger
suites (some with enormous timber decks) to
luxury six-bed dorms with bathrooms where
each bunk has its own USB charger and reading
light. A cavernous pub-restaurant serves great
bar food (mains €12 to €29). Spa treatments
use hand-harvested seaweed and the property's
own mountain spring water. There's a good cafe
here as well.

Connemara National Park ⑧

🛏 Lough Inagh Lodge Lodge €€

(📞095-34706; www.loughinaghlodgehotel.ie;
off R344; s/d from €140/170; P 🛜) Set in huge
grounds against a hill, this atmospheric lodge
has rich colour schemes, an oak-panelled dining
room and open log fires. Several of its 13 grand
rooms face the lake. You can also dine (mains
€17 to €33) in style. It's midway up the Lough
Inagh Valley, 9km north of Recess.

Inishbofin ⑩

🛏 Dolphin Hotel & Restaurant Inn €€

(📞095-45991; www.dolphinhotel.ie; d €110;
🕙Apr-Sep; 🛜) Bedrooms at this 11-room inn
have light, cream-coloured fabrics and a good
deal of space. Solar panels on the roof provide
power, while its organic kitchen garden provides
ingredients to team with a wealth of local
seafood (lunch mains €6 to €19, dinner two-/
three-courses €25/30). There's a two-night
minimum stay at weekends. Pick up from the
pier is included in the price.

🛏 Lapwing House B&B €€

(📞095-45996; www.inishbofin.com/bandb/
lapwing.html; d from €80; 🛜) Named after the
local bird species that breeds on the island, this
lovely family-run B&B in a whitewashed building
500m north from the pier has just two rooms
(one double and one twin), each with a private
bathroom. Views extend over the sheep-flecked
hillside to the harbour. Homemade breakfast
pancakes come with maple syrup.

North Mayo & Sligo

Travel from country-cosmopolitan Westport to nature at its most visceral on windswept Achill Island. Then, carry on via superb surfscapes to Sligo, Yeats' beloved adopted home town.

26

TRIP HIGHLIGHTS

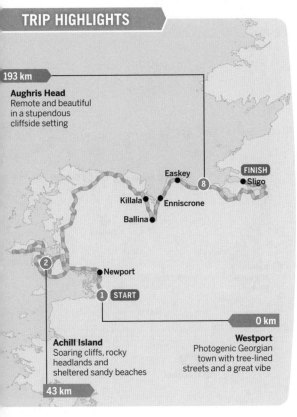

193 km

Aughris Head
Remote and beautiful in a stupendous cliffside setting

Easkey

FINISH
Sligo

Killala

Enniscrone

Ballina

Newport

START

0 km

Achill Island
Soaring cliffs, rocky headlands and sheltered sandy beaches

Westport
Photogenic Georgian town with tree-lined streets and a great vibe

43 km

4–5 DAYS
266KM / 165 MILES

GREAT FOR...

BEST TIME TO GO
In early autumn crowds have abated and the sea is warmest.

ESSENTIAL PHOTO
Wild Atlantic rollers at sunset on Easkey beach.

BEST FOR OUTDOORS
Achill Island and Easkey offer surf and blustery beach walks.

Easkey Rocky coastline of one of Ireland best surfing destinations

287

26 North Mayo & Sligo

This area has something quietly special – the rugged and remote Atlantic scenery of the west, but with fewer crowds. Grab a board and face off an invigorating roller at Achill, take a restorative seaweed bath at Enniscrone, walk in WB Yeats' footsteps round the 'Lake Isle of Innisfree' at the foot of Benbulben and enjoy the unpretentious company of lively Westport.

TRIP HIGHLIGHT

① Westport

Bright and vibrant even in the depths of winter, Westport is a photogenic Georgian town with tree-lined streets, riverside walkways and a great vibe. With an excellent choice of accommodation and restaurants and pubs renowned for their music, it's an extremely popular spot, yet has never sold its soul to tourism. A couple of kilometres west on Clew Bay, the town's harbour, Westport Quay

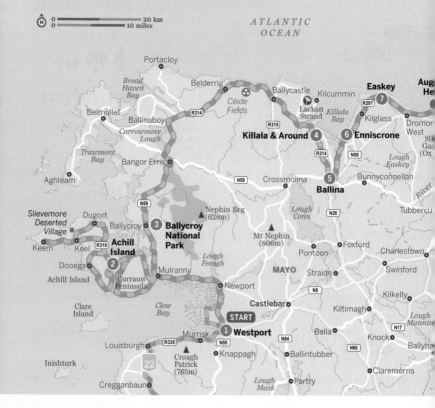

is a picturesque spot for a sundowner.

Westport House (p250), built in 1730 on the ruins of the 16th-century castle of Grace O'Malley (p290), is a charming Georgian mansion that retains much of its original contents and has some stunning period-styled rooms. The house is set in glorious gardens. Children will love the **Pirate Adventure Park**, complete with a swinging pirate ship, a 'pirate's playground' and a rollercoaster-style

flume ride through a water channel.

🍴 p256 p293

The Drive » A wiggling 12km drive north of Westport is the picturesque 18th-century village of Newport. Then comes Mulranny village on a narrow isthmus overlooking the 365 islands of Clew Bay. Just before the main R319 to Achill Island take the scenic route left (signed Ocean Rd). Once on Achill, cut left again to pick up Atlantic Dr, signed Wild Atlantic Way.

- - - - - - - - - - - - - - - - - -

TRIP HIGHLIGHT

2 Achill Island

Ireland's largest offshore island, Achill (An Caol), is connected to the mainland by a short bridge. Despite its accessibility, it has plenty of that far-flung-island feeling: soaring cliffs, rocky headlands, sheltered sandy beaches, broad expanses of blanket bog and rolling mountains. **Slievemore Deserted Village** (⊙dawn-dusk), at the foot of Slievemore Mountain, is a poignant reminder of the island's past hardships. In the mid-19th century, as the

Potato Famine took hold, starvation forced the villagers to emigrate, or die. Except in the height of the holiday season, the Blue Flag beaches at **Dooega**, **Keem**, **Dugort** and **Golden Strand** are often pretty much deserted.

🍴 🛏 p293

The Drive » The superbly scenic R319 bounces past broad inlets and high hills back towards the mainland. At the junction with the N59, turn left towards Ballycroy National Park. You're now deep amid beautifully bleak boglands dotted with drystone walls and sheep. About 14km later follow signs for the Ballycroy National Park Visitor Centre, and its cafe, Ginger & Wild.

- - - - - - - - - - - - - - - - - -

3 Ballycroy National Park

Covering one of Europe's largest expanses of blanket bog, **Ballycroy National Park** (🕿098-49888; www.ballycroynationalpark.ie; off N59, Ballycroy; ⊙10am-5.30pm Mar-Oct) is a gorgeously scenic region, where the River Owenduff wends its way

LINK YOUR TRIP

27 Sligo Surrounds
Continue from Sligo to explore the county's rich megalithic remains, blustery beaches and Yeats' old stomping ground.

22 Best of the West
The crème de la crème of Ireland's west coast; pick up this route in Westport for a scenic and cultural feast.

through intact bogs. The park is home to a diverse range of flora and fauna including peregrine falcons, corncrakes and whooper swans. A nature trail with interpretation panels leads from the visitor centre across the bog with great views to the surrounding mountains. If you wish to explore further, the challenging, 40km **Bangor Trail** crosses the park and leads to some of its most spectacular viewpoints.

The Drive ≫ Ballycroy is 18km south of Bangor Erris on the N59. Continuing north from here on to the R314, you'll pass the magnificent Stone Age monument at Céide Fields before heading through Ballycastle and on to the historic town of Killala.

- - - - - - - - - - - - - - - -

④ Killala

The town itself is pretty enough, but Killala is more famous for its namesake **bay** nearby, and for its role in the

French invasion, when in 1798 more than 1000 French troops landed at Kilcummin in Killala Bay. It was hoped that their arrival would inspire the Irish peasantry to revolt against the English. The rebellion though was short-lived; the events are marked by signs at Killala Quay – follow signs to it from the centre of town.

Lackan Strand, just to the west, is a stunning expanse of golden sand. There's good surf here, but you'll need to bring your own equipment.

The Drive ≫ Back on the R314, it's only 12km or so down to the provincial hub of Ballina, a busy market town.

- - - - - - - - - - - - - - - -

⑤ Ballina

Mayo's second-largest town, Ballina, is synonymous with salmon. If you're here during fishing season, you'll see droves of green-garbed waders, poles in hand, heading

for the River Moy – one of the most prolific rivers in Europe for catching the scaly critters – which pumps right through the heart of town. You'll also spot salmon jumping in the Ridge (salmon pool), with otters and grey seals in pursuit.

One of the best outdoor parties in the country, the five day **Ballina Salmon Festival** (www. ballinasalmonfestival.ie) takes place in mid-July.

The Drive ≫ Taking the N59 northeast out of town towards Enniscrone, cut back up to the coast on to the small R297, which you'll meet just over 4km from Ballina.

THE PIRATE QUEEN

The life of Grace O'Malley (Gráinne Ní Mháille or Granuaile; 1530–1603) reads like an unlikely work of adventure fiction. Twice widowed and twice imprisoned for acts of piracy, she was a fearsome presence in the troubled landscape of 16th-century Ireland, when traditional chieftains were locked in battle with the English for control of the country. Grace was ordered to London in 1593, whereupon Queen Elizabeth I granted her a pardon and offered her a title: she declined, saying she was already Queen of Connaught. **Westport House** (p250) now resides on the ruins of Grace's 16th-century castle.

WONDERFUL PICTURES/SHUTTERSTOCK ©

Slievemore Deserted Village, Achill Island

6 Enniscrone

Enniscrone is famous for **Kilcullen's Seaweed Baths** (☏096-36238; www.kilcullenseaweedbaths.net; Cliff Rd; bath from €25; ☺10am-9pm Jun-Aug, noon-8pm Mon-Fri, 10am-8pm Sat & Sun Sep-May, closed Tue & Wed Nov-Mar), an Edwardian bathhouse that is one of the best and most atmospheric in the country. A stunning beach known as the **Hollow** stretches for 5km. Surf lessons and board hire are available from Enniscrone-based **Seventh Wave Surf School** (☏087 971 6389; www.surfsligo.com; Enniscrone Beach; lessons adult/child from €30/25; ☺Apr-Oct).

The Drive » Some 14km north you'll come to the little village of Easkey.

7 Easkey

Easkey seems blissfully unaware that it's one of Europe's best year-round surfing destinations. Pub conversations revolve around hurling and Gaelic football, and facilities are few. The beach is signed from the eastern edge of town. It's overlooked by a 19m-high 12th-century ruined castle tower, the remains of a formidable stronghold. The upper-most level is known as the Sailor's Bed.

The Drive » From Easkey, hug the winding coast road (R297) until you see signs for Aughris Head.

TRIP HIGHLIGHT

8 Aughris Head

An invigorating 5km walk traces the cliffs around remote Aughris Head, where dolphins and seals can often be seen swimming into the bay. Birdwatchers should look out for kittiwakes, fulmars, guillemots, shags, storm petrels and curlews along the way. In a stupendous setting on the lovely beach by the cliff walk, the Beach Bar is tucked inside a 17th-century thatched cottage, with cracking traditional music sessions and superb seafood.

 p293

The Drive » From Aughris rejoin the N59 heading broadly east and on to the N4 towards Sligo until you see a sign for Dromahair (R287). Take this small, leafy road east, skirting the south of Lough Gill.

- - - - - - - - - - - - - - - - -

9 Lough Gill

The mirrorlike 'Lake of Brightness', Lough Gill is home to as many legends as fish. One that can be tested easily is the story that a silver bell from the abbey in Sligo was thrown into the lough and only those free from sin can hear it pealing. (We didn't hear it...)

Two magical swathes of woodland – **Hazelwood** and **Slish Wood** – have loop trails; from the latter, there are good views of Innisfree Island, subject of WB Yeats' poem 'The Lake Isle of Innisfree'. You can take a cruise on the lake from **Parke's Castle**.

The Drive » Having soaked up the atmosphere of Yeats' backyard, make your way a few kilometres north, via the R288 and R286, to the hub of Yeats country, Sligo town.

- - - - - - - - - - - - - - - - -

10 Sligo Town

Sligo town is in no hurry to shed its cultural traditions but it doesn't sell them out, either. Pedestrian streets lined with inviting shopfronts, stone bridges spanning the River Garavogue,

and *céilidh* (sessions of traditional music and dancing) spilling from pubs contrast with contemporary art and glass towers rising from prominent corners of the compact town. A major draw of Sligo's **County Museum** (☏071-911 1679; www.sligoarts.ie; Stephen St; ⊙9.30am-12.30pm Tue-Sat, plus 2-4.50pm Tue-Sat May-Sep) is the Yeats room, which features photographs, letters and newspaper cuttings connected with the poet WB Yeats, as well as drawings by his brother Jack B Yeats, one of Ireland's most important modern artists.

✗ 🛏 p58, p72, p293, p301, p351

IRELAND'S SEAWEED BATHS

Ireland's native spa therapy is the stuff of mermaid (or merman) fantasy. Part of Irish homeopathy for centuries, steaming your pores open then submerging yourself in a seaweed bath is said to help rheumatism and arthritis, thyroid imbalances, even hangovers. Certainly it leaves your skin feeling baby-soft: seaweed's silky oils contain a massive concentration of iodine, a key presence in most moisturising creams.

Seaweed baths are prevalent along the west coast but two places stand out. **Kilcullen's Seaweed Baths** (p291), set within a grand Edwardian structure in Enniscrone, is the most traditional and has buckets of character. It seems perfectly fitting to sit with your head exposed and your body ensconced in an individual cedar steam cabinet before plunging into one of the original gigantic porcelain baths filled with amber water and seaweed.

For an altogether more modern setting, try **Voya Seaweed Baths** (☏071-916 8686; www.voyaseaweedbaths.com; Shore Rd; bath from €28; ⊙10am-8pm), which has a beachfront location.

If too much relaxation is barely enough, both establishments also offer the chance to indulge in various other seaweed treatments, including body wraps and massages.

Eating & Sleeping

Westport ❶

✖ Pantry & Corkscrew · Irish €€

(📞098-26977; www.thepantryandcorkscrew.com; The Octagon; mains €17-24; ⏱5-10pm daily May-Sep, Wed-Sun Oct-Apr; 🍴) The heart of Mayo's slow-food movement is found at this narrow storefront with a turquoise exterior and interior walls crammed with pictures. The kitchen works culinary magic with seasonal, local and organic produce to rustle up stout-braised beef, maple-glazed pork and arancini with jalapeño and Aran islands feta. Book ahead. The early-evening menu (5pm to 6.30pm; 2/3 courses €22/25) is superb value.

Achill Island ❷

✖ Chalet · Seafood €€

(📞087 230 7893; www.keembayfishproducts.ie; Keel; mains €17-30; ⏱6-10pm summer, shorter hours rest of year) The proprietors of Keem Bay Fish Products have been serving up their acclaimed smoked local salmon and other delicacies at this restaurant for decades. The menu changes with what's fresh, but expect a meal of the very best seafood.

🛏 Pure Magic Achill Island · Guesthouse €€

(📞085 243 9782; www.puremagic.ie; Slievemore Rd; s/d/f from €60/80/120; 🛜) There's a fun vibe at this lively 10-room spot near Dugort thanks to a buzzing bar and cafe with excellent pizza. Bedroom themes range from Moroccan and Brazilian to French, and you can arrange lessons in kite-surfing (per three hours €130) and stand-up paddleboarding (SUP; per hour €40) and rent out SUPs (per hour €15).

Aughris Head ❽

✖ Beach Bar · Seafood €€

(📞071-917 6465; www.thebeachbarsligo.com; Aughris Head; mains €12-25; ⏱food served noon-8pm daily summer, Fri-Sun winter; 🛜) In a sheltered setting on the curving beach by the cliff walk, the pub in this 17th-century thatched cottage hosts lively traditional-music sessions and serves superb seafood, including creamy chowder and poached salmon. The owners also run the **Aughris House B&B** (tent/van sites from €12/22, s/d from €40/80; 🛜) next door, with seven comfy, wi-fi-enabled rooms and an adjacent camp site.

Sligo Town ❿

✖ Hargadons · Pub Food €€

(📞071-915 3709; www.hargadons.com; 4/5 O'Connell St; mains €10-25; ⏱food noon-3.30pm & 4-9pm Mon-Sat) You'll have a hard time leaving this superb 1868 inn with its winning blend of Old World fittings and gastropub style. The uneven floors, peat fire, antique signage, snug corners and bowed shelves laden down with ancient bottles lend it a wonderful charm. The great-value food is renowned, transforming local ingredients such as oysters with continental flair.

✖ Kate's Kitchen · Cafe €

(📞071-914 3022; www.kateskitchen.ie; 3 Castle St; mains from €7; ⏱8.30am-5.30pm Mon-Sat) Only the best local foodstuffs are served at this welcoming, contemporary cafe-store. All the ingredients for a prime picnic are there along with prepared foods. The tiny cafe is a cheery spot for punchy coffee and home-made lunch..

🛏 An Crúiscin Lan · Guesthouse €€

(📞087 233 1573; www.bandbsligo.ie; Connolly St; s/d €50/85; 🅿🛜) A friendly welcome, fair-sized rooms, good location and parking all add to the appeal at this convivial B&B, as do the porridge and Irish fry-ups for breakfast. Some rooms share bathrooms.

Sligo Surrounds

27

Sligo is as varied as a county this size gets. On top of exceptional beaches, there's a wealth of prehistoric sites and Yeats literary heritage, along with fine traditional bars.

TRIP HIGHLIGHTS

98 km

Drumcliff
Yeats' final resting place in the shadow of Benbulben

116 km

Mullaghmore
Dive-friendly fishing village with sweeping arc of dark-gold sand

Grange

Rosses Point

Sligo

START/FINISH

Riverstown

28 km

Carrowkeel Megalithic Cemetery
Sacred prehistoric site dotted with stone circles and passage cairns

**5 DAYS
155KM / 96 MILES**

GREAT FOR...

BEST TIME TO GO
May, June or September for fewer crowds and better weather.

 ESSENTIAL PHOTO
Drumcliff cemetery with Benbulben in the background.

☑ **BEST FOR ANCIENT HISTORY**
South Sligo is stacked with megalithic dolmens and burial grounds.

Drumcliff Graveyard with view of Benbulben

Carrowkeel, just 5km south of Sligo town). Some 20km later turn right in Castlebaldwin at McDermott's Restaurant, then head left at the fork and follow the signs. The cemetery is 2km uphill from the car park.

27 Sligo Surrounds

Sligo offers wild beauty, but with a sense of quietude. Lush fields, lakes and flat-topped mountains provided inspiration for William Butler Yeats – a literary legacy that resounds to this day. And among the stretches of golden sands and legendary breaks that lure the surfing cognoscenti, you'll find a bounty of prehistoric sites, luxury spa treatments, elegant Georgian towns, little fishing villages and good old-fashioned country hospitality.

1 Sligo Town

For a small provincial hub, Sligo, with its galleries, museums and atmospheric old pubs, is quite the cultural magnet. Thanks largely to WB Yeats' childhood affection for, and his association with, the area, Sligo attracts visitors keen to learn more about the poet's formative environment. In the **Yeats Memorial Building** (☎071-914 2693; www.yeatssociety.com; Hyde Bridge; €3; ☺10am-5pm Mon-Fri), in a pretty setting near Hyde Bridge, you can visit the **WB Yeats Exhibition**, with a video presentation and valuable draft manuscripts;

the exhibition catalogue makes a good souvenir of Sligo. The charming **tearoom** has outdoor tables overlooking the river. One of Ireland's leading contemporary-arts centres, the **Model** (☎071-914 1405; www.themodel.ie; The Mall; admission varies; ☺10am-5pm Tue-Sat,10.30am-3.30pm Sun) houses an impressive collection of contemporary Irish art, including works by Jack B Yeats (WB's brother), as well as a program of experimental theatre, music and film.

🗙 🛏 p58, p72, p293, p301, p351

The Drive ›› The N4 cuts south, then southeast towards Carrowkeel Megalithic Cemetery (don't confuse it with the other

TRIP HIGHLIGHT

2 Carrowkeel Megalithic Cemetery

With a God's-eye view of the county from high in the Bricklieve Mountains, it's little wonder this hilltop site was sacred in prehistoric times. The windswept location is simultaneously eerie and uplifting, its undeveloped, spectacular setting providing a momentous atmosphere. Dotted with around 14 passage cairns, Carrowkeel dates from the late Stone Age (3000 to 2400 BC). Climbing up from the car park the first tomb you'll reach is Cairn G. Above its entrance is a **roof-box** aligned with the midsummer sunset, which illuminates the inner chamber. The only other such roof-box known in Ireland is that at Newgrange in County Meath. Everywhere you look across the surrounding hills you'll see evidence of early life here, including about 140 **stone circles**, all that remain of the foundations of a large village thought to have been inhabited by the builders of the tombs.

The Drive ›› From the Carrowkeel turning, rejoin

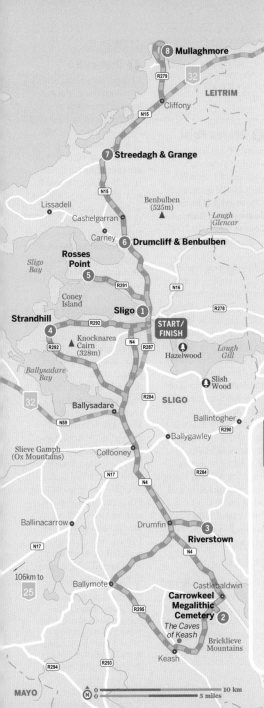

the country lane, turning left initially, heading south then west to Keash (sometimes spelt Kesh). At the R295 turn right for Ballymote; immediately the Caves of Keash appear high on the ridge on your right. After Ballymote lanes lined with moss-topped walls lead you across the N4 to Riverstown and signs for the Sligo Folk Park.

③ Riverstown

The endearing **Sligo Folk Park** (☎071-916 5001; www.sligofolkpark.com; Millview House, Riverstown; adult/child €5/4; ☺10am-5pm Mon-Fri, plus Sat Jun-Aug) revolves around a lovingly restored 19th-century cottage. Humble thatched structures complement this centrepiece, along with scattered farm tools and an exhibit that honours the old country life. Another fine reason to come here is to attend a nonfaith monastic retreat

LINK YOUR TRIP

32 **Northwest on Adrenaline**

There's plenty more surf to be found on Donegal's beach beauties. From Grange stick north on the N15.

25 **Loughs of the West**

From the northwest's wild coast, turn it down a little for a tour of the west's serene lakelands, from Sligo on the N17.

GALWAY & THE WEST OF IRELAND **27** SLIGO SURROUNDS

297

or a course on hemp lime plastering at the green-roofed **Gyreum** (📞087 328 0789; www.gyreum.com; Corlisheen, Riverstown; per 2 nights from €40; **P**), a pudding-shaped eco-lodge hidden by the surrounding hills.

The Drive ≫ Returning to the N4, follow the Sligo road for some 15km till you veer off on to the R292 to the seaside resort of Strandhill.

- - - - - - - - - - - - - - - -

④ Strandhill

The great Atlantic rollers that sweep the shorefront of Strandhill make this long, red-gold **beach** unsafe for swimming. They have, however, made it a magnet for surfers. Gear hire and lessons can be arranged through **Strandhill Surf School** (📞071-916 8483; www.strandhillsurfschool.com; Shore Rd; lessons adult/child from €35/25; 🕑Apr-Oct). Alternatively, take a gentler, warmer dip in the Voya Seaweed Baths (p292). A few kilometres towards Sligo, you can walk – at low tide only! – to **Coney Island**. Its New York namesake was supposedly named by a man from Rosses Point. The island's wishing well is reputed to have been dug by St Patrick (who, if all these tales are to be trusted, led a *very* busy life). Check tide times to avoid getting stranded.

✕ 🛏 p301

The Drive ≫ Continue along the R292 before picking up the R291 out of Sligo town to cruise the coast to Rosses Point, 8km northwest of Sligo. This road can get busy with holidaymakers in summer.

- - - - - - - - - - - - - - - -

⑤ Rosses Point

Rosses Point has two wonderful beaches and one of Ireland's most challenging and renowned golf links, **County Sligo Golf Course** (📞071-917 7134; www.countysligogolfclub.ie; Rosses Point; 18 holes €175-195; 🕑mid-Mar–Oct), which attracts golfers from all over the world. Fringed by the Atlantic and lying in the shadow of Benbulben, this is one of Ireland's greatest and most picturesque golf links. Offshore, the odd **Metal Man** beacon dates from 1821. **Harry's Bar** (📞071-917 7173; www.harrysrossespoint.com; Rosses Point; 🕑11am-11pm, shorter hours Oct-Apr; 🛜), on your right as you enter town, has a historic well, an aquarium and maritime bric-a-brac. The Yeats Country Hotel (p301), just up the hill, serves good bar food.

🛏 p301

The Drive ≫ Returning via the R291 you'll pick up the busy N15 as you head north to the quaint town of Drumcliff, Yeats' final resting place, at the foot of Benbulben. It's 10km in all.

- - - - - - - - - - - - - - - -

⑥ Drumcliff

Visible right along Sligo's northern coast, **Benbulben** (525m) resembles a table covered by a pleated cloth: its limestone plateau is uncommonly flat, and its near-vertical sides are scored by earthen ribs. Benbulben's beauty was not lost on WB Yeats. Before the poet died in Menton, France, in 1939, he had requested that, should he die there, 'after a year or so' he be dug up and brought to Sligo. Someone was buried here, but there is an ongoing debate as to whether it was actually Yeats or not. Still, **Yeats' grave** (📞071-914 4956; off N15; 🕑dawn-dusk) is next to the doorway of the Protestant church in Drumcliff, and his youthful bride Georgie Hyde-Lee is buried alongside. Historic **Lissadell House** (📞071-916 3150; www.lissadellhouse.com; Ballinful; adult/child house & grounds €14/6, grounds €10/5; 🕑10.30am-6pm Easter-Oct), west of Drumcliff off the N15 just past Yeats Tavern, was recently restored by its private owners and is now open to visitors.

The Drive ≫ The light on Benbulben, looming in the distance inland, often changes it from dark blue to purple or a mossy shade of green. Continue on the N15 less than 9km into the small village of Grange.

MICHAEL QUIRKE: WOODCARVER OF WINE STREET

The inconspicuous **studio** (☎071-914 2624; Wine St; ⏲9.30am-12.30pm & 3-5.30pm Mon-Sat) of Michael Quirke, woodcarver, raconteur and local character, is filled with the scents of locally felled timbers and offcuts of beech stumps. A converted butcher shop on Wine St in Sligo town, it retains some of the implements of the butcher's trade, including an electric bone saw. Quirke, himself formerly a butcher, began to use his tools for cutting and carving wood in 1968. He divided his time between his twin callings for 20 years, after which he gave up meat, so to speak. Quirke's art is inspired by Irish mythology, a subject about which he is passionate and knowledgeable, and as he carves he readily chats with the customers and the curious who enter his shop and end up staying for hours. He draws unforced connections between Ireland's shifting myths, music, history, flora, fauna and contemporary events, as well as comparisons in the wider world, such as Australian Aboriginal and Native North American lore. As he talks and carves, Quirke frequently pulls out a county map, pointing to places that spring from the conversation, leading you on your own magical, mystical tour of the county.

❼ Grange

From the village of Grange, signs point towards **Streedagh Strand**, a grand crescent of sand that saw some 1100 sailors perish when three ships from the Spanish Armada were wrecked nearby. Views extend from the beach to the cliffs at Sliabh Liag (Slieve League) in Donegal. Locals regularly swim here, even in winter. Don't leave Grange without stopping into **Langs pub** (☎071-916 3105; www.langs.ie; Main St, Grange; ⏲4-11.30pm Mon, Wed & Thu, 12.30-11.30pm Fri-Sun) for a bite or to water the horses in the well-preserved front bar, with bottles of Guinness among the old washing powder and cereal boxes. It's one of the county's finest old grocery-draper-bars.

The Drive » Keep heading north on the N15 until you reach the sleepy crossroads of Cliffony. In the centre of the village take a left, following signs for the R279 to Mullaghmore.

TRIP HIGHLIGHT

❽ Mullaghmore

The sweeping arc of dark golden sand and the safe shallow waters make the pretty fishing village of Mullaghmore a popular family destination. Take time to drive the scenic road looping around Mullaghmore Head, where wide shafts of rock slice into the Atlantic surf. En route you'll pass **Classiebawn Castle** – closed to the public – a neo-Gothic turreted pile built for Lord Palmerston in 1856 and later home to the ill-fated Lord Mountbatten, who was killed here in 1979 when the IRA rigged his boat with explosives. **Mullaghmore Head** is becoming known as one of Ireland's premier **big wave surf** spots, with swells of up to 30m allowing for Hawaiian-style adventure. Mullaghmore's clear waters, rocky outcrops and coves are also ideal for diving.

🛏 p301

The Drive » Once back on the N15 it's a straight run for some 27km back to Sligo, where you can enjoy a creamy pint in a snug at one of the region's finest traditional pubs, Thomas Connolly on Holborn St.

Eating & Sleeping

Sligo Town ❶

✕ Miso Sligo Japanese €

(☎071-919 4986; Stephen St; mains from €7; ⏱noon-3pm & 5-10.30pm Tue-Fri, 3-10.30pm Sat, 5-10pm Sun; ✏) The exterior in a modern block may look uninviting, but the Japanese/Korean food here is good. To gyoza (dumplings) add good sushi and excellent miso ramen.

✕ Fabio's Ice Cream €

(☎087-177 2732; Wine St; treats from €2.50; ⏱11am-6pm Mon-Thu, to 6.30pm Fri & Sat, noon-6pm Sun) Local hero Fabio makes arguably Ireland's best Italian gelato and sorbets from mostly local and natural ingredients. The frequently changing flavour offer is remarkable: from white chocolate and pistachio crunch to raspberry lime sorbet. In summer he's often open till 7pm.

🛏 Railway Hostel Hostel €

(☎087 690 5539; www.therailway.ie; 1 Union Pl; dm/s/tw from €20/27/46; ℗☎) Great rates, a clutch of parking spaces and cosy dorms – many featuring single beds as well as bunk beds – sit inside this cheery hostel, where the train-themed decor meshes with the name. A basic breakfast of tea, coffee and cereal is included in the price.

🛏 Sligo Park Hotel Hotel €€

(☎071-919 0400; www.sligoparkhotel.com; Pearse Rd; s/d/f from €110/120/145; ℗☎☂) Landscaped grounds, mature trees, and an array of facilities help lend this modern hotel a country-club air. The pretty, tastefully decorated rooms are bright and modern. It's 3km south of town.

Strandhill ❹

✕ Stoked Irish €€

(☎071-912 2734; Shore Rd; mains €15-26; ⏱6-10pm Wed-Sun; ✏) With its surf-chic vibe, stripped wooden tables and primary colour scheme, the eatery above Strandhill's shoreside Strand Bar is winning over legions of local fans. Expect everything from whole spatchcock chicken and juicy steaks, to seared scallops and chargrilled sea bream. Book.

🛏 Strandhill Lodge & Suites Guesthouse €€

(☎071-912 2122; www.strandhilllodgeandsuites.com; Top Rd; s €99, d €120-130, ste €130-150; ℗☎) This excellent hillside guesthouse offers 22 bright, spacious rooms with king-sized beds, hotel-quality design and trendy neutral styling. Room sizes vary, but most have terraces or balconies and fabulous ocean views.

🛏 Surf & Stay Lodge & Hostel Lodge €

(☎085 851 0889; www.surfnstay.ie; Shore Rd; hostel dm/d €25/50, lodge s €55, d €50-85; ☎) Surfers thaw out by the open fire in the common room of the 34-bed hostel portion of this two-building complex. Rooms in the adjoining lodge are B&B-style and, while small, are comfortable; some share bathrooms. The beach is close and there's an on-site surf school. Surfing lessons cost from €25 to €40; stand-up paddleboard sessions start at €40.

Rosses Point ❺

🛏 Yeats Country Hotel Hotel €€

(☎071-911 7100; www.yeatscountryhotel.com; Rosses Point; d/f €139/148; ☂) A commanding presence on Rosses Point overlooking the beach and County Sligo Golf Course makes this huge three-star hotel a big hit with familes and golfers. Many of the large, modern rooms have fine sea views. There's a popular restaurant; food is also served at its two bars.

Mullaghmore ❽

🛏 Pier Head Hotel Hotel €€

(☎071-916 6171; www.pierheadhotel.ie; Mullaghmore Harbour; s/d from €90/140; ⏱closed late Dec; ☎☂) The panoramic views from this gorgeous quayside hotel are magnificent. The 40 smart rooms feature clean lines, artful lighting and bright colour schemes; the best have extensive ocean or harbour views. Other draws include a sweeping rooftop terrace with hot tub, spa and indoor pool, and very decent food (mains from €11 to €22).

County Clare

28

Experience scenic coastline including the breathtaking Cliffs of Moher, the Aran Islands, market towns with cracking pubs and Clare's jewel, the geological wonder of The Burren.

TRIP HIGHLIGHTS

110 km

Inishmaan
Little-visited, breathtakingly beautiful and rich in mythology

Ballyvaughan

Cliffs of Moher

148 km

Ennistimon
An authentic market town with the Cascades at its centre

Ennis

START/FINISH

Kilrush

218 km

Loop Head
Spectacularly windswept and cliff-fringed

8–9 DAYS
299KM / 185 MILES

GREAT FOR...

BEST TIME TO GO
Spring for the awakening of nature in The Burren.

ESSENTIAL PHOTO
A sunset shot over the Atlantic from Dun Aengus, Inishmore.

BEST FOR RAMBLING
Take blustery cliff walks, or cross The Burren on foot.

Inishmore Cliffs of Dun Aengus

28 | County Clare

From friendly market towns Ennis and Ennistimon down the cliff-fringed coast of Clare to its southernmost tip, the raggedly beautiful Loop Head, you'll encounter sandy strands and quiet coves just begging for company. In the summer you can island-hop between the Aran Islands, discovering historic relics and a taste of a simpler life, before returning to the mainland's homely resorts of Kilrush and Kilkee.

❶ Ennis

Ennis (Inis) is the busy commercial centre of Clare. It lies on the banks of the smallish River Fergus, which runs east, then south into the Shannon Estuary. It's the place to stay if you want a bit of urban flair; a little short on sights, Ennis' strengths are its food, lodging and traditional entertainment. The town's medieval origins are indicated by its irregular, narrow streets. Its most important historical site is **Ennis**

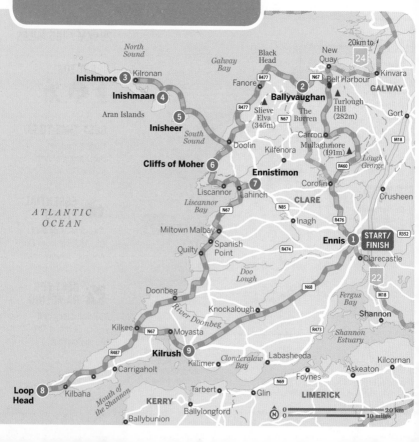

Friary (065-682 9100; www.heritageireland.ie; Abbey St; adult/child €5/3; ⏱10am-6pm Easter-Sep, to 5pm Oct), founded in the 13th century by the O'Briens, kings of Thomond, who also built a castle here.

 p45, p268, p309

The Drive >> A jaunt north, initially on the R476 towards Corofin, opens up the wondrous karst limestone of The Burren's heartland. Make sure you stop and take in primroses and other flora dotted in the crevices in spring. Skirting the Burren National Park, you'll turn left on to the N67 to get to Ballyvaughan. some 55km in all.

- - - - - - - - - - - - - - - - - - -

❷ Ballyvaughan

Something of a hub for the otherwise dispersed charms of The Burren, Ballyvaughan (Baile Uí Bheacháin) sits between the hard land of the hills and a quiet leafy corner

LINK YOUR TRIP

22 Best of the West
Having sampled the delicious Clare coast take a wild southerly bite of Kerry and West Cork from Limerick down.

24 Mountains & Moors
If you like The Burren, you'll love Connemara. Join this trip at Ballyvaughan and wander west at Galway.

of Galway Bay. Just west of the village's junction is the **quay**, built in 1829 at a time when boats traded with the Aran Islands and Galway, exporting grain and bacon and bringing in turf – a scarce commodity in the windswept rocks of The Burren.

 p309

The Drive >> From Ballyvaughan the R477 clings to the coast, a leisurely 40-minute, shore-side ride down to Doolin, offering sweeping views over to the Aran Islands on your right. At Doolin, park and catch one of the ferries that run (between mid-March and October) to Inishmore, the first of three splendid castaway isles.

- - - - - - - - - - - - - - - - - - -

❸ Inishmore

Most visitors who venture out to the islands don't make it beyond 14km long Inishmore (Inis Mór) and its main attraction, Dun Aengus (p266), the stunning stone fort perched perilously on the island's towering cliffs. The arid landscape west of Kilronan (Cill Rónáin), Inishmore's main settlement, is dominated by stone walls, boulders, scattered buildings and the odd patch of deep-green grass and potato plants. It gets pretty crowded in summer but on foot or bike (for hire at the pier), you can happily set your own pace. There's an EU Blue Flag white-sand beach (awarded for cleanliness)

at Kilmurvey, peacefully situated west of bustling Kilronan. A **craft village** (Kilmurvey; ⏱hours vary), where you'll find local women hand-knitting traditional Aran sweaters, sits nearby.

 p59, p93, p269, p309

The Drive >> Prebook your seasonal interisland boat ticket (€10 to €15) with one of the ferry companies and check their sailing schedules for the latest crossing times.

- - - - - - - - - - - - - - - - - - -

TRIP HIGHLIGHT

❹ Inishmaan

The least-visited of the islands, with the smallest population, Inishmaan (Inis Meáin) is a rocky respite. Early Christian monks seeking solitude were drawn to Inishmaan, as was the author JM Synge, who spent five summers here over a century ago. The island they knew largely survives today: stoic cows and placid sheep, impressive old forts and warm-hearted locals, who may tell you with a glint in their eye that they had a hard night on the whiskey the previous evening. Inishmaan's scenery is breathtaking, with a jagged coastline of startling cliffs, empty beaches, and fields where the main crop seems to be stone. **Teach Synge** (☎099-73036; €3; ⏱by appointment Apr–mid-Sep), a thatched cottage on the road just before you head up to the fort, is where JM Synge spent his summers.

📖 p309

⑤ Inisheer

Inisheer (Inis Oírr), the smallest of the Aran Islands with a population of only around 200, has a palpable sense of enchantment, enhanced by the island's deep-rooted mythology, devotion to traditional culture and ethereal landscapes. Wandering the lanes with their ivy-covered stone walls and making discoveries here and there is the best way to experience the island. At **O'Brien's Castle** (Caisleán Uí Bhriain), a 100m climb to the island's highest point yields dramatic views over clover-covered fields to the beach and harbour. Much more modern is an iconic island sight – the freighter, **Plassy**, that was thrown up on the rocks in 1960 in a storm. An aerial shot of the wreck was used in the opening sequence of the seminal TV series *Father Ted*.

🍴 📖 p269, p309

The Drive ≫ Back on the mainland, it's back behind the wheel. From Doolin, it's a scenic 10-minute cruise on the coastal R478 to the famed, unmistakable Cliffs of Moher.

- - - - - - - - - - - - - - - -
⑥ Cliffs of Moher

Star of a million tourist brochures, the Cliffs of Moher (Aillte an Mothair, or Ailltreacha Mothair) are one of Ireland's most visited sights. But, as at many at-times overcrowded attractions, you have to get beyond the coach parties to experience what's drawn visitors in the first place – entirely vertical cliffs that rise to a height of 214m, with edges falling away abruptly into the constantly churning sea. A series of heads, the dark limestone seems to march in a rigid formation that amazes, no matter how many times you look. Luckily crowds thin the further you get from the coach park. And if you're willing to walk for 10 minutes south past the end of the 'Moher Wall', there's a trail along the cliffs to Hag's Head – few venture this far. A vast **visitor centre** (☎065-708 6141; www.cliffsofmoher.ie; R478; adult/child incl parking €8/free; ☻8am-9pm May-Aug, to 7pm Mar, Apr, Sep & Oct, 9am-5pm Nov-Feb) is set back into the side of a hill, Hobbit house style. For uncommon views of the cliffs and wildlife you might consider a **cruise**. The boat operators in Doolin offer popular tours of the cliffs.

The Drive ≫ A 10km drive through an ever-flattening landscape takes you to the

small seaside resort of Lahinch. From there the N67 darts 4km due east to the authentic rural market town of Ennistimon.

- - - - - - - - - - - - - - - -
TRIP HIGHLIGHT
⑦ Ennistimon

Ennistimon (Inis Díomáin; sometimes spelt Ennistymon) is a genuinely charming market town. Here a postcard-perfect main street is lined with brightly coloured shopfronts and traditional pubs that host fantastic trad sessions throughout the year. From the roaring Cascades (p263), the stepped falls of the River Inagh, there are picturesque walks downstream. Each Saturday morning the stalls of a farmers market fill Market Sq.

🍴 📖 p268, 309

The Drive ≫ Next comes a 74km picturesque trip down the coastal N67 and then the R487. The landscape between the old-fashioned resort of Kilkee and Loop Head in the south has subtle undulations that suddenly end in dramatic cliffs falling off into the Atlantic. It's a windswept place with timeless striations of old stone walls.

- - - - - - - - - - - - - - - -
TRIP HIGHLIGHT
⑧ Loop Head

Discriminating travellers are coming here for coastal views that are in many ways more dramatic than the Cliffs of Moher. On a clear day, Loop Head (Ceann Léime), Clare's southernmost point, has magnificent

Teach Synge cottage, Inishma

GETTING TO & FROM THE ARAN ISLANDS

Flights and ferries serve the Aran Islands. Seasonal boats shuttle regularly from Doolin to the islands; ferries also run year-round from Rossaveal in County Galway.

From mid-March to October, **Doolin 2 Aran Ferries** (☎065-707 5949; www.doolin2aranferries.com; Doolin Pier) and the **Doolin Ferry Co** (O'Brien Line; ☎065-707 5555; www.doolinferry.com; Doolin Pier) link the Arans with the mainland – they also run interisland services.

It takes around half an hour to cover the 8km from Doolin to Inisheer; a boat from the mainland to Inishmore takes at least 1¼ hours, while ferries from Doolin to Inishmaan take up to an hour. Expect to pay €20 to €25 return. Interisland boats cost €10 to €15. Each firm has an office at Doolin Pier or you can book online.

The ferry firms also offer various combo trips and Cliffs of Moher boat tours, which are best done late in the afternoon when the light is from the west.

Year-round, ferries also run to the Aran Island from Rossaveal, 37km west of Galway. **Aran Island Ferries** (☎091-568 903; www.aranislandferries.com; one-way/return €15/25) has two to three crossings daily; a shuttle bus is available from Galway city.

Aer Arann Islands (☎091-593 034; www.aerarannislands.ie; one-way/return €25/49) has flights to each of the islands up to six times a day; the journey takes about 10 minutes and can be done as a day trip. Flights go from **Connemara Regional Airport** (Aerfort Réigiúnach Chonamara; NNR; ☎091-593 034; Inverin); a shuttle bus links it with Galway city, 30km to the east.

views south to the Dingle Peninsula crowned by Mt Brandon (952m), and north to the Aran Islands and Galway Bay. There are bracing walks in the area including heritage trails around Kilkee and a 15km clifftop circuit. A working **lighthouse** (complete with fresnel lens) is the punctuation on the far southwestern point.

The Drive ≫ A scenic 40km drive north on the R487 and east on the N67 brings you to the bustling local resort of Kilrush.

9 Kilrush

Kilrush (Cill Rois) is a small, atmospheric town that overlooks the Shannon Estuary and the hills of Kerry to the south. From the town's big **marina**, you can head out on cruises run by **Dolphin Discovery** (☎065-905 1327; www.discoverdolphins.ie; Kilrush Marina; adult/child €26/14; ☺late May–mid-Oct) to see the pods of bottlenose dolphins that live in the estuary, an important calving region for the mammals. The remarkable 'lost'

Vandeleur Walled Garden
(☎065-905 1760; www.vandeleurwalledgarden.ie; Killimer Rd; ☺10am-5pm Tue-Sat) was the private domain of the wealthy Vandeleur family – merchants and landowners. The gardens are just east of the centre and have been redesigned and planted with colourful tropical and rare plants.

✗ p309

The Drive ≫ After all that sea air and seafood you'll be ready for a straight 40-minute jaunt (on the N68) inland back to Ennis.

Eating & Sleeping

Ennis ❶

✖ Ennis Gourmet Store — Deli €

(📞065-684 3314; www.ennisgourmet.com; 1 Old Barrack St; dishes €8-16; ⏰10am-8pm Mon-Wed, to 10pm Thu-Sat, noon-6pm Sun) Gourmet produce – from Burren smoked salmon and whiskey marmalade to fine French wines – fills the shelves of this delightful deli, which has a handful of seats inside and out.

⛏ Ardilaun Guesthouse — B&B €

(📞065-682 2311; purcells.ennis@eircom.net; Ballycoreet; s/d €44/68; 🅿️ 📶) Drop a line into the River Fergus or just watch the sunset from the rear deck of this B&B around 3km north of the centre, off the R458. Pluses include an on-site fitness room and sauna, and friendly owners who can help arrange transport into town.

Ballyvaughan ❷

⛏ Gregan's Castle Hotel — Hotel €€€

(📞065-707 7005; www.gregans.ie; N67; d €240-325, ste €377-447; 🅿️ 📶) This hidden Clare gem is housed in a grand 18th-century manor, 5km south of Ballyvaughan at the aptly named, twisting Corkscrew Hill. The 21 rooms and suites combine antiques with contemporary countrified furnishings (and purposely no TVs); some open to private garden areas.

Inishmore ❸

⛏ Aran Islands Camping & Glamping — Campground €€

(📞086 189 5823; www.irelandglamping.ie; Frenchman's Beach; camp sites per person €10, glamping hut €150-160) At this smart, modern campground with direct access to a sweeping white-sand beach, you can stay in a beehive-shaped glamping hut inspired by an early Christian stone *clochán*. Sleeping up to four people, the nine timber huts have bathrooms, kitchenettes, double beds and pull-out sofas, along with sea views from the front decks.

Inishmaan ❹

⛏ Inis Meáin — Inn €€€

(📞086 826 6026; www.inismeain.com; d 2/3/5 nights from €1000/1350/2300; ⏰Mar-Sep; 📶) Everything about Inis Meáin gives a boutique twist to Aran's wild heart. Five suites sit among curving, stacked stone walls and feature wrap-around windows, crisp styling and cinematic views. The acclaimed restaurant (dinner at 8pm Wednesday, Friday and Saturday) is bold enough to deliver pared-down combinations of own-grown veg, freshly harvested shellfish and home-reared meat.

Inisheer ❺

✖ Teach an Tae — Cafe €

(📞099-75092; www.cafearan.ie; dishes €5-12; ⏰11am-5pm May–early Nov) Wild island raspberries and blackberries, home-grown salads, eggs from the cafe's chickens and apples from its heritage orchard are used in dishes here. Treats include net-fresh local mackerel, a herby Aran goat's cheese tart and an Irish porter cake that's laced with Guinness.

Ennistimon ❼

⛏ Byrne's Inn — Inn €€

(📞065-707 1080; www.byrnes-ennistymon. ie; Main St; d from €105; 🅿️ 📶) Facing Main St out front and the rushing waters of the town's Cascades out back, this historic guesthouse has one of Ennistimon's most colourful facades, in vibrant shades of violet, orange, aqua and sky-blue. Up the steep stairs are six large, stylish, rooms – some with Cascades views.

Kilrush ❾

✖ Buttermarket Cafe — Cafe €

(📞065-905 1822; Burton St; mains €5-12; ⏰10am-4pm Mon-Thu, to 5pm Fri & Sat, 11am-4pm Sun; 📶) A courtyard that's a suntrap in fine weather might draw you here. That or hot specials including stews and shepherd's pie, or drinks spanning salted caramel lattes, cinnamon hot chocolates, and mint-mocha frappuccinos.

STRETCH YOUR LEGS
GALWAY

Start/Finish Spanish Arch

Distance 1.8km

Duration 2 hours

The best way to soak up Galway's convivial atmosphere is to wander its cobblestoned streets. This walk takes you from the city's medieval roots, through its cafe- and bar-lined heart to some of its finest historic buildings.

Take this walk on Trips

Spanish Arch & Medieval Walls

Framing the river east of Wolfe Tone Bridge, the Spanish Arch (1584) is thought to be an extension of Galway's medieval walls. The arch appears to have been designed as a passageway through which ships entered the city to unload goods, such as wine and brandy from Spain. Today, the lawns and riverside form a gathering place for locals and visitors on any sunny day.

The Walk >> A mere step from the Spanish Arch, you can't miss the modernist Galway City Museum. For cake and coffee before you go, Ard Bia, right opposite, will hit the spot beautifully.

Galway City Museum

The **Galway City Museum** (☎091-532 460; www.galwaycitymuseum.ie; Spanish Pde; ⏱10am-5pm Tue-Sat, plus noon-5pm Sun Easter-Sep) is in a glossy, glassy building that reflects the old walls. Exhibits trace aspects of daily life through Galway's history; especially good are the areas dealing with life – smelly and otherwise – during medieval times. Look for the photos of President John F Kennedy's 1963 visit to Galway, including one with dewy-eyed nuns looking on adoringly.

The Walk >> A few minutes' walk from here, crossing the plaza and heading up bustling Quay St, take the first right at the Quays Pub onto Druid Lane, also home to the acclaimed Druid Theatre.

Hall of the Red Earl

Back in the 13th century when the de Burgo family ran the show in Galway, Richard – the Red Earl – had a large **hall** (www.galwaycivictrust.ie; Druid Lane; ⏱9am-4.45pm Mon-Fri, 11am-3pm Sat) built as a seat of power. The hall fell into ruin and was lost until 1997 when expansion of the city's Custom House uncovered its foundations. It now gives a fascinating sense of Galway life some 900 years ago.

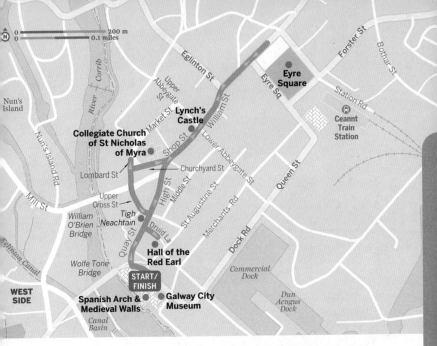

The Walk ≫ Back on Quay St walk up as far as Tigh Neachtain's, and left onto Cross St where you continue for 50m. You'll spot the Church of St Nicholas on your right.

Collegiate Church of St Nicholas of Myra

Crowned by a pyramidal spire, the **Collegiate Church of St Nicholas of Myra** (☎086-389 8777; www.stnicholas.ie; Lombard St; by donation; ☺9am-7pm Mar-Dec, to 5pm Jan & Feb) is Ireland's largest medieval parish church still in use. Dating from 1320, the church has been rebuilt and enlarged over the centuries. St Nicholas is the patron saint of sailors – Christopher Columbus reputedly worshipped here in 1477.

The Walk ≫ Outside on Lombard St, head east along Churchyard St to Shop St and straight up to Eyre Sq, 600m from the church.

Eyre Square

Galway's central public square is an open space with sculptures and pathways. The eastern side is taken up almost entirely by the Hotel Meyrick, an elegant grey limestone pile. Guarding the upper side of the square, **Browne's Doorway** (1627), a classy, if forlorn, fragment is from the home of one of the city's merchant rulers.

The Walk ≫ From north of the square, make your way back down Shop St. Not far down on the right-hand side you'll spot the stone facade of Lynch's Castle, now a bank.

Lynch's Castle

Considered the finest town castle in Ireland, the old stone **Lynch's Castle** (Shop St; ☺10am-4pm Mon-Wed & Fri, to 5pm Thu) was built in the 14th century. The Lynch family was the most powerful of the 14 ruling Galway 'tribes'. Stonework on the castle's facade includes ghoulish gargoyles and many coats of arms.

The Walk ≫ It may take you a while to navigate the pleasant bustle of Shop St, with its many buskers and shoppers. Return to the Spanish Arch via High St, stopping at Tigh Neachtain for a sup en route.

Belfast & the North of Ireland

IRELAND'S NORTH IS MADE FOR ROAD TRIPS. Routes swoop from hard, stark hills to soft, sandy shores, and cliff-clinging roads snake into wild lands peppered with loughs, glens and bogs.

These epic routes link blockbuster sights. The Giant's Causeway, romantic castles and stately homes are just an exhilarating drive from surfing, hiking or horseback riding across golden sand. Within easy reach are Belfast and Derry, once crippled by sectarian violence but now inspirational in their progress towards peace.

In this compelling corner of Ireland you might get a little lost, but that's more than made up for by what you'll find.

Causeway Coast, County Antrim
PETER ZELEI IMAGES/GETTY IMAGES ©

Belfast & the North of Ireland

 DON'T MISS

Arranmore Island

Ancient pubs, turf fires and late-night music sessions make overnighting special. Do a Robinson Crusoe on Trip 29

Glenariff Forest Park

Many visitors bypass this dramatic gorge. Let them. It will make your wander beside waterfalls even more tranquil on Trip 34

Belfast

When previously warring communities have the courage to strive for peace, it's inspiring. Witness that transformation on Trips 29 33

Malin Head

Don't miss beachcombing for semiprecious stones near Ireland's most northerly point. Try your luck on Trip 31

Enniscrone's Seaweed Baths

This Edwardian spa will have you steaming and soaking amid therapeutic seaweed on Trip 32

Kilcullen's Seaweed Baths, Enniscrone

Classic Trip

The North in a Nutshell

29

*The North's must-do trip takes in unmissable
cities and big-name sights. It also heads off the
tourist trail, revealing secret beaches, quaint
harbours, waterfalls and music-filled pubs.*

TRIP HIGHLIGHTS

455 km

Arranmore Island
A castaway island
where music plays into
the night

110 km

Giant's Causeway
An extraordinary
outcrop of ancient,
geometric rock

Horn
Head

Mamore's
Gap

Derry

Glencolumbcille
FINISH

START

Carrigart
Ride horseback
across wide,
golden sands

370 km

Belfast
Experience the
transformed capital of
the North

0 km

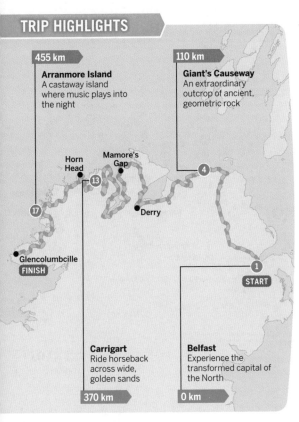

**10 DAYS
470KM / 292 MILES**

GREAT FOR...

BEST TIME TO GO

March to June and
September mean
good weather but
fewer crowds.

**ESSENTIAL
PHOTO**

Crossing the Carrick-
a-Rede Rope Bridge
as it swings above the
waves.

**BEST FOR
SCENERY**

Stops 16 to 20 head
into the heart of wild,
wind-whipped Donegal.

arrick-a-Rede The famous rope bridge, County Antrim

29 The North in a Nutshell

On this road-trip-to-remember you'll drive routes that cling to cliffs, cross borders and head high onto mountain passes. You'll witness Ireland's turbulent past and its inspiring path to peace. And you'll also explore rich faith, folk and music traditions, ride a horse across a sandy beach, cross a swaying rope bridge and spend a night on a castaway island. Not bad for a 10-day drive.

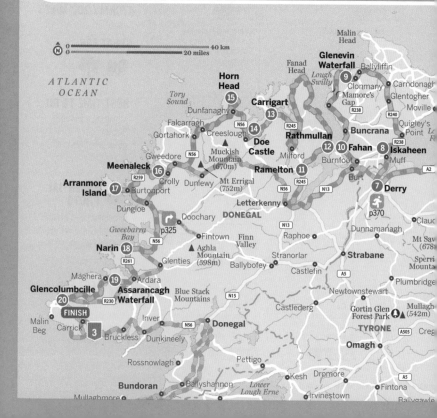

❶ Belfast

In bustling, big-city Belfast the past is palpably present – walk the city's former sectarian battlegrounds (p368) for a profound way to start exploring the North's story. Next, cross the River Lagan and head to the Titanic Quarter. Dominated by the towering yellow Harland and Wolff (H&W) cranes, it's where RMS *Titanic* was built. **Titanic Belfast** (www.titanicbelfast.com; Queen's Rd; adult/child £18.50/8; ☺9am-7pm Jun & Jul, to 8pm Aug, to 6pm Apr, May & Sep, 10am-5pm Oct-Mar; 🚇G2) is a stunning multisensory experience: see bustling shipyards, join crowds at *Titanic's* launch, feel temperatures drop as it strikes that iceberg, and look through a glass floor at watery footage of the vessel today. Slightly to the west, don't miss the **Thompson Graving Dock** (www.titanicsdock.com; Queen's Rd; adult/child £5/3.50; ☺10am-5pm Apr-Oct, 10.30am-4pm Nov & Dec, 10.30am-5pm Jan & Feb; 🚇G2), where you descend into the immense dry dock where the liner was fitted out.

The Drive » As you drive the M3/M2 north, the now-familiar H&W cranes recede. Take the A26 through Ballymena; soon the Antrim Mountains loom large to the right. Skirt them, following the A26 then the A44 into Ballycastle, 96km from Belfast.

❷ Ballycastle

Head beyond the sandy beach to the harbour at the appealing resort of Ballycastle. From here, daily **ferries** (☎028-2076 9299; www.rathlinballycastleferry.com; return trip adult/child/bicycle £12/6/3.30) depart for Rathlin Island, where you'll see sea stacks and thousands of guillemots, kittiwakes, razorbills and puffins.

🛏 p327

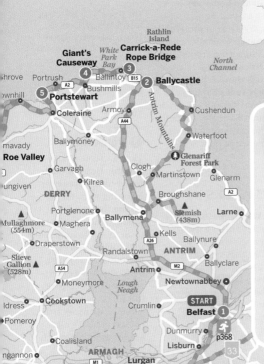

LINK YOUR TRIP

33 From Bangor to Derry

Encounter seaside fun, a grand stately home and the Queen's official residence. Begin 20km east of Belfast at Bangor.

3 Tip to Toe

Take in the cream of Irish music and poetry. Start where this trip stops: Glencolumbcille.

Classic Trip

The Drive » Pick up the B15 towards Ballintoy, which meanders up to a gorse-dotted coastal plateau where hills part to reveal bursts of the sea. As the road plunges downwards, take the right turn to the Carrick-a-Rede Rope Bridge (10km).

- - - - - - - - - - - - - -

❸ Carrick-a-Rede Rope Bridge

The **Carrick-a-Rede Rope Bridge** (☎028-2073 3335; www.nationaltrust.org.uk/ carrick-a-rede; 119 Whitepark Rd, Ballintoy; adult/child £9/4.50; ⏰9.30am-6pm Apr-Oct, to 3.30pm Nov-Mar) loops across a surging sea to a tiny island 20m offshore. This walkway of planks and wire rope sways some 30m above the waves, testing your nerve and head for heights. The bridge was originally put up each year by salmon fishers to help them set their nets,

and signs along the 1km clifftop hike to the bridge detail the fascinating process. Declining stocks have put an end to fishing, however. If you want to cross the bridge, it's best to book a ticket online in advance as numbers are limited.

The Drive » The B15 then the A2 snake west along clifftops and past views of White Park Bay's sandy expanse. Swing right onto the B146, passing Dunseverick Castle's fairy-tale tumblings, en route to the Giant's Causeway (11km).

- - - - - - - - - - - - - -

TRIP HIGHLIGHT

❹ Giant's Causeway

Stretching elegantly out from a rugged shore, the **Giant's Causeway** (www. nationaltrust.org.uk; ⏰dawn-dusk) is one of the world's true geological wonders. Clambering around this jetty of fused geometric rock chunks, it's hard to believe it's not human-made. Legend says Irish giant Finn McCool built the Causeway to cross the sea to fight Scot-

tish giant Benandonner. More prosaically, scientists tell us the 60-million-year-old rocks were formed when a flow of molten basaltic lava cooled and hardened from the top and bottom inwards. It contracted and the hexagonal cracks spread as the rock solidified.

Entry to the Causeway site is free, but to use the National Trust car park you'll need to buy a ticket that includes the **Giant's Causeway Visitor Experience** (☎028-2073 1855; www.nationaltrust.org. uk; 60 Causeway Rd; adult/ child £12.50/6.25; ⏰9am-7pm Jun-Sep, to 6pm Mar-May & Oct, to 5pm Nov-Feb).

The Drive » Continue west, through Bushmills, with its famous distillery, picking up the A2 Coastal Causeway route, signed to Portrush. You'll pass wind-pruned trees, crumbling Dunluce Castle and Portrush's long sandy beaches before arriving at Portstewart (16km).

- - - - - - - - - - - - - -

❺ Portstewart

Time for some unique parking. Head through resort-town Portstewart, following signs for the **Strand** (beach). Eversandier roads descend to an immense shoreline that doubles as a car park for 1000 vehicles. It's a decidedly weird experience to drive and park (£6.50) on an apparently endless expanse of hardpacked sand. It's also at your own risk, which

---

CAUSEWAY COAST WALKS

The official **Causeway Coast Way** (www.walkni.com) stretches for 53km from Ballycastle to Portstewart, but individual chunks can be walked whenever you feel like stretching your legs. Day hikes include the supremely scenic 16.5km section between Carrick-a-Rede and the Giant's Causeway – one of the finest coastal walks in Ireland. Shorter options also abound, including a 2km ramble around Portrush, a 1.5km stroll on sandy White Park Bay and a 300m scramble around ruined Dunluce Castle.

doesn't deter the locals (but do stick to central, compacted areas). Nearby, a 1km **walking trail** meanders up a sand ladder, through huge dunes and past marram grass and occasional orchids.

📭 p327

The Drive » Take the A2 west, through Coleraine towards Downhill. About 1km after the Mussenden Temple's dome appears, take Bishop's Rd left up steep hills with spectacular Lough Foyle views. Descend, go through Limavady and onto the B68 (signed Dungiven). Soon a brown Country Park sign points to Roe Valley (42km).

6 Roe Valley

This beguiling **country park** (Dogleap Rd; ⏰9am-dusk) is packed with rich reminders of a key Irish industry: linen production. The damp valley was ideal for growing the flax that made the cloth; the fast-flowing water powered the machinery.

The **Green Lane Museum** (📞028-7776 0650; Dogleap Rd, Roe Valley Country Park; ⏰1-4.45pm Sat-Thu Jun-Aug, 1-4.45pm Sat & Sun Apr, May & Sep), near the car park, features sowing fiddles, flax breakers and spinning wheels. Look out for nearby watchtowers, built to guard linen spread out to bleach in the fields, and Scutch Mills, where the flax was pounded.

The Drive » Head back into Limavady to take the A2 west to Derry (28km). Green fields give way to suburbs then city streets.

7 Derry

Northern Ireland's second city offers another powerful insight into the North's troubled past and the remarkable steps towards peace. It's best experienced on foot (p370). Partway round, drop into the **Tower Museum** (www.derrystrabane.com/towermuseum; Union Hall Pl; adult/child £3/1.50; ⏰10am-5.30pm, last entry 4pm). Its imaginative Story of Derry exhibit leads you through the city's history, from the 6th-century monastery of St Colmcille (Columba) to the 1960s Battle of the Bogside.

✕📭 p72, p327, p359

The Drive » The A2 heads north towards Moville. Soon speed-limit signs switch from mph to km/h: welcome to the Republic of Ireland. Shortly after Muff take the small left turn, signed Iskaheen, up the hill. Park beside Iskaheen church (11km).

8 Iskaheen

It's completely off the tourist trail, but Iskaheen church's tiny **graveyard** offers evidence of two of Ireland's most significant historical themes: the poverty that led to mass migration and the consequences of sectarian violence. One gravestone among many is to the McKinney family, recording a string of children dying young: at 13 years, 11 months, nine months and six weeks. It also bears the name of 34-year-old James Gerard McKinney, one of 13 unarmed civilians shot dead when British troops opened fire on demonstrators on Bloody Sunday, 1972.

The Drive » Rejoin the R238 north, turning onto the R240 to Carndonagh, climbing steeply into rounded summits. After quaint Ballyliffin and Clonmany, pick up the Inis Eoghain Scenic Route signs towards Mamore's Gap, and park at the Glenevin Waterfall car park.

TOP TIP: THE BORDER

Driving 20 minutes north out of Derry will see you entering another country: the Republic of Ireland. On road signs, be aware speed limits will suddenly change from mph to km/h, while wording switches from English to Irish and English. Stock up on euros in Derry or visit the first post-border ATM.

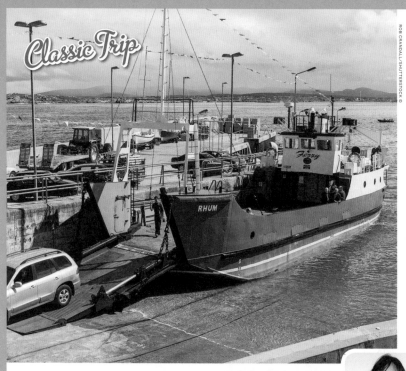

Classic Trip

WHY THIS IS A CLASSIC TRIP
ISABEL ALBISTON, WRITER

Starting in Belfast, a city whose turbulent history seems finally to come second to its flourishing future, this trip gives a sense of the north's past and present while showcasing a stunning natural landscape so old – the striking hexagonal rocks of the Giant's Causeway date back 60 million years – it makes the region's troubles seem like a blip on the timeline.

Above: Arranmore Island ferry
Left: Giant's Causeway, County Antrim
Right: Thompson Graving Dock, Belfast

ATTILA JANDI/SHUTTERSTOCK ©

⑨ Glenevin Waterfall

Welcome to Butler's Bridge – from here a 1km trail winds beside a stream through a wooded glen to Glenevin Waterfall, which cascades 10m down the rock face. It's an utterly picturesque, gentle, waymarked route – the perfect leg stretch.

🛏 p327

The Drive ›› The Inis Eoghain snakes south up to Mamore's Gap, a high-altitude, white-knuckle mountain pass that climbs 260m on single-lane, twisting roads, past shrines to the saints. After a supremely steep descent (and glorious views) go south through Buncrana, and onto Fahan (37km), parking beside the village church.

⑩ Fahan

St Colmcille founded a monastery in Fahan in the 6th century. Its creeper-clad ruins sit beside the church. Among them, hunt out the beautifully carved **St Mura Cross**. Each face of this 7th-century stone slab is decorated with a cross in intricate Celtic weave. The barely discernible Greek inscription is the only one known in Ireland from this early Christian period and is thought to be part of a prayer dating from 633.

The Drive ›› Take the N13 to Letterkenny, before picking up the R245 to Ramelton (aka

Classic Trip

Rathmelton), a 10km sweep north through the River Swilly valley. Turn off for the village, heading downhill to park beside the water in front of you (50km).

- - - - - - - - - - - - - - - - -

⑪ Ramelton

In this picture-perfect town, rows of Georgian houses and rough-walled stone warehouses curve along the River Lennon. Strolling right takes you to a string of three-storey, three-bay Victorian warehouses; walking back and left up Church Rd leads to the ruined **Tullyaughnish Church** with its Romanesque carvings in the eastern wall. Walking left beside the river leads past Victorian shops to the three-arched, late-18th-century Ramelton Bridge.

🛏 p327

The Drive » Cross the town bridge, turning right (north) for Rathmullan. The hills of the Inishowen Peninsula rise ahead and Lough Swilly swings into view – soon you're driving right beside the shore. At Rathmullan (11km), make for the harbour car park.

- - - - - - - - - - - - - - - - -

⑫ Rathmullan

Refined, tranquil Rathmullan was the setting for an event that shaped modern Ireland. In 1607 a band of nobles boarded a ship here, leaving with the intention of raising an army to fight the occupying English. But they never returned. Known as the Flight of the Earls, it marked the end of the Irish (Catholic) chieftains' power. Their estates were confiscated, paving the way for the Plantation of Ulster with British (Protestant) settlers. Beside the sandy beach, look for the striking modern **sculpture**, depicting the earls'

departure, waving to their distressed people as they left.

The Drive » Head straight on from the harbour, picking up Fanad/Atlantic Dr, a roller-coaster road that surges up Lough Swilly's shore, round huge Knockalla, past the exquisite beach at Ballymastocker Bay and around Fanad Head. It then hugs the (ironically) narrow Broad Water en route to Carrigart (74km), with its village-centre horse-riding centre.

- - - - - - - - - - - - - - - - -

TRIP HIGHLIGHT

⑬ Carrigart

Most visitors scoot straight through laid-back Carrigart, heading for the swimming beach at Downings. But they miss a real treat: a horse ride on a vast beach. The **Carrigart Riding Centre** (☎087 227 6926, 074-915 3583; per hour adult/child €20/15; ⏰10am-6pm) is just across the main street from sandy, hill-ringed Mulroy Bay, meaning you can head straight onto the beach for an hour-long ride amid the shallows and the dunes. Trips go on the hour, but it's best to book.

🛏 p327

The Drive » Head south for Creeslough. An inlet with a creamy, single-towered castle soon pops into view. The turnoff comes on the plain, where brown signs point through narrow lanes and past farms to Doe Castle (12km) itself.

NORTH WEST 200 ROAD RACE

Driving this delightful coast can have its challenges, so imagine doing it at high speed. Each May the world's best motorcyclists do just that, going as fast as 300km/h in the **North West 200** (www.northwest200.org), which is run on a road circuit taking in Portrush, Portstewart and Coleraine. This classic race is Ireland's biggest outdoor sporting event and one of the last to take place on closed public roads anywhere in Europe. It attracts up to 150,000 spectators; if you're not one of them, it's best to avoid the area on the race weekend.

🔟 Doe Castle

The best way to appreciate the charm of early-16th-century **Doe Castle** (📞086 843 7533; Sheephaven Bay; tour €3; ⊙grounds 9am-6pm, castle tours Jul & Aug only) is to wander the peaceful grounds, admiring its slender tower and crenellated battlements. The castle was the stronghold of the Scottish MacSweeney family until it fell into English hands in the 17th century. It's a deeply picturesque spot: a low, water-fringed promontory with a moat hewn out of the rock.

The Drive » Near Creeslough, the bulk of Muckish Mountain rears up before the N56 to Dunfanaghy undulates past homesteads, loughs and sandy bays. Once in Dunfanaghy, with its gently kooky vibe, welcoming pubs and great places to sleep, look out for the signpost pointing right to Horn Head (25km).

🔟 Horn Head

This headland provides one of Donegal's best clifftop drives: along sheer, heather-clad quartzite cliffs with views of an island-dotted sea. A circular road bears left to the coastguard station – park to take the 20-minute walk due north to the signal tower. Hop back in the car, continuing east – around 1km later a viewpoint tops cliffs 180m high.

There's another superb vantage point 1km further round – on a fine day you'll see Ireland's most northerly point, Malin Head.

The Drive » The N56 continues west. Settlements thin out, the road climbs and the pointed peek of Mt Errigal fills more and more of your windscreen before the road swings away. At tiny Crolly follow the R259 towards the airport then turn right, picking up signs for Leo's Tavern (35km).

🔟 Meenaleck

You never know who'll drop by for one of the legendary singalongs at **Leo's Tavern** (📞074-954 8143; www.leostavern.com; Meenaleck, off R259, Crolly; mains €10.50-14.50; ⊙kitchen 5-8.45pm Mon-Fri, from 1pm Sat & Sun, bar 4pm-midnight Mon-Fri, from noon Sat & Sun; 🛜) in Meenaleck. It's owned by Bartley

Brennan, brother of Enya and her siblings Máire, Ciaran and Pól (aka the group Clannad). The pub glitters with gold, silver and platinum discs and is packed with musical mementos – there's live music nightly in summer.

The Drive » Continue west on the R259 as it bobbles and twists beside scattered communities and an at-first-boggy then sandy shore. Head on to the pocket-sized port of Burtonport, following ferry signs right, to embark for Arranmore Island (25km).

TRIP HIGHLIGHT

🔟 Arranmore Island

Arranmore (Árainn Mhór) offers a true taste of Ireland. Framed by dramatic cliff faces, cavernous sea caves and clear sandy beaches, this 9km-by-5km island sits 5km offshore. Here you'll discover a prehistoric

DETOUR: FINTOWN RAILWAY

Start: 🔟 Arranmore island

You've been driving for days now – time to let the train take the strain. The charming **Fintown Railway** (📞074-954 6280; www.antraen.com; off R250, Fintown; adult/child €8/5; ⊙11am-4pm Mon-Sat, 1-5pm Sun Jul & Aug, Thu-Sun only Jun & Sep) runs along a rebuilt 5km section of the former County Donegal Railway track beside picturesque Lough Finn. It's been lovingly restored to its original condition and a return trip in the red-and-white, 1940s diesel railcar takes around 40 minutes. To get to the railway, head east on the R252, off the N56 south of Dungloe. Then settle back to enjoy the ride.

triangular fort and an off-shore bird sanctuary fluttering with corncrakes, snipes and seabirds. Irish is the main language spoken, pubs put on turf fires and traditional-music sessions run late into the night. The **Arranmore Ferry** (☎074-954 2233, 074-952 0532; www.arranmoreferry.com; Burtonport; return adult/child €15/7, car & driver €30; ⏱4-8 daily sailings year-round) takes 20 minutes and runs up to eight times a day.

🛏 p327

The Drive » The R259 bounces down to Dungloe, where you take the N56 south into a rock-strewn landscape that's backed by the Blue Stack Mountains. After a stretch of rally-circuit-esque road, the sweep of Gweebarra Bay emerges. Take the sharp right towards peaceful Narin (R261), following signs to the beach (*trá*), 45km from Arranmore Island.

18 Narin

You've now entered the beautiful Loughrea Peninsula, which glistens with tiny lakes cupped by undulating hills. Narin has a spectacular 4km-long, wishbone-shaped

Blue Flag beach, the sandy tip of which points towards **Iniskeel Island**. You can walk to the island at low tide along a 500m sandy causeway. Your reward? An intimate island studded with early Christian remains: St Connell, a cousin of St Colmcille, founded a monastery here in the 6th century.

🛏 p327

The Drive » Continue south on the R261 through tweed-producing Ardara. Shortly after leaving town, take the second turning (the first turning after the John Malloy factory outlet), marked by a hand-painted sign to 'Maghera', following a road wedged between craggy hills and an increasingly sandy shore. In time the Assarancagh Waterfall (14km) comes into view.

19 Assarancagh Waterfall

Stepping out of the car reveals just what an enchanting spot this is. As the waterfall streams down the sheer hillside, walk along the road (really a lane) towards the sea. This 1.5km route leads past time-warp farms – sheep bleat and the tang of peat smoke scents the air. At tiny Maghera head through the car park, down a track, over a boardwalk

and onto a truly stunning expanse of pure-white sand. This exquisite place belies a bloody past. Some 100 villagers hid from Cromwell's forces in nearby caves – all except one were discovered and massacred.

The Drive » Drive west through Maghera on a dramatic route that makes straight for the gap in the towering hills. At the fork, turn right, heading deeper into the remote headland, making for Glencolumbcille (20km).

20 Glencolumbcille

The welcome in the scattered, pub-dotted, bayside village of Glencolumbcille (Gleann Cholm Cille) is warm. This remote settlement also offers a glimpse of a disappearing way of life. **Father McDyer's Folk Village** (www.glenfolkvillage.com; Doonalt; adult/child €6/5; ⏱10am-6pm Mon-Sat, from noon Sun Easter-Sep, 11am-4.30pm Oct) took traditional life of the 1960s and froze it in time. Its thatched cottages re-create daily life with genuine period fittings, while the Craft Shop sells wines made from such things as seaweed, as well as marmalade and whiskey truffles – a few treats at your journey's end.

/ SHUTTERSTOCK ©

Eating & Sleeping

Ballycastle ❷

🛏 An Caislean Guesthouse
Guesthouse ££

(☎028-2076 2845; www.ancaislean.co.uk; 42 Quay Rd; s £35, d £70-80; 🅿 🛜) Originally two guesthouses, now linked by a covered walkway, An Caislean has a large guest lounge and a warm and welcoming family atmosphere. Rooms are spacious and comfortable, if a bit creaky in the floorboard department, but the trump card is the location, just a few minutes' walk from the beach.

Portstewart ❺

🛏 Saltwater House
B&B £££

(☎028-7083 3872; www.saltwaterhouse.co.uk; 63 Strand Rd; d £130-150) More like a boutique hotel than a B&B, Saltwater House has four beautiful wooden-shuttered rooms with pale grey and blue hues, bike rental and an ocean-facing terrace. It also serves scrumptious organic and/or free-range breakfasts.

Derry ❼

🛏 Merchant's House
B&B ££

(☎028-7126 9691; www.thesaddlershouse.com; 16 Queen St; d from £75; @ 🛜) This historic, Georgian-style townhouse is a gem of a B&B. It has an elegant lounge and dining room with marble fireplaces and antique furniture, TV, coffee-making facilities, homemade marmalade at breakfast and bathrobes in the bedrooms.

Glenevin Waterfall ❾

🛏 Glen House
Guesthouse €€

(☎074-937 6745; www.glenhouse.ie; Straid, Clonmany; d €90-100; 🅿 🛜) Despite the grand surroundings and luxurious rooms, you'll find neither pretension nor high prices at this gem of a guesthouse, where rooms are a lesson in restrained sophistication and the setting is totally tranquil. Rooms at the front have gorgeous views of the lough, and the walking trail to Glenevin Waterfall and the Urris Hills is right next door.

Ramelton ⓫

🛏 Frewin House
B&B €€

(☎074-915 1246; www.frewinhouse.com; Rectory Rd; s €125, d €160-180; ☺Mar-Oct; 🅿 🛜) This fine Victorian rectory in secluded grounds would make every weepy heroine's dreams come true. The house combines antique furniture and open fires with contemporary style. The bedrooms are pretty but uncluttered.

Downings ⓭

🛏 Beach
Hotel €€

(Óstán na Trá; ☎074-915 5303; www.beachhotel.ie; R248, Downings; s €80-100, d €110-130; 🅿 🛜) The bright, modern rooms at this large family-run hotel come in calming neutral tones; many have ocean views. You can refuel in its restaurant (mains €12 to €23).

Dunfanaghy ⓮

🛏 Corcreggan Mill
Guesthouse €

(☎074-913 6409; www.corcreggan.com; Castlebane, off N56; campsites €17.50, r €95, glamping from €80; @ 🛜) As well as spotless double and family rooms (only some with private bathrooms) in the lovingly restored former mill-house, Corcreggan has sites for camping and a number of quirky glamping cabins.

Arranmore Island ⓱

🛏 Claire's Bed & Breakfast
B&B €

(☎074-952 0042; www.clairesbandb.wordpress.com; Leabgarrow; r from €60; 🛜) This modern house with simple rooms is right by the ferry port.

Narin ⓲

🛏 Carnaween House
B&B €€

(☎074-954 5122; www.carnaweenhouse.com; Narin; s/d from €50/90, cottage from €155, restaurant mains €16.50-26.50; ☺kitchen 6-9pm Thu-Sun, 1-4pm Sun Jun-Sep, shorter hours Oct-May; 🛜) Carnaween House glows with brilliant white bedrooms in a luxury beach-house style – indeed, the sands on the adjoining beach are *almost* as white.

Delights of Donegal

Supremely scenic (sometimes scary) roads lead from sandy shores to exposed mountains, taking in horse rides, boat trips and world-class art along the way.

30

TRIP HIGHLIGHTS

280 km

Dunfanaghy
Go for a gallop across soft, white sand

245 km

8

Tory Island
Discover Irish traditions on this rock outcrop

9

FINISH
Buncrana

12

Letterkenny

350 km

Glebe House & Gallery
Enjoy world-class art amid picture-perfect mountains and loughs

Ardara

Sliabh Liag

2

20 km

Rossnowlagh
START

Donegal Bay
Delight in charismatic Donegal town's scenic location

7 DAYS
423KM / 263 MILES

GREAT FOR...

BEST TIME TO GO

Easter to October – sights and activities are open; weather might be better.

ESSENTIAL PHOTO

Riding a horse across Dunfanaghy beach.

BEST TWO DAYS

From tweed town via mountain to classic Irish island: stops 6 to 8 deliver the essence of Donegal.

Dunfanaghy Horse riders on the beach at Dunfanaghy

30 | Delights of Donegal

This trip prompts diverse sensations: looming Mt Errigal is overwhelming; a beach horse ride feels liberating; and driving the high mountain passes is heart-in-the-mouth stuff. Relax on boat trips around Donegal Bay to 600m-high sea cliffs and an island, then encounter international art, Ireland's traditional industries and piles of hand-cut peat beside the road. On this trip you gain a true insight into delightful Donegal.

ATLANTIC OCEAN

1 Rossnowlagh

There's more to the happy-go-lucky resort of Rossnowlagh than its superb 3km sandy beach. Deep in a forest (signed off the R231 south of town), a **Franciscan Friary** (📞071-985 1342; www. franciscans.ie; off R231) offers tranquil gardens, a small museum and the Way of the Cross walk, which meanders up a hillside smothered with rhododendrons for spectacular views.

The Drive » The R231 heads north through a gently rolling landscape, joining the N15 for a smooth run into Donegal town (19km). Head for the waterfront, parking near the pier.

TRIP HIGHLIGHT

2 Donegal Town

With its handsome castle, waterside location and Blue Stack Mountains backdrop, Donegal town is a delightful stop. Drink in the beauty of Donegal Bay on the **Donegal Bay Waterbus** (📞074-972 3666; www.donegalbaywaterbus. com; Donegal Pier; adult/child €20/7; ⏰Easter-Oct), a 1¼-hour boat tour that will see you gazing at historic sites, seal-inhabited coves, an island manor and a ruined castle.

The Drive » Take the N56 west. The Blue Stack Mountains retreat in your wing mirror, an open coast road unfurls and soon the wafer-thin St John's peninsula comes into view. Turn

off left, heading out to its tip for 32km.

3 St John's Point

This improbably thin finger of land pokes into the sea, culminating at St John's Point. Driving the 11km lane to the tip feels like driving into the ocean. The point itself has a small sandy beach,

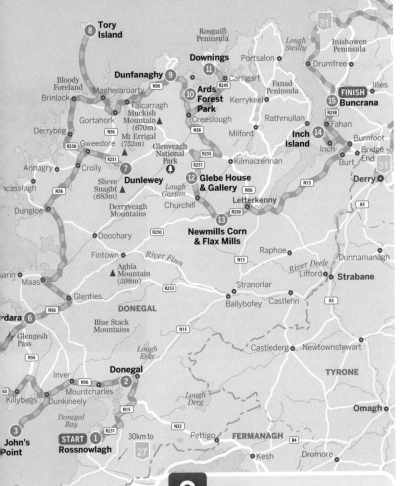

rich bird and plant life, total tranquillity and (inevitably) remarkable, wraparound views.

📖 p335

The Drive » Continue west on the N56 then take the R263 through fish-scented Killybeggs. After its harbour full of trawlers, signs appear for Sliabh Liag, the towering mountains that loom ever closer ahead. After Carrick

LINK YOUR TRIP

27 **Sligo Surrounds**

A five-day meander through culture-packed Sligo. Head for Sligo town, 50km south of this trip's start.

31 **Inishowen Peninsula**

An exhilarating foray onto a remote headland. Start in Derry, 20km east of this trip's finish.

comes tiny Teelin (Tieleann), 34km from St John's Point.

- - - - - - - - - - - - - - - - -

❹ Sliabh Liag

From the road so far, Sliabh Liag (Slieve League) has looked like an impressive mountain range, but these sheer 600m-high sea cliffs are utterly awe-inspiring when seen from the water at their base. Boats leave from Teelin; book with **Nuala Star** (📞087 628 4688; www.sliabhleagueboattrips.com; Teelin Pier; tours per person €20-25; 🕑Apr-Oct).

The Drive » Back at Carrick, edge west on the R263 before turning left on the minor route signed Malin Beg (Málainn Bhig). It cuts behind the massive peaks of Sliabh Liag (Slieve League), threading through an increasingly remote landscape, dotted with isolated farms and scored by strips of hand-cut turf (peat). It's 12km to Malin Beg.

- - - - - - - - - - - - - - - - -

❺ Malin Beg

Malin Beg is one of Donegal's wildest spots, which is quite something in a county crammed with them. An undulating sea-monster-like headland snakes in the waves; Sligo's coast appears distant to the south, and a creamy lighthouse sits just offshore. The bay below is bitten out of low cliffs; descend 60 steps to firm, red-tinged sand, a spot sheltered from Malin Beg's howling winds.

🛏 p335

The Drive » Go north through Glencolumbcille (Gleann Cholm Cille), picking up signs for Glengesh Pass. A steep climb past bogs and wandering sheep leads to a plunging road, winding into the valley below. Go north onto the N56 to reach Ardara (34km).

- - - - - - - - - - - - - - - - -

❻ Ardara

Heritage-town Ardara is the heart of Donegal's traditional tweed industry; the **Heritage Centre** (📞087 286 8657; Main St; 🕑 usually 10am-5pm Mon-Fri, 11am-4pm Sat Easter-Sep) charts its transformation from cottage industry to global product. Turn right out of the centre and stroll up the hill to the **Eddie Doherty** (📞087 699 6360; www.handwoventweed.com; Main St; 🕑10am-6pm Mon-Sat, sometimes Sun) shop to see a vast loom, piles of rugs and rolls of cloth. Staff will happily explain more.

The Drive » The N56 sweeps north towards Dungloe (signed Glenties). After Dungloe, Mt Errigal's pyramidal peak rears from a lough-studded landscape. Turn onto the R251, climbing steadily towards it and Dunlewey (70km).

- - - - - - - - - - - - - - - - -

❼ Dunlewey

Isolated, exposed lough-side Dunlewey (Dún Lúiche) offers a true taste of mountain life. The scenery overwhelms everything here; human habitation seems very small. Experience the

landscape's full impact on a boat trip run by the **Dunlewey Centre** (Ionad Cois Locha; 📞074-953 1699; www.dunleweycentre.com; Dunlewey; cottage or boat trip adult/child €7.25/5.25, cottage & boat €13.50/9.50; 🕑10.30am-5.30pm Easter-Sep, to 4.45pm Oct; 👶), as a storyteller expounds on ghoulish folklore.

🛏 p72, p335

The Drive » Rejoin the N56, heading briefly west before taking the R258 around Bloody Foreland (Cnóc Fola), a spectacular shore so named because sunsets turn its rocks crimson. Turn towards the tiny harbour (Magheraroarty, 32km) that eventually swings into

DESIGN PICS INC/GETTY IMAGES ©

Tory Island, County Donegal

view. From here the 35-minute crossing to Tory Island on the ferry can be wild.

TRIP HIGHLIGHT

8 Tory Island

Some 11km offshore, craggy Tory Island (Oileán Thóraí) is a fiercely independent community with its own Irish dialect, tradition of electing a 'king' and style of 'naive' art, plus early Christian remains and 100 seabird species.

The Drive » The N56 undulates north past loughs to Dunfanaghy in a sheep-grazed landscape where the ever-present bulk of Muckish

Mountain looms to the right. Once in Dunfanaghy (37km), make for the central Arnold's Hotel.

TRIP HIGHLIGHT

9 Dunfanaghy

Along with chilled-out pubs and arty shops, cheerful Dunfanaghy offers the chance to ride along pristine sweeps of white sand. **Dunfanaghy Stables** (📞074-910 0980; www.dunfanaghystables. com; Arnolds Hotel, Main St; adult/child per hour €35/30; ⏰Easter-Oct) at Arnold's Hotel is just across the road from the beach; book for an unforgettable ride.

✖ ⊨ p58, p327, p335

The Drive » Continue east through Dunfanaghy; 5km later turn left into Ards Forest Park.

----

10 Ards Forest Park

From the main **park** (off N56; parking €5 - €1 & €2 coins only; ⏰8am-9pm Apr-Sep, 10am-4.30pm Oct-Mar) car park, pick up the trail that meanders east through ash and oak towards a Capuchin Friary. Follow the path further down still and you'll stumble upon the exquisite Isabella's Cove then Lucky Shell Bay. Allow two hours return.

The Drive » Rejoin the N56 east, before taking the R245, an increasingly windy road backed by the rugged hills of the Fanad Peninsula, to Carrigart (Carraig Airt). Head through amiable Carrigart to Downings, 24km from Ards Forest Park.

⑪ Downings

The **beach** at Downings (or Downies) is simply superb: rolling green hills meet an immense curl of bright-white sand. It's also, unlike many local beaches, safe to swim here; the Atlantic makes for a chilly, but memorable, dip.

The Drive » Return to the N56, turning towards Letterkenny, with the Derryveagh Mountains gathering ahead. Turn onto the R255 (signed Glenveagh National Park), climbing towards those peaks. Turn left onto the R251, which descends, revealing a glittering Lough Gartan. At the water's edge, follow Glebe Gallery signs right (40km).

TRIP HIGHLIGHT

⑫ Glebe Gallery

This is a true treat: the top-notch artwork at **Glebe Gallery** (☎074-913 7071; www.heritageireland.ie; Church Hill; adult/child €5/3; ⏰11am-6.30pm daily Easter, Jul & Aug, Sat-Thu Jun & Sep, last admission 5.30pm) belonged to English painter Derrick Hill. Works include pieces by Tory Island's 'naïve' artists, plus Picasso, Landseer, Hokusai, Jack B Yeats and Kokoschka.

The Drive » The R251 winds south through woodland, hugging the lough shore. Turn onto the R250 towards Letterkenny; soon you'll see Newmills Corn and Flax Mills signed on your right (11km).

⑬ Newmills Corn and Flax Mills

A whirring, creaking, gushing delight, this restored, three-storey, water-powered **corn mill** (☎074-912 5115; www.

heritageireland.ie; R250; ⏰10am-6pm late May–Sep) is full of in-motion grinding stones, drive shafts, cogs and gears.

The Drive » After Letterkenny join the N13 east towards Derry. The River Swilly uncurls to your left. Take the R238/239 turn, then the left towards Inch Island (signed 'Inch Island Wildfowl Reserve'). Once over the causeway the (signed) road to Inch Pier (53km) snakes along tranquil, tree-lined lanes.

⑭ Inch Island

At Inch's tiny pier, park on the right (don't block the fishers' track to the left). Few tourists make it to this compact crescent of sand. It's a place to rest, skim stones and watch waves.

The Drive » Return to the R238, which sweeps north past a 5km sandy beach to Buncrana. By now Lough Swilly is stretching far ahead. Head for Buncrana's shoreline (20km).

⑮ Buncrana

Bustling Buncrana provides a fitting trip finale, courtesy of stunning sunsets; locals will tell you the ones over Lough Swilly are the best around. A path leads beside the water to pint-sized, 1718 **Buncrana Castle** – it and neighbouring **O'Doherty's Keep** provide ideal sun-going-down vantage points.

✕ 🛏 p335, p343

TOP TIP:
GLENVEAGH NATIONAL PARK

Glebe House and Gallery sits beside the stunning **Glenveagh National Park** (Páirc Náisiúnta Ghleann Bheatha; www.glenveaghnationalpark.ie). This 16,500-sq-km wilderness features forests, mountains, shimmering lakes and green-gold bogs, and makes for magnificent walking. The **visitor centre** (☎076-100 2537; www.glenveaghnationalpark.ie; off R251; ⏰9am-5.30pm Apr-Oct, 8.30am-5pm Nov-Mar) provides free maps.

Eating & Sleeping

St John's Point ③

🛏 Castle Murray   Boutique Hotel €€
(📞074-973 7022; www.castlemurray.com; St John's Point; r from €120; 🛜) Overlooking the ruins of the 15th-century McSwyne's Castle, Castle Murray is not a castle, but a boutique hotel in a sprawling modern beach house. Most of the 10 guest rooms have fine sea views. Breakfast is a feast of homemade bread and locally sourced produce. It's 1.5km south of Dunkineely on a minor road leading to St John's Point.

Malin Beg ⑤

🛏 Áras Ghlean Cholm Cille   B&B €
(📞074-973 0077; www.arasgcc.com; Malinmore; s/d from €32/60; 🛜) This large place in peaceful Malinmore, between Malin Beg and Glencolumbcille, is a good choice, with a large variety of rooms from small but serviceable singles to larger doubles, twins and triples. There's a large kitchen and lounge, and breakfast is an extra €5. A shuttle service to local pubs is offered and bikes can be rented (per day €15).

Dunlewey ⑦

🛏 Glen Heights B&B   B&B €
(📞074-956 0844; www.glenheightsbb.com; s €50, d €70-80; 🛜) The three rooms are bright and inviting, and the Donegal charm is in full swing at this fine choice run by Kathleen. Your breakfast may well go cold on the plate in front of you as you stare at the breathtaking views of Dunlewey Lake and the Poisoned Glen from the conservatory. It's down a minor road off R251, 2km east of the Dunlewey centre.

Dunfanaghy ⑨

✕ Rusty Oven   Pizza €
(www.facebook.com/therustyoven; Main St; pizzas €10-12; 🕐5-9.30pm Fri-Sun; 🍴) Arrive early to avoid a long wait at this popular place serving artisan sourdough pizzas, cooked in a wood-fired oven, with toppings like goat's cheese and pepper, and pear and walnut. Eat in the garden or at one of the indoor tables in the stove-heated, shabby-chic shed. It's located behind **Patsy Dan's** (Main St; 🕐11am-midnight). Sourdough loaves are available to takeaway.

🛏 Arnold's Hotel   Hotel €€
(📞074-913 6208; www.arnoldshotel.com; Main St, Dunfanaghy; s/d from €80/115; 🅿🛜) Open since 1922, this family-run hotel at the east end of the village has 30 comfortable and stylish rooms. The hotel's restaurant serves up traditional seafood, roasts and grills (mains €15 to €26). Next door, **Arnou** serves breakfasts (€6 to €8) and lunches (€7 to €12.50) daily, plus gourmet burgers on Saturday and Sunday nights (€13 to €14).

🛏 Whins   B&B €€
(📞074-913 6481; www.thewhinsdunfanaghy. com; off N56; s/d €50/80; 🛜) About 750m east of the town centre opposite the golf course, the colourful, individually decorated rooms at the Whins have patchwork quilts and a real sense of character. A wide choice of breakfasts is served upstairs in a room with a view towards Horn Head. Cash only.

Letterkenny ⑫

🛏 Pearse Road B&B   B&B €
(📞074-912 3002; Pearse Rd; r €80-85; 🅿🛜) This tidy guesthouse has rooms spread over two buildings close to Main St. Rooms are well equipped and there's a speedy laundry right next door.

Buncrana ⑮

🛏 Caldra Bed & Breakfast   B&B €€
(📞074-936 3703; www.caldrabandb.com; Pillar Park; s/d from €50/80; 🅿🛜) This large, modern B&B has four spacious rooms ideal for families. The public rooms feature impressive fireplaces and gilt mirrors while guest rooms are more sedate and understated. The garden and patio overlook Lough Swilly and the mountains.

Inishowen Peninsula

This thrilling route heads deep into Ireland's wild lands. You'll encounter clifftop hikes, shipwrecks, a fort and superb seafood then return exhilarated to the comforts of town.

31

TRIP HIGHLIGHTS

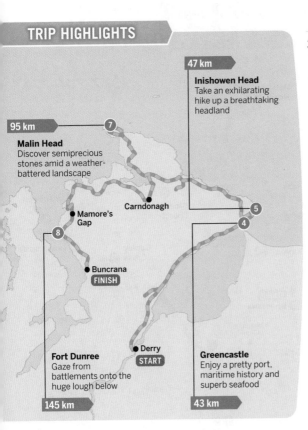

47 km

Inishowen Head
Take an exhilarating hike up a breathtaking headland

95 km ⑦

Malin Head
Discover semiprecious stones amid a weather-battered landscape

Carndonagh

Mamore's Gap
⑧

Buncrana
FINISH

Fort Dunree
Gaze from battlements onto the huge lough below

145 km

Derry
START

Greencastle
Enjoy a pretty port, maritime history and superb seafood

43 km

⑤
④

---

3 DAYS
165KM / 103 MILES

GREAT FOR...

BEST TIME TO GO

Easter to October should have better weather, and more things are open.

📷 ESSENTIAL PHOTO

The gorgeous sandy-bay views from Inishowen Head.

✅ BEST DRIVE

The white-knuckle ascent up mountainous Mamore's Gap.

Mamore's Gap A white-knuckle mountain ascent

31 Inishowen Peninsula

This trip isn't about skimming Ireland's surface through big-name sights. Instead it's a route to the heart of the country's compelling narratives: faith, poverty, mass migration, territorial disputes, the Troubles. With unsigned, cliff-side roads that look more like farm tracks, you'll probably get a little lost. But locals are helpful if you do – and asking for directions is a great conversation starter.

❶ Derry

Kick-start your Inishowen trip by exploring the story of one of the coast's most famous victims: *La Trinidad Valenciera*. This Venetian trader was the second-biggest vessel in the Spanish Armada and was shipwrecked at Kinnagoe Bay in 1588 – a spot you'll see later. Derry's Tower Museum (p321) tells the vessel's story and features poignant wreck finds: pewter tableware, wooden combs, olive jars, shoe soles. In the Story

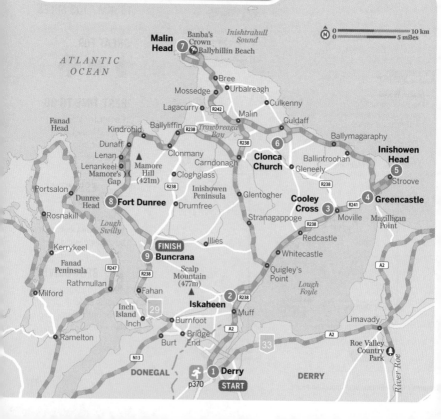

of Derry exhibition, well-thought-out exhibits and audiovisuals lead you through the city's history, from the founding of the monastery of St Colmcille (Columba) in the 6th century to the Battle of the Bogside in the late 1960s. Make time to explore vibrant, fascinating Derry, Northern Ireland's second city.

The Drive » Take the A2 north towards Moville. Derry's retail parks quickly give way to fields and mountain views, and the silvery Lough Foyle emerges to your right. Soon road signs switch from mph to km/h: welcome to the Republic of Ireland. Shortly after Muff, turn left to Iskaheen (11km), head up the hill and park beside the village church.

❷ Iskaheen

Head across the road, through the creaking gate and into the old

LINK YOUR TRIP

29 The North in a Nutshell

The cream of the north in one glorious route; pick it up from this trip's end at Buncrana.

33 From Bangor to Derry

Belfast and the sight-packed Antrim Coast. It stops where this trip starts: Derry.

graveyard. There you'll see evidence of spectres that have long stalked Ireland: poverty, high death rates and the Troubles. Among many gravestones recording multiple deaths, hunt out the broad memorial to the McKinney family. Its losses include a 24-year-old woman, a nine-month-old boy and three girls, aged 13 years, 11 months and six weeks. It also commemorates 34-year-old James Gerard McKinney, one of 13 unarmed demonstrators shot dead by British troops in Derry on 30 January 1972 – Bloody Sunday.

The Drive » Head back to the R238 drinking in the panorama of Lough Foyle as you go. Next comes a 15-minute, scenic shoreside cruise north to Moville. Just before town, take the left turn, signed Cooley Cross, which appears next to a small lay-by on the right, 20km from Iskaheen.

❸ Cooley Cross

The 3m-high cross you've parked beside has an unusual ringed head – through it negotiating parties are said to have shaken hands to seal agreements. The atmospheric tumbling of ruins beyond features the remnants of an early monastery founded by St Patrick. At the foot of the enclosure, set against some great lough views, sits the tiny, hut-like **Skull House**. This roofed,

gabled structure is a tomb-shrine associated with St Finian, an abbot of the early monastery.

 p343

The Drive » Rejoin the R238, heading left for the 10-minute drive along the shore to Greencastle. Opposite, Magilligan Point's sandy beaches curl into view. Soon after entering Greencastle (5km) take the right to the Maritime Museum.

❹ Greencastle

Packed with boats and top seafood restaurants, the thriving port of Greencastle also has a fine **Maritime Museum** (☏074-938 1363; www.inishowenmaritime.com; off R241; adult/child museum €5/3, museum & planetarium show €10/6; ☉9.30am-5pm Mon-Fri year-round, plus to 5.30pm Sat & from noon Sun Easter-Sep). It explores the history of the surrounding seas, with fascinating exhibits from the sunken wrecks of Lough Foyle, exhibitions exploring the demise of the Spanish Armada and examples of Drontheim fishing boats, once produced en masse in Greencastle and widely used along Ireland's north coast and beyond.

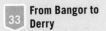 p343

The Drive » Continue north. Just after the Fisheries College take the right, following signs to Inishowen Head. Houses thin out and the road narrows before the black-and-white Inishowen lighthouse edges into your windscreen. Park just beyond, beside Stroove Beach (5km).

- - - - - - - - - - - - - - - - -

5 Inishowen Head

From Stroove Beach's curling sands, join the footpath that winds north, initially on the road then onto a track,

up towards Inishowen Head itself. This stiff 2.5km climb reveals spectacular views over Lough Foyle to the immense ribbon of sand framing Magilligan Point. On clear days you can spot Scotland's islands to the northeast. Edge high enough and you'll see the jagged rocks and golden sands of Kinnagoe

Bay – where *La Trinidad Valenciera* came to grief.

✕ p343

The Drive ›› Motor north, initially along your walk route, before curving left. Opposite the Maritime Museum turning, head up an unsigned, steep, narrow, roller-coaster road (it even has grass in the middle) to Culdaff. This is a difficult to navigate route with very steep hills; an alternative is to backtrack to

Maritime Museum & Planetarium, Greencastle, County Donegal

Moville via the R241 coastal road and take the R238 to Culdaff. At Culdaff, take the R238 towards Gleneely. Turn right 1km along, opposite the modern church. Clonca Church appears 1km later.

- - - - - - - - - - - - - - - - -

❻ Clonca Church

The towering gable ends and huge windows of the roofless shell of 17th-century Clonca Church frame views of the Donegal mountains.

AMAZING GRACE

John Newton, the composer of 'Amazing Grace', was inspired to write his legendary song after his ship the *Greyhound* took refuge in the calm waters of Lough Swilly during a severe storm in 1748. He and his crew were welcomed in Buncrana after their near-death experience and his spiritual journey from slave trader to antislavery campaigner had its beginnings here. He went on to become a prolific hymn writer and later mentored William Wilberforce in his fight against slavery. For more on the story, visit www.amazinggrace.ie.

Inside sits the intricately carved tombstone of Scott Magnus Mac-Orristin – spot the carved writing sloping down the side, and the sword and hurling-stick motifs. Outside, a tall cross stands in a field; clamber down to decipher the depiction of the loaves-and-fishes miracle on its weathered face, amid ornate swirls and zigzags.

The Drive » The R238/R243 leads from Culdaff to quaint Malin village. Next make for Malin Head (25km from Clonca Church), a spectacular drive through Trawbreaga Bay's lowlands, past massive dunes at Five Fingers Strand and the hulk of Knockamany. You emerge onto a rugged coast dotted with whitewashed cottages. Take the right, signed Banba's Crown.

TRIP HIGHLIGHT

Malin Head

Open your car door at Malin Head and step into a weather-battered landscape of tumbling cliffs and sparse vegetation – welcome to Ireland's most northerly point. The clifftop tower beside you was built in 1805 by the British admiralty and later used as a Lloyds signal station. WWII lookout posts are dotted around. To the west a path leads to Hell's Hole, a chasm where the incoming

waters crash against rock formations. Just to the east of the head sits Ballyhillin Beach, known for its semiprecious stones.

📖 p343

The Drive » From Malin village take the R238 through Carndonagh to Clonmany then follow signs to Mamore's Gap, heading straight for the by-now-large-looming mountains. At the crossroads the Inis Eoghain Scenic Route goes up what looks like a farm track. Wayside shrines and another first-and-second-gear ascent follow, before a brake-burning descent. At the plain, head right to Dunree Head (50km).

TRIP HIGHLIGHT

⑧ Fort Dunree

Dunree Head overlooks Lough Swilly, a highly strategic stretch of water that's been navigated by Norsemen, Normans, Ireland's fleeing aristocracy and part of Britain's WWI naval fleet. The 19th-century **Fort Dunree** (📞074-936 1817; www.dunree.pro.ie; Dunree Head; adult/child €7/5; ⏰10.30am-4.30pm Mon-Fri, noon-5pm Sat & Sun) commands the water. Along with some menacing artillery, films explore the fort's past, while an underground bunker conjures up daily life. The scenery and the birdlife are stunning.

 p343

The Drive » Head south to Buncrana, past the mountains of Bulbin and Aghaweel, rising up to your left. The waters of Lough Swilly sweep off to the right, backed by the ranges of the Fanad Peninsula. At the appealing town of Buncrana (19km) head for the shore, initially signed Swilly Ferry, and park opposite the leisure centre.

⑨ Buncrana

From the car park a path leads across the grass and along the coast, with Lough Swilly and the Fanad Peninsula's hills stretching out in front of you.

Make for **Buncrana Castle**, built in 1718. Wolfe Tone was imprisoned here following the unsuccessful French invasion in 1798. Beside the castle you'll find **O'Doherty's Keep**, a 15th-century tower built by the local O'Doherty chiefs, but burned by the English and rebuilt for their own use.

From here, the waymarked **Shore Walk** continues north for 4km to **Straghill Strand**, a remote beach with beautiful views across the lough,

🍴 📖 p335, p343

Eating & Sleeping

Moville ③

🛏 Redcastle Hotel & Spa   Hotel €€
(☏074-938 5555; www.redcastlehoteldonegal.com; R238, Redcastle; s/d from €90/140; 📶🐕) The peninsula's smartest luxury resort is on the coast 7km southwest of Moville and tucked away off the main road near Cooley Cross. The 93 rooms are comfortable and spacious; some look straight out to the water. Restaurants include the **Edge**, which has excellent views and modern Irish cuisine.

Greencastle ④

🍴 Kealy's Seafood Bar   Seafood €€
(☏074-938 1010; www.kealysseafoodbar.ie; The Harbour; mains €16-29, early-bird set menu €24-28.50; ☺12.30-3pm & 5-9.30pm Wed-Sun; 📶) Family-run for over 25 years, this bistro offers locally caught seafood so fresh you almost have to fight the harbourside seals for it. Its unpretentious nautical-style polished-timber decor belies its numerous culinary awards. It's a splendid spot for anything from a bowl of chowder to monkfish tagine, and every meal has a side serve of delicious views.

Culdaff ⑤

🛏 McGrory's of Culdaff   Guesthouse €€
(☏074-937 9104; www.mcgrorys.ie; Malin Rd/R238; s/d from €84/118, mains €14-18; ☺kitchen 12.30-9pm; 📶) This landmark hotel and bar has 17 bright, modern rooms. Catch live music in the **Backroom**, which books international singer-songwriters and traditional music. McGrory's classic Irish cuisine, served in the **Front Room**, is the best for miles around; the seafood chowder with homemade Guinness bread is especially good. .

Malin Village ⑦

🍴 Wild Strands Caife   Cafe €
(☏085 105 3893; www.malinheadcommunity.ie/wild-strands-caife; Carnmalin, Malin Head Community Centre; flatbread €9-11; ☺10am-5pm Fri, Sat & Mon, 11am-4pm Sun; 🖐) At the Malin Head Community Centre on the road to Malin Head, Wild Strands Caife is a worthwhile stop for delicious, home-cooked organic food.

🛏 Whitestrand B&B   B&B €
(☏086 822 9163, 074-937 0335; www.whitestrand.net; off R242, Middletown; s €35-37, d €70-74; 📶) Perfectly placed amid the bluffs and hills leading to Malin Head, this comfy B&B has three fine bedrooms. As a welcome you'll receive a hot beverage and home-baked treats.

Carndonagh ⑧

🍴 Caffe Banba   Cafe €
(☏074-932 9277; www.caffebanba.com; Main St; mains €5.50-8; ☺8am-5.30pm Mon-Fri, from 9am Sat, 10am-5pm Sun; 📶) This welcoming, wood-panelled cafe makes a good stop for breakfasts, lunchtime sandwiches, quiche, sausage rolls and home-baked cakes.

Buncrana ⑨

🍴 Tank & Skinny's   Bistro €€
(☏074-936 1583; www.facebook.com/tankandskinnysseaside; Swilly Rd; mains lunch €8-10, dinner €12-14.50; ☺9am-9pm daily Jun-Sep, to 4.30pm Mon-Wed, to 8pm Thu-Sun Oct-May) With picture windows overlooking the lough, this cafe-bistro can easily be your destination for the day. Breakfast, including fluffy pancakes and freshly baked croissants, is served until midday, followed by lunch of salads and sandwiches and evening burgers and pizzas.

🛏 Tullyarvan Mill   Hostel €
(☏074-936 1613; www.tullyarvanmill.com; off R238; dm/d €17/50; 📶) Set amid riverside gardens, this purpose-built 51-bed hostel is housed in a modern building attached to the historic Tullyarvan Mill. It also hosts regular cultural events and art exhibits.

🛏 Westbrook House   B&B €€
(☏074-936 1067; www.westbrookhouse.ie; Westbrook Rd; s/d from €55/85; 📶) A handsome Georgian house set in beautiful gardens, Westbrook features chandeliers and antique furniture, giving it a refined sophistication. It's opposite the entrance to Swan Park.

Northwest on Adrenaline

This high-octane trip sees you surfing, hiking and gazing at 600m-high cliffs, driving through mountain passes and along remote roads – an action-packed, unforgettable drive.

32

TRIP HIGHLIGHTS

345 km

Mt Errigal
Scramble to the top of this pyramidal peak

240 km

Killybegs
Feast on fine seafood in this bustling fishing port

195 km

Rossnowlagh
Learn to surf beside a vast sandy beach

● **Erris Head**
START

95 km

Enniscrone
Steam and soak amid seaweed in this Edwardian spa

9
FINISH

Glengesh
Pass ●

Donegal ●

Sliabh ●
Liag

7

5

3

4 DAYS
345KM / 214 MILES

GREAT FOR...

BEST TIME TO GO
Easter to October means better weather and opening hours.

 ESSENTIAL PHOTO

The 600m-high sea cliffs at Sliabh Liag are a photographer's dream.

 BEST FOR OUTDOORS

Stops 3 to 8 for surfing, clambering around cliffs and soaking in seaweed baths.

Northwest on Adrenaline

If you're after an Irish adventure, this trip delivers in spades. Along with adrenaline-fuelled surfing and hiking, you'll take in Donegal's highest mountain, Ireland's highest sea cliffs and the world's largest Stone Age monument. Other heritage crowds in, too: an abbey, a castle and a seafaring past. And then there's the drive itself, from sand-dusted seaside lanes to exhilarating mountain roads – it's a roller-coaster ride.

1 Erris Head

Where better to start a road trip than at the end of the road – literally. The parking area for Erris Head (Ceann Iorrais) appears where the rough lane peters out. From there waymarks (posts with purple arrows) direct you on a two-hour, 5km loop walk around this wind-buffeted headland. The path leads over footbridges and earth banks, across fields and along sheep tracks. The views from the high cliffs are spectacular, taking in islands, sea stacks and rock arches. **Belmullet Tourist Office** (☑097-20494; www.visiterris.ie; Chapel St, Belmullet;

☺9am-4pm Mon-Sat Jun-Aug, 9am-4pm Mon-Fri Sep-May) has free guides; to get to the trailhead from Belmullet, initially follow signs to An Baile Glas, then pick up signs for Ceann Iorrais.

The Drive » Motor southeast across the narrow neck of land that fuses Belmullet to the rest of County Mayo. Soon, turn left onto the R314, towards Ballycastle. After it climbs a lush ravine and attaches itself to the coast, a wood and glass pyramid suddenly pops up on the right. It's your next stop: Céide Fields (45km).

2 Céide Fields

Céide Fields (☑096-43325; www.heritageireland.ie; off R314; adult/child €5/3; ☺visitor centre 10am-6pm

Jun-Sep, to 5pm Easter-May & Oct, last tour 1hr before closing) is considered the world's most extensive Stone Age monument. Half a million tonnes of rock make up the field boundaries, houses and megalithic tombs that have been found so far. Today it's a barren, wind-blasted spot, but five

ATLANTIC
OCEAN

FINISH
Mt Errigal
9

Dunlewy

Slieve
Snaght
(683m)

Dungloe Derryveagh
Mountains

Crohy
Head

Narin Glenties

Ardara

Blue Stack Lough
Mountains Eske

Glencolumbcille Glengesh
Pass

DONEGAL

Donegal
6

Malin Beg Carrick

Inver

Kilcar
Sliabh 7
Liag 8

Killybegs Dunkineely

St John's
Point

Rossnowlagh
5

Donegal
Bay

Ballyshannon

Bundoran

Belleek

Mullaghmore Rosscor

Inishmurray

Lough
Melvin

Cliffony Rossinver

Grange Truskmore
(643m)

Dartry
Mountains

Manorhamilton

Cashelgarran Benbulben
Drumcliff (525m)

LEITRIM

Céide Downpatrick
Fields Head
2

Kilcummin

Dromore
West

Rosses Point

Strandhill

4 **Sligo**

Dromahair

Ballycastle

Killala
Bay

Kilglass

Ballysadare

Castlebaldwin

Lough
Allen

Killala
3 **Enniscrone**

Slieve Gamph
(Ox Mountains) Colloney

Drumfin

MAYO

Crossmolina

Bunnyconnellan

SLIGO

3

Lough
Conn **Ballina**

Ballymote

millennia ago a thriving
farming community lived
here, growing wheat and
barley and grazing sheep
and cattle. Although
important, this story is
hard to tell engagingly
(to the uninitiated the
site could resemble tum-
bles of stone) but a sleek,
award-winning visitor
centre cleverly re-creates

**LINK
YOUR
TRIP**

3 **Tip to Toe**
Wind south to
Wexford, past the pick of
Ireland's historic sites.
Join it at stop 4: Sligo
town

30 **Delights of
Donegal**
Head further north for
exquisite beaches and
a sandy horseback ride.
Pick it up where this trip
stops: towering
Mt Errigal.

347

life in early farming communities. Better still, take a guided tour.

The Drive » The R314 heads east, revealing a vast sea stack at Downpatrick Head. Gradually, exposed hills give way to rolling fields. After one-street Ballycastle comes congested Ballina, where you take the N59 north (signed 'Sligo'). Soon the R297 peels off to Enniscrone, 56km from Céide Fields. Drive up the main street, passing several signs to the beach, before turning left at the sign for Cliff Rd.

TRIP HIGHLIGHT

❸ Enniscrone

Right beside Enniscrone's stunning 5km beach sits **Kilcullen's Seaweed Baths** (☎096-36238; www.kilcullenseaweedbaths.net; Cliff Rd; bath from €25; ☉10am-9pm Jun-Aug, noon-8pm Mon-Fri, 10am-8pm Sat & Sun Sep-May, closed Tue & Wed Nov-Mar). Step into this Edwardian spa and soon you'll be steaming away in a cedar cabinet then submerging yourself in a gigantic porcelain bath filled with orangey water and bits of seaweed. It's used to treat arthritis and rheumatism, but the baths' high iodine content means this traditional natural therapy also acts as an intense moisturiser. It's also a great way to recover from, and prepare for, this trip's adventures.

🛏 p351

The Drive » You could head south back to the N59, but it's more fun to stay on the R297 as it bobbles and twists beside flat coastal fields. Eventually it rejoins the N59 to sweep east to Ballysadare. There take the N4 to Sligo (56km); Sligo Abbey is signed from the ring road.

❹ Sligo Town

Sligo town is an inviting stop: stone bridges frame the river; pedestrian streets are lined with attractive shops; and pub music sessions overflow onto the footpath. In the centre is **Sligo Abbey** (☎071-914 6406; www.heritageireland.ie; Abbey St; adult/child 5/3; ☉10am-6pm Apr-Oct), a Dominican friary founded around 1252. The abbey survived the worst ravages of the Tudor era and it has the only sculpted altar to survive the Reformation. The doorways reach only a few feet high at the abbey's rear – the ground around it was swollen by mass graves from years of famine and war.

🍴🛏 p58, p72, p293, p301, p351

The Drive » Heading north out of Sligo town on the N15 sees the mountains of Benbulben and Truskmore looming ever larger. At Ballyshannon take the R231 to Rossnowlagh. When sand starts edging onto the road, you know you're near the resort's Blue Flag beach. Make for the graffiti-art designs of Fin McCool Surf School, a total trip of 53km.

TRIP HIGHLIGHT

❺ Rossnowlagh

Rossnowlagh's spectacular 3km-long beach is a wide, sandy stretch beloved by families, walkers and surfers throughout the year. The gentle rollers are great for learning to ride the waves, or to hone your skills. **Fin McCool Surf School** (☎071-985 9020; www.finmccoolsurfschool.com; Beach Rd; board & wetsuit rental per day €39, 2hr lesson incl gear adult/child €35/25; ☉10am-5pm daily Jun-Aug, Sat & Sun Sep-May) offers tuition and gear hire; the

Surfers at Rossnowlagh, County Donegal

waters of Donegal Bay offer an exhilarating ride.

✕ ⤙ p351

The Drive >> From Rossnowlagh's sand-dusted road, the R231 winds north through rolling fields before rejoining the N15. This sweeps on towards Donegal town, with the Blue Stack Mountains now appearing behind. On the roundabout on its fringes, pick up the signs for Donegal (20km).

---

❻ Donegal Town

Mountain-backed, pretty Donegal town was for centuries the stamping grounds of the chiefs who ruled northwest Ireland from the 15th to 17th centuries: the O'Donnells. They built **Donegal Castle** (☎074-972 2405; www.heritageire-land.ie; Castle St; adult/child €5/3; ⏲10am-6pm daily East-er–mid-Sep, 9.30am-4.30pm Thu-Mon mid-Sep–Easter) in 1474 and it served as the seat of their formidable power until 1607, when the English ousted Ireland's chieftains. Rory O'Donnell torched his own castle before leaving for France in the infamous Flight of the Earls. Their departure paved the way for the Plantation of Ulster by thousands of Scots and English Protestants, creating divisions still felt today. The castle was rebuilt in 1623 and it's a wonderfully atmospheric place to visit, with rooms furnished with French tapestries and Persian rugs.

✕ ⤙ p351

The Drive >> As the N56 heads west the Blue Stacks range to your right and more mountains shade the horizon ahead. For now though it's a gently rolling road that leads towards Killybegs. Take the R263 into town (30km); the Maritime and Heritage Centre is signed soon after the fishing-boat-packed harbour.

TOP TIP:
GAELTACHT

This part of Ireland is the Donegal Gaeltacht, one of many areas where Irish culture and language are championed. Initially you'll notice it mostly in road signs, as here they tend to be in Irish only (elsewhere it's Irish and English). We use English transliterations with Irish names included in brackets.

TRIP HIGHLIGHT

7 Killybegs

Killybegs is a sensory summation of the sea – the scent of fish hangs in the air, and seagulls wheel overhead in this, Ireland's largest fishing port. A visit to the **International Carpet Making & Fishing Centre** (☏074-974 1944; www.visitkillybegs.com; Fintra Rd; adult/child €5/3; ⏰9.45am-5pm Mon-Fri, weekends by appointment) is a must. You'll hear the personal accounts of local fishers and see evocative sepia images of the industry's heyday. The best bit though is to step aboard the simulation of a fishing-trawler wheelhouse, where you'll try navigating into port amid choppy seas – driving seems easy after that.

🍴 🛏 p351

The Drive ≫ The R263 heads west, tracing the shore before cutting inland to a peak-lined landscape threaded with rough stone walls. Gradually the brooding Sliabh Liag (Slieve League) mountains come to dominate the view. At Carrick turn left, signed Sliabh Liag, and nudge round the mountain edge to the lower car park (16km).

8 Sliabh Liag

The Cliffs of Moher get more publicity, but the spectacular polychrome sea cliffs at Sliabh Liag (Slieve League) are higher – some of the highest in Europe, plunging 600m to the sea. From the lower car park, a path skirts up around the near-vertical rock face to the aptly named **One Man's Pass** – look out for two rocks nicknamed the 'school desk and chair'. Sunset can be stunning, with waves crashing dramatically far below and the ocean reflecting the day's last rays. It's a strenuous hike to the summit, and rain and mist can appear unexpectedly, making conditions slippery. You can drive further up to the second car park, but be sure to close the gate behind you.

The Drive ≫ Pick up the (signed) Glengesh Pass road, a long climb into a wild landscape that crests to reveal sweeping valley views. A dizzying, hairpin descent lurches to the N56 and towards Mt Errigal, the massive pointed peak that edges ever nearer. The R251 climbs through Dunlewey village; when Errigal is directly on your left, turn into the small, walled parking area (83km).

TRIP HIGHLIGHT

9 Mt Errigal

Towering Mt Errigal (752m) seemingly dares you to attempt the tough but beautiful climb to its pyramid-shaped peak. Watch the weather: it's a dangerous trek on misty or wet days, when visibility is minimal. The easiest path to the summit covers 5km and takes around three hours (two up, one back); the Dunlewey Centre (p332) can direct you to the starting point. Even if you don't climb, drink in this remarkably exposed, remote landscape of peaks, loughs and bogs.

🛏 p351

Eating & Sleeping

Enniscrone ❸

🛏 Seasons Lodge   B&B €€
(📞096-37122; www.seasonslodge.ie; Bartragh;
s/d/ste €71/97/118; 🅿 🛜) This friendly and
welcoming B&B right by Enniscrone Golf Links
and a short walk from the beach has large and
very pleasant rooms; excellent breakfasts are
another plus.

Sligo Town ❹

🍴 Montmartre   French €€
(📞071-916 9901; www.montmartrerestaurant.ie;
1 Market Yard; mains €17-26; ☺5-11pm Tue-Sat)
Tucked away on a back road by the market sits an
excellent French restaurant serving unpretentious
but top-quality food. The menu spotlights local
meats, but seafood lovers are well catered for too.
Book ahead.

Rossnowlagh ❺

🍴 Gaslight Inn   Irish €€
(📞071-985 1141; www.gaslightinnrossnowlagh.
com; Highfield, Coolmore; mains lunch €9-15,
dinner €13-36, rooms s/d €85/110; ☺11am-late
daily Jun-Sep, from 5pm Fri, from 11am Sat &
Sun Oct-May) Set on the clifftop, the Gaslight
Inn offers an extensive menu of well-cooked
comfort food and spectacular views over the
bay. Upstairs, the B&B has five pleasant rooms;
front rooms have killer sea views.

🛏 Smugglers Creek   B&B €€
(📞071-985 2367; www.smugglerscreekinn.
com; Cliff Rd; s €50-65, d €80-110, mains €13-25;
☺pub daily Apr-Sep, Thu-Sun Oct-Mar; 🛜) This
combined pub-restaurant-guesthouse perches
on the hillside above the bay. It's justifiably
popular for its excellent food and sweeping
views (room 4 has the best vantage point and
a balcony).

Donegal Town ❻

🍴 Olde Castle Bar   Irish €€
(📞074-972 1262; www.oldecastlebar.com;
Castle St; mains €11-32; ☺ kitchen noon-9pm;

🚶) This ever-busy pub off the Diamond serves
some of the area's best food. Look for classics
such as Donegal Bay oysters or mussels, Irish
stew and seafood platters (€32), plus steaks
and burgers. The pub is always rollicking with
locals and serves its own excellent pale ale: Red
Hugh Brew.

🛏 Cove Lodge   B&B €€
(📞074-972 2302; www.thecovelodgebandb.
com; R267, Drumgowan; r €90; ☺Apr-Oct;
🛜) You'll find subtle floral patterns and rustic
charm in the four ground-floor rooms of this
tranquil and pretty stone and stucco B&B 2.5km
south of town in a rural setting, offering a taste
of Irish country living.

Killybegs ❼

🍴 Seafood Shack   Fish & Chips €
(📞089 239 3094; www.facebook.com/
killybegseafoodshack; Killybegs Harbour; fish
& chips €9-12; ☺4-8.30pm Wed, 12.30-8pm
Thu-Sun) Superfresh seafood cooked to order
is available at this roadside fish and chips
stand. Find it next to the harbour on Shore Rd,
opposite the very fishing boats that caught the
haddock, cod, scampi and calamari in its fryers.

🛏 Ritz   Guesthouse €
(📞074-973 1309; www.theritz-killybegs.com;
Chapel Brae; s/d €40/65; 🛜) The name might
be ironic and this isn't Piccadilly, but this
superbly run guesthouse in the town centre has
ritzy facilities, including an enormous kitchen,
colourful rooms with private bathroom and TV,
and a laundry. The tastefully decorated rooms
all have private bathroom.

Mt Errigal ❾

🛏 Errigal Hostel   Hostel €
(📞074-953 1180; www.anoige.ie; off R251;
dm/s/d €20/32/53; ☺Mar-Oct; 🛜) At the
foot of magnificent Errigal Mt, this gleaming,
excellent and purpose-built 60-bed An Óige
hostel has superb facilities including a self-
catering kitchen, a large laundry room for your
muddy climbing gear, light-filled common areas,
and pristine dorms and private rooms.

From Bangor to Derry

33

From seaside to mountainside, via ruined castles, stately homes, museums and the Giant's Causeway – this trip blends cracking coastal scenery with blockbuster historic sights.

TRIP HIGHLIGHTS

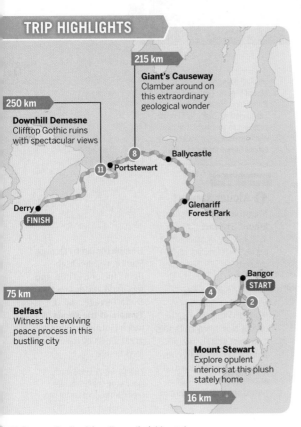

215 km

Giant's Causeway
Clamber around on this extraordinary geological wonder

250 km

Downhill Demesne
Clifftop Gothic ruins with spectacular views

Ballycastle

⑧ Portstewart
⑪

Derry ●
FINISH

Glenariff Forest Park

Bangor
START

75 km

Belfast
Witness the evolving peace process in this bustling city

④
②

Mount Stewart
Explore opulent interiors at this plush stately home

16 km

**4 DAYS
295KM / 183 MILES**

GREAT FOR...

BEST TIME TO GO

March to October brings better weather; avoid August to dodge holiday crowds.

ESSENTIAL PHOTO

The spectacular Giant's Causeway, your must-have north-coast snap.

BEST TWO DAYS

Stops 8 to 11 take in the Causeway, castles, ruins and golden sands.

33 From Bangor to Derry

This drive delivers a true taste of Ireland's gloriously diverse north: the must-see stops of the Giant's Causeway and Carrick-a-Rede; castles and historic homes at Mount Stewart, Hillsborough, Dunluce and Downhill; and superb scenery, from Slemish to sea-sprayed cliffs and immense sand dunes. While in Belfast and Derry, you'll experience two vibrant cities progressing beyond a painful past.

❶ Bangor

Start your journey through the north's scenic and historic highlights at a stop with a pop-culture twist. Pedal round the ornamental lake at Bangor's kitsch-rich **Pickie Funpark** (☎028-9145 0746; www.pickiefunpark.com; Marine Gardens; attractions £1.50-4.50; ⊙9am-9pm Jun-Aug, to 7pm Apr-May & Sep, to 4pm Oct-Mar;) in one of its famous swan-shaped boats then do a road-trip warm-up by putting a track full of electric cars through their paces.

The Drive » From Bangor's pastel-painted seafront terraces, pick up the A21 south to Newtownards. From there

the A20 runs south towards Mount Stewart (initially signed Portaferry). Soon the vast, island-dotted Strangford Lough emerges to your right; the road clings to its winding shore to Mount Stewart House (16km).

TRIP HIGHLIGHT

❷ Mount Stewart

Magnificent,18th-century **Mount Stewart** (☎028-4278 8387; www.nationaltrust.org.uk; Portaferry Rd; adult/child £10.50/5.75; ⊙house 11-5pm daily Mar-Oct, 11am-3pm Sat & Sun Nov-Feb, grounds 10am-5pm daily Mar-Oct, to 4pm Nov-Feb) is one of Northern Ireland's grandest stately homes. Lavish plasterwork combines with antiques and artworks that include a painting of the racehorse

Hambletonian by George Stubbs. Garden highlights include griffin and mermaid statues on the Dodo Terrace, and the **Temple of the Winds**, a mock Gothic ruin with great views of the Strangford Lough.

The Drive » Head north, back along the A20 beside scenic Strangford Lough into

ATLANTIC
OCEAN

SCOTLAND

Rathlin
Island

Ballintoy

Giant's
Causeway

Carrick-a-Rede
Rope Bridge

Ballycastle

Portrush

Portstewart

Bushmills

Dunluce
Castle

Downhill

Downhill
Demesne

A2

Coleraine

Armoy

Knocklayd
(514m)

Cushendun

North Channel

Ballymoney

Slievanorra
(511m)

A43

Cushendall

Waterfoot

Limavady

Roe Valley
Country Park

Newtown
Crommelin

Glenariff
Forest
Park

Carnlough

RRY

Garvagh

Clogh

Martinstown

Glenarm

Kilrea

B94

A42

Dungiven

A6

Broughshane

ullaghmore
(554m)

Portglenone

Ballymena

Slemish

Ballygally

Maghera

Gracehill

Larne

Portmuck

rrin Mountains

Draperstown

Kells

ANTRIM

Slieve
Gallion
(528m)

Randalstown

Ballyclare

Ballynure

Whitehead

Magherafelt

Antrim

Carrickfergus

Moneymore

M2

Newtownabbey

Belfast
Lough

A505

Coagh

Bangor

START

Donaghadee

Creggan

Cookstown

Crumlin

p368

A21

Millisle

omeroy

Lough
Neagh

Belfast

Newtownards

Coalisland

Dunmurry

M1

Comber

A2

Ballywalter

Dungannon

Lisburn

B178

Lisbane

Mount
Stewart

Ballygawley

Moira

Saintfield

A20

Aughnacloy

Lurgan
Craigavon

Hillsborough

A21

Strangford
Lough

Portaferry

Portadown

Dromore

Ballynahinch

ARMAGH

A1

DOWN

Strangford

Newtownards. There, take the A21 southwest through Comber. Soon the B178 to Hillsborough (40km) cuts off to the right, across a lush landscape of fields, woods and farms.

- - - - - - - - - - - - - - - -

❸ Hillsborough

Set in elegant Hillsborough, the rambling, late-Georgian **Hillsborough Castle** (☏028-9268 1300;

 LINK YOUR TRIP

29 The North in a Nutshell

Head west to wild Donegal for sandy shores, live-music sessions and a castaway island. Pick it up at this trip's end in Derry.

31 Inishowen Peninsula

Drive north onto a remote headland with exquisite scenery, shipwrecks and white-knuckle drives. Start in Derry.

www.hrp.org.uk; Main St; adult/child £11.40/5.70; ⊘9.30am-6pm Apr-Oct, to 4pm Nov-Mar) is the Queen's official residence in Northern Ireland. Book ahead for guided tours taking in opulent state drawing and dining rooms and the Lady Grey Room, where former UK prime minister Tony Blair and former US president George W Bush had talks on Iraq. Garden delights include yew- and lime-tree walks, an icehouse and a lake.

 p359

The Drive ≫ Head north on the A1 then join the M1 for Belfast. Exit onto the A55/Outer Ring, then follow signs for Queens University, Botanic Gardens or your destination, Ulster Museum (16km).

TRIP HIGHLIGHT

④ Belfast

Bustling Belfast has big-city appeal. As well as walking through its former sectarian strongholds (p368), drop by the **Ulster Museum** (www.nmni.com; Botanic Gardens, Stranmillis Rd; ⊘10am-5pm Tue-Sun; 🚻; 🚌8A to 8D), one of Belfast's biggest

---

draws. Highlights of its beautifully designed displays are the Armada Room; Takabuti, a 2500-year-old Egyptian mummy; the Bann Disc; and the Snapshot of an Ancient Sea Floor.

 p58, p359

The Drive ≫ From Belfast, pass the Grand Opera House (which was bombed by the IRA in the 1990s). Take the M2 north, then the A26 to Ballymena and then the A42 to Broughshane. There, turn right onto the B94, following the hard-to-see sign to Slemish. Follow another sign, which points left almost immediately, before the mountain itself emerges, an immense, hump-topped plateau of rock (67km).

---

⑤ Slemish

Craggy Slemish (438m) is where Ireland's patron saint St Patrick is said to have tended goats. On St Patrick's Day, thousands make a pilgrimage to its summit. It's a steep but pleasant 30-minute climb that's rewarded with fine views.

The Drive ≫ Head back to Broughshane then peel off right onto Knockan Rd towards

---

Clogh. Next take the A43 north towards Waterfoot. In time the road suddenly rises, settlements thin out and you're in the glens: sweeping ridges of steep-sided hills. After a steep valley descent, emerge onto the coast to go north to Cushendall (32km), parking beside its beach.

---

⑥ Cushendall

From Cushendall's beach, walk 1km north, scrambling up the coast path to the picturesque ruins of **Layde Old Church**. Here views stretch as far as the Scottish coast. Founded by the Franciscans, Layde was used as a parish church from the early 14th century. Today the picturesque ruins have grand memorials to the MacDonnells (earls of Antrim from 1620) in the graveyard, and an ancient, weathered ring-cross by the gate.

 p359

The Drive ≫ The A2 heads north, through pretty Cushendun, before climbing steeply to open heathland. At the holiday resort of Ballycastle, pick up the B15, which winds beside fields and windswept cliffs to the Carrick-a-Rede Rope Bridge (34km).

---

⑦ Carrick-a-Rede Rope Bridge

A wobbling bridge is an unusual spot to stretch your legs, but it's unforgettable nonetheless. The Carrick-a-Rede Rope

---

TOP TIP:
GIANT'S CAUSEWAY

The causeway is stunning but it can get overwhelmed by visitor numbers. If you can, visit midweek or out of season to experience it at its most evocative. Sunset in spring and autumn is the best time for photographs.

Ulster Museum, Belfast

Bridge (p320) is a 20m-long, 1m-wide contraption of wire and planks that stretches 30m above rock-strewn water. It sways and bounces beneath your feet before you emerge onto a tiny island dotted with reminders of its past as a salmon fishery. Book your ticket to cross the bridge online in advance.

The Drive >> Rejoin the B15 then the A2 before turning right onto the scenic B146, which clings to the coast, passing ruined Dunseverick Castle en route to the Giant's Causeway (11km).

TRIP HIGHLIGHT

8 Giant's Causeway

The Giant's Causeway (p320) is this coast's must-see sight: a remarkable, ragged ribbon of regular, closely packed, hexagonal stone columns that dips gently beneath the waves. The spectacular rock formation is Northern Ireland's only Unesco World Heritage site and is one of Ireland's most impressive and atmospheric landscape features. To park on-site you'll need to buy a ticket to the Giant's Causeway Visitor Experience (p320).

The Drive >> Head through Bushmills, with its historic distillery and great sleeping options, onto the A2 to Portrush. Soon sea views flood in, then Dunluce Castle's ragged ruins (8km) spring suddenly into view. Be aware: the castle turnoff comes immediately afterwards, down a sloping track on the right.

9 Dunluce Castle

The atmospheric remains of **Dunluce Castle** (87 Dunluce Rd; adult/child £5.50/3.50; ⊙10am-5pm Feb-Nov, to 4pm Dec & Jan, last entry 30 min before closing) cling to a dramatic basalt crag. Built between the 15th and 17th centuries, it was once the coast's finest castle and the seat of the powerful MacDonnell family. A narrow bridge leads from the mainland courtyard across a dizzying gap to the main fortress, where you can roam the shells of buildings and listen to the sea pounding on the cliffs.

The Drive » Taking the A2 towards Portrush, you're soon sandwiched between creamy cliffs and a huge golden beach far below. At Portrush (6km), sand dunes dotted with golf courses take over; head for the central East (Curran) Strand car park.

⑩ Portrush

You can't leave the Antrim coast without some head-clearance time beside the sea. The East Strand car park borders the 3km Curran Strand, a dune-backed golden ribbon of sand that makes for a glorious walk. Or make for nearby **Troggs Surf Shop** (☏028-7082 5476; www.troggs.com; 88 Main St; ⊙10am-6pm Mon-Sat, closed Tue Oct-Mar), which runs lessons (bookings advised) and hires out bodyboards/surfboards (per day £6/12) and wetsuits (per day £8).

✖ ⊨ p359

The Drive » The A2 heads west, passing through seaside Portstewart and shop-packed Coleraine. Next the cupola of Downhill Demesne's Mussenden Temple eases into the windscreen. Go past the Bishop's Gate entrance, turning off into the Lion's Gate (24km).

TRIP HIGHLIGHT

⑪ Downhill Demesne

In 1774 the eccentric Bishop of Derry built himself a palatial, clifftop home: **Downhill Demesne** (www.nationaltrust.org.uk; Mussenden Rd; adult/child £6.20/3.10; ⊙dawn-dusk). It burnt down in 1851, was rebuilt in 1876 and finally abandoned after WWII. Today it features follies (ornamental buildings), mausoleums and a giant, ruined house. Trails lead past a dovecote onto a grassy headland and the elegant **Mussenden Temple**. From inside, the cliff-edge views are extraordinary, reaching from Portrush round to the shores of Lough Foyle.

The Drive » The A2 continues west, through the fertile lowlands that frame Lough Foyle, and onto the city of Derry (41km).

⑫ Derry

Northern Ireland's second city surprises some with its riverside setting and impressive, 17th-century walls. The best way to explore them, and the city's inspiring progress beyond sectarian violence, is by walking (p370). Make sure you drop into **St Columb's Cathedral** (www.stcolumbscathedral.org; 17 London St; suggested donation £2; ⊙9am-5pm Mon-Sat Mar-Oct, 10am-2pm Nov-Feb). This stately church was completed in 1633, making it Derry's oldest building. In the porch look for the hollow mortar shell fired into the churchyard during the Great Siege of 1688. Inside the shell were the terms of a surrender that never came.

✖⊨ p72, p327, p359

DERRY OR LONDONDERRY?

Derry-Londonderry is a city with two names. Nationalists always use Derry, and the 'London' part of the name is often crossed through on road signs. Some staunch Unionists insist on Londonderry, which is still the city's (and county's) official name. All the same, most people, regardless of political persuasion, call it Derry in everyday speech. Traditionally, road signs in Northern Ireland point to Londonderry and those in the Republic point to Derry (or Doíre in Irish). Attempts by the council to change the city's official name to Derry were foiled by a 2007 High Court ruling that the city's legal name could only be changed by legislation or royal prerogative. Many local businesses, as well as buses and trains, use the clunky Derry-Londonderry.

Eating & Sleeping

Hillsborough ❸

🍴 Hara
Modern Irish ££

(📞028-7116 1467; www.harahillsborough.
co.uk; 16 Lisburn St; mains £15-28; ⏰5-9.30pm
Thu, noon-2.30pm & 5-9.30pm Fri & Sat,
12.30-6.30pm Sun) Hara gets even the little
details right: the wheaten bread is served
warm from the oven and the side orders are
divine. The menu changes regularly, but usually
features unusual and creative dishes alongside
more classic Irish cooking highlighting local
ingredients.

Belfast ❹

🍴 Muddlers Club
Modern Irish £££

(📞028-9031 3199; www.
themuddlersclubbelfast.com; Warehouse Lane,
off Waring St; 6-course tasting menu £55, with
wine pairings £90; ⏰noon-2.45pm & 5.30-10pm
Tue-Sat; 🚍3A, 4D, 5A, 6A) Industrial-style
decor, friendly service and rustic dishes that
allow fresh local ingredients to shine are a
winning combination at one of Belfast's best
restaurants. The Muddlers Club is named after
a society of Irish revolutionaries co-founded by
Wolfe Tone who held meetings at the same spot
in the 1790s.

🛏 Merchant Hotel
Hotel £££

(📞028-9023 4888; www.themerchanthotel.
com; 16 Skipper St; d/ste from £180/350;
P @ 🛜; 🚍3A, 4D, 5A, 6A) Belfast's most
flamboyant hotel occupies the palatial
former Ulster Bank head office. Rooms are
individually decorated with a fabulous fusion
of contemporary styling and old-fashioned
elegance; those in the original Victorian building
have opulent floor-length silk curtains while
newer rooms have an art deco–inspired theme.

Cushendall ❻

🍴 Harry's Restaurant
Bistro ££

(📞028-2177 2022; 10 Mill St; mains lunch
£11-14, dinner £12-22; ⏰noon-9pm; 🛜) With
its cosy lounge-bar atmosphere and friendly

welcome, Harry's is a local institution, serving
pub grub staples from noon to 5pm, plus an à
la carte evening menu that ranges from steak
to seafood.

Portrush ❿

🍴 55 Degrees North
International ££

(📞028-7082 2811; www.55-north.com; 1
Causeway St; mains £9-17; ⏰12.30-2.30pm &
5-8.30pm Mon-Fri, 12.30-9pm Sat, noon-8.30pm
Sun; 🍴) Floor-to-ceiling windows allow you
to soak up a spectacular panorama of sand
and sea. The bistro-style food (burgers,
steaks, fish and chips) doesn't quite match the
sophisticated setting.

🛏 Shola Coach House
B&B £££

(📞028-7082 5925; www.sholabandb.com;
110A Gateside Rd; r £110-140) Housed in a
converted stable block dating from 1840, this
luxurious B&B has four gorgeous guest rooms
and a stylish lounge with wooden beams and a
welcoming fire. There are home-baked cakes
on arrival and the breakfast menu includes
porridge with Bushmills whiskey and locally
sourced smoked salmon and pork sausages. It's
3km south of Portrush.

Derry ⓬

🍴 Primrose Restaurant
Irish ££

(📞028-7137 3744; www.primrose-ni.com; 53-55
Strand Rd; mains lunch £6.50-11.50, dinner
£12-18; ⏰8am-5pm Mon & Tue, 8am-9.30pm
Wed-Sat, 10am-5pm Sun) In its chic new Strand
Rd premises, Primrose has expanded beyond
home baking and brunches. Owners Ciaran (a
butcher) and Melanie (a baker) Breslin have
designed a sophisticated lunch and dinner
bistro menu using mostly local ingredients.

🛏 Saddler's House
B&B ££

(📞028-7126 9691; www.thesaddlershouse.com;
36 Great James St; d from £75; 🛜) Centrally
located within a five-minute walk of the
walled city, this friendly B&B is set in a lovely
Victorian townhouse. All seven rooms have
private bathrooms, and you get to enjoy a huge
breakfast in the family kitchen.

The Antrim Coast

34

This trip encompasses Antrim's big sights and some surprises: a hideaway island, a gorgeous glen and a clifftop walk where you'll hardly see another soul.

TRIP HIGHLIGHTS

107 km

Giant's Causeway
Unmissable, incredible – one of Ireland's biggest sights

93 km

Carrick-a-Rede Rope Bridge
Traverse a swaying rope bridge high above the waves

Rathlin Island

Fair Head

Cushendun

Cushendall

Bushmills
Toast your trip's end with a top whiskey tot

Ballymena **START**

Glenariff Forest Park
Stroll beside waterfalls and steep gorges

110 km

23 km

**3 DAYS
110KM / 68 MILES**

GREAT FOR...

BEST TIME TO GO

Avoiding August means less-crowded sights; Easter to July and September should mean brighter days.

ESSENTIAL PHOTO

Standing on the Giant's Causeway's basalt columns.

BEST FOR SOLITUDE

Stops 4 and 5 see you well away from the crowds.

34 The Antrim Coast

Many visitors belt around the Antrim coast, cramming the big-name sights into a day. But this trip can be taken slowly, allowing time to marvel at less-obvious sights and discover a side to Antrim that many people miss. This mystical landscape's extraordinary rock formations, ruined castles and wooded glens have made the region an atmospheric backdrop for the TV series *Game of Thrones*, with numerous filming locations here.

❶ Ballymena

Start exploring the Antrim coast with the superb potted history offered by the **Braid** (Mid-Antrim Museum; 📞028-2563 5077; www.thebraid.com; 1-29 Bridge St; ⏰10am-5pm Mon-Fri, to 4pm Sat) museum. Audiovisual displays evoke a rich history stretching from the county's prehistoric inhabitants to the present. Prepare for stories of Irish chiefs, the mass settlement of Scottish and English Protestants (called Plantation) and

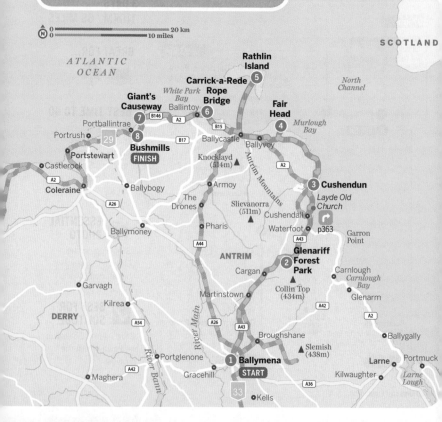

the historic events behind the island's political banners – both Unionist/Loyalist (mostly Protestants who want to preserve the union with Britain) and Nationalist/Republican (mostly Catholics who want the north to be part of the Irish Republic). The *Modern Times* film montage is another highlight, encompassing the *Titanic,* WWI, the Depression, Civil Rights, footballer George Best and former US president Bill Clinton.

The Drive ›› As the A43 heads north towards Waterfoot, the Antrim Mountains rise closer. Suddenly there's a landscape shift: houses peter away, the road climbs and trees thin out, revealing rock ridges and plunging valleys. Turn right into Glenariff Forest Park (23km), onto a track that winds between

LINK YOUR TRIP

29 The North in a Nutshell

Head west to Donegal's wild, beach-fringed coast. Begin where this trip ends: Bushmills.

33 From Bangor to Derry

Take in seaside fun, history-rich Belfast and two stately homes. Start 60km southeast of Ballymena, at Bangor.

DETOUR: LAYDE OLD CHURCH

Start: ② Glenariff Forest Park

In a coast full of big sights it's worth hunting out some hidden delights. In central Cushendall, turn right to park beside its beach. Then walk 1km north up the coast path, enjoying views across to the Scottish coast. The path leads to Layde Old Church. Founded by the Franciscans, it was in use from the early 14th century until 1790. The graveyard features grand memorials to the MacDonnells (earls of Antrim from 1620) and an ancient, weathered ring-cross, much older than the 19th-century inscription on its shaft.

dense conifers. The trees clear abruptly, exposing plummeting hills.

TRIP HIGHLIGHT

② Glenariff Forest Park

The pick of the trails at Glenariff Forest Park is the **Waterfall Walk**. From the car park (surely one of the north's most scenic; parking £5) this 3km, waymarked, circular trail goes beside the Glenariff River and past the Ess-na-Larach and Ess-na-Crub waterfalls, along paths cut into the sheer gorge sides, up stairways and along boardwalks set on stilts on the water. The forest is a mix of native species (look out for oak, elm and hazel) and introduced trees, notably pine and Douglas fir. You've a fair chance of spotting red squirrels, hen harriers and Irish hares dart-

ing among the trees. The teahouse beside the car park offers the chance to refuel and see more stunning gorge views.

 p367

The Drive ›› Continue on the A43, descending steeply through hairpin bends into a wide, U-shaped glacial valley with suddenly revealed sea views. Follow the A2 north along the shore, through the busy little town of Cushendall to Cushendun (17km).

----

③ Cushendun

Follow the shoreline to the right, past the fisher's cottage on the south side of pretty Cushendun, until you reach a series of caves sculpted from porous rock; *Game of Thrones* fans will recognise this as a filming location for the Stormlands. Head back along the seafront and over the bridge, this time going straight on to the village itself. Its central cluster of Cornish-style cottages was built between 1912 and 1925 and designed by Clough Williams-Ellis, the architect of Portmeirion in north Wales. They were commissioned by Lord Cushendun and his Cornish wife, Maud. Her grave in the village churchyard bears the inscription, 'To a Cornish woman who loved the Glens and their people'.

p367

The Drive » Pick up the (signed) Torr Head Scenic Route, a heart-in-the-mouth route of winding first-gear gradients that clings to increasingly stark cliffs. Ignore the Torr Head turnoff and instead peel off right to Murlough Bay (signed), reaching a car park 300m after the turning (16km).

4 Fair Head

By now the 180m-high basalt cliffs of Fair Head rear to your left. Walk towards them, following a 1km moderate clifftop path (waymarked by yellow circles) to the top. Once there, look out for rock climbers (this is one of the region's best climbing sites) and the spectacular gully bridged by a fallen rock, called Grey Man's Path. A stunning panorama sweeps from Rathlin Island in the west to Scotland's Mull of Kintyre in the east. Keep an eye out for whales and dolphins swimming offshore.

RICCAR/GETTY IMAGES ©

The Drive » Heading west on the A2, the landscape becomes steadily less rugged. Soon golf courses replace sheep-grazed hills and sandy beaches replace that precipitous shore. At the cheery resort of Ballycastle (20km), park in the ferry-terminal car park or in a free harbourside long-stay bay (some have time limits, so double-check).

5 Rathlin Island

Time to leave the car behind and stay overnight on Rathlin Island (Reachlainn, www.rathlincommunity.org), a 6.5km-by-4km windswept slab of rock, 6km offshore. From mid-April to August it's home to hundreds of seals and thousands of nesting

Glenariff Forest Park, County Antrim

seabirds. The Royal Society for the Protection of Birds' **Rathlin West Light Seabird Centre** (028-2076 3948; www.rspb.org.uk/rathlinisland; adult/child £5/2.50; 10am-5pm May-Aug, 11am-4pm Apr & Sep) provides extraordinary views of sea stacks thick with guillemots, kittiwakes, razorbills and puffins.

Scottish hero Robert the Bruce hid here in 1306 after being defeated by the English. Inspired by a spider's determined web-spinning, he subsequently triumphed at Bannockburn. His cave is beneath the East Lighthouse.

From July to August, 10 ferries (p319) a day (eight daily in April, May and September and five daily from October to March) make the 25- to 45-minute crossing. Book in advance.

p367

The Drive » From the Rathlin Island ferry terminal the B15 climbs north towards Ballintoy. As Rathlin Island recedes behind you, a coastal plateau of rugged heathland unfurls. The plateau runs along then steeply down to the Carrick-a-Rede Rope Bridge turn (19km) on the right.

➎ Carrick-a-Rede Rope Bridge

The Carrick-a-Rede Rope Bridge (p320) is a 20m-long, 1m-wide assemblage of wire rope and planks that sways 30m above rock-strewn water. It spans a chasm between cliffs and a tiny island that sustained a salmon fishery for centuries – fishers used the bridge to stretch their nets out from the island's tip to intercept migrating salmon. Declining stocks have now put an end to fishing, however. Now firmly on the tour-bus route, Carrick-a-Rede has become so popular that the National Trust has introduced ticketed one-hour time slots to visit the bridge. Book your ticket online in advance, especially during high season.

It's a heart-in-the-mouth walk across the bridge. Once on the island the panorama includes last night's stop, Rathlin Island, and the site of your walk the day before: the sheer cliffs of Fair Head.

The Drive ⟫ Heading west, the B15 then the A2 deliver more bursts of rugged coastal driving – the golden beach unfurling below is White Park Bay. Turn onto the B146, getting even closer to the shore. This road glides past ruined Dunseverick Castle en route to the coast's big draw: the Giant's Causeway (11km).

TRIP HIGHLIGHT

➐ Giant's Causeway

When you first see it you'll understand why the ancients believed the causeway (p320) couldn't be a natural feature. The spectacular expanse of regular, closely packed, hexagonal stone columns dipping gently beneath the waves looks for all the world like the handiwork of giants. The phenomenon is explained in the Giant's Causeway Visitor Experience (p320).

It's a sloping 1km walk to the causeway. Once you've clambered around on the geometric rocks, don't miss the stack of pipe-like basalt columns known as the **Organ** – you can access them on the lower coastal path that heads towards the

Amphitheatre Viewpoint at Port Reostan.

Visiting the causeway itself is free of charge but you pay to use the car park on a combined ticket with the visitor centre.

The Drive ⟫ Rejoin the A2 for a 3km uphill drive inland to the small town of Bushmills. Signs point towards the world-famous distillery on its western edge.

TRIP HIGHLIGHT

➑ Bushmills

What better way to finish a trip full of the flavour of the Antrim coast than with a true taste of Ireland – Bushmills Irish Whiskey? **Old Bushmills Distillery** (☎028-2073 3218; www.bushmills.com; 2 Distillery Rd; tour adult/child £9/5; ⏱9.15am-4.45pm Mon-Sat, noon-4.45pm Sun) is the world's oldest legal distillery. During ageing, the alcohol content drops from around 60% to 40%. The spirit lost through evaporation is known as 'the angels' share'. Tours include a sample of a 12-year-old Single Malt Distillery Reserve, only available on-site.

✕ ⌂ p367

Eating & Sleeping

Glenariff Forest Park ②

✕ Laragh Lodge   Irish ££

(☎028-2175 8221; www.laraghlodge.co.uk; 120 Glen Rd; mains £12-16; ⊙11am-9pm Mar-Oct; 🖶) A renovated Victorian tourist lodge, the Laragh dates from 1890 and serves hearty meals like steak sandwiches, burgers and fish and chips, as well as a traditional roast lunch on Sunday – perfect after a long walk. It's on a side road off the A43, 3km northeast of the main Glenariff Forest Park entrance.

Cushendun ③

✕ Mary McBride's   Pub Food ££

(☎028-2176 1511; www.facebook.com/Mcbridescushendun; 2 Main St; bar mains £10-15, restaurant mains £14-35; ⊙food noon-6pm Wed, 11am-9pm Thu-Sat, 11am-6pm Sun) The original bar here (on the left as you go in) is the smallest in Ireland (2.7m by 1.5m), but there's plenty of elbow-bending room in the rest of the pub. Good pub grub is served downstairs and there's live music on weekends. Upstairs is the **Little Black Door** (6pm to 9pm Thursday to Saturday), specialising in seafood and steak.

⮕ Cloneymore House   B&B ££

(☎028-2176 1443; ann.cloneymore@btinternet.com; 103 Knocknacarry Rd; s £60, d £75-85; [P][🖥]) A traditional family B&B on the B92 road 500m southwest of Cushendun, Cloneymore has three spacious and spotless rooms named after Irish and Scottish islands – Aran is the biggest. There are wheelchair ramps and a stairlift, and rooms are equipped for visitors with limited mobility.

⮕ Villa Farmhouse   B&B £

(☎028-2176 1252; www.thevillafarmhouse.com; 185 Torr Rd; s/d £35/70; [P][🖥]) This lovely old whitewashed farmhouse is set on a hillside 1km north of Cushendun, with great views over the bay and the warm atmosphere of a family home, decorated with photos of children and grandchildren. The owner is an expert chef, and breakfast will be a highlight of your stay.

Rathlin Island ⑤

⮕ Coolnagrock B&B   B&B ££

(☎028-2076 3983; www.rathlin-island.co.uk/margaret; Coolnagrock; s/d from £40/70; ⊙Apr-Oct; [🖥]) Views stretch across the sea to the Mull of Kintyre from this well-appointed guesthouse in the eastern part of the island. It's a 15-minute walk from the ferry, but you can arrange for the owner to pick you up. Book ahead.

⮕ Manor House   Guesthouse ££

(☎028-2076 0046; www.manorhouserathlin.com; Church Bay; s £70-80, d £130-145) Rathlin's 18th-century manor house has been fully renovated and transformed into a stylish 11-room guesthouse with stunning views across Church Bay. Rooms combine modern furnishings with period features and the bright reception area has a welcoming fire. There's also a good restaurant serving fresh local seafood.

Bushmills ⑧

✕ Bushmills Inn   Irish ££

(☎028-2073 3000; www.bushmillsinn.com; 9 Dunluce Rd; mains lunch £7-13, dinner £14-28; ⊙noon-9.30pm Mon-Sat, 12.30-3pm & 5-9.30pm Sun; [🖥]) Set in the old 17th-century stables of the Bushmills Inn, this haven has intimate wooden booths and blazing fires, and uses fresh local produce in dishes like Greencastle cod, Laney Valley lamb and traditional Dalriada Cullen Skink (wood-smoked haddock poached in cream, with poached eggs and new potatoes). Book ahead. There's trad music in the bar on Saturday nights.

⮕ Bushmills Inn Hotel   Hotel £££

(☎028-2073 3000; www.bushmillsinn.com; 9 Dunluce Rd; d/ste from £220/360; [P][@][🖥]) The Bushmills Inn is an old coaching inn dating to around 1608, complete with peat fires, gas lamps, a secret library and a round tower. The old part of the hotel has been given over to the restaurant; the luxurious accommodation is in the neighbouring, modern Mill House complex. Low-season discounts cut room rates in half.

STRETCH YOUR LEGS
BELFAST

Start/Finish Belfast City Hall

Distance 5km

Duration 3 hours

For decades Belfast's murals symbolised a violent sectarian divide. On this walk you'll see passions painted large, but also remarkable progress towards peace. Although safe, this walk crosses West Belfast's Peace Lines (walls with gates) – best avoided after dark.

Take this walk on Trips

City Hall

Start at the 1906 classical Renaissance **City Hall** (028-9027 0456; www.belfastcity.gov.uk; Donegall Sq; 9.30am-5pm Mon-Fri, 10am-5pm Sat & Sun, to 8pm Thu Jun-Sep; Donegall Sq), fronted by a dour Queen Victoria accompanied by bronzes symbolising Belfast's textile and shipbuilding industries.

The Walk » Go up Donegall Pl, turning left on Castle St, which becomes Falls Rd; you've entered Catholic West Belfast. After the huge murals of the Solidarity Wall, which champion global civil rights movements, stop at Sevastopol St.

Sinn Féin Headquarters

This red-brick building is the base of the Irish Republican party, which is committed to ending British rule in Northern Ireland. It features a vast mural of Bobby Sands, the West Belfast MP who died on a hunger strike in 1981.

The Walk » Pass the Royal Victoria Hospital, which developed expertise in treating gunshot wounds during the Troubles. The Cultúrlann McAdam Ó Fiaich comes soon after, on the left.

Cultúrlann McAdam Ó Fiaich

The welcoming **Cultúrlann McAdam Ó Fiaich** (www.culturlann.ie; 216 Falls Rd; 9am-6pm Mon-Thu, to 9pm Fri & Sat, 11am-4pm Sun; G1) features a shop selling Ireland-related books and crafts and a good cafe-restaurant.

The Walk » At nearby Islandbawn St the Plastic Bullet Mural commemorates 17 people, including eight children, killed by security-service plastic-baton rounds. Beechmount Ave is two streets on.

Beechmount Avenue

Absorbed by Beechmount Ave's murals, most visitors miss the hand-painted 'RPG Avenue' sign beside the street name. 'RPG' stands for 'rocket-propelled grenade', a nickname awarded because the street offered sight lines for IRA rocket attacks on security forces based nearby.

The Walk » Go back up Falls Rd, noticing dual Irish-English street names. After 1km, turn left into

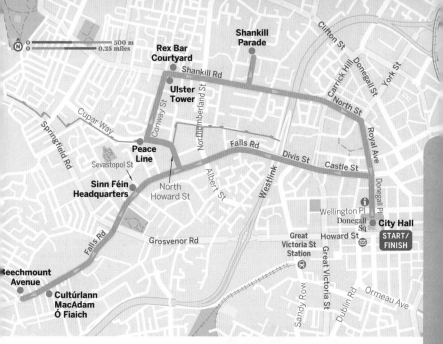

North Howard St and go through the gate in the towering steel fencing. Turn left beside it, walking 150m.

Peace Line

This imposing 6m-high, 4km-long barrier has divided West Belfast's Catholic and Protestant communities for more than four decades. Now sections are a focus for reconciliation; here you'll find local peoples' testimonies and spaces for adding your own peace message.

The Walk » Turn off the main road into residential (unsigned) Conway St. You're now in Loyalist, Protestant West Belfast. Stop at the junction of Shankill Rd.

Ulster Tower

The gable end is covered by a huge picture depicting a creamy, poppy-fringed fort, the Ulster Tower. It emphasizes Protestant loyalty to Britain by highlighting Ulster regiments' WWI losses.

The Walk » Cross Shankill Rd to the photograph-filled courtyard beside the Rex Bar.

Rex Bar Courtyard

Photographic and textual displays here describe the signing of the Ulster Covenant, a mass petition against limited Irish self-government in 1912, and the formation of the Ulster Volunteer Force in 1913.

The Walk » Head down Shankill Rd, passing batches of murals, tributes to the Queen and masses of red, white and blue. After the Gospel Hall, turn left into Shankill Pde.

Shankill Parade

Murals covering the entire gable ends of houses pack this housing estate. The Protestant King William III rides a prancing white horse on the left, while on the right sits **Remember, Respect, Resolution**, three metal columns representing the communities' willingness to embrace Northern Ireland's future. Several paramilitary murals have now been replaced by local community artworks.

The Walk » Shankill Rd crosses the dual carriageway. Head straight on, turning right down Royal Ave and on to City Hall.

STRETCH YOUR LEGS
DERRY

Start/Finish Butcher's Gate, City Walls

Distance 3km

Duration 3 hours

This walk winds along 17th-century city walls and past former sectarian battlegrounds, revealing a vivid history, startling political murals and the inspiring steps being taken towards peace.

Take this walk on Trips

Butcher's Gate

Derry's immense **city walls** (⏱ dawn-dusk) were built in 1619 to secure the settlement of immigrant Protestants. In 1688 they helped residents repel a 105-day siege by Catholic forces. The Protestants' slogan, 'No Surrender', remains a Loyalist battle cry today.

The Walk » Climb the gateside steps, walking downhill along the top of the walls, high above the streets, to the first corner.

Magazine Gate

The Tower Museum (p321) rears up to the right. On the left, the red-brick, neo-Gothic **Guildhall** (☎028-7137 6510; www.derrystrabane.com/Guildhall; Guildhall St; ⏱10am-5.30pm) was formerly home to the Londonderry Corporation, which institutionalised anti-Catholic discrimination over housing and jobs.

The Walk » After the next corner, the wall-top walk climbs steeply, passing bastions occupied by huge cannons. As you near the crest of the rise, look down left over the wall.

Fountain Housing Estate

You're now looking onto the last significant Protestant community on the River Foyle's western bank. Immediately obvious is the massive slogan, 'West Bank Loyalists Still Under Siege. No Surrender'.

The Walk » After more bastions and massive cannons, the walls widen, revealing a plinth that's been empty since the IRA blew up a statue of one of Derry's siege-era governors. Go down the Butcher's Gate steps, through the arch, into Waterloo St.

Peadar O'Donnell's

Time to refuel. **Peadar O'Donnell's** (www.facebook.com/Peadarsderry; 59-63 Waterloo St; ⏱11.30am-1.30am Mon-Sat, 12.30pm-12.30am Sun) is done up as a typical Irish pub-cum-grocer. It's alive with traditional music on weekends.

The Walk » William St cuts left to Rossville St, a junction dubbed Agro Corner, where security forces and residents of the Catholic Bogside housing estate routinely clashed. Some 120m on, the Bloody Sunday Memorial commemorates

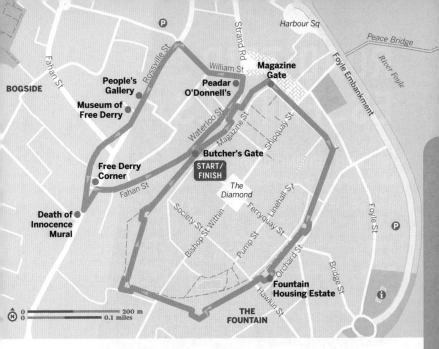

where British soldiers shot dead 13 unarmed demonstrators in 1972.

People's Gallery

The huge murals you can now see are part of the People's Gallery and were painted by three Bogsiders who lived through the Troubles. Ahead is a huge monochrome **Civil Rights** mural; behind you a rioter and armoured car clash in **Saturday Matinee**.

The Walk » Cut between these murals, into the Museum of Free Derry.

Museum of Free Derry

This excellent **museum** (www.museumof freederry.org; 55 Glenfada Park; adult/child £6/5; 9.30am-4.30pm Mon-Fri, 1-4pm Sat year-round, plus 1-4pm Sun Jul-Sep) chronicles the Bogside's history, the Civil Rights Movement and the events of Bloody Sunday, through interactive displays, the accounts of first-hand witnesses, and photographs, including some of the original images that inspired the murals of the nearby People's Gallery.

The Walk » Pass more murals: the sledgehammer drama of *Operation Motorman*; *Bloody Sunday*, where a priest tries to shepherd one of the dying to safety; and a boy in a gas mask (*Petrol Bomber*). Look to the left.

Free Derry Corner

The roundabout contains a house remnant bearing the words 'You Are Now Entering Free Derry'. This stems from the late 1960s, when Bogsiders declared themselves independent of the authorities and barricaded the streets.

The Walk » Continue down Rossville St, looking back up to the gable ends to your right.

Death of Innocence Mural

This mural depicts 14-year-old Annette McGavigan, who was killed in crossfire between the IRA and the British Army in 1971. The downward-pointing, broken rifle symbolises the failure of violence; the butterfly symbolises the peace process.

The Walk » Return to Free Derry Corner then head up Fahan St, back to Butcher's Gate.

ROAD TRIP ESSENTIALS

Ireland Driving Guide

The motorway system makes for easy travelling between major towns, but the spidery network of secondary and tertiary roads makes for the most scenic driving.

DRIVING LICENCE & DOCUMENTS

EU licences are treated like Irish ones. Holders of non-EU licences from countries other than the US or Canada should obtain an International Driving Permit (IDP) from their home automobile association.

You must carry your driving licence at all times.

INSURANCE

All cars on public roads must be insured. Most hire companies quote basic insurance in their initial quote. If you are bringing your own vehicle, check that your insurance will cover you in Ireland. When driving your own car, you'll need a minimum insurance known as third-party insurance.

HIRING A CAR

Compared with many countries hire rates are expensive in Ireland; you should expect to pay around €250 a week for a small car (unlimited mileage), but rates go up at busy times and drop off in quieter seasons. The main players:

Avis (www.avis.ie)

Budget (www.budget.ie)

Europcar (www.europcar.ie)

Hertz (www.hertz.ie)

Sixt (www.sixt.ie)

Thrifty (www.thrifty.ie)

The major car-hire companies have different web pages on their websites for different countries, so the price of a car in Ireland can differ from the same car's price in the USA or Australia. You have to surf a lot of sites to get the best deals. **Nova Car Hire** (www.novacarhire.com) acts as an agent for Alamo, Budget, European and National, and offers greatly discounted rates.

➡ Most cars are manual; automatic cars are available, but they're more expensive to hire.

➡ If you're travelling from the Republic into Northern Ireland, it's important to be sure that your insurance covers journeys to the North.

➡ The majority of hire companies won't rent you a car if you're under 23 and haven't had a valid driving licence for at least a year.

➡ Some companies in the Republic won't rent to you if you're aged 74 or over; there's no upper age limit in the North.

➡ Motorbikes and mopeds are not available for hire in Ireland.

Driving Fast Facts

➡ **Right or left?** Drive on the left

➡ **Manual or automatic?** Manual

➡ **Legal driving age** 18

➡ **Top speed limit** 120km/h (motorways; 70mph in Northern Ireland)

➡ **Best radio station** RTE Radio 1

Ireland Playlist

Virtually every parish and hamlet has a song about it. Here are our favourites:

Carrickfergus Traditional Irish folk song

Galway Girl Steve Earle

Raglan Road Luke Kelly

Running to Stand Still U2

The Fields of Athenry Paddy Reilly

The Town I Loved So Well The Dubliners (about Derry)

BRINGING YOUR OWN VEHICLE

It's easy to take your own vehicle to Ireland and there are no specific procedures involved, but you should carry a vehicle registration document as proof that it's yours.

MAPS

You'll need a good road map; we recommend getting one even if you have a sat-nav system.

Michelin's 1:400,000-scale Ireland map (No 923) is a decent single-sheet map, with clear cartography and most of the island's scenic roads marked. The four maps (North, South, East and West) that make up the Ordnance Survey Holiday map series at 1:250,000 scale are useful if you want more detail. Collins also publishes a range of maps covering Ireland.

The Ordnance Survey Discovery series covers the whole island in 89 maps at a scale of 1:50,000.

These are all available at most big bookshops and tourist centres throughout Ireland as well as at www.osi.ie.

ROADS CONDITIONS

Irish road types and conditions vary wildly. The road network is divided into the following categories:

Regional Roads Indicated by an R and (usually) three numbers on a white background, these are the secondary and tertiary roads that make up the bulk of the road network, generally splintering off larger roads to access even the smallest hamlet. Blind corners, potholes and a width barely enough for two cars are the price for some of the most scenic routes in all of Ireland; whatever you do, go slow. In Northern Ireland, these are classified as B-roads.

Road Distances (Km)

	Athlone	Belfast	Cork	Derry	Donegal	Dublin	Galway	Kilkenny	Killarney	Limerick	Rosslare Harbour	Shannon Airport	Sligo	Waterford
Belfast	227													
Cork	219	424												
Derry	209	117	428											
Donegal	183	180	402	69										
Dublin	127	167	256	237	233									
Galway	93	306	209	272	204	212								
Kilkenny	116	284	148	335	309	114	172							
Killarney	232	436	87	441	407	304	193	198						
Limerick	121	323	105	328	296	193	104	113	111					
Rosslare Harbour	201	330	208	397	391	153	274	98	275	211				
Shannon Airport	133	346	128	351	282	218	93	135	135	25	234			
Sligo	117	206	336	135	66	214	138	245	343	232	325	218		
Waterford	164	333	126	383	357	163	220	48	193	129	82	152	293	
Wexford	184	309	187	378	372	135	253	80	254	190	19	213	307	61

National Roads Indicated by an N and two numbers against a green background, these were, until the construction of the motorway network, the primary roads in Ireland. They link most towns and are usually single lane in either direction, widening occasionally to double lane (usually on uphill stretches to allow for the overtaking of slower vehicles). In Northern Ireland, these are classified as A-roads.

Motorways Indicated by an M and a single digit against a blue background, the network is limited to the major routes and towns. Most motorways are partially tolled. Motorways in Northern Ireland are not tolled.

ROAD RULES

A copy of Ireland's road rules is available from tourist offices. Following are the most basic rules:

➡ Drive on the left, overtake to the right.

➡ Safety belts must be worn by the driver and all passengers.

➡ Children aged under 12 aren't allowed to sit on the front seats.

➡ Motorcyclists and their passengers must wear helmets.

➡ When entering a roundabout, give way to the right.

➡ On motorways, use the right lane for overtaking only.

➡ Speed limits are 120km/h on motorways (70mph in Northern Ireland), 100km/h on national roads (60mph in Northern Ireland), 80km/h on regional and local roads (60mph in Northern Ireland) and 50km/h (30mph in the North) or as signposted in towns.

➡ The legal alcohol limit is 50mg of alcohol per 100ml of blood or 22mg on the breath (roughly two units of alcohol for a man and one for a woman); in Northern Ireland the limit is 80mg of alcohol per 100ml of blood.

PARKING

All big towns and cities have covered and open short-stay car parks that are conveniently signposted.

➡ On-street parking is usually by 'pay and display' tickets available from on-street machines or disc parking (discs, which rotate to display the time you park your car, are usually provided by rental agencies). Costs range from €1.50 to €6 per hour; all-day parking in a car park will cost around €25.

➡ Yellow lines (single or double) along the edge of the road indicate restrictions. Double yellow lines mean no parking at any time. Always look for the nearby sign that spells out when you can and cannot park.

➡ In Dublin, Cork and Galway, clamping is rigorously enforced; it'll cost you €85 to have the yellow beast removed. In Northern Ireland, the fee is £100 for removal.

FUEL

The majority of vehicles operate on unleaded petrol; the rest (including many hire cars) run on diesel.

Road Trip Websites

AUTOMOBILE ASSOCIATIONS

Automobile Association (AA; www. theaa.ie) Roadside assistance and driving tips.

Royal Automobile Club (RAC; www.rac.co.uk) Roadside assistance, route planner and accommodation.

ROAD RULES

Road Safety Authority (www.rsa. ie) Rules, tips and information in case of accident.

CONDITIONS & TRAFFIC

AA Roadwatch (www.theaa.ie) Up-to-date traffic info.

Traffic Watch Northern Ireland (www.trafficwatchni.com) Traffic news, maps and live cameras.

MAPS

AA Route Planner (www.theaa.ie) Map your route for the whole island.

APPS

Both the AA and the RAC have mobile apps for Android and IOS that track traffic and allow you to report breakdowns.

Cost In the Republic, petrol costs range from €1.30 to €1.50 per litre, with diesel usually €0.10 cheaper. Fuel is marginally more expensive in Dublin. In Northern Ireland, petrol costs between £1.20 and £1.30 per litre, but diesel is slightly more expensive (between £1.25 and £1.35 per litre).

Service Stations These are ubiquitous on all national roads, usually on the outskirts of towns. They're increasingly harder to find in cities, and the motorway network has only three or four spread across the entire system. In the North, the big supermarket chains have gotten into the fuel business, so you can fill your car before or after you shop. There are service stations along the North's motorway network.

SAFETY

Although driving in Ireland is a relatively pain-free experience, hire cars and cars with foreign registrations can be targeted by thieves looking to clean them of their contents. Don't leave any valuables, including bags and suitcases, on display. Overnight parking is safest in covered car parks.

BORDER CROSSINGS

Border crossings between Northern Ireland and the Republic are unnoticeable; there are no formalities of any kind. This may change, however, once Brexit occurs in 2019.

RADIO

The Irish love radio – up to 85% of the population listens in on any given day. Following are the national radio stations:

Newstalk 106-108 (106-108FM) News, current affairs and lifestyle.

RTE Radio 1 (88.2-90FM) Mostly news and discussion.

RTE Radio 2 (90.4-92.2FM) Lifestyle and music.

RTE Lyric FM (96-99FM) Classical music.

Today FM (100-102FM) Music, chat and news.

Regional or local radio is also very popular, with 25 independent local radio stations available, depending on your location.

In Northern Ireland, the BBC rules supreme, with BBC Radio Ulster (92.7-95.4FM) flying the local flag in addition to the four main BBC stations.

Local Expert: Driving Tips

Conor Faughnan, Director of Consumer Affairs with the Automobile Association, shares his tips for hassle-free driving in Ireland:

➡ The motorway network is excellent, but there aren't nearly enough rest areas so check that you have a full tank of fuel before setting off. Off the motorway network there is a good supply of service stations, often open 24 hours, but less so in more remote areas.

➡ The real driving fun is on Ireland's network of secondary roads, where road conditions vary – make sure you're equipped with a good map along with your sat-nav, and beware of potholes, poor road surfaces and corners obscured by protruding hedges! You may also encounter farm machinery and even livestock on rural roads.

➡ Although it rarely snows, winter conditions can be testing (particularly when roads are icy).

➡ A driver may flash their hazard lights once or twice as an informal way to say 'thank you' for any kind of road courtesy extended to them.

Driving Problem-Buster

What should I do if my car breaks down? Call the service number of your car-hire company and a local garage will be contacted. If you're bringing your own car, it's a good idea to join the Automobile Association Ireland, which covers the whole country, or, in Northern Ireland, the Royal Automobile Club (RAC), which can be called to attend breakdowns at any time.

What if I have an accident? Hire cars usually have a leaflet in the glovebox about what to do in case of an accident. Exchange basic information with the other party (name, insurance details, driver's licence number, company details if the car's a rental). No discussion of liability needs to take place at the scene. It's a good idea to photograph the scene of the accident, noting key details (damage sustained, car positions on the road, any skid markings). Call the police (☏999) if required.

What should I do if I get stopped by police? Always remain calm and polite: police are generally courteous and helpful. They will want to see your passport (or valid form of ID), licence and proof of insurance. In the Republic, breath testing is mandatory if asked.

What if I can't find anywhere to stay? If you're travelling during the summer months, always book your accommodation in advance. If you're stuck, call the local tourist office's accommodation hotline.

How do I pay for tollways? Tolls are paid by putting cash in the bucket as you pass. If you don't have exact change, at least one booth is staffed.

Ireland Travel Guide

GETTING THERE & AWAY

AIR

Ireland's main airports:

Cork Airport (☎021-431 3131; www.corkair
port.com) Airlines servicing the airport include
Aer Lingus and Ryanair.

Dublin Airport (☎01-814 1111; www.
dublinairport.com) Ireland's major international gateway airport, with direct flights from
the UK, Europe, North America and the Middle
East.

Shannon Airport (SNN; ☎061-712 000;
www.shannonairport.ie; ☎) Has a few direct
flights from the UK, Europe and North America.

Northern Ireland's airports:

Belfast International Airport (Alder-
grove; ☎028-9448 4848; www.belfastairport.
com; Airport Rd) Has direct flights from the
UK, Europe and North America.

Car hire firms are well represented at all
major airports. Regional airports will have
at least one internationally recognised firm
as well as local operators.

Book Your Stay Online

For more accommodation reviews
by Lonely Planet authors, check
out http://hotels.lonelyplanet.com.
You'll find independent reviews, as
well as recommendations on the
best places to stay. Best of all, you
can book online.

SEA

The main ferry routes between Ireland and
the UK and mainland Europe:

➡ Belfast to Liverpool (England; eight hours)

➡ Belfast to Cairnryan (Scotland; 1¾ hours)

➡ Cork to Roscoff (France; 14 hours; April to
October only)

➡ Dublin to Liverpool (England; fast/slow
four/8½ hours)

➡ Dublin & Dun Laoghaire to Holyhead (Wales;
fast/slow two hours/3½ hours)

➡ Larne to Cairnryan (Scotland; two hours)

➡ Larne to Troon (Scotland; two hours; March
to October only)

➡ Larne to Fleetwood (England; six hours)

➡ Rosslare to Cherbourg/Roscoff (France;
18/20½ hours)

➡ Rosslare to Fishguard & Pembroke (Wales;
3½ hours)

Competition from budget airlines has
forced ferry operators to discount heavily
and offer flexible fares. A useful website
is www.ferrybooker.com, which covers all
sea-ferry routes and operators to Ireland.

Main operators include the following:

Brittany Ferries (www.brittanyferries.com)
Cork to Roscoff; April to October.

Irish Ferries (www.irishferries.com) It has
Dublin to Holyhead ferries (up to four per day
year-round) and France to Rosslare (three
times per week).

P&O Ferries (www.poferries.com) Daily sailings year-round from Dublin to Liverpool, and
Larne to Cairnryan. Larne to Troon runs March
to October only.

Stena Line (www.stenaline.com) Daily
sailings from Holyhead to Dublin Port, from
Belfast to Liverpool and Cairnryan, and from
Rosslare to Fishguard.

Arriving in Ireland

Dublin Airport Private coaches run every 10 to 15 minutes to the city centre (€6). Taxis take 30 to 45 minutes and cost €20 to €25.

Dun Laoghaire Ferry Port Public bus takes around 45 minutes to the centre of Dublin; DART (suburban rail) takes about 25 minutes. Both cost €3.

Dublin Port Terminal Buses are timed to coincide with arrivals and departures; they cost €3.50 to the city centre.

Belfast International Airport Airport Express 300 bus runs hourly (one way/return £8/11.50, 30 to 55 minutes). A taxi costs around £30.

George Best Belfast City Airport Airport Express 600 bus runs every 20 minutes (one way/return £2.60/4, 15 minutes). A taxi costs around £10.

DIRECTORY A–Z

ACCOMMODATION

Accommodation options range from bare and basic to pricey and palatial. The spine of the Irish hospitality business is the ubiquitous B&B, in recent years challenged by a plethora of midrange hotels and guesthouses. Beyond Expedia, Booking.com, Trivago and other hotel price comparison sites, Ireland-specific online resources for accommodation include the following:

Daft.ie (www.daft.ie) Online property portal includes holiday homes and short-term rentals.

Elegant Ireland (www.elegant.ie) Specialises in self-catering castles, period houses and unique properties.

Imagine Ireland (www.imagineireland.com) Holiday cottage rentals throughout the whole island, including Northern Ireland.

Irish Landmark Trust (www.irishlandmark.com) Not-for-profit conservation group that rents self-catering properties of historical and cultural significance, such as castles, tower houses, gate lodges, schoolhouses and lighthouses.

Lonely Planet (www.lonelyplanet.com/Ireland/hotels) Recommendations and bookings.

Dream Ireland (www.dreamireland.com) Lists self-catering holiday cottages and apartments.

B&Bs & Guesthouses

Bed and breakfasts are small, family-run houses, farmhouses and period country houses, generally with fewer than five bedrooms. Standards vary enormously, but most have some bedrooms with private bathroom at a cost of roughly €40 to €60 (£35 to £50) per person per night (at least €100 in Dublin). In luxurious B&Bs, expect to pay €70 (£60) or more per person. Off-season rates – usually October through to March – are usually lower, as are midweek prices.

Guesthouses are like upmarket B&Bs, but a bit bigger. Facilities are usually better and sometimes include a restaurant.

Other tips:

➡ Facilities in B&Bs range from basic (bed, bathroom, kettle, TV) to beatific (whirlpool baths, rainforest showers) as you go up in price. Wi-fi is standard and most have parking (but check).

➡ Most B&Bs take credit cards, but the occasional rural one might not; check when you book.

➡ Advance reservations are strongly recommended, especially in peak season (June to September).

➡ Some B&Bs and guesthouses in more remote regions may only be open from Easter to September or other months.

➡ If full, B&B owners may recommend another house in the area (possibly a private house taking occasional guests, not in tourist listings).

➡ To make prices more competitive at some B&Bs, breakfast may be optional.

Camping & Caravan Parks

Camping and caravan parks aren't as common in Ireland as they are elsewhere in Europe. Some hostels have camping space for tents and also offer house facilities, which makes them better value than the main camping grounds.

At commercial parks the cost is typically somewhere between €15 and €25 (£12 to £20) for a tent and two people. Prices given for campsites are for two people unless stated otherwise. Caravan sites cost around €20 to €30 (£17 to £25). Most parks are open only from Easter to the end of September or October.

Hostels

Prices quoted for hostel accommodation apply to those aged over 18. A high-season dorm bed generally costs €12 to €25, or €18 to €30 in Dublin (£15 to £20 in Northern Ireland). Many hostels now have family and double rooms.

Relevant hostel associations:

An Óige (www.anoige.ie) HI-associated national organisation with 26 hostels scattered around the Republic.

HINI (www.hini.org.uk) HI-associated organisation with five hostels in Northern Ireland.

Independent Holiday Hostels of Ireland (www.hostels-ireland.com) Fifty-five tourist-board-approved hostels throughout all of Ireland.

Independent Hostel Owners of Ireland (www.independenthostelsireland.com) Independent hostelling association.

ELECTRICITY

220V/50Hz

FOOD

The 'local food' movement was pioneered in Ireland in the 1970s, notably at the world-famous Ballymaloe House. Since then the movement has gone from strength to strength, with dozens of farmers markets showcasing the best of local produce, and restaurants all over the country highlighting locally sourced ingredients.

A 'Standard' Hotel Rate?

There is no such thing. Prices vary according to demand – or have different rates for online, phone or walk-in bookings. B&B rates are more consistent, but virtually every other accommodation will charge wildly different rates depending on the time of year, day, festival schedule and even your ability to do a little negotiating. The following price ranges have been used in our reviews of places to stay. Prices are all based on a double room with private bathroom in high season.

Budget	Republic	Dublin	Northern Ireland
Budget (€)	<€80	<€150	<£50
Midrange (€€)	€80–180	<€150-250	£50–120
Top end (€€€)	<€180	<€250	<£120

When to Eat

Irish eating habits have changed over the last couple of decades, and there are differences between urban and rural practices.

Breakfast Usually eaten before 9am, as most people rush off to work (though hotels and B&Bs will serve until 10am or 11am Monday to Friday, and till noon at weekends in urban areas). Weekend brunch is popular in bigger towns and cities.

Lunch Urban workers eat on the run between 12.30pm and 2pm (most restaurants don't begin to serve lunch until at least midday). At weekends, especially Sunday, the midday lunch is skipped in favour of a substantial mid-afternoon meal (called dinner), usually between 2pm and 4pm.

Tea Not the drink, but the evening meal – also confusingly called dinner. This is the main meal of the day for urbanites, usually eaten around 6.30pm. Rural communities eat at the same time but with a more traditional tea of bread, cold cuts and, yes, tea. Restaurants follow international habits, with most diners not eating until at least 7.30pm.

Supper A before-bed snack of tea and toast or sandwiches, still enjoyed by many Irish folk, though urbanites increasingly eschew it for health reasons. Not a practice in restaurants.

Vegetarians & Vegans

Ireland has come a long, long way since the days when vegetarians were looked upon as odd creatures; nowadays, even the most militant vegan will barely cause a ruffle in all but the most basic of kitchens. Which isn't to say that travellers with plant-based diets are going to find the most imaginative range of options on menus outside the bigger towns and cities – or in the plethora of modern restaurants that have opened in the last few years – but you can rest assured that the overall quality of the homegrown vegetable is top-notch and most places will have at least one dish that you can tuck into comfortably.

LGBTQI+ TRAVELLERS

Ireland is a generally tolerant place for the LGBTQI+ community. Bigger cities such as Dublin, Galway and Cork have well-established gay scenes, as do Belfast and Derry in Northern Ireland. Same-sex

Eating Price Ranges

The folllowing price indicators, used throughout this guide, represent the cost of a main dish:

Budget	Republic/ Dublin	Northern Ireland
Budget (€)	<€12/15	<£12
Midrange (€€)	€12–25/ €15–30	£12–20
Top end (€€€)	<€25/30	<£20

marriage has been legal in the Republic since 2015; Northern Ireland is the only region of the United Kingdom where it is not.

While the cities and main towns tend to be progressive and tolerant, you'll still find pockets of homophobia throughout the island, particularly in smaller towns and rural areas.

Resources include the following:

Gaire (www.gaire.com) Message board and info for a host of gay-related issues.

Gay & Lesbian Youth Northern Ireland (www.cara-friend.org.uk) Voluntary counselling, information, health and social-space organisation for the gay community.

Gay Men's Health Service (☑01 921 2730; www.hse.ie/go/GMHS) Practical advice on men's health issues.

National LGBT Federation (NLGF; ☑01-671 9076; http://nxf.ie) Publishes the monthly *Gay Community News* (www.gcn.ie).

Northern Ireland Gay Rights Association (☑028-9066 5257; www.nidirect.gov.uk; 9-13 Waring St) Represents the rights and interests of the LGBTQ community in Northern Ireland. It offers phone and online support, but is not a call-in centre.

Outhouse (☑01-873 4999; www.outhouse.ie; 105 Capel St; ☺10am-6pm Mon-Fri, noon-5pm Sat; ⛺all city centre) Top LGBTI+ resource centre in Dublin. Great stop-off point to see what's on, check noticeboards, visit the cafe and library, and meet people. The website has listings and support links.

Dining Etiquette

The Irish aren't big on restrictive etiquette, preferring friendly informality to any kind of stuffy to-dos. Still, the following are a few tips to dining with the Irish:

Children All restaurants welcome kids up to 7pm, but pubs and some smarter restaurants don't allow them in the evening. Family restaurants have children's menus; others have reduced portions of regular menu items.

Returning a dish If the food is not to your satisfaction, it's best to politely explain what's wrong with it as soon as you can. Any respectable restaurant will offer to replace the dish immediately.

Paying the bill If you insist on paying the bill for everyone, be prepared for a first, second and even third refusal to countenance such an exorbitant act of generosity. But don't be fooled: the Irish will refuse something several times even if they're delighted with it. Insist gently but firmly and you'll get your way!

HEALTH

No jabs are required to travel to Ireland. Excellent health care is readily available. For minor, self-limiting illnesses, pharmacists can give valuable advice and sell over-the-counter medication. They can also advise when more specialised help is required and point you in the right direction.

EU citizens equipped with a European Health Insurance Card (EHIC), available from health centres or UK post offices, will be covered for most medical care – but not non-emergencies or emergency repatriation. While other countries, such as Australia, also have reciprocal agreements with Ireland and Britain, many do not.

In Northern Ireland, everyone receives free emergency treatment at accident and emergency (A&E) departments of state-run NHS hospitals, irrespective of nationality.

INTERNET ACCESS

Wi-fi and 3G/4G networks are making internet cafes largely redundant (except to gamers). The few that are left will charge around €6 per hour. Most accommodation places have wi-fi, either free or for a daily charge (up to €10 per day).

MONEY

The Republic of Ireland uses the euro (€). Northern Ireland uses the pound sterling (£), though the euro is also accepted in many places. Although notes issued by Northern Irish banks are legal tender throughout the UK, many businesses outside of Northern Ireland refuse to accept them and you'll have to swap them in British banks.

ATMs

All banks have ATMs that are linked to international money systems such as Cirrus, Maestro or Plus. Each transaction incurs a currency-conversion fee, and credit cards can incur immediate and exorbitant cash-advance interest-rate charges. Watch out for ATMs that have been tampered with, as card-reader scams ('skimming') have become a real problem.

Credit & Debit Cards

Visa and MasterCard credit and debit cards are widely accepted in Ireland. American Express is only accepted by the major chains, and very few places accept Diners or JCB. Smaller businesses, such as pubs and some B&Bs, prefer debit cards (and will charge a fee for credit cards), and a small number of rural B&Bs only take cash.

Exchange Rates

The Republic of Ireland uses the euro.

Australia	A$1	€0.62
Canada	C$1	€0.68
Japan	Y100	€0.83
New Zealand	NZ$1	€0.60
UK	£1	€1.12
USA	US$1	€0.89

Northern Ireland uses the pound sterling.

Australia	A$1	£0.55
Canada	C$1	£0.61
Europe	€1	£0.89
Japan	Y100	£0.74
New Zealand	NZ$1	£0.53
US	US$1	£0.80

For current exchange rates see www.xe.com.

OPENING HOURS

Banks 10am–4pm Monday to Friday (to 5pm Thursday)

Pubs 10.30am–11.30pm Monday to Thursday, 10.30am–12.30am Friday and Saturday, noon–11pm Sunday (30 minutes 'drinking up' time allowed); closed Christmas Day and Good Friday

Restaurants noon–10.30pm; many close one day of the week

Shops 9.30am–6pm Monday to Saturday (to 8pm Thursday in cities), noon–6pm Sunday

PHOTOGRAPHY

➡ Natural light can be very dull, so use higher ISO speeds than usual, such as 400 for daylight shots.

➡ In Northern Ireland get permission before taking photos of fortified police stations, army posts or other military or quasi-military paraphernalia.

➡ Don't take photos of people in Protestant or Catholic strongholds of West Belfast without permission; always ask and be prepared to accept a refusal.

➡ Lonely Planet's *Guide to Travel Photography* is full of helpful tips for photography while on the road.

PUBLIC HOLIDAYS

Public holidays can cause road chaos as everyone tries to get somewhere else for the break. It's wise to book accommodation in advance for these times.

The following are public holidays in both the Republic and Northern Ireland:

New Year's Day 1 January

St Patrick's Day 17 March

Easter (Good Friday to Easter Monday inclusive) March/April

May Holiday 1st Monday in May

Christmas Day 25 December

St Stephen's Day (Boxing Day) 26 December

St Patrick's Day and St Stephen's Day holidays are taken on the following Monday when they fall on a weekend. Nearly everywhere in the Republic closes on Good Friday even though it isn't an official public holiday. In the North most shops open on Good Friday, but close the following Tuesday.

Practicalities

Smoking Smoking is illegal in all indoor public spaces, including restaurants and pubs.

Time Ireland uses the 12-hour clock and is on Western European Time (UTC/GMT November to March; plus one hour April to October).

TV & DVD All TV in Ireland is digital terrestrial; Ireland is DVD Region 2.

Weights & Measures In the Republic, both imperial and metric units are used for most measures except height, which is in feet and inches only. Distance is measured in kilometres, but people can refer to it colloquially in miles. In the north, it's imperial all the way.

Republic

June Holiday 1st Monday in June
August Holiday 1st Monday in August
October Holiday Last Monday in October

Northern Ireland

Spring Bank Holiday Last Monday in May
The Twelfth 12 July
August Holiday Last Monday in August

SAFE TRAVEL

Ireland is safer than most countries in Europe, but normal precautions should be observed.

➡ Don't leave anything visible in your car when you park.

➡ Skimming at ATMs is an ongoing problem; be sure to cover the keypad with your hand when you input your PIN.

➡ In Northern Ireland exercise extra care in 'interface' areas where sectarian neighbourhoods adjoin.

➡ Best avoid Northern Ireland during the climax of the Orange marching season on 12 July. Sectarian passions are usually inflamed and even many Northerners leave the province at this time.

TAXES & REFUNDS

Non-EU residents can claim Value Added Tax (VAT, a sales tax of 21% added to the purchase price of luxury goods – excluding books, children's clothing and educational items) back on their purchases, so long as the store operates either the Cashback or Taxback refund program (they should display a sticker). You'll get a voucher with your purchase that must be stamped at the *last point of exit* from the EU. If you're travelling on to Britain or mainland Europe from Ireland, hold on to your voucher until you pass through your final customs stop in the EU; it can then be stamped and you can post it back for a refund of duty paid.

VAT in Northern Ireland is 20%; shops participating in the Tax-Free Shopping refund scheme will give you a form or invoice on request to be presented to customs when you leave. After customs have certified the form, it will be returned to the shop for a refund and the cheque sent to you at home.

TELEPHONE

When calling Ireland from abroad, dial your international access code, followed by ☎353 and the area code (dropping the 0). Area codes in the Republic have three digits, eg ☎021 for Cork, ☎091 for Galway and ☎061 for Limerick. The only exception is Dublin, which has a two-digit code (☎01).

To make international calls from Ireland, first dial 00 then the country code, followed by the local area code and number. Always use the area code if calling from a mobile phone, but you don't need it if calling from a fixed-line number within the area code.

In Northern Ireland the area code for all fixed-line numbers is ☎028, but you only need to use it if calling from a mobile phone or from outside Northern Ireland. To call Northern Ireland from the Republic, use ☎048 instead of ☎028, without the international dialling code.

	Republic	Northern Ireland
Country Code	☎353	☎44
International Access Code	☎00	☎00
Directory Enquiries	☎11811/ ☎11850	☎118 118/ ☎118 192
International Directory Enquiries	☎11818	

Mobile Phones

➡ Ensure your mobile phone is unlocked for use in Ireland.

➡ Pay-as-you-go mobile phone packages with any of the main providers start around €40 and usually include a basic handset and credit of around €10.

➡ SIM-only packages are also available, but make sure your phone is compatible with the local provider.

TOURIST INFORMATION

In both the Republic and the North there's a tourist office or information point in almost every big town. Most can offer a variety of services, including accommodation and attraction reservations, currency-changing services, map and guidebook sales and free publications.

In the Republic the tourism purview falls to **Fáilte Ireland** (☏Republic 1850 230 330, UK 0800 039 7000; www.discoverireland.ie); in Northern Ireland, it's **Discover Northern Ireland** (☏head office 028-9023 1221; www. discovernorthernireland.com). Outside Ireland both organisations unite under the banner Tourism Ireland (www.tourismireland.com).

TRAVELLERS WITH DISABILITIES

All new buildings have wheelchair access, and many hotels (especially urban ones that are part of chains) have installed lifts, ramps and other facilities such as hearing loops. Others, particularly B&Bs, have not invested in making their properties accessible.

In big cities, most buses have low-floor access and priority space on board, but the number of kneeling buses on regional routes is still relatively small.

Trains are accessible with help. In theory, if you call ahead, an employee of Irish Rail (Iarnród Éireann) will arrange to accompany you to the train. Newer trains have audio and visual information systems for visually impaired and hearing-impaired passengers.

The **Citizens' Information Board** (☏0761 079 000; www.citizensinformation-board.ie) in the Republic and **Disability Action** (☏028-9029 7880; www.disabilityac-tion.org; 189 Airport Rd W, Portside Business Pk; 🚌28) in Northern Ireland can give some advice to travellers with disabilities.

Lonely Planet's free Accessible Travel guide can be downloaded here: http://lptravel.to/AccessibleTravel.

VISAS

If you're a European Economic Area (EEA) national, you don't need a visa to visit (or work in) either the Republic or Northern Ireland. Citizens of Australia, Canada, New Zealand, South Africa and the US can visit the Republic for up to three months, and Northern Ireland for up to six months. They are not allowed to work, unless sponsored by an employer.

Full visa requirements for visiting the Republic are available online at www.dfa.ie; for Northern Ireland's visa requirements see www.gov.uk/government/organisa-tions/uk-visas-and-immigration.

To stay longer in the Republic, contact the local *garda* (police) station or the **Garda National Immigration Bureau** (☏01-666 9100; www.garda.ie; 13-14 Burgh Quay, Dublin; ⏰8am-9pm Mon-Fri; 🚌all city centre). To stay longer in Northern Ireland, contact the Home Office (www.gov.uk/government/organisations/uk-visas-and-immigration).

Language

Irish (Gaeilge) is the country's official language. In 2003 the government introduced the Official Languages Act, whereby all official documents and street signs must be either in Irish or in both Irish and English. Despite its official status, Irish is really only spoken in pockets of rural Ireland known as the Gaeltacht, the main ones being Cork (Corcaigh), Donegal (Dún na nGall), Galway (Gaillimh), Kerry (Ciarraí) and Mayo (Maigh Eo).

Ask people outside the Gaeltacht if they can speak Irish and nine out of 10 of them will probably reply, '*ah, cupla focal*' (a couple of words), and they generally mean it – but many adults also regret not having a greater grasp of it. Irish is a compulsory subject in schools for those aged six to 15. In recent times, a new Irish curriculum has been introduced cutting the hours devoted to the subject but making the lessons more fun, practical and celebratory.

Irish divides vowels into long (those with an accent) and short (those without), and also distinguishes between broad (a, á, o, ó, u) and slender (e, é, i and í), which can affect the pronunciation of preceding consonants. Other than a few clusters, such as mh and bhf (both pronounced as w), consonants are generally pronounced the same as in English.

Irish has three main dialects: Connaught Irish (in Galway and northern Mayo), Munster Irish (in Cork, Kerry and Waterford) and Ulster Irish (in Donegal). Our pronunciation guides are an anglicised version of modern standard Irish, which is essentially an amalgam of the three – if you read them as if they were English, you'll be able to get your point across in Gaeilge without even having to think about the specifics of Irish pronunciation or spelling.

BASICS

Hello.
Dia duit.　　deea gwit

Hello. (reply)
Dia is Muire duit.　　deeas moyra gwit

Good morning.
Maidin mhaith.　　mawjin wah

Good night.
Oíche mhaith.　　eekheh wah

Goodbye. (when leaving)
Slán leat.　　slawn lyat

Goodbye. (when staying)
Slán agat.　　slawn agut

Yes.
Tá.　　taw

No.
Níl.　　neel

It is.
Sea.　　sheh

It isn't.
Ní hea.　　nee heh

Thank you (very) much.
Go raibh (míle)　　goh rev (meela)
maith agat.　　mah agut

Excuse me.
Gabh mo leithscéal.　　gamoh lesh scale

I'm sorry.
Tá brón orm.　　taw brohn oruhm

Do you speak (Irish)?
An bhfuil (Gaeilge) agat?　　on wil (gaylge) oguht

I don't understand.
Ní thuigim.　　nee higgim

What is this?
Cad é seo?　　kod ay shoh

Want More?

For in-depth language information and handy phrases, check out Lonely Planet's *Irish Language & Culture*. You'll find it at **shop.lonelyplanet.com**, or you can buy Lonely Planet's iPhone phrasebooks at the Apple App Store.

Signs

Dúnta	Closed
Fir	Men
Gardaí	Police
Leithreas	Toilet
Mná	Women
Ná Caitear Tobac	No Smoking
Oifig An Phoist	Post Office
Oifig Eolais	Tourist Information
Oscailte	Open
Páirceáil	Parking

What is that?
Cad é sin? · kod ay shin

I'd like to go to ...
Ba mhaith liom · baw wah lohm
dul go dtí ... · dull go dee ...

I'd like to buy ...
Ba mhaith liom ... · bah wah lohm ...
a cheannach. · a kyanukh

another/one more
ceann eile · kyawn ella

nice
go deas · goh dyass

MAKING CONVERSATION

Welcome.
Ceád míle fáilte. · kade meela fawlcha
(lit: 100,000 welcomes)

Bon voyage!
Go n-éirí an bóthar leat! · go nairee on bohhar lat

How are you?
Conas a tá tú? · kunas aw taw too

I'm fine.
Táim go maith. · thawm go mah

... please.
... más é do thoil é. · ... maws ay do hall ay

Cheers!
Slainte! · slawncha

What's your name?
Cad is ainm duit? · kod is anim dwit

My name is (Sean Frayne).
(Sean Frayne) is · (shawn frain) is
ainm dom. · anim dohm

Impossible!
Ní féidir é! · nee faydir ay

Nonsense!
Ráiméis! · rawmaysh

That's terrible!
Go huafásach! · guh hoofawsokh

Take it easy.
Tóg é gobogé . · tohg ay gobogay

DAYS OF THE WEEK

Monday	*Dé Luaín*	day loon
Tuesday	*Dé Máirt*	day maart
Wednesday	*Dé Ceádaoin*	day kaydeen
Thursday	*Déardaoin*	daredeen
Friday	*Dé hAoine*	day heeneh
Saturday	*Dé Sathairn*	day sahern
Sunday	*Dé Domhnaigh*	day downick

NUMBERS

1	*haon*	hayin
2	*dó*	doe
3	*trí*	tree
4	*ceathaír*	kahirr
5	*cúig*	kooig
6	*sé*	shay
7	*seacht*	shocked
8	*hocht*	hukt
9	*naoi*	nay
10	*deich*	jeh
11	*haon déag*	hayin jague
12	*dó dhéag*	doe yague
20	*fiche*	feekhe
21	*fiche haon*	feekhe hayin

387

BEHIND THE SCENES

SEND US YOUR FEEDBACK

We love to hear from travellers – your comments help make our books better. We read every word, and we guarantee that your feedback goes straight to the authors. Visit **lonelyplanet. com/contact** to submit your updates and suggestions.

Note: We may edit, reproduce and incorporate your comments in Lonely Planet products such as guidebooks, websites and digital products, so let us know if you don't want your comments reproduced or your name acknowledged. For a copy of our privacy policy visit lonelyplanet.com/privacy.

WRITER THANKS

FIONN DAVENPORT

Dublin's forever changing, and to update it properly I needed more than two eyes and one brain, so a huge thanks to everyone who helped me along. To the staff in the Dublin office, thanks for your tips, suggestions and recommendations; to Nicola Brady, for her invaluable assistance in knowing all of the right places to eat; and to Cliff Wilkinson, the ever-present, ever-helpful editor who answered all of my questions.

ISABEL ALBISTON

Huge thanks to Caroline Wilson for the foodie tips, to Hazel at Dunluce Castle for the tour and to Philip Bingham for helping with endless bus prices. Most of all, thanks to my family for all their help and support, for lending me the car and for accompanying me to restaurants and windswept castles.

BELINDA DIXON

To everyone encountered along the way: *go raibh maith agat* for the warmth and wit that makes your wild, creative country so irresistible. To Cliff for these fantastic opportunities, my sincere thanks; it's been a blast. All LP's in-house teams: thank you so much for helping turn my rain-sodden notes into beautiful books, maps and tech. To fellow LP writers: shall we meet for a pint next time? And to Laura for keeping me grounded and making me laugh.

CATHERINE LE NEVEZ

Sláinte first and foremost to Julian, and to all of the locals and fellow travellers throughout Ireland who provided insights, information and great times. Huge thanks too to Cliff Wilkinson and the Ireland team, and to everyone at LP. As ever, *merci encore* to my parents, brother, *belle-sœur*, *neveu* and *nièce*.

NEIL WILSON

Thanks to the friendly and helpful tourist office staff in Cork, Kerry, Limerick and Tipperary; to Mortimer at Mannix Point; to Warren at Curraghchase; to Hilary at Fleming's; to George at Glen of Aherlow; and, as ever, to Carol Downie. Thanks also to my co-authors and to Cliff and the editorial team at Lonely Planet.

ACKNOWLEDGEMENTS

Climate map data adapted from Peel MC, Finlayson BL & McMahon TA (2007) 'Updated World Map of the Köppen-Geiger Climate Classification', *Hydrology and Earth System Sciences*, 11, 163344.

Front cover photographs: (clockwise from top): Rock of Cashel, Riccardo Spila/4Corners Images©; B&B, Skibbereen, Andy Gibson/Alamy Stock Photo©; Austin car, Ballydehob, Andy Gibson/Alamy Stock Photo©. Back cover: Lough Corrib, George Karbus Photography©.

THIS BOOK

This 3rd edition of *Ireland's Best Trips* was researched and written by Fionn Davenport, Isabel Albiston, Belinda Dixon, Catherine Le Nevez and Neil Wilson. This guidebook was produced by the following:

Destination Editor Clifton Wilkinson

Product Editor Paul Harding

Senior Cartographer Mark Griffiths

Assisting Cartographer Julie Dodkins

Book Designer Gwen Cotter

Assisting Editors Andrew Bain, Imogen Bannister, Nigel Chin, Michelle Coxall, Kate Daly, Carly Hall, Kellie Langdon, Rosie Nicholson, Kristin Odijk, Gabrielle Stefanos, Simon Williamson

Cover Researcher Naomi Parker

Thanks to Hannah Cartmel, Shona Gray, Jessica Ryan

INDEX

Y

Z

BELINDA DIXON

Only happy when her feet are suitably sandy, Belinda has been (gleefully) travelling, researching and writing for Lonely Planet since 2006. It's seen her navigating mountain passes and soaking in hot-pots in Iceland's Westfjords, marvelling at Stonehenge at sunrise; scrambling up Italian mountain paths; horse riding across Donegal's golden sands; gazing at Verona's frescoes; and fossil hunting on Dorset's Jurassic Coast. Then there's the food and drink: truffled mushroom pasta in Salo; whisky in Aberdeen: Balti in Birmingham, grilled fish in Dartmouth; wine in Bardolino. And all in the name of research. Belinda is also a podcaster and adventure writer and helps lead wilderness expeditions. See her blog posts at belindadixon.com.

CATHERINE LE NEVEZ

Catherine's wanderlust kicked in when she roadtripped across Europe from her Parisian base aged four, and she's been hitting the road at every opportunity since, travelling to some 60 countries and completing her Doctorate of Creative Arts in Writing, Masters in Professional Writing, and postgrad qualifications in Editing and Publishing along the way. Over the past decade-and-a-half she's written scores of Lonely Planet guides and articles covering Paris, France, Europe and far beyond. Her work has also appeared in numerous online and print publications. Topping Catherine's list of travel tips is to travel without any expectations.

NEIL WILSON

Neil was born in Scotland and has lived there most of his life. Based in Perthshire, he has been a full-time writer since 1988, working on more than 80 guidebooks for various publishers, including the Lonely Planet guides to Scotland, England, Ireland and Prague. An outdoors enthusiast since childhood, Neil is an active hill-walker, mountain-biker, sailor, snowboarder and rock-climber, and a qualified fly-fishing guide and instructor. He has climbed and tramped in four continents, including ascents of Jebel Toubkal in Morocco, Mount Kinabalu in Borneo, the Old Man of Hoy in Scotland's Orkney Islands and the Northwest Face of Half Dome in California's Yosemite Valley.

OUR WRITERS

OUR STORY

A beat-up old car, a few dollars in the pocket and a sense of adventure. In 1972 that's all Tony and Maureen Wheeler needed for the trip of a lifetime – across Europe and Asia overland to Australia. It took several months, and at the end – broke but inspired – they sat at their kitchen table writing and stapling together their first travel guide, *Across Asia on the Cheap*. Within a week they'd sold 1500 copies. Lonely Planet was born.

Today, Lonely Planet has offices in Franklin, London, Melbourne, Oakland, Dublin, Beijing, and Delhi, with more than 600 staff and writers. We share Tony's belief that 'a great guidebook should do three things: inform, educate and amuse'.

FIONN DAVENPORT

Irish by birth and conviction, Fionn has spent the last two decades focusing on the country of his birth and its nearest neighbour, England, which he has written about extensively for Lonely Planet and others. In between writing gigs he's lived in Paris and New York, where he was an editor, actor, bartender and whatever else paid the rent. When he returned to Ireland in the late 1990s, he tried his hand at radio, which landed him a series of presenting gigs, most recently as host of *Inside Culture* and regular travel contributor to the mid-morning *Sean O'Rourke Show*, both on RTE Radio 1. He moved to Manchester a few years ago where he lives with his wife, Laura, but he commutes back and forth to Dublin, only 40 minutes away.

Read more about Fionn at https://auth. lonelyplanet.com/profiles/fionndavenport

ISABEL ALBISTON

After six years working for the *Daily Telegraph* in London, Isabel left to spend more time on the road. A job as writer for a magazine in Sydney, Australia was followed by a four-month overland trip across Asia and five years living and working in Buenos Aires, Argentina. Isabel started writing for Lonely Planet in 2014 and has contributed to 12 guidebooks. She's currently based in Ireland.

Read more about Isabel at https://auth. lonelyplanet.com/profiles/IsabelAlbiston

← MORE WRITERS

Published by Lonely Planet Global Limited
CRN 554153
3rd edition – March 2020
ISBN 978 1 7870 135 44
© Lonely Planet 2020
Photographs © as indicated 2020
10 9 8 7 6 5 4 3 2 1
Printed in China